Riefenstahl Screened

Riefenstahl Screened

An Anthology of New Criticism

edited by
Neil Christian Pages, Mary Rhiel, and Ingeborg Majer-O'Sickey

NEW YORK • LONDON

2008

The Continuum International Publishing Group Inc
80 Maiden Lane, New York, NY 10038

The Continuum International Publishing Group Ltd
The Tower Building, 11 York Road, London SE1 7NX

www.continuumbooks.com

Printed in the United States of America

Library of Congress Cataloging-in-Publication Data

Riefenstahl screened : an anthology of new criticism / edited by Neil Christian Pages, Mary Rhiel, and Ingeborg Majer-O'Sickey.

p. cm.

Includes bibliographical references and index.

ISBN-13: 978-0-8264-2800-4 (hardcover : alk. paper)

ISBN-10: 0-8264-2800-2 (hardcover : alk. paper)

ISBN-13: 978-0-8264-2801-1 (pbk. : alk. paper)

ISBN-10: 0-8264-2801-0 (pbk. : alk. paper) 1. Riefenstahl, Leni—Criticism and interpretation. I. Pages, Neil Christian. II. Rhiel, Mary, 1949- III. Majer O'Sickey, Ingeborg, 1944- IV. Title.

PN1998.3.R54R54 2008
791.4302'33092—dc22

2008004189

Contents

Acknowledgments

The essays in this volume do not represent a unified critical voice. Instead, they are evidence of diverse reflections on the theoretical, historical, and aesthetic problems raised by the figure and films of Leni Riefenstahl. The editors thank the contributors for creating what we hope will be a continued dialogue on the issues invoked in this book. Our thanks go to Bärbel Dalichow, Georg Seesslen, and Martina Thiele for the cooperation and permissions that assisted us in presenting their work here for the first time in English translation. The rights for some of the texts and images were provided by Seemann Henschel GmbH & Co. KG of Leipzig and by the Filmmuseum Potsdam. We received support for the preparation of the volume from Binghamton University, State University of New York. We are immensely grateful to David Barker, Katie Gallof, and Gabriella Page-Fort at Continuum for their enthusiasm, advice, and patience. Finally, we would like to thank our families for their support as we spent hours with one another in virtual and physical work environments: Mike Arnold, Vincent Greiber, Emily Rhiel, and Patrick Clary, the last of whom served as poet-in-residence and personal chef for the project.

Contributors

Celia Applegate is Associate Professor of History at the University of Rochester. Her books include *A Nation of Provincials: The German Idea of Heimat* (1990) and *Bach in Berlin: Nation and Culture in Mendelssohn's Revival of the St. Matthew Passion* (2005). She edited (with musicologist Pamela Potter) the anthology *Music and German National Identity* (2002). Applegate's research focuses on the political culture of modern Germany and the history of German nationalism and national identity. She is now at work on a study of musical culture in Germany from the eighteenth century to the present.

David Bathrick is the Jacob Gould Schurman Professor of German and Theater at Cornell University. His is author of *The Dialectic and the Early Brecht* (1976), *Modernity and the Text: Re-Visions of German Modernism* (1989, co-edited with Andreas Huyssen), and *The Powers of Speech: The Politics of Culture in the GDR* (1995), which was awarded the 1996 DAAD/GSA Book of the Year Prize. He has also written numerous articles on twentieth-century European culture. Bathrick is also co-founder and co-editor of the journal *New German Critique*. His forthcoming book, *Rescreening the Holocaust*, addresses the visual culture of the Nazi period.

Wulf Kansteiner is Associate Professor of History at Binghamton University SUNY. His work as a cultural-intellectual historian of twentieth-century Europe focuses on media history and comparative genocide studies in Germany. In addition to many articles on the intersections of history, memory, and politics, Kansteiner is the author of *In Pursuit of German Memory: History, Television, and Politics after Auschwitz* (2005) and co-editor of *The Politics of Memory in Postwar Europe* (2006).

Lutz Koepnick is Professor of German, Film, and Media Studies at Washington University in St. Louis. He has published widely on German literature, film, media, and visual culture, and is author of *Framing Attention: Windows on Modern German Culture* (2007), *The Dark Mirror: German Cinema between Hitler and Hollywood* (2002), and *Walter Benjamin and the Aesthetics of Power* (1999). His co-edited anthologies include *The Cosmopolitan Screen: German Cinema and the Global Imaginary, 1945 to the Present* (2007), and *Sound Matters: Essays on the Acoustics of Modern German Culture* (2004). His current book project explores strategies of deceleration in media of twentieth- and twentieth-first-century artistic practice.

Ingeborg Majer-O'Sickey is Associate Professor of German and Faculty Director of Women's Studies at Binghamton University SUNY. Her scholarly and teaching interests include German cinema and literature and contemporary feminist theory. She has authored numerous articles on German cinema and co-edited *Triangulated Visions: Women in Recent German Cinema* (1998) and *Subversive Subjects: Reading Marguerite Yourcenar* (2004). Her current book project is titled *Women in Nazi Cinema: Engendering Heimat, Genderizing Nation.*

Guinevere Narraway received her Ph.D. in German Studies and Visual Culture from Monash University in Melbourne, Australia. She is currently a Research Associate in the Department of Media and Communications at Goldsmiths, University of London. Her doctoral thesis, "Making Nature: Visions of Mastery in Third Reich Cinema," examines the representation and instrumentalization of modernity in film under National Socialism. Her teaching and research interests include visual culture in Weimar and Nazi Germany, gender and sexuality in cinema, and discourses in cultural production surrounding technology and nature.

Neil Christian Pages is Associate Professor of German and Comparative Literature at the Binghamton University SUNY, where he teaches courses in European literature, literary theory, and cultural history. His publications include essays on Kierkegaard, Nietzsche, Georg Brandes, and W. G. Sebald. He is currently at work on a manuscript on memorials, public memory, and commemorative practice, titled *On Commemoration: Memory.Identity.Ideology.*

Eric Rentschler is the Arthur Kingsley Porter Professor of Germanic Languages and Literatures at Harvard University. His many publications cover film history, theory, and criticism, with particular emphasis on German cinema during the Weimar Republic, the Nazi period, and the postwar and post-Wall eras. He is the author of numerous books, including *The Films of G. W. Pabst* (1990) and *The Ministry of Illusion: Nazi Cinema and Its Afterlife* (1996). At present he is working on two book projects, *The Enduring Allure of Nazi Attractions* and *Film in the Federal Republic of Germany, 1962–1989.*

Mary Rhiel is Associate Professor of German at the University of New Hampshire. Her research interests in German film and colonial narratives, particularly those set in China, have led to publications on film, biography, and autobiography, and on the problems of teaching Leni Riefenstahl. Her books include *Re-Viewing Kleist: The Discursive Construction of Authorial Subjectivity in West German Kleist Films* (1991) and the co-edited volume *The Seductions of Biography* (1996).

Georg Seesslen is a German cultural critic, film scholar, and theorist widely known for his critical works on popular film. A prolific writer and critic, Seesslen's publications range from best-selling books on Stanley Kubrick, Steven Spielberg, Quentin Tarrantino, and David Lynch to reflections on the social and cultural mechanisms of popular culture. A frequent contributor to leading German newspapers and magazines, he is also the author of numerous book-length studies, including *Orgasmus und Alltag* (*Orgasm and Everyday*

Life, 2000), *Kino. Detektive im Film* (*Murder in the Cinema: Detectives in Film*, 1981), and *Natural Born Nazis* (1996).

Carsten Strathausen is Associate Professor of German and English at the University of Missouri, Columbia. He is the author of numerous articles on aesthetics, political philosophy, European intellectual history, and cinema. His books include *The Look of Things: Poetry and Vision around 1900* (2003) and the edited volume *A Leftist Ontology* (forthcoming). His current book project, *The Aesthetics of New Media: Art and Politics in the Digital Age*, situates contemporary media aesthetics within leftist political discourse.

Martina Thiele teaches media studies and communications at the University of Salzburg and has also taught at universities in Bern and Göttingen. Her research interests include cinema, media history, comparative media studies, politics, and the media, and the role of the media in identity construction. Her book *Publizistische Kontroversen über den Holocaust im Film* (*Controversies on the Holocaust in Film in the Publishing Industry*) is now in its second edition. She has also published articles on print and other media cultures in Germany and Austria and on the representation of the Shoah in the popular press.

Valerie Weinstein is Associate Professor of German at the University of Nevada, Reno. Her research interests include German visual and popular culture, popular music as represented in music videos, gender, ethnicity, and aging. At present she is working on a research project on the aging of the World War II generation in Germany. She is the author of articles on Ernst Lubitsch, philosemitic film in the Weimar period, German precolonial literature in the Pacific, and on the Turkish-German author Saliha Scheinhardt. She is currently at work on a book project entitled *Mistaken Identities: Wilhelmine, Weimar and Nazi Film.*

INTRODUCTION: Screening Riefenstahl—Riefenstahl Screened

This anthology emerged from our assumption that there were enough monographs and biographies of Leni Riefenstahl, but that there was a dearth of critical, scholarly volumes dealing with her work and persona. Predicting that the biography wave was declining, we looked forward to entering the era in which "Riefenstahl" had lost her power to turn our heads. We have been proven wrong. Two new books on Leni Riefenstahl appeared in 2007. Both the English translation of Jürgen Trimborn's *Riefenstahl. Eine deutsche Karriere* and Steven Bach's *Leni Riefenstahl: A Life* were met with considerable media attention, solid reviews, and radio and television interviews. At the same time, media reports told of Jodie Foster's apparent intention to return to her plan to produce and star in a Riefenstahl biopic. Dead indeed. Though Riefenstahl died in 2003 at the age of 101, at the beginning of the twenty-first century, it would seem that we are still very much intrigued by her. From the lure of her persona as it enters our homes via television to our pleasure at the recognition of film images in advertising and at rock concerts, to her place as part of the history of the Nazi period, Riefenstahl lives on in our imaginations and in our cultural productions.

But what is the nature of that afterlife, the reverberations of Riefenstahl in the twenty-first century? To be sure, the continued fascination with Riefenstahl makes it all the more crucial that we continue to think about the issues that are invoked by her legacy. Indeed, *Riefenstahl Screened* also came about as an attempt to think about "Riefenstahl" beyond the compartmentalization of a biographical project or the divisions of academic disciplines. We aimed to gather a set of essays that would maneuver around the impasse that has characterized the debates around the meaning of her films and her biography. Thinking about Riefenstahl in gender terms, for instance, we noted her uncanny oscillation between disempowerment and empowerment. That is to say, she strategically instrumentalized advantages associated with "femininity" at the same time that she challenged patriarchal dicta as part of a strategy to create a different "reality" for herself. As a result, Riefenstahl's masks make it difficult to "screen" her as a fixed object of scholarly inquiry just as the proliferation of her images in popular culture has been largely impossible to control, no matter the litigious nature of the filmmaker herself, who sought doggedly to control the crafting of her persona in the public sphere.

Screening, of course, implies hiding, protecting, and projecting simultaneously. Our title, then, speaks to the problem of masking and to our cultural investment in unmasking Riefenstahl, in catching her in the act, as it were. For decades, writing about Riefenstahl has been motivated by a desire to have the final word about her and her films. In contrast, this volume seeks to be conscious of this projecting and hiding and to analyze the historical issues that motivate our need to "discover" Riefenstahl's secret. For us, there is no essential Riefenstahl, no discourse, whether scholarly or pop, that can give the final word on her. Indeed, these are also historical questions.

Let us turn to the period in which Riefenstahl emerged as an artist—Weimar Germany—and to the aesthetic and political discourses of that historical and cultural context. Riefenstahl was in many ways typical of the Weimar "New Woman," whose supposed transgressive gender-bending is assumed to have rewritten the patriarchal grammar of self-presentation. This was part of an emancipatory project associated with modernity. While that project was probably within the grasp of a minority of women in the period, namely those in urban centers and on the covers of the illustrated magazines, it was not the rule for most women. Riefenstahl is a fascinating case here, because she in many ways embodies the contradictions of the time in which she began her career. Although Alice Schwarzer would try to make her into a kind feminist icon in the pages of the magazine *Emma* in 1999, Riefenstahl herself had already used the power of her various positions in a feminist movement that had only one constituent, namely Leni Riefenstahl.[1] What we find intriguing (and confounding) about her is how limited her imagination seems to have been in the historical and artistic context in which she worked.

Although she represents a break from the exclusion of women from the development of technological media in the early twentieth century, Riefenstahl's films employ technology in largely derivative ways, in approaches that reinstall power structures instead of challenging them. Consistently enough, her postwar attempts at the rehabilitation of her person and her career stubbornly worked not to reflect on patriarchal history, but rather to portray "Riefenstahl" as a victim of the very structures she helped to (re)produce. This repetition, then, is also a re-*petitioning* through which the filmmaker reappears in an array of postwar cultural productions as she tries to repackage herself as victim, genius, innovator, and pop culture icon.

The editors recognize that there is little to be learned from a resuscitation of Leni Riefenstahl's dichotomous image as "Hitler's filmmaker," as a "Nazi pinup girl," or as a misunderstood, naïve artist. Indeed, Ian Buruma got it right when he noted recently, "The fact that Leni Riefenstahl was rather a monster is not really in dispute."[2] Thus, we by no means see this project as part of a compilation of evidence for or against the person or work of Leni Riefenstahl.

As the remark above indicates, these debates are largely over, largely because postwar controversies surrounding "Riefenstahl" have run their course.

Historical studies have also influenced our approach to questions of art and Nazism by redefining the object of study as we continue to refine our understanding of National Socialism and its aftermath. Historical inquiry has moved away from trying to construct and give a name to a coherent, unitary system of Nazi politics and aesthetics. Instead, in examining the interrelations between cultural productions and ideologies, we now recognize the generative potential of the inconsistencies, vicissitudes, and complexities of everyday life and politics in the Nazi period. Reflecting on these issues must necessarily bring us to ask different questions of the person whose films helped to define what we have come to understand as "fascist aesthetics." In thinking about these problems, though, we bear in mind that "fascist aesthetics" is itself a problematic category. There is no coherent aesthetic strategy behind "fascist aesthetics." Nevertheless, their political effects, however predictable they are, do indeed generate a "counteraesthetic" that could be useful for our understanding of the relation between art and politics.

As we have learned from the work of scholars like Linda Schulte-Sasse, Sabine Hake, Lutz Koepnick, Eric Rentschler, and Hans Dieter Schäfer, films from the Nazi period, even the films of Leni Riefenstahl, reveal the gap between visual culture and what it purports to represent. Ruptures, fissures, breaks, and lapses remind us that the seemingly uniform surface of fascism is itself yet another fiction. Nevertheless, studies of Riefenstahl's texts (dance, film, photography, memoirs) still can teach us something about the workings of Nazi culture and how its mechanisms live on well past 1945 in a range of contexts and citations. Although there is no "totality" of Nazi fascism, although there is indeed its historical reality (Saul Friedlander), the representational issues connected to the texts and figures of complicity will always be re-energized by our changing theories of the relationship of art and ethics.[3]

What, then, is in dispute in the context of the persona and films of the woman who is arguably the most recognized German filmmaker of all time? What is there left to say about Leni Riefenstahl in this period—postwar, post-Wall, post-Sontag, post-Riefenstahl? In response to these questions, the essays in this collection explore our highly invested discursive struggles over the meaning of Leni Riefenstahl and the images she created. The first part of the anthology, "Aesthetics," looks in new ways at the intersections of politics and aesthetics as well as the problem of reception in Riefenstahl's work. This section opens with German media critic Georg Seesslen's widely cited and acclaimed work on the influence of Riefenstahl's films from the perspective of contemporary pop culture. Seesslen's essay originally appeared in the catalogue for the first exhibition on Leni Riefenstahl in Germany, which opened at the Filmmuseum Potsdam in December 1998. It appears here for the first time in English translation. In his reflections Seesslen demonstrates how Riefenstahl's films anticipate pop culture in the way in which their images abolish any link to historical referentiality, thus underscoring the continuities between pop and fascism. Like pop culture productions, Riefenstahl's images circulate freely, carrying none of the weighty historical signification of the context in which they were produced. Unlike Seesslen's work, Carsten Strathausen's essay argues that Riefenstahl criticism (and with it, "fascist" art) can no longer serve as a foil with and against which we construct prescriptions for theorizing the relevance of art for ethical praxis. He asserts that the aesthetic binaries associated with modernity are no longer viable as guidelines or tools for resistance to political tyranny. With the contention that Riefenstahl is historically irrelevant for our time, Strathausen theorizes how we might rethink the relation of art and politics. Working with questions of aesthetics and their production, Lutz Koepnick's essay probes Riefenstahl's aesthetic via the use of slow-motion photography in the film *Olympia*. Taking as his vantage point the acceleration of play on the contemporary soccer field, Koepnick finds in *Olympia* an example of a point at which the Riefenstahl "aesthetic" fails to capture what it seeks to represent. The game of soccer, he argues, eludes Riefenstahl's cinematic strategies. Koepnick's interventions show what this aesthetic cannot do with a sport that deconstructs forward movement through "fluid movements of discrete bodies across extended spaces." This scholar takes on a specific historical link between Riefenstahl's films and fascism that represents a break that has been overlooked by critics.

The second section of the volume, "Afterlife," is organized around the reception of Riefenstahl and her position as a cipher in popular culture's construction of our cultural memory of the Nazi period. It is a commonplace among those who write on Riefenstahl to note that she has been influential in a range of cultural practices, from fashion advertising to art photography, from sportscasting to the theatrics of politics, to the representation of celebrity in our time. The essays in this section investigate the specific ways in which her work reverberates in contemporary settings. Film scholar David Bathrick begins his essay with an analysis of *Triumph of the Will*. He asserts that the film gives voice to an inchoate, unexplicated trauma. Bathrick shows through careful analysis how the iconic images from the film were picked up by other filmmakers and at times employed in unexpected, sometimes jarring, contexts. His close readings of seminal films by Chaplin, Wilder, Resnais, and others show that the filmmakers' citation of *Triumph* created new binaries that limit the ability of many of the films to offer a deeper critique of fascism. Through careful historical research, Bathrick exposes how major postwar films used Riefenstahl images in their historical reconstruction of the Shoah. Working with and against the documentary genre as seen on German television, historian Wulf Kansteiner provides a sociological view on the present state of German collective memory and its representation in historiographic work. His essay shows that the popular demonization of Riefenstahl has everything to do with her function in the entertainment industry. In the context of the programming made by the German television channel ZDF, Kansteiner critiques a kind of *Vergangenheitsbewältigung* (coming to terms with the past) that defines Nazism as the product of the machinations of an evil clique that included Riefenstahl. This warm-up exercise brings Kansteiner to a contentious and intriguing assessment of a film that has been central to how we think of this historical figure, namely the 1993 Emmy-winning biopic *The Wonderful, Horrible Life of Leni Riefenstahl* (*Die Macht der Bilder*) by Ray Müller, which he concludes is a "terrible documentary." Like Kansteiner, Valerie Weinstein approaches the contemporary state of German popular culture in order to uncover its continued investment in the images of Riefenstahl. In this case it is the heavy metal band Rammstein that provides a focus for this scholar's investigation into how the image of the filmmaker and the images she created were recycled in German hard rock. The essay explores how the German media condemned the band Rammstein for its use of images from *Olympia* and *Triumph of the Will* in its music videos. Weinstein's close reading of the videos in question suggests that although the group did indeed rely on the antimodern themes of Riefenstahl's films in these works, it did so in a far more ironic and self-reflective manner than most German music critics would have it. In the end, the essay shows that the reception of the music and videos tells us more about the state of post-Wall German memory culture than it does about the supposed "fascist aesthetics" of Riefenstahl's work.

The essays in "Continuities," the third section of the volume, turn to specific historical and theoretical perspectives on Riefenstahl's oeuvre. These scholars focus on artistic and aesthetic practices as a historically grounded means to understand Riefenstahl's "texts" as manifestations of their time and context. Returning to his seminal work on Riefenstahl's *The Blue Light* from his 1996 *The Ministry of Illusion: Nazi Cinema and Its Afterlife*, Eric Rentschler reflects anew on his contention that Riefenstahl's aesthetic in this film anticipates fascism's combining of the antimodern with the technological. His comprehensive discussion of the debates surrounding the filmmaker's status in the postwar world now takes into consideration the recent release of a DVD of *The Blue Light* that contains both the version of the film that premiered in 1932, long thought lost, as well as a shorter postwar release. Rentschler explains how Riefenstahl's first feature is indeed the cornerstone upon which the filmmaker crafts her own biography as legend. Moving from movie to sound, historian Celia Applegate's reflections on the status of music in Riefenstahl's Nazi-era "documentaries" provides English-speaking readers with new research on this ignored aspect of these iconic films. Putting to rest the myth that Richard Wagner provided the "sound track for the Third Reich," Applegate gives us a detailed account of the early history of musical composition for the cinema and ends with the compelling story of Herbert Windt's contributions to *Triumph of the Will*. Applegate touches upon the role of dance in understanding Riefenstahl's musical tastes, but Mary Rhiel zooms in on dance rhythm and repetition as central to the aesthetic of the films both in terms of theory and historical practice. Rhiel's argument begins with an interrogation of Riefenstahl's vexing memoirs, in which she locates a particular narrative rhythm. She then links this beat to the filmmaker's foundational training in modern dance. Having done the historical legwork on dance in the Weimar period and earlier, this scholar, through a discursive reading of Freud's *fort/da* paradigm, teases out fresh connections between movement and politics in Riefenstahl's style.

"Riefen-Star," the final section of the volume, is in no way intended as a closure. As the essays here indicate, there remains much to be done in terms of questioning the existing scholarship on Riefenstahl and the filmmaker's own attempts at controlling her legacy in the postwar period. Guinevere Narraway's critical overview of Riefenstahl's postwar photography cannily locates these images in the contexts of both their historical settings and in recent thought on ethnography and postcoloniality. As a site for examining these problematic images she sees Riefenstahl's Nuba photographs as occupying a liminal position between the traditions of ethnographic photography and touristic photographs. Beginning with the narrative of how Riefenstahl sought to rehabilitate herself in the postwar period, the author shows how the photographer's trips to Africa and her expeditions to coral reefs were part of her postwar autobiographical mythmaking. Narraway offers some needed contextualization of Riefenstahl's postwar projects. In a similar vein, media scholar Martina Thiele works with a more recent phenomenon of image making and presentation, that of Leni Riefenstahl's Web site. In her discussion she gives a useful summary of Riefenstahl's (auto)biography and develops the beginnings of how one might consider the filmmaker's self-presentation in cyberspace. This look at Riefenstahl's latest work of self-fashioning appears here in English translation for the first time and gives readers a sense of the interest in Riefenstahl among scholars in media studies in Germany. The anthology ends with an important document from a particular historical moment for the reception of Leni Riefenstahl, the comprehensive exhibit on her life and work at the Filmmuseum Potsdam. Ingeborg Majer-O'Sickey's interview with the exhibition's curator, Bärbel Dalichow, reflects on the show from a number of perspectives but also documents some of the key themes of this important exhibit, which ran from December 1998 to March 1999, among them the visit of Riefenstahl herself to the exhibit. That tense day and the fact that a newly founded museum in what was the German Democratic Republic had taken on the organization and presentation of such a contentious show on a controversial living artist are the topics of some of Dalichow's pointed reflections on her work as a curator of the troublesome "Riefenstahl." This contribution to the volume contains previously unpublished documentation of what the editors see as a turning point in the public presentation and perception of Riefenstahl in post-Wall Germany. It serves as something of a bookend to the anthology's opening contribution by Georg Seesslen, whose essay comes from the exhibition's catalogue.

The contributions to this volume make clear that the phenomenon "Riefenstahl" has entered our collective memories in ways not necessarily apparent on the surface of contemporary cultural productions and the scholarly discourses that aim to analyze and understand them. These essays gathered here should serve to illuminate the trajectories that informed Riefenstahl's own work and to investigate the palimpsest of Riefenstahl's films, photographs, and persona in her aftermath. The following texts, then, aim both to excavate what has gone unsaid or unstudied in Riefenstahl's body of work and to build upon existing scholarship in order to think about how this contentious figure will be received in the future.

THE EDITORS

NOTES

1. See Alice Schwarzer, "Leni Riefenstahl. Propagandistin oder Künstlerin?" *Emma* 1 (1999): 34–47.
2. Ian Buruma, "Fascinating Narcissism," Review of *Leni: The Life and Work of Leni Riefenstahl*, by Steven Bach (New York: Knopf, 2007) and *Leni Riefenstahl. A Life*, by Jürgen Trimborn, trans. Edna McCown (New York: Faber and Faber, 2007), *New York Review of Books* 10 (14 June 2007): 49–52: 49.
3. See Saul Friedlander, *Memory, History, and the Extermination of the Jews of Europe* (Bloomington, IN: Indiana University Press, 1993).

Part One

Aesthetics

Chapter 1

Blood and Glamour

Georg Seesslen
Translated by Neil Christian Pages

I.

In the nineteenth century, industrial society produced, in addition to the three great systems of cultural communication—high culture, religious culture, and folk culture—a fourth, namely pop culture. Consistent with the very spirit of that age, pop culture was manufactured in an industrial process, distributed as a commodity, and intended for immediate consumption. It feeds off its predecessors and simultaneously transcends them. Objections to entertainment, popular culture, mass culture, or in short, pop culture, are equally strong on the left and on the right. In the case of the latter, the very "cannibalism" of pop culture is seen as a constant threat. While the one side critiques the permeability, ambivalence, and triviality of pop culture, the other warns of its manipulative tendencies, its essential complicity with real life under the conditions of exploitation and capital, and finally, its role as preparation and training for an escape or flight from reality.

All aspects of the social have the potential to become "pop"—politics as well as sex, theology as well as technology. "Pop" can emerge from every form of aesthetic production, from art to the semiotics of machines. "Pop will eat itself" is not only the melancholic-sarcastic statement of pop consciousness in the postmodern era, but also the consequence of a sensory system that inherited in the conditions of its production an element of voracity. Everything can become pop, and pop wants to become everything.

But are there things, like the historical and moral processing of German fascism, for example, that resist such a utilization in pop culture? Apparently not. While one can still debate the representation of fascist mass murder as soap opera (the miniseries *Holocaust*) in a moral and somewhat dignified manner, concentration camp porn, Hitler masquerades, and Nazi chic circulate without reaching the definable limits of a public consensus. Further, the self-staging of German fascism, its "aesthetics," seems to have been especially predestined for pop culture. This is so firstly because fascism perpetuated itself immediately (as in the continuity represented by the postwar German cinema of the Adenauer period), and secondly because the "camp" character of the painting and sculpture of the fascist era could be rediscovered, as it were, as pop. Nazi pop was born in the museum of history in an impossibly "pure" (and malignant) form that would have been impossible otherwise. This conspicuous transformation occurs again and again in both national and international pop culture.

The problem with what we call "fascist aesthetics" has something to do with the fact that the boundaries drawn in bourgeois culture between high culture, religion, folk tradition, and entertainment no longer apply. These meld into an aesthetic system to which there can no longer be any kind of alternative. Fascist aesthetics are a peculiar subspecies of pop that do not consume themselves, but rather demand eternal validity. This aesthetic no longer forms an open system, but rather produces kitsch, which is then treated according to the laws of religious art.

The films and photography of Leni Riefenstahl are one of the most difficult and perpetually "fascinating" interfaces between pop culture and fascism. They also lead to ever newer attempts at disassociation and interpretation, incorporation and "discovery." That probably has something to do with the fact that Riefenstahl's films, along with their elements of propaganda, kitsch, and a deeply personal and abhorrent political "conviction," always already carried the pop germ in themselves. In this sense the films were in the time of their production more modern than most fascist "art" and propaganda (these two are nearly inseparable in terms of the historical conditions of their production), which conveyed the antimodern of its form quite conspicuously as content.

On the one hand, Riefenstahl's films can be seen as a "lived" ideology, as the work of a natural-born fascist (and thus as the most authentic example among the works from the aesthetic production of German fascism: free material for aesthetic, semiotic, and psychoanalytic interpretation); on the other hand, one can view them as "works of art" (ones that probably sold themselves out to false ideas and codes, but that in their context are also in one way or another a part of an avant-garde); they can be seen as documents that demonstrate how propaganda appropriates and uses a technically inflated, private mythology for its own purposes. Finally, the films can be regarded as an endless erotic dream, as masked female-phallic desire. These differing perspectives are unlikely to result in a reliable whole, which is precisely why they render comprehensible something about the conditions of aesthetic production in German fascism.

To consider Riefenstahl's films in light of pop discourse is not as simple as it might seem. It is impossible to come to any easy conclusions in this context, because the question as to how much pop there is in fascist aesthetics must lead directly to the question as to how much fascism there can be in pop. The question, then, is to what extent fascism itself generated a bizarre and distorted form of pop aesthetics, a particular form of kitsch whose dominance is assured through the repression of every other kind of aesthetics. It has, moreover, been elevated to the status of "art" by an organized philistinism of the bloodiest sort. Furthermore, we must pose the question as to whether and how pop culture could be contained at all—that is to say, pop culture as a form of aesthetic production that begets no consciousness of its own, or that either does not want to be understood or that wants to be understood as "self-evident." To answer these questions it may be useful to compile a catalogue of the conditions of pop discourse:

1. The semiotics of pop are serial. The question of authorship is relevant only in as far as the commodity can be compared to a personal mythology. The author in pop discourse functions more like a "brand" than an artistic-moral authority. The principle is not originality, but rather an intertwining of the repetition compulsion and the pressure to innovate in a competitive struggle. Pop, unlike art, does not "speak" to us as autonomous interlocutors, but rather returns our anxieties and desires repackaged as a network of images. Pop always turns the consumer into a co-producer. That means that the conditions of consumption receive at least as much attention as those of production.
2. Genre as an organizing system is part of the serial nature of pop discourse. Genre is not comparable to the typologies of bourgeois culture. Rather, it is a dynamic ordering system of fantasies and signs, driven by an "arrangement" made between production and consumption that systematically organizes the use of these signs. This arrangement is negotiated in the market of images and texts in which the state or other systems of order intervene, sometimes more, sometimes less. Usually, pop culture genres mediate between the needs and anxieties of the individual, social structures, and the demands of the state. The positive fantasy of pop culture satisfies the desires of people who are recognized by society, and who serve the state accordingly (the human being who can be simultaneously happy and useful). The negative fantasy of pop culture allows unresolved contradictions to return in the form of demons and synthetic bogeymen who are then to be vanquished in symbolic acts. If, however, as in the case of German fascism, these contradictions are no longer resolved through compromise but rather through violence (through the killing off of everything about the individual that contradicts the unity of state and society), then pop culture obviously turns away completely from individual expression and becomes blind to the actual human being.
3. Pop culture is intertextual. One system refers to the other, enhances it, and cites it. The different parts of pop culture are organized vertically according to the stages of life and horizontally with respect to class. At the same time these parts repeatedly attempt to capture the middle, where individual impulses converge in consumption.
4. A "statement" in pop culture is always playfully "trivial" [*frivol*]; it expresses its own tentative, nonbinding nature as part of its utterance.
5. A "statement" in pop culture is temporary. It awaits its replacement by the next statement.

6. A "statement" in pop culture is simultaneously regressive-foundational (it seems "definitive") and polyvalent (its legibility is arbitrary).
7. "Statements" in pop culture attend to very different needs, which relate to one another as pretext, text, and subtext. Among other things they involve:

   - the longing for "justice"
   - the real presence of the "miraculous" in the everyday world
   - the pleasure of a sadistic proximity to the other
   - desire and its guises
   - the enjoyment of life via laughter (and simultaneously: exclusion via laughter)
   - the fascination with sin, punishment, and redemption
   - the adventure of travel and the feeling of territorial belonging.

8. Pop culture is accessible and available. No effort is needed in order to gain access to its products. Pop assumes neither a prior acquisition of sophisticated aesthetic codes nor does it produce them (which in no way means that there is no refinement in popular culture).
9. Pop discourse creates an interface between the transcendental and the profane, the public and the private. Pop means both to peek into your neighbor's pot and into his soul, and at the same time to watch the gods at work.
10. The crux of pop discourse is myth, a weaving together of social and historical contradiction in eternity and nature.
11. The structure of perception in pop discourse comes from neither the real nor the dream. Rather, it most resembles a controlled daydream that has been constructed from the processing of anxieties, the masking of desire, the construction of a "livable" parallel world (*Heimat*), and finally, from ideology as therapy. Ideology changes its character in pop discourse. It latches on to a myth that claims to feed off eternity and nature, and still remains simultaneously both provisional and "useful."
12. Kracauer's notion of the "lobby" or anteroom [*Vorraum*] could be used to describe the individual parts of pop culture. One is always in the condition of the "not yet," in which the "real" happens only behind the next door. Pop resides before that holy space (temple as well as bedroom). Once the threshold is crossed, the pop myth crumbles.
13. The psycho-aesthetic compulsions of pop culture are fear and desire. Each pop product balances these two forces with great precision and links them into a new metafeeling, namely eroticized fear and panicked eroticism.
14. Pop culture mirrors the existing state of technology in the way it is produced and in its aesthetics. It continually employs the latest techniques in order to reach fundamental fantasies that seem to change only gradually. In the end, even the most state-of-the-art computer animation only generates the same old dragons.

15. Pop culture is connected to a longing for paradoxical fulfillment: for the construction of "the good old days" and the acceleration of images and sensations. Pop culture depicts the innovations of modernization, along with the production of winners and losers, by continuously linking them back to the victory of "traditional" values.
16. As much as all imaginable ideological signs in pop culture are able to "spook," they still refer clearly to the two basic values of the free market, namely "democracy" and "capitalism." Despite the fact that pop culture prefers to dream of the old, dependable, feudal, and familiar systems of domination, its center still contains a notion of liberation. The opposition between "people" and "power" is constantly and repeatedly suspended in pop culture. Part of the essence of pop culture is that it is freely and collectively accessible. It excludes no one from taking part in it, not even for economic reasons. Pop culture is cheap culture.
17. Pop sees no hidden truth in things. It initiates no analytical processes. Pop simulates "integrity" (and is, in fact, the essence of an aesthetic of fragmentation itself). Pop sees the spectacular and the exotic. Pop is utterly in love with the superficial. Sign and signified are identical. Whoever is good is also beautiful. Whoever is evil is also ugly. Everything else is part of a masquerade that will dissolve in the end.
18. Pop culture is usually part of the "antimodern" that is built into the processual nature of the modern. The antimodern longs both for a return to a preindustrial time, and for a time before society even existed. Its vision of civilization is a beautiful barbarism.
19. In addition to the notion of genre, pop culture produces the star. The star is a lived myth, an answer to the many questions that seethe unresolved in the audience. Here the star functions as problem solver (John Wayne), as rebel (James Dean), as a controlled ambivalence (Marlene Dietrich), as masked desire (Marilyn Monroe). Even more common is the merging of different impulses of release and identification in one figure: The star is not just an actor/performer [*Darsteller*], nor is s/he an instance of self-fashioning and self-exposure [*Selbstdarsteller*]. The appeal of the star occurs more at the margins and in the interstices. Part of what it means to be a star is the ritual of the audience. The star is a "king" whose only power is to transmit splendor. Although the star stands above the mass of his admirers, he is still "one of us." His star-ness is always tied to a passion that makes him completely vulnerable and utterly dependent upon us. He is a god without transcendental essence. Where the gods elude us, and even forbid human beings to make images of them, the star is all presence and image. Unlike an emperor or a pope, the star, in his strange oscillation between dominance and submission, exists in his pure representational function.
20. Popular culture functions melodramatically. In a non-transcendental, mechanical manner it transmits a moral in which good redeems and evil is punished.

II.

There are several points of contact between the aesthetic productions of German fascism and pop discourse. At the same time there are also a series of pronounced differences. Excluded from the aesthetic production of fascism is the frivolous and transitory nature of pop culture, to which we constantly adapt and adjust ourselves, even to the point of accepting the undesirable along with the fascinating (since, after all, it is "only" pop), or the play of pop culture with taboo and sin. Such is the paradox of a pop culture that has been raised to the level of an aesthetic-political doctrine.

A Riefenstahl film, placed in pop discourse (and thereby offered up as trivial, tantalizing, and mythologized), breaks apart into many different individual facets that are incompatible with one another—like an image that looks back at us from a greater and greater distance the closer the proximity from which we attempt to get a look at it. To be sure, the Nuba photographs and the myth that Leni Riefenstahl wove around this society of "natural fascists" are a direct continuation of the idealized images of the fascist stage set that she designed for the Nuremberg Rally film. But now this mythology has become pop. The "Nuba" dream involves no obligation. Rather, it creates pure theater from the connecting of sexuality, violence, nature, and myth; it creates a dream of a barbarism that does not necessarily call for a political praxis. Riefenstahl, then, has "learned nothing"—neither morally nor aesthetically—but now her statements can be associated only with the social space of consumption (even if that other human discourse, which appears to have learned just as little as she, assigns an artistic or even an anthropological value to her images).

To consider Riefenstahl films and the aesthetic of their images in the context of pop discourse could mean that we largely negate their political content. This seems possible to a certain extent, given the fact that their appellative character is minimal. The warlike and the fascist, the racist and the monumental are, then, only material for an inconsequential, quasi-empty organization of seething impulses, as if these were in fact oppositions that function entirely according to whether one dreams of fascism or whether one practices it. There is only one advantage to considering Riefenstahl in the context of pop discourse: We no longer have to act as if what we are contemplating is "art" (that would mean, among other things, that we would recognize as a fact an autonomous culpability on the part of the author "entity"). The "beautiful" that Leni Riefenstahl repeatedly invokes, a beauty capable of not only disregarding but also of transcending its own environment—this complete rejection of reflection [*Widerspiegelung*] suggests such a disassociation with a fervor that should make us suspicious. Does the cynicism of popular culture, in which everything can be turned into material—the crime, the misadventure, the heroic deed, and the harmony of movement itself—imply a kind of *carte blanche* for the author? And is Leni Riefenstahl really as wicked and as inconsequential as all the pop culture dreams of the beautiful and the evil?

The momentary, the playfully trivial, and the serial nature of pop discourse, however, trips itself up when it comes to other instances of perception, like "reality" for example. Only there can the pop commodity become an element of the pop circulatory system, in which the image is more powerful than the thing it represents. The image does not convey the social praxis. Instead, it replaces it just as the constantly running television film replaces everyday reality more than it comments on it. Riefenstahl's contention that her films are "more beautiful than reality" itself betrays art to pop discourse. She negates the concept of the artist's responsibility and sees the aesthetic as beyond morality. Leni Riefenstahl approaches her material with pop flippancy by serving not that which is represented but rather the image itself. Of course, it is utterly absurd to attempt to derive from this strategy a form of political absolution.

Perhaps it might be possible to work through the pop discourse catalogue anew with the aid of Leni Riefenstahl's films. This time we will try to do so in regard to both the production of the films and in light of the renaissance they have enjoyed recently in pop culture.

1. The films are parts of a series and are linked, insofar as they develop neither their own narration nor their own aesthetic. (In both of these, Leni Riefenstahl continually failed, despite her contention that it was the resistance of the Nazi Party leadership to her ideas that caused that failure.) Rather, her films are pre-staged performances of the kind disseminated by other media of the time as well. They connected a pretext ("beauty") and a subtext ("eroticism") and thereby elevated—to excess, as it were—a staged social production to the status of a myth.

   Just as pop represents pure surface but always depends on the material reality of that which is represented, Leni Riefenstahl is an "artist" who pretends to search for an abstract and morally neutral "beauty," but who can only extract it from the given, just as myth always requires its own "remnant of reality" (Barthes). The Riefenstahl aesthetic captures beauty not in abstraction, but rather in the serial organization of the concrete. Her gaze is turned toward the socially preformed, toward social reality. It permits no concrete artistic rebellion. If she is asked about the message of her images, she maintains that they only represent what was already there. If one points out the fact that she betrayed "that which was already there," then she cites her interest in abstraction. She claims for herself the artist's privilege of ignoring reality, and refuses to accept the artist's responsibility insofar as she—utterly consistent with popular culture—describes herself as only a medium. She poses as an author while simultaneously refusing to be one.
2. Thus, the author operates in a genre to whose development she admittedly made a significant contribution. Her task was to be faithful to the "Olympics film" genre while at the same time surpassing it. The dramatic staging of power and its representation, which she cultivated in the Nuremberg Rally films, has been a genre in popular culture for as long as it has existed. To a great extent

both genres continued to evolve because of the stimulus they received from Riefenstahl's images.

What differentiated Riefenstahl's *Olympia* films from their predecessors in the genre was more than the immense technical evolution of the medium itself and their stringent aesthetic concept (at once a political concept), which was not content to provide a mere documentation of athletic events. More than that, she transformed athletics from an autonomous space of corporeal experience into a succession of mythical acts that continually produced an aesthetic exaltation of the body. It was undoubtedly viewed with a desiring gaze. In addition, the films involved a melodramatization of athletic competition in which, from this point forward, there would always also be some kind of "story." In the Riefenstahl aesthetic the athlete becomes an actor whose individuality has almost no possibility to express itself. In pop culture, sports—conveyed via the Riefenstahl aesthetic—become image and melodrama. Both open a path not only for mass mediation as a supra-individual and supra-corporeal drama, but also as the image [*Abbild*] of an ideology. The dramatization through which Riefenstahl brings pressure to bear on her material makes clear that the individual competition in its exaggerated form could never be explained in and through itself, but rather only as the replica [*Abbild*] of something else.

3. Riefenstahl's stagings of sports and politics referred directly to other historically determined forms, above all to the images and entertainment created from what was known at the time about the culture of the ancient Greeks. In the corresponding sequences, the erotic subtext becomes particularly pronounced (a simultaneously sensual and morbid play of the body and the phallic symbol). Its intertextuality simultaneously blurs and mythologizes a whole series of analogies (purity, aristocracy, origin, clarity, etc.) between the past and the present, and lends the events on the field the character of an "eternal return."

In the temporal distance, through the use of imposing technology and sophisticated editing techniques, Riefenstahl's films seem to be more original and more autonomous than they really are. In a crossover act, Riefenstahl transfers the mysticism of the Alpine film onto a political stage. This technique of (pop) citation becomes even more apparent when we compare the *Olympia* films to amateur scientific works on the Greeks or illustrated books on *Ausdruckstanz* from the period. Even the spectacular camera angles are not unusual for the photography of the time. Finally, the "mass ornament" shown in the Nuremberg Rally films and prefabricated in the world of advertising and in the installations of New Objectivity [*neue Sachlichkeit*], is nothing more than the application of an "aesthetic of the object" to the aesthetic of the human body. The innovation here was linked back to the familiar, and even Riefenstahl's Nuba photographs have (admitted) models in the photographs of George Rodger (who rejected the images of his imitator: "They are certainly good photographs, but they have no warmth"). Only myth makes of Leni

Riefenstahl that dubious "artist" who at the same time is said to have "invented" fascist aesthetics.

4. "Modernity" is present in Riefenstahl's films in the conspicuousness of their technical devices and in the very direct manner in which the power of the medium itself is represented (in their abstract clarity: the medium is the message). The action in the *Olympia* films is endlessly dissolved. The camera does not adhere to the reality of time and space. The camera finds its "impossible" perspective up in a dirigible and its "impossible" movement through the technique of slow motion. "The camera lenses must penetrate the event in the strictest sense of the word," the director remarked back then. In the process that which is depicted [*das Abgebildete*], the phallic and necrophilic performance, repeats itself in the image [*Abbildung*]. (In the Nuremberg Rally film, the camera seems to be fascinated when it moves to capture close-ups of the skulls on the SS standards.) The exaltation of the subject matter is simultaneously its trivialization; the borders between performance and documentation blur, and the image speaks so narcissistically of itself that we find ourselves far less in the presence of a reality, and more in the midst of Leni Riefenstahl's dream of a male body that achieves victory as it perishes. The bulk of Hollywood cinema tells of nothing else.

   The propaganda effect of Riefenstahl's films can certainly be called into question, given the trivial nature of the treatment. The goal is not expressly stated, but rather self-explanatory in as far as it only appears to speak of that which speaks in everything and everyone. Unlike *Jud Süß* or *Kolberg*, the images do not present an argument. In fact, they remain tentative and nonbinding in as far as they refuse any rational reconstruction.

   In democratic pop culture, this kind of trivialization leads to a condition in which the spectator leaves the cinema with the conscious knowledge that "it was only a dream." The Riefenstahl aesthetic forecloses this very awakening just as much as any fascist performance does. The weighty signs form a closed system that achieves just the opposite: The performance categorically replaces reality, not as an alternative but as the real. In order to enter Leni Riefenstahl's dream, we must accept the closed nature of its aesthetic devices (if we follow the hand movements with which Riefenstahl describes the musical movements of the camera, then we soon have the imaginary construction of a closed space). Today this closed space of staging and performance is an element of pop with which we are utterly familiar. There is no exit from the *Lindenstraße* [a popular German television soap opera], and there is almost no way to establish a playful distance from it.

5. The Nuremberg Rally and the *Olympia* films cannot be seen as preliminary or temporary [*vorläufig*]. The immense amount of time devoted to finishing the *Olympia* films in postproduction made any idea of their speedy consumption impossible. The result is a paradoxical divide between the transitory nature of the events themselves and the claim to timelessness. The contradiction in the relationship between pop and fascism is this: Nothing threatens the

"fascisization" of images of the masses and of bodies more than the serial repetition of their occasions. In Riefenstahl's *Olympia* films, it was as if one had to feel that this was not *an* but *the* Olympics; this would be the last one. Pop will eat itself. But after the production of the "picturesque image," necrophilic Riefenstahl pop tolerates only the dead original. Even the objects of her next image world—the Nuba—had to die once the penetrating camera lenses closed. And the fish and corals that she chose as her next object? It is only as objects doomed to die that they have that aesthetic and mythic value that the author assigns to them.

Even in the direct reproduction of sports the social and historical is excluded: There is the aspect of "beauty" and that of suffering, but work and strategy are missing. The one who wins does so not because of some inherent quality; he merely repeats an age-old drama. Thus, the Riefenstahl aesthetic may be a kind of pop aesthetic that both monumentalizes, itself, and that also vehemently objects to its own transient and time-bound nature. Instead of relying on the cyclical return of fear and desire in ever newer forms, it bets on the construction of the "ultimate image."

6. The myth of a restaged and reenacted Olympics, like the Nuremberg Rally, is obvious: The event transcends itself and slips from time into the surreal (which Riefenstahl doggedly confuses with the beautiful). Anything that cannot be covered by the "beauty" of this myth is excluded from the image. In the Riefenstahl aesthetic both the Olympics and the Nuremberg Rally remain pop productions that, at best, only become "clear" by mistake. The staged production speaks of everything except its own intentions. The arbitrary legibility of its content is suppressed by the unambiguous nature of its form.
7. All of the "building blocks" of entertainment are present in Riefenstahl's films, of course with some significant displacements. These building blocks construct a network in democratic pop culture, where one element can always be used as a means of escape if the dominance of the other element becomes too great (every *Titanic* is followed by a *Titanic* parody). In the case of Riefenstahl, these building blocks are subjugated to a totality that negates all that is ironic and temporary [*vorläufig*].

The simple mythology of Riefenstahl's films and images, from the Alpine films to the Nuba photographs, is the search for the "savage man," the man who becomes a warrior. This form of corporeal mythology appears again and again in pop culture—Tarzan, Conan the Barbarian, the stars of professional wrestling, Schwarzenegger, and Stallone. The ideal of beauty is a paradox, since the man is not really obtainable for the woman. He is a sculpture. He refers only to himself. How can a woman approach such a man, one who transcends himself? As a competitor (the barbarian woman who wields a sword even more powerfully than the man does), as "Amazon," as mother, companion, subordinate, victim? Riefenstahl escapes the contradictory nature of her desire by fleeing into myth. That this desire can never be fulfilled leads to a double way out: The man must be sacrificed. He must be made less and less real. The human being becomes the body, the body becomes a sculpture, the sculpture is made into a war monument, the monument becomes an eternal repetition of the man as the masses, which then leads from the masses to the Führer. Without leaving pop discourse and without really becoming conscious of themselves ideologically, Riefenstahl's films describe a mythical answer to the fate of a female desire from an eroding bourgeoisie and in the "fascisization" of perception.

Is it not the case that Riefenstahl's films accomplished one of the main tasks of popular culture, namely the fulfillment of secret wishes? It is in pop discourse at the latest that these films become recognizable as both an abstract game with a "cold aesthetic" of bodies and masses, and as female erotic fantasies in which the male body becomes an object just like the female body had become through the male gaze in thousands of other productions—an object of both accessible, available desire and of a mythical disassociation.

The second mythical vanishing point, the erotic veneration of the meta-man Hitler, corresponds to the incursion of the magical [*des Wunderbaren*] into popular culture's world of desire and fear. Often in her films, Riefenstahl stages acts of deflowering and creation through the sheer gaze of the Führer. This gaze opens women's hearts and their sexes. The gaze overcomes all the weaknesses of the male body. It organizes the armies of bodies and deploys the mass ornament. With a clarity deserving our gratitude she describes her inner vision when she sees the Führer for the first time. Hitler and the masses—that is the symbol of that "super-orgasm" that this particular bourgeois daughter, who grew up in the shadow of her father (in the shadow of his very *Bürgerlichkeit*), was not permitted to have.

This form of image making corresponds directly to pop culture's strategy of relegating sexuality to the pretext (the heroic installation) and the subtext (the play of signs). The gaze of the Führer leaves us awestruck. At the same time, the gazes themselves repeatedly serve to create the Führer. The staging of the bodies and the Führer is tied to the appearance of light. The films [*Lichtspiele*] of Steven Spielberg work in much the same way. The trivializing use of the religious is an essential characteristic of pop culture. The chain of signs moves from the light of the sun (that awakens and forms the bodies) to the Olympic fire that now becomes visible as a fascist symbol, as that eternally blazing phallus that will soon have to go out into the world in order to consume it in its flames.

"Adolf Hitler Superstar" would experience a renaissance in postwar pop culture only as a demon or a clown, stripped of that erotic fascination Riefenstahl configured less in the "figure" of the Führer and more in the interaction of gazes. The Adolf Hitler of post-fascist pop culture is the negative of the Riefenstahl superstar. The Riefenstahl aesthetic does not produce its own code. There is no one who does not "get" a Riefenstahl image. The Riefenstahl aesthetic is built around a complex and paradoxical contradiction of artistic will and code. She is only looking, she says, for the "beautiful," the "picturesque";

she sees in the Nuremberg Rally and in the coral reef only the "stylized." In the nomenclature of pop culture, this surface fixation is called "glamour." However, in that discourse it is usually the case that the one who wears the mask can take it off again. What is more, the glamour of Marlene Dietrich's face only works as long as we know that it will dissolve once the spotlights are turned off. In democratic pop the dialectic of human being and mask is an open game.

8. The private is absent from Riefenstahl's production of the world of the strong and the beautiful. The image is planned together with the event and is produced in a manner similar to the event itself, just as a television show features its own audience. Of course, Riefenstahl, the personality and the writer of memoirs, delivers plenty of the private. In that context, she privatizes history just as radically as she monumentalizes the private in her own images. The pop discourse that Leni Riefenstahl over-fulfills demands a sublation of the dialectic of the two in favor of a symbiotic and mythical relationship. Riefenstahl always spoke of *Das blaue Licht* (*The Blue Light*) as her own (magical) biography. Just as desire can be read from the monumental stagings of the Nuremberg Rally and *Olympia* films, hurt can be read from *The Blue Light* (and from some of the images of female bodies, including those from the Nuba series). Private pain and public desire are connected by a myth that Riefenstahl conveyed already in her early career as a dancer and an actress. This is the world before its "demystification" (Kracauer's "*Entzauberung*"). This is nothing less than a classic pop-Reich.
9. The mythical manner in which Riefenstahl tells her stories composes a magical unity out of the elements of technology and nature, elements that are seen as contradictory in bourgeois culture. The mountain is the meta-body that men must tame and on which they sacrifice themselves, and it is simultaneously part of Riefenstahl's technique. She did not need to invent this symbol, because it was thoroughly anchored in the popular culture of the time. Even the images of bodies and the dance and sport scenes from the *Olympia* films are not original Riefenstahl creations. Nonetheless, she is indeed the woman in a group of men, one who has virtually doubled herself. While she is inwardly defiled, she is outwardly triumphant, a survivor. That the defiled woman herself turns toward the phallic is a virulent narrative topos in popular culture. This is the metaphysics of pop: The fulfillment of wishes and the processing of pain are condensed into one image that excludes categorically the question of the causes of that pain.

Riefenstahl's images of the body seem to liberate it, or at least rid it of the bourgeois strictures of clothing, only to confine it anew. As a star, Riefenstahl is the answer to the contradictions of a bogged-down project of female emancipation. She symbolically acts out wounds and desires at the place where it is the least conspicuous, namely in the company of men [*im Männerbund*]. What this myth depicts is the suspension of the contradiction between narcissism and submission. But does not every pop performance, once it attracts public attention and a mass audience, function according to the same model? Every rock concert and every carnival party? Is not every interaction between pop star and audience the very alternation between movement and virile pose? Is not every soccer game the orgiastic interplay between powerful forces and uniformly clad marionettes? If so, then Riefenstahl would have created the perfect form of the total pop event twice. And conversely, would it require an enormous effort to resist this "fascist" element in pop events? It seems that pop events are moving toward crossing the line at which there is no longer any lighthearted play, any freedom from obligation and commitment. That there is a "built-in" fascism in the productions of pop culture and that there are similarities between these and a Riefenstahl film is, to be sure, reflected in popular culture. There are films about it (*Wild in the Streets*) and stories like those of Philip K. Dick. It seems impossible to talk about pop culture while remaining silent about Leni Riefenstahl.

10. Coldness is not an error, but rather the essence of Riefenstahl films. They are perfect, but they are uninhabitable. From them we can cull glamour, but not *Heimat* (or home), fascination but no sense of security or belonging. It is no coincidence that ice is such a suitable metaphor in the films. However, it would be incorrect to maintain that the Riefenstahl aesthetic transported or produced an ideology. The Riefenstahl aesthetic is already ideology itself to such an extent that it can no longer become conscious of its own ideological nature, even if it wanted to. Just as "beauty" replaces experience, ideology takes the place of feeling [*Empfindung*].
11. Leni Riefenstahl's films do not describe fascism, but rather the "lobby" to fascism. Riefenstahl's constant blindness is the blindness of pop to all consequences. The threshold before the "actual" space is not crossed (in her memoirs this image returns repeatedly—the refusal to enter the "actual" space).
12. In the Riefenstahl aesthetic, the driving forces of fear and desire are suspended in a monumentalized world of images. "Beauty" and violence take their place. The aesthetic concept is apathy. The gaze is selective, not empathetic. This is the "imitation" of a gaze, the imitation of the foreign and powerful gaze onto one's own or another's culture that has been a part of cinema ever since the Lumière brothers brought their audience a view that moved from the executive suite to the workers leaving the factory. Pop in fascism is also the uncoded imitation of the gaze of the Führer upon the masses.
13. The "beauty" of the Riefenstahl aesthetic is, like that of futurism, the result of mechanical production. However, it is not the beauty of the machine that is discovered and extolled in the process, but rather the transformation of the human being into a machine. Happiness lies in the annihilation of the "bourgeois" entities of person, ego, soul, conscience. The eternal popular culture dream of a perfected, soulless parallel human being, of Frankenstein's monster, cyborgs, replicas, is in this case represented as a quasi-documentary truth. Leni Riefenstahl's people are nothing more than those beautiful monsters that

spook us in the nightmares of bourgeois pop culture—"zombies among cannibals."

14. In the Riefenstahl aesthetic we return to a state of nature in which the bourgeois ambivalence of desire and alienation is no more. No arcadia and no revelation. The "good old days" are fascism in raw form—the natural is the warlike.
15. There is a fantasy of "liberation" in the Riefenstahl aesthetic (it is at the core of her biographical legend), but this liberation does not ask what it is supposed to liberate itself from, nor where such a liberation will lead. It is the liberation of nature from civilization, the liberation of the id from the ego. Thus, the "flight from civilization"—a constant in pop culture—leads to a paradoxical metacivilization, to the paradoxical image of an organized barbarism.
16. The Riefenstahl aesthetic spells the absolute domination of the gaze over the image, a relation that pop culture simultaneously desires and fears. The world is utterly devoid of secrets and ordered; the sign has murdered the signified. The body is not the expression of life. Rather, life is in the service of the characterization and marking of the body. Riefenstahl is completely blind to the spiritual background of the Nuba masks and rituals. The other side of ritual, namely chaos, is absent.
17. The antimodern in Riefenstahl's dream worlds has been transferred from the level of a lost paradise into the projection of the only true world. The (bourgeois) problem with the modern no longer exists, because everything modern finds its sole application as a means for the production of the antimodern.
18. In her image worlds, Leni Riefenstahl consciously and repeatedly distinguishes the individual from the mass. However, unlike democratic pop culture, she does not do so in order to make the individual into a star, into a "hero for a day." Rather, the sole, absolute star of her films is Adolf Hitler. He is not the icon in these films (the image that reproduces itself endlessly but that remains the same), but rather quite directly the man in erotic contact with his two lovers, the woman and the masses. This superstar, the answer to all of our questions (the final linkage of man and god), cannot tolerate any kind of individual image in his proximity, since every individual represents an unresolved question.
19. All of Leni Riefenstahl's films, images, and texts—because they are to such a large extent masked desire—function melodramatically in the negative. If the ideal of the melodramatic is to create virtue through terror (and even if it is only the terror of "fate"), then terror itself, in the case of Riefenstahl, has been elevated to the status of a virtue. It is not that the virtuous is victorious in the end, but rather that the victory is virtuous.

III.

The Riefenstahl aesthetic, although it certainly treats its material in a trivial manner, does not allow itself to be trivialized. It can best be described as the bastard of pop culture, one that helps itself to the advantages of its pedigree without sticking to the rules of that parentage. It crosses the borders of pop not just in its monumentality and aggressiveness, not only in its necrophilia, but also through the reinterpretation of its precepts [*Vorgaben*].

The Riefenstahl aesthetic becomes a negative key to the question as to whether pop culture is capable of creating meaning at all, or whether it, in fact, means—at least from the perspective of the democratic and capitalist consensus—"everything and nothing." Is pop culture, then, automatically fascist at that point at which it seeks to get beyond itself? The "intensified" version of pop would have to discover at least that part of fascist aesthetic production that functioned less according to fantasies about conspiracies and eliminatory bogeymen, and more in the sense of self-stylization. These are questions of production and simulation that arise in the context of the postmodern relation to pop, and for which the Riefenstahl aesthetic, through all sorts of circuitous routes, has been rediscovered as "avant-garde."

The rediscovery of Leni Riefenstahl and her crossover into pop discourse took place in the 1970s, when the divide between affliction [*Betroffenheit*] and entertainment opened wider than ever, a time at which the alliance between pop avant-garde, youth culture, and leftist revolution ended. Paradoxically, through entertainment, affliction developed to the point that it began to take on the characteristics of entertainment. One was "afflicted" and moved by the "sheer" pleasure felt when viewing Riefenstahl's films. Whereas in the 1970s the crucial question was whether something could be both "art" and fascist, the main concern later became the acceptance of the superficial charms of pop language and the negation of the fascist core. After a brief phase in which Riefenstahl's films were seen as "campy" (which also means that the dangerous, the abyssal, and even the evil in these films was consciously included in the reproduction process), the films were regarded in pop discourse as both harmless and ("somehow") rebellious. That was indeed the case, since the rebellion in the films had lost its content; it had become a matter of form.

The "cold pop" of the 1970s, which distanced itself from the slightly stuffy warmth of the hippies, must have felt challenged by Riefenstahl's closed aesthetic system. During this period, pop and art danced uncomfortably around one another. For Andy Warhol, art could reemerge from pop by merely declaring that it was art and through an act of isolation. This is exactly what Riefenstahl seems to have shown with her films by permitting the biographical individual to appear only as the material for a cinematic sculpture. She made from the human being the same thing Andy Warhol made from the tomato soup can when he added the element of New Objectivity to the concatenation of "objects."

David Bowie radicalized the transitory nature of life in the pop cosmos ("hero for a day") and accepted the Riefenstahl aesthetic for its very coldness, which allowed for an exit from the closed space. Many of the pop heroes of the time were fascinated by Riefenstahl—Francis Ford Coppola, Mick Jagger, Susan Sontag, Bryan Ferry—and their veneration functioned through very different strategies. For Mick Jagger, it was "Sympathy for the Devil." In the case of Coppola, it was a fascination that led him to choose Richard Wagner's "Ride of the Valkyries" as an accompaniment to helicopter attacks in Vietnam. For Bryan Ferry, it was the attitude of the cool dandy, aloof to bodies and emotions. Susan Sontag even intended to purify Riefenstahl of fascist dross. Of course, this veneration of Riefenstahl on the part of 1970s pop heroes was itself pop through and through—frivolous, transitory, and quickly replaced by new points of reference. In the end, Riefenstahl herself became a pop icon, a image of pure surface. In Los Angeles in 1977, a group of teenagers founded a Riefenstahl fan club, complete with T-shirts bearing Leni Riefenstahl's face. A group from the "German New Wave" thought it was amusing to call itself "Reifenstahl." And, in fact, Riefenstahl's photographs of Mick and Bianca Jagger are just as trivial as her work from the 1972 Munich Olympics. Pop discourse has no interest in the outcome; it is interested only in the event.

Nineteen eighty-two and 1983 were the big years of Nazi chic in the West. The duo *Deutsch-Amerikanische Freundschaft* (German-American Friendship) sang "*Tanz den Adolf Hitler*" ("Do the Adolf Hitler") and "*Unsere Stiefel sind so schwarz*" ("Our Boots Are So Black"), and posed for photographs as fascist dictators in front of a flag with a black fantasy emblem. All signs were meant to lose their political content. In the period, critical engagement with the films of Riefenstahl was almost completely absent, and the films were thoroughly trivialized. Leni Riefenstahl became "current" once again in that she was rediscovered as a photographer whose aesthetic came closest to fitting a structure without content. She was celebrated as the producer of "empty images," whether one found words to describe them or not.

The identity-obsessed early 1970s discovered Leni Riefenstahl as an individual (and even as a person in a feminist imaginary; one text even spoke of her as "sister"). The 1980s, however, saw the form of her aesthetic more "abstractly," since "content" belonged to a long gone aesthetic epoch. What made the films of Leni Riefenstahl so readable specifically in the 1980s, then, was their coldness, their lack of identity. The aspects of the Riefenstahl aesthetic cited by the pop culture of the late 1970s and early 1980s suited above all two ideas: the "athletic" stylization of the body and the staged space. This is the sense in which the first episode of the *Star Wars* saga in particular functioned quite clearly according to the Riefenstahl aesthetic. It shows the transformation of the male body into a monument to itself and, particularly in the last sequence in the throne room, the staging of empty space as the installation of a "positive" force.

In the end, the pop quality of the Riefenstahl aesthetic can be understood most clearly in the admiration for her two large photography series. The Nuba photographs are a mercilessly sadistic and fascist world of images that depicts absolutely nothing that has to do with a foreign culture. Rather, these photographs depict a fascist culture in a mythically reconstructed (simulated) and raw state. Anything that could disturb the eroticized vision of the militant, steeled, young warrior-man and of the woman as his "reward" (or as his inventor) is removed in a fade-out. Here, of course, Riefenstahl makes an antipop argument: The elimination of the weak, the sick, and the "unaesthetic" exists not thanks to the staging but rather thanks to the "reality" of Nuba culture. The Riefenstahl aesthetic that emerged at the end of the decade in the world of advertising as well no longer requires this move of "documentary" deception and disguise. Thus, ideology in Riefenstahl's pop staging is unmistakably the endless flight between the discourses of the documentary, the artistic, and the pop dream of a beautiful aesthetic surface [*vom schönen Schein*].

Riefenstahl's Nuba photographs always aim for the staging of the body as the essential. They "read" neither faces nor landscapes. They permit no processes of time and individuality. They are very similar to the hero comics of the 1940s and again to those of the 1970s. Finally, they are reminiscent of the academic studies of the male body in the "Tarzan" comics of Burne Hogarth. Riefenstahl's photographs offer a message that wants nothing to do with itself. In their very monumentality, the images empty themselves *stante pede* when placed under any kind of analytical scrutiny. The "fascination" of Riefenstahl's images emerges, then—and here they become a paradigm of fascist aesthetics as such—from the fact that they sell pop as art. The message is a surface without substance. The form is the content. In the end that means that the aesthetic becomes incomprehensible, evading each and every analytical approach by fleeing into another segment in the production of meaning.

Even the second of Riefenstahl's image worlds, the fish in the sea, begets fascist content from a process of becoming pop (from the concealing of contents also). The images declare nature part of the repertoire of the beautiful and the exotic. It suits the misconceptions of pop myth to view nature as nothing more than art in a raw state. In the best case, this misunderstanding produces kitsch. In the worst case, it leads to the idea that violence is the aesthetic staging of nature. Even in her deep-sea images, Riefenstahl does not want to "see" anything that is not inherent in the production of the image itself. She shows us a "nature" that imitates her "art."

From the process of perfecting the staged image itself, the image of fascism without historicity emerges. This is a fascism that exhausts itself in the production of its own image: fascism as pure pop event. To accept this means to complete the emptying of the images. Riefenstahl in pop discourse—that means something different for every decade, for every pop era. In the 1950s, she was indeed shunned and isolated. She had to pay a price by serving as a stand-in for a number of other "artists" of the Third Reich who seem to have escaped punishment far more easily than Riefenstahl did and who were permitted to work before she was. The fact that she learned nothing in the process, was never introspective, that she never abandoned the attitude of innocent victim, that she took umbrage instead of grieving, that she filed lawsuits instead of offering to participate in dialogue—all of that made her into a key figure of the old right-wingers. She armored herself. She became unreachable, untouchable. She allowed no one to look into her (and perhaps she could not look into herself either). The only thing she was able to rescue in this period was her complete identification with the martyr role. In the 1960s, we saw the first attempts to establish some distance from her person and to understand her aesthetic nonetheless. Psychoanalytic offerings were made to the artist of "phallic narcissism" (Mitscherlich). But her armor only became stronger. The first wave of the 1970s pop renaissance was at least partially aware of the danger of playing with her images. Above all it was a cold fascination that was at issue here; at the end of the century, a process began that would find its climax in the 1980s: the devaluation of content and the fascination with form. At the time, it was apparent that the Nuba photographs could be read in myriad ways. They satisfied the hunger for nature in the post-hippie generation. In fact, the images seemed appropriate as part of the advocacy on behalf of threatened indigenous peoples. Thus, they were free of fascism. These simultaneously anticipated the body culture of the "me generation," which repaired to the fitness studio as the setting for its social and erotic rivalries.

At that time, Leni Riefenstahl herself became the myth of someone who ignores her age and had not "let herself go." As such, she was celebrated in high society, which saw in her the embodiment of a whole series of dreams. She becomes the prophet for an entire generation of nature boys like Reinhold Messner, who are themselves media sculptures. What contributed in no small part to the transference of Leni Riefenstahl into pop discourse during the 1980s was the revival of the 1930s and 1940s. The very feeling of dancing on the edge of the abyss created a space for the immense pleasure of provocation and simulation. Punk and New Wave devalued political signs generally, and people collected everything that was reminiscent of the "weighty signs" of the political past, from peace signs to swastikas. In the same vein, Riefenstahl's films seemed relevant and timely because they were perfect simulations. Yes, it was clear that there would never again be an opportunity to fabricate such a perfect simulation in film, because in the *Olympia* and the Nuremberg Rally films the entire world became simulation through the concentrated power of medium and mastery. The age of simulative narcissism was bound to find a kinship in fascist aesthetics, with which it now engaged "only" aesthetically and semiotically, and no longer politically, morally, and historically.

Leni Riefenstahl experienced a completely different kind of rebirth in the pop discourse of the 1990s (a time with no noteworthy opposition to the process). Here the complete opposite of the 1980s phenomenon is palpable: Whereas the Riefenstahl aesthetic was once admired for its very coldness and stoniness, it now became charged with emotion. The friendly, plucky, grand old lady is more than happy to volunteer for a game of mother-and-son, particularly if it involves young men of the "1989 generation." But this is now not only a matter of fun and games. The well-protected Riefenstahl and her innocence are tenaciously defended. Her synthetic biography is unwavering in its defense of Leni Riefenstahl. It now assumes the status of truth—a pop truth that, in its unreasonable attempt at rationalization, is itself an act of malfeasance. A certain Joachim Lottman addressed Riefenstahl in the pages of the magazine *Münchner*: "Dear Ms. Riefenstahl, I couldn't care less about Adolf Hitler and all that, and I know the same goes for you. From your biography I can see that you never even spoke to the Führer for more than a few minutes." That is the response, even though the biography is nothing more than the disguised, endlessly convoluted and twisted love story of Leni and Adolf—a love story that was never allowed to happen.

In the 1990s, the Riefenstahl devotees take off their gloves. They adopt not only the lie that is her life [*ihre Lebenslüge*], they also raise Riefenstahl to absolute purity. Leni Riefenstahl and the traces of her aesthetic in miniature form in pop culture seem finally to have arrived at the point at which these remnants are consecrated in pop recycling. The Riefenstahl myth is no longer necessary for the production of the Riefenstahl aesthetic. She has the absolutely "perfect" images for the undeclared civil war of neoliberalism. She is the absent mother of the German yuppies. It is this very absolute lack of human empathy, of tenderness, of responsibility, and of warmth that is now being sentimentalized and valorized as a part of the new brutality of neoliberalism. Like Leni Riefenstahl herself, her latest acolytes venerate only the beautiful and the strong in pop culture. For the first time, the Riefenstahl aesthetic seems freely accessible. No longer devoid of content, it is re-ideologized in sports, in advertising, in computer games.

The playful triviality of the game is now over. We know that the signs mean something again. We also know, even if we excuse her as a primary perpetrator, that flirting with Leni Riefenstahl the person and the creator of a particular aesthetic strategy is anything but innocent. Even now, attempts are underway to reinvent Riefenstahl as a pop product or as a producer of pop—obviously using other paradigms. The Italian newspaper *Corriere della Sera* titled an exhibition in Milan "The Untamed Leni." The German newsmagazine *Der Spiegel* wrote of the Nuremberg Rally film that one could not "quite divest oneself of the suspicion that the masses danced less to tune of the Führer and more to that of Leni Riefenstahl." The myth of the strong woman has taken the place of the myth of the artist who was intoxicated by beauty, whose innocence was led astray. The questions as to Riefenstahl's aesthetic legacy are now posed in a new way. The new fascism, and its echo of the old fascism, has now arrived at the point where it means business—it fills the trivialized, devalued signs with meaning again, and it has recently transformed—as in the "culture" of the new right wing—what was once the trivial invocation of fascist aesthetics into the commitment to a "worldview."

Leni Riefenstahl in pop discourse? The question must always return us to the fundamental elements of the production and consumption of popular culture itself.

Chapter 2

Riefenstahl and the Face of Fascism

Carsten Strathausen

Leni Riefenstahl as "Junta" in *Das blaue Licht (The Blue Light)*, as seen in the illustrated film programs for the original 1932 version of the film and for its 1938 release.

I.

Let me begin by looking at a photograph. It depicts Riefenstahl in her role as Junta in *The Blue Light* from 1932. One of her best known, the portrait plays a crucial role in the diegesis of this film, where it appears on the cover of the innkeeper's book that purportedly preserves the memory of Junta for later generations. The picture of Junta not only graces the cover of Riefenstahl's memoirs, which appeared in English translation in 1992, it also plays a prominent role in Ray Müller's 1993 documentary *Die Macht der Bilder* (*The Wonderful, Horrible Life of Leni Riefenstahl*). Irritated by Müller's persistent questions about her involvement in the Third Reich, Riefenstahl points to the poster of Junta behind her and likens her own biographical fate to that of her fictive creation: "Just as Junta lost her ideals, in the same way I lost my ideals at the end of the war. To that extent the film was indeed a premonition of my own destiny."

Riefenstahl repeatedly sought to dodge the fierce criticism of her accusers by means of such analogues, which are perpetuated by friends and foes alike.[1] The latter, of course, advance a completely different interpretation of her persona, according to which Riefenstahl's picture can be read as the ambiguous emblem of Nazi culture as such: beautiful, yet treacherous, an embellished mask covering up the horrors underneath. In this sense, one might say that to look at Riefenstahl is to stare into the face of fascism itself, her cross-eyed gaze (her *Silberblick*) symbolizing the perfidious, double-edged nature of her work. Just as critics have read *Triumph of the Will* as a deceptive veneer that concealed the regime's true barbarism, Riefenstahl's cinematic portrait is but a pretty mask that hides her true face.

The problem with such a reading is that it unwittingly doubles the Nazis' own rhetoric about the alleged two faces of the Jew, expressed most vividly in Veit Harlan's notorious *Jew Süss* from 1940 during the conversation between the Duke and Süss:

Duke: Hm, what kind of look is he giving me? As if his face were that of a hypocrite.

Süss: What kind of face?

Duke: Hm, he should take off his mask, my dear fellow!

Süss: What mask?

Duke: The last one, the last one! Ha, what does he really look like, what does he really look like?

Süss: How am I really supposed to look?[2]

This parallel, in my view, highlights the ambivalent nature of the traditional effort to "unmask" the fascist aesthetics allegedly operating in Riefenstahl's work. For this approach can easily be reversed to lend credibility to Riefenstahl's self-stylization as an innocent scapegoat for the wrath of zealous antifascists or antifeminists or antiaesthetes who allegedly persecute her much like the Nazis persecuted the Jews. Convincing or not, the logic of the argument remains the same in either case, since this line of reasoning can be applied to whatever position one chooses to support. This inherent reversibility—not to say arbitrariness—of traditional *Ideologiekritik* is not the least reason for the stale rigidity that has characterized the Riefenstahl debate over the last few decades.[3]

In the following, I would like to explore this impasse as symptomatic of a larger crisis of *Ideologiekritik* in general (section II) and promote a different aesthetic approach that tries to avoid it (section III). Since my overall goal is to remobilize critical discourse and push beyond its established positions, I shall discuss the relationship between stasis and mobility in Riefenstahl's films in the context of contemporary art and aesthetics (sections IV and V).

II.

There are two reasons why Riefenstahl's work continues to fascinate even after her death and receives the copious attention it has throughout much of the twentieth and into the twenty-first century. The first relates to the contemporary political situation. The events of 9/11 and the U.S.-American military involvement in the Middle East have prompted what President Bush calls a "war of ideas" between Islamic fundamentalists and Western liberal democracies. Haunted by the specter of the Vietnam War, the U.S. has drastically increased its propagandistic efforts to improve its damaged reputation all over the world, paying journalists in Iraq to disseminate prearranged and preapproved information by the Pentagon as independent news reports while, at the same time, censoring public broadcasts about American and Iraqi casualties at home. (Just recall the administration's strong reaction against the allegedly "illegal" proliferation of pictures in the Internet in 2004, which showed the arrival of flag-draped coffins carrying the remains of fallen American soldiers.) In such a climate, Riefenstahl's aesthetic embellishment of the Nazi regime cannot but arouse interest, be it in order to learn more about the use of televised propaganda in general (as did Frank Capra back in 1940 when he drew inspiration from Riefenstahl's *Triumph of the Will* for his own *Why We Fight* series that sought to justify America's engagement in World War II), or be it in order to emphasize the inherent dangers of state-sanctioned propaganda for all liberal-democratic societies, both then and now.

But there is another, more historical reason for Riefenstahl's continued presence on the contemporary agenda. It concerns the proverbial "aestheticization of politics" (Walter Benjamin) under German fascism. For decades, scholars have scrutinized Hitler's obsession with art and architecture and the Nazis' effective use of modern media in an effort to come to terms with the nature of a "fascist aesthetics." Riefenstahl's work in particular has been pivotal to this effort, and one might consider the continued scholarly and public interest in Riefenstahl as a symptom for a deep-seated fear that haunts the history of aesthetic discourse: the fear that art is not ethical as such, but can be made to serve the most inhumane and barbaric policies. Ever since Plato, the relationship between aesthetics and ethics has remained a highly charged matter of debate particularly in Germany, and there is little hope that the issue will be settled soon.[4] In Riefenstahl's case, this fear about the potentially unethical dimension of art is exacerbated by the century-old humanist suspicion of technological media as inherently ideological and prone to political abuse. According to Vilém Flusser, twentieth-century "techno-images"—as opposed to traditional media such as books or paintings—are determined by soulless apparatuses whose interior mechanism few of us fully understand or control.[5] Flusser's concern about the disastrous and deeply antidemocratic impact of techo-image-proliferation in Western culture was and still is shared by a number of media critics, among them Guy Debord, Jean Baudrillard, and

Neil Postman.[6] Put differently, Riefenstahl's work becomes the locus where these two humanist qualms—the one concerning the ethical frailty of traditional art and the other regarding the manipulative nature of technological media—coincide and reinforce each other. This, in my view, distinguishes her case from that of other Nazi collaborators like Arno Breker, Albert Speer, Ernst Jünger, or in the French tradition, Louis-Ferdinand Céline.[7]

The hope to exorcise this fear is the hidden motor that powers the search for a "fascist aesthetics." The latter, according to Walter Benjamin, grants the masses their (aesthetic) self-expression, but not their (politico-economic) rights.[8] Trying to substantiate this claim, traditional *Ideologiekritik* has sought to expose the "totalitarian" effects produced by the hidden mechanical apparatus operating underneath the Nazi's celebration of the *Volk*. We find an excellent example of this *Ideologiekritik* in Müller's documentary *The Wonderful, Horrible Life of Leni Riefenstahl*, which includes video footage documenting the making of his own film. Müller thus alludes to a crucial difference between the most radical avant-garde techniques of the 1920s and 1930s and Riefenstahl's ambition of seamlessness and aesthetic closure. Contrary to any of Riefenstahl's movies, Müller's film features *the making of the film as an essential part of the film*.[9] In other words, he includes the recording of the production process within the exhibition of the final product. Müller's effort to increase the aesthetic transparency of his film is anathema to Riefenstahl's style. One of the reasons why Riefenstahl later disavowed and actually sought to "erase" from memory the making of her first Nazi propaganda film *Victory of Faith* from 1933 was precisely the rough or unrefined quality of the film, where power cables are visible and people stumble into position right in front of the camera. By contrast, Soviet filmmakers like Dziga Vertov and Sergei Eisenstein, much like Müller himself, reveled in this deliberate deconstruction of their own movies.

On the basis of this juxtaposition, many scholars—either implicitly or explicitly—advance the following argument: The Soviet deconstructive approach activates the critical faculties of the audience to evaluate what they see, whereas Riefenstahl's classicism numbs these faculties and instead seduces the audience to embrace the ideological message of the film. One school uses montage critically so as to raise the consciousness of the "awakened" proletarian class, whereas the other only appeals to the masses' base, subconscious instincts, thereby turning them into mindless automatons.

I have several misgivings about this argument. First, one ought not to forget that the Soviet style at the time also included outright propaganda films. This is not to deny or diminish the ideological differences between Nazism and Stalinism, but to argue that the kind of consciousness propagated and raised in Soviet film was a streamlined one steeped in party rationale rather than the exercise of free, independent, and critical thinking. Second, the juxtaposition of Eisenstein's critical versus Riefenstahl's affirmative cinematography all too easily merges with another problematic assumption of some film critics, namely that the classical Hollywood style of the mid-1930s to the mid-1950s—defined by the shot/reverse shot paradigm and cinematic suture—is inherently more ideological than avant-garde cinema. One hides the constitutive mechanism of its cinematic effect, whereas the other highlights and thus exposes this mechanism. But obviously there are numerous Hollywood films from the classical period that resist this simple equation of form and function.[10] To argue otherwise is to condemn film-realists like André Bazin as vicious ideologues or to return to the ahistorical and metatheoretical vision of the cinematic apparatus as a gigantic interpellation machine that conditions film audiences to become mindless consumers of basic ideological beliefs, as Christian Metz, Jean-Louis Baudry, and other Lacanian-inspired theorists argued in the 1970s.[11] My point is that we cannot simply equate (aesthetic) form with (socio-ideological) function without considering the specific historical circumstances in each case. In the words of Karsten Witte: "Instead of determining which features constitute a fascist film, we need to examine how films functioned under fascism or rather, in the context of fascism."[12]

We are now able to reverse the proposition I advanced above, according to which Riefenstahl's work conjures a humanist fear about the (missing) ethical dimension of art and aesthetics, a fear that needs to be exorcised through rational discourse. The fact that there continues to be broad interest in Riefenstahl testifies to the futility of this effort; otherwise, the issue would have been settled long ago. This effort—which Wolfgang Fritz Haug once correctly diagnosed as indicative of the "helplessness of antifascists" with regard to art in the Third Reich[13]—is futile because Nazi aesthetics cannot be positively identified with a fixed set of tangible characteristics or stylistic patterns. Albert Speer's monumental neo-classicism, Arno Breker's glorification of naked bodies, and Riefenstahl's cinematic montage idealizing a *völkisch* community are examples of attempts to define such stylistic qualities. However, there is no distinct Nazi style of art that could be abstracted from its historical context in this way. There is only a multifaceted Nazi aesthetics that envelops and informs this art to serve a specific sociopolitical function at a particular moment in time. The overall goal was to redefine the very concept of "reality" and the human perception of that reality by means of an overpowering *Gesamtkunstwerk* of intersecting media (what Bertolt Hinz rightly calls a *Medienverbund*) considered more perfect than reality itself.[14] Put differently, the falsity of Nazi aesthetics lies not in its attempt to distort or idealize reality (that being the proper task of all art and aesthetics), but in its unwillingness to allow for other distortions or idealizations of reality besides its own. Nazi aesthetics sought to close down what must remain an essentially open discourse regarding the experience of difference.

This brings me to my central argument. The rejection of Riefenstahl's aestheticized style far too quickly and reductively identifies what seems to be at stake in aesthetic discourse: an immediate rationalization about the critical—which is to say the cognitive—potential of art. Sensibility and the sensible, by contrast, are quickly subordinated to this allegedly superior goal better to understand the world. I argue against this tendency, not so as to denounce the critical aspects of art *tout court*, but to reject its exclusivity or superior role in aesthetic discourse. This strong focus on the rational potential of art is particularly unhelpful in the case of Nazi aesthetics, which openly acknowledged their "un-critical" nature. In 1937, Goebbels officially prohibited the use of the term *art criticism*, speaking instead of the "art-report." The task of art, according to Paul Schultze-Naumburg, Alfred Rosenberg, and other cultural conservatives in the Nazi regime, was *not* to mirror the existing status quo, but to visualize the fascist ideal of a higher reality underneath the everyday.[15] The goal of Nazi culture was to achieve a "naturalization of the ideal, and simultaneously an idealization of nature," as Bertolt Hinz has rightly argued.[16]

This conflation of reality and the ideal explains why Nazi ideologues could herald *Triumph of the Will* as an authentic documentary of the 1934 party rally. In fact, everyone acknowledged—and Riefenstahl herself repeatedly emphasized—the constructed nature of the film, since many scenes were rehearsed, while others were restaged after the actual events had already occurred. Martin Loiperdinger addresses this paradox by pointing to the specific understanding of "documentation" in Nazi ideology, which does not "refer to a truthful representation of a historical event, but to the successful implementation of a particular intention: to address the spectator such that he feels himself part of the portrayed event."[17] The goal of the film, then, was to leave a strong impression on the audience. The stronger this impression, the more "true" was the depicted reality on the screen, because it would entice ever more people to join the movement and realize its goals. It is precisely this allegedly transformative and self-realizing power of images and ideas that defines the "Nazi myth" in Philippe Lacoue-Labarthe and Jean-Luc Nancy's sense of the term. The Nazi "myth is only true when it is *lived*," they argue, meaning that the Nazi "*Weltanschauung* must be absolutely embodied" in and through the people who actively participate in the rallies.[18]

This crucial shift in Nazi cultural theory from a production-oriented toward a reception-oriented approach that aims to "capture" the audience also explains the lack of a discernable style in Nazi cinema, as film experts such as Eric Rentschler, Linda Schulte-Sasse, and Sabine Hake have shown. For once you focus on the creation of a certain atmosphere or mood as the goal of artistic production, all aesthetic styles and materials become available to serve this goal. Hake is correct when she concludes that the Nazi identification of filmic reality with perceptual and emotional effects "closed the gap between ideologized constructions of the real in the state-commissioned film and the conventional techniques of illusionism associated with popular entertainment."[19] In other words, the classical normative distinction between state propaganda and popular art disintegrates. In this regard, Nazi culture confronts us with an all-encompassing process of aestheticization not unlike that which we face today.

III.

This correlation seems to leave us with only two choices: The first is to recoil from aestheticization in general and to denounce *all* of its forms as potentially fascist. This is exactly what Adorno had in mind when he spoke of fascism coming to America in the guise of Mickey Mouse. The second option is to embrace this aestheticization and to agree with Gilles Deleuze and Félix Guattari that "art is sensation and nothing else."[20] The methodological consequences of this dictum have been clarified recently by Brian Massumi, who argues that "techniques of negative critique [must] be used sparingly" in cultural studies in order "to shift to [more] affirmative methods" of investigation.[21] As for most Deleuzians, Massumi's underlying assumption seems to be that the more thoughts and ideas we produce, the more relationships will form and the more multiplicity will exist in the world. However, this is clearly not the case. Unfettered growth often entails self-destructive tendencies. After all, there is cancerous growth—global capitalism is a good example. Thus, the overall goal must be a particular kind of growth (or productivity), one that enables connectivity and fosters sustainable relationships among the existing parts. The ethico-political dimension of art is to increase—rather than decrease—the level of complexity in the world. In the words of Heinz von Förster, "Always act in such a way that the number of possibilities is increased."[22] Both art and aesthetic discourse should abide by this dictum.

In order to achieve this goal, "affirmative" thinking and production is as important as the judicious reevaluation of what already exists. By contrast, the term *Ideologiekritik* is best avoided altogether—not because our analyses aim to be uncritical, but because these terms still carry along the traditional Marxist connotation of some objective rationality able to look through the ideological veil of art or aesthetics in order to discover its allegedly "true" meaning. Based upon an antiquated nineteenth-century (Hegelian-hermeneutic) epistemology, this goal of objectivity remains unattainable for any form of scientific or humanist criticism. The latter is always bound to a particular perspective, some of which are better than others merely in the sense that they produce a richer and more complex reading that enables a higher degree of interconnectivity among ideas.

Aesthetic discourse, then, is neither Derridean nor Deleuzian, but always—and necessarily—both. The ratio between these two aspects—the critical and the affirmative—remains problematic for aesthetic theory. Or, to borrow a term from Roland Barthes, I would say it remains "obtuse." In an essay discussing some Eisensteinian film stills, Barthes defines the obtuse meaning of an image as that which disrupts its "obvious" (informational or symbolic) meaning. "A signifier without a signified," the obtuse meaning remains "outside (articulated) language," because its function is not to criticize or explain a particular content but to disrupt "the whole practice of meaning" as such. "In short," Barthes concludes, "what the obtuse meaning disturbs, sterilizes, is metalanguage ([that is] criticism)."[23] Barthes here alludes to the fact that *aisthesis*, or the study of perception, cannot render its object fully transparent without losing what it hopes to grasp. Otherwise, it would become superfluous in much the same way as Hegel once predicted the "end of art" in his lectures on aesthetics. There, Hegel claimed that "art is and remains for us . . . a thing of the past."[24] For Hegel, the ultimate goal of art was the dissolution of sensuous substance into philosophical ideas, of matter into thought. I would make the exact opposite claim, namely that art resists this conversion, and that it is the responsibility of aesthetic discourse to look after this resistance. In my view, sensing difference or making difference sensible is precisely *not* the same as to explain it or define it or understand it. Art, and the ethics of art and *aisthesis*, lingers within this difference. It *is* this difference.

I realize that some critics may judge my plea to respect this "obtuse" difference antithetical to academic research, whose task, after all, is to bring light to darkness and render explicit our aesthetic experiences by means of rational analyses. I agree, yet would insist that these analyses must remain innovative and probing rather than apathetic and redundant. Otherwise, we might fall prey to the opposite danger of reducing aesthetics to what we know, and that would be just as disastrous as the willful obfuscation of the knowledge we seek. In the context of Riefenstahl, at least, there is nothing to be gained anymore from rehearsing the same old debate about her personal guilt or innocence vis-à-vis the horrors of German fascism, about whether her works are "art" or "propaganda," about her alleged use of concentration camp victims in *Tiefland* (1945; 1954; *Lowlands*), for example. The point is not to deny that these are meaningful and important questions. But, by now, the positions have become so reified and the arguments so redundant—who could possibly afford *not* to quote Kracauer or Benjamin or Sontag in this context?—that scholars often begin and end their reassessment with a synopsis of the same opposing views that have structured the debate for the last half century, without, however, moving beyond them.[25]

To do so, we need a fresh look at Riefenstahl's work from today's perspective, one that recognizes Riefenstahl's symptomatic character for the problematic of art, ethics, and politics and thus uncouples the discussion from biographical and moral issues. We might begin by recognizing the fact that the aesthetics of montage has lost its ethico-political edge today. Once we acknowledge the importance of montage in Riefenstahl's works and recognize the intimate relationship between Nazi aesthetics and postmodern pop culture,[26] then many of the idealist assumptions about the intimate relationship between aesthetic form and sociopolitical function—assumptions that once motivated the historical avant-garde and fascinated Marxist theorists like Eisenstein and Vertov, Benjamin and Brecht—become more than questionable. "Dialectical montage," "critical montage," or any other kind of "open montage" that seeks to "deconstruct" or "parody" or "reflect upon" contemporary society have all been coopted by the very socioeconomic mechanism they sought to expose. The once "critical," but now "affirmative" trinity of dialectical thinking, montage aesthetics, and speed is doomed—at least for now. It has lost the potential to teach us anything that we have not already been taught by the experts of commercial advertising and pop culture.

However, this ability to teach us how to experience the world differently remains the crucial asset of art and aesthetics alike, as contemporary philosophers rightly point out. "When you have an artistic event," Alain Badiou explains,

> sensibility is organized in a new way because something which was . . . not formalized is accepted as a new form. . . . So we can say in the field of artistic creation the affirmative split is finally something like a new disposition between what is a form and what is not. And the becoming of a positive form of something, which was not a form is the affirmative dimension of an artistic event.[27]

Art (or, in Badiou's terms, the artistic event) must contain both this evaluative and this affirmative-productive dimension so as to redress existing aesthetic forms in a new light.

Similar to Badiou, Jacques Rancière argues that aesthetics *(aisthesis)* concerns the "distribution of the sensible" in a given society.[28] Its normative task is both to reveal the constructedness of social reality and to offer alternative possibilities for reconstructing it otherwise. Philosophically speaking, Rancière's model revisits Kant via Foucault. He seeks to delineate the set of rules and regulations that prescribe what can become the object of experience in a given society. However, Rancière differs from Kant insofar as these rules are not hardwired into our cognitive apparatus; rather, they are historically constructed and thus changeable. Like Foucault, Rancière points us to a "historical *a priori*" or a kind of immanent transcendentalism whose "laws" can be challenged most effectively in the realm of art. [29] Hence Rancière's claim that the "aesthetic regime" puts the "entire system of norms into question."[30] Or, in John Dewey's words from his 1931 lectures on *Art as Experience*: "The conception that objects have fixed and unalterable values is precisely the prejudice from which art emancipates us."[31]

This is the reason why aesthetic changes cannot *not* reverberate across the whole (political, cultural, economic) field of a given society. Let me emphasize that I am not referring here to a radical epistemic rupture that completely alters the entire social structure, as the early Foucault might have argued. Rather, aesthetic changes could be minuscule, almost imperceptible, and they might coexist with other, regressive tendencies for quite some time. But I nonetheless maintain that if there is an ethics of art and *aisthesis*, it can only consist in engendering difference and in making this difference palpable, experienceable, sensible. It is literally a question of learning to see things differently. So, aesthetic practice should "deconstruct" a given sensibility only in the service of new modes of perception and experiences. By contrast, a purely negative deconstruction or critique of aesthetic sensibility remains ineffective and thus, simply put, worthless. This insight is certainly one reason why supporters of Derrida increasingly insisted on the "affirmative" dimension—or what John Caputo calls the "Yes, Yes"—of deconstruction during the 1990s.[32] The central point is that critical negativity must be balanced by an affirmative power. Both aspects belong together, because one cannot produce the new without rearranging the old. But neither should one take apart the old without creating and seizing upon a space for the new.

But who or what decides about artistic newness? Which cultural objects are considered new, and what exactly are the selection criteria? In his study *On the New*, the German philosopher and art historian Boris Groys argues that what counts as a cultural innovation is decided by "an ideologically neutral, purely technical system" whose goal is to include precisely those works "that have demonstrated their particularity, originality, and individuality" in comparison to previously known practices.[33] In other words, what decides about the value of a particular artwork is not its so-called truth-dimension or its critical potential vis-à-vis our social reality. Rather, the new is a purely relational category *within* a given system of cultural production. "Hence, the central question in assessing the value of a cultural work is its relation to cultural tradition, that is, the success of its positive or negative assimilation into this system," Groys concludes.[34] No doubt, there are fierce battles among artists, critics, collectors, public administrators, and museum visitors about which artistic practices and products are really "new." But the crucial point is that such debates always presuppose and never question the importance of newness as such. Even works that denounce the "new" will have to do so in innovative ways; otherwise, they will have no chance of being admitted into our cultural archives.

Most important, without this admission, a particular work of art cannot become an artistic event in Badiou's or Rancière's sense of the term either. Every event worthy of its name must sooner or later be recuperated into the very system from which it originally took leave. For if an artistic event were to remain forever outside the system of cultural (re)production, how could we possibly judge it to be artistic at all? To be named an event, the production of a particular work must always already have been identified as such. To put it in paradoxical terms, we might say that art transcends the cultural realm precisely to the degree to which it is recognized and incorporated therein. For in order to change a society's ways of saying and doing, as Rancière and Badiou insist it does, art requires an institutional system of support, even if—or precisely because—its entire purpose is to break out of this system. In this sense, art not only affirms the new, but the old as well, and thus once again highlights the problematic nature of these binary oppositions (between new and old, critique and affirmation) in aesthetic discourse.

Returning to the case of Riefenstahl, we quickly realize that her work remains timely today precisely because it was never unconditionally admitted into the cultural archive to begin with. The persisting humanist suspicion that her work is mere propaganda—and thus not art—never allowed for it to become "old" or traditional in Groys's sense. Put differently, Riefenstahl's symbolic status in the perennial debate about the ethico-political dimension of art effectively prevented the intellectually more interesting, but emotionally less charged discussion of whether or not her work still yields insights into the "distribution of the sensible" in our own aestheticized society. "Actualizing" Riefenstahl thus means to situate her work outside the well-known context of German fascism and Nazi aesthetics—*not* in order to exonerate Riefenstahl, but in order to ask what else her work has to tell us about our ways of saying and doing things today.

Like all aesthetic inquiries, the pursuit of this question is an exercise in augmentation, not substitution. It is based on the premise that an artistic event is not simply "there" objectively, but remains an active construction of those who engage with what they claim to perceive. This construction changes over time, simply because art always functions within changing (social, political, historical) contexts. And since aesthetics discourse attempts to discern this function with reference to *both* its cognitive and affective dimension, it must move beyond a merely historical analysis of her work toward a more contemporary one.

IV.

In order to do so, I will use what Laura Mulvey calls "delayed cinema." By this, she means our increased awareness of a film's individual frames due to the arrival of digital technology that allows us to slow down or pause the movie on our DVD player at will. According to Mulvey, these "new ways of consuming old movies on electronic and digital technologies should bring about a 'reinvention' of textual analysis."[35] One consequence she draws is to dismiss, as I did above, the traditional juxtaposition of avant-garde cinema with Hollywood, because she recognizes that "the aesthetics of cinema have a greater coherence across its historic body in the face of new media technologies" than before (7). Another consequence of these new technologies is to shift emphasis from the analysis of cinematic montage toward the "relation between movement and stillness in cinema" (7). In other words, Mulvey implicitly rejects the Deleuzian ideal of a genuine "movement-image" allegedly inherent in cinema. [36] Instead, she turns our gaze once again to the constitutive role of still images for analog film and thus toward the tension between stasis and movement that defines cinema.[37]

No one knew that better than Riefenstahl, whose work not only exhibits a strong photographic quality, but also makes frequent use of slow motion. Her directorial debut, *The Blue Light* from 1932, is full of shots that appear like portrait-photographs, revealing her obsession with facial close-ups that lasted until her later photographs of the Nuba in the 1960s and beyond.[38] Brigitte

Peucker, too, has called attention "to the recurrent presence of tableau vivant moments" in Riefenstahl's filmmaking, arguing that the human bodies in *Triumph of the Will* "function as images even when they are subjected to motion."[39] And Thomas Elsaesser rightly claims that *Triumph of the Will* "strikes one as a camera(wo)man's film, introducing a certain *photographic aesthetic* into the hitherto shunned areas of crowds, power and politics."[40] In the remainder of this essay, I want to investigate the aesthetic power of this "box of photographer's tricks" (Elsaesser 190) in Riefenstahl's oeuvre.

What, then, does "delayed cinema" look like? *The Matrix* (1999) immediately comes to mind—except that the Brothers Wachowski use slow motion for precisely the opposite effect, namely to teach the audience how to appreciate the infinite mega-speed of life in the future. Their ideal is speed, not slowness. A temporal logic of suspension, by contrast, aims at "perceiving the present—not as one unified trajectory speeding us into the future—but as a simultaneity of multiple temporalities and durations, a heterogeneous and open-ended moment that cannot be contained within one single frame of reference," as Lutz Koepnick puts it.[41] The best-known example of such a temporal multiplicity stems from Vertov's *Man with the Movie Camera*, which remains an important point of reference for Mulvey's study. In particular, she discusses the scene in which Vertov shows a series of individual frames (the face of a child, among others) *within* the celluloid strip that constitutes the film as a whole. Mulvey argues that Vertov

> seems to touch the point between the aesthetic of photography and the cinema. In their stillness, the repeated images belong to the photograph, to the moment of registration, but in their sequence they signify poignantly the indivisibility of these individual moments from a larger whole, an integral part of the shift into movement. (Mulvey 15)

Again, the point is not just that Vertov includes film stills in his film, but that he depicts these stills *as part of and integrated within the very filmstrip* that the audience gets to see before and after this sequence. In doing so, he lets different media and temporalities collide and intermingle before our eyes. This technique serves to remind us of the indexicality of photography and film—the fact that the "referent must have been there" (Barthes)—which is presently undermined by digital technology, as Mulvey rightly points out. But the reverse is true as well, for Vertov's sequence also reveals the power of modern media to define the very reality it merely claims to index. "Media define what is real," Friedrich Kittler declares, and there is widespread agreement among media theorists that our notion of reality is filtered through a variety of apparatuses that include not only our sensory organs and the brain, but also the technological machines we invent (quoted in Mulvey 10).

Thus, the Vertov sequence takes on various—even contradictory—meanings in our own media-controlled time. By presenting images simultaneously as photographs and filmstrips, Vertov highlights the fact that pictures both authenticate *and* aestheticize reality, render it present *and* absent at the same time. But it also enables us to *see* something most of us rarely do anymore: an unprojected strip of 16 mm film—the raw material of the medium itself. This may have been novel in 1927, but it is even more intriguing today, at a time when even film buffs and experts rarely get to put their hands on this outdated technology. It is an unusual sight, not due to the skilled use of cinematic technique, but because of the seeming absence of this technique—never mind the fact that the filmstrip itself is, of course, part of the projected film we are watching.

Another, more recent example that similarly exhibits "a simultaneity of multiple temporalities" is Tom Tykwer's *Lola rennt* (1998; *Run Lola Run*). At various points in the movie, Tykwer includes a series of snapshots/photographs of some of the characters Lola encounters while running through Berlin. Several temporalities intersect at these points: While we assume that Lola keeps on running (in supposedly "real," i.e., *continuous* time), we both witness the *instantaneous freezing* of time in a snapshot-photograph (indicated by the clicking sound of a camera) and are presented with yet another narrative, one composed of a series of such snapshots shown in quick succession, that is, through the *lapse of time* between them. Thus, three different temporalities—continuous, frozen, and elliptical time(s)—coincide during these sequences and create the kind of perceptual rupture and aesthetic openness that characterize artistic events in Badiou's and Rancière's sense.

By contrast, Riefenstahl never quite achieves—or attempts to achieve—this heterogeneous simultaneity in her own work. Take the opening sequence of *Olympia I. Fest der Schönheit* (*Festival of Beauty*), which depicts Myron's famous statue of the *Diskobolus* in the Acropolis slowly coming to life in front of the camera. This transition is accomplished by superimposing as precisely as possible the image of a living athlete (Ernst Huber) over the contours of the ancient statue. Thus, the temporal distance between the two points in time is cancelled and transformed into a chronological narrative of linear succession. Riefenstahl's goal is to emphasize the continuity between classical antiquity and modern (Nazi) Germany, a reincarnation of the old within the new, which leaves no space for the simultaneous presence of both past and present. Similarly, the numerous slow-motion sequences and superimpositions used here and elsewhere in the film serve to extend or bridge temporal succession, but never to rupture it or let it "escape" in unforeseen directions. The famous depiction of the high dive toward the end of the film is a case in point. During the interview with Ray Müller, Riefenstahl explains how she consistently slowed down the speed of the depicted dives and later even spliced in a few frames in reverse order, causing the figures to "fly" up into air or appear to hover there "like birds in the sky," as Riefenstahl herself puts it during the interview. But showing footage in reverse has been a well-known trick ever since Georges Méliès. Although Riefenstahl's sequence is visually pleasing, it pales in comparison to what audiences are used to seeing in today's digitally enhanced movies. Likewise, the affective quality of *Triumph of the Will* is virtually zero for most youngsters today, as the bored reactions of all those students who had to suffer through a full-length showing of the film seems to indicate.

Hence, I generally agree with Peucker's assessment of *Triumph of the Will*: "By promoting the part only in relation to the whole, Riefenstahl's film contains and neutralizes the heterogeneity of *tableaux vivants*" (284). Yet I do not believe it necessary to connect this missing heterogeneity to a lack "of self-consciousness that disrupts and critiques" her film (284). Nor should we identify the hierarchical relationship of stasis and movement in these films with "the psychosexual dynamic of fascist art" (293) in general. As argued above, such attributions are difficult to sustain. For what exactly are the criteria to prove (the lack of) self-consciousness in any work of art? Or what about the intimate relationship of Italian futurism—whose works, unlike Riefenstahl's, feature a highly complex relationship between stasis and movement—with Italian fascism? Or how should we evaluate Vertov's involvement in Stalinism?

In my view, Peucker's generalized assertions about the alleged nature of fascist art are unnecessary to sustain our major point, namely that Riefenstahl ultimately subsumes stillness into motion and thus reduces the temporal complexity of both *Triumph of the Will* and *Olympia*. It suffices to conclude that Riefenstahl's films give the eye less to see and the mind less to play with in terms of temporality than Vertov's or Tykwer's. The avoidance of such terms as "fascist art" or "self-consciousness" may seem trivial, but it serves to prevent the undue rationalization of aesthetic discourse I deplored earlier. Otherwise, there is the danger of ending up, once again, with some kind of "dialectical critique" that would focus on hitherto "oppressed" moments of slowness and standstill in European modernism. But since there is no "whole" of society and no absolute principle that governs cultural production at any time—neither then nor now—it follows that an aesthetic of slowness and standstill is not inherently "better" or "more political" than one of speed and montage. It is just more pertinent to our own times and thus more productive for investigation.

Let me emphasize also that at issue here is not a simple juxtaposition between (boring) old and (exciting) new films. Aesthetic affect cannot just be reduced to the effect of ever-more-sophisticated technological gimmicks. The experimental nature of Vertov's *Man with the Movie Camera* renders it much richer in both affect and meaning than Riefenstahl's productions during the Nazi period, in spite of the fact that both are more than seventy years old. Contrary to Vertov, Riefenstahl focuses almost exclusively on producing "grandiose" visual effects that were ingenuous at the time, but have since lost much of their appeal. Why? Because her use of slow-motion and still photography is always subservient to her fascination with movement. The latter merely serves to highlight the former, but does not achieve the self-sufficiency necessary to attract and sustain our curiosity. The various forms of temporality are present only to be sooner or later reabsorbed into the dominant movement of linear time.[42]

V.

This becomes all the more obvious if we once again look at Riefenstahl's directorial debut, *The Blue Light*, where the relationship between stasis and movement is less hierarchical and more complex than in her other films. In her memoirs, Riefenstahl tells of her fascination with the Sarntal peasants engaged to perform in the movie, and the film repeatedly includes short series of quasi-photographs focusing on their motionless faces (for example, during the scene in which Junta first appears in the village). Yet this photographic quality also applies to Vigo and Junta, whose faces are likewise framed in portrait-like photographs. Thus, the obvious juxtaposition between the fast-moving, agile Junta and the sedate, cloddish peasants is undermined. Instead, a complex interplay of movement and stasis pervades all the characters in the film: at times the quiet peasants are quickly transformed into a fierce mob while Junta is changed into a serene figure as soon as she sets foot in the cave.[43]

The exceptional status of *The Blue Light* is particularly evident in the photograph of "Junta" I mentioned at the beginning of this essay. Eric Rentschler's seminal reading of *The Blue Light* from the early 1990s focuses on Junta's death mask at the end of the film and its transposition onto the cover of the innkeeper's book. This transition, he argues, marks Junta's resurrection and immortalization as a martyr who dies for the benefit of the village and thus anticipates the propagation of Nazi martyrdom that was soon to follow. Similarly, Peucker argues that "the filmic image [of the dead Junta's face] is held, becomes a still—and is finally revealed to the film's spectator as a framed photograph" (292). There is, however, an important difference between these two still images: Junta's eyes are closed in the first, yet open in the second. One might say that the final portrait once again bestows upon Junta the power of her gaze looking back at the beholder.

This gaze is significant for a variety of reasons. First, there is the overall centrality of "looking" for *The Blue Light* in general, whose photographic style also establishes a semiotics of the gaze, so to speak. On the diegetic level, the various "looks" exchanged among the characters express the sexual desire of the young men for Junta much like the older people's hatred for her or Vigo's love and Junta's childlike innocence. On the formal level, these gazes also serve to mobilize the otherwise static quality of the film, since they are usually directed sideways into the off-screen rather than directly toward another character on screen with whom the spectator could identify. In other words, the shot/counter-shot dialectics do not apply. Rather, we as spectators observe the visual exchange from the outside and thus create a triangular rather than bilateral structure. The (sexual, abject, loving) tension among the characters travels along these gazes until it passes a critical threshold and suddenly bursts into action (i.e., the villagers chasing Junta; sons defying their parents' orders, etc.). The explosive potential of the gaze haunts *The Blue Light* and renders it dynamic in spite of its photographic style.

This tension, however, is absent in the final portrait of Junta, whose direct gaze at the beholder grants it a special status not only in the context of *The Blue Light*, but in Riefenstahl's oeuvre in general. Riefenstahl usually tends to avoid the subject's gaze and instead relegates it to the off-space. It is evident from her conversations with Müller that Riefenstahl considers an actor's direct gaze into the camera un-aesthetic and un-cinematic.[44] Indeed, there is an undeniable aesthetic continuity here between Riefenstahl's earlier films and her later photographs of the African Nuba: In both media, Riefenstahl's subjects rarely, if ever, return the viewer's gaze. However, it would be a mistake to regard this similarity as nothing but further evidence for Susan Sontag's claim about the inherently fascist character of Riefenstahl's work both before and after the war.[45] Nor should we conclude that Riefenstahl's later photography objectifies its subjects by refusing to grant them the power of the gaze. Doing so would prevent us from realizing that the status of the human gaze has changed dramatically over the last century.

For much of twentieth-century philosophy, the reciprocal gaze either evoked a direct, nonalienated relationship among all beings or served to expose the absence of this relationship.[46] From Benjamin and Adorno to Heidegger, Lacan, and Levinas, to face the look of the Other was to experience an ethical command emanating from a realm beyond positive law. Both Dorothea Lange's and Lewis Hine's photographic works before and during the Great Depression render this figurative motif literal. They depict people in need who look back at the beholder, pleading for or demanding both our attention and our respect. Thus, the direct gaze used to carry both a mythical and a social-historical charge. At stake was never just the fate of a particular individual, but always that of an entire social group or of humanity at large. The gaze was a reminder about some unfulfilled human potential and "a world where things would be different," as Adorno once phrased it.[47] Traditionally, then, "the portrait photograph is fraught with ambiguity," because it must negotiate between the concrete and the abstract, the single individual and the social group.[48] The Western portrait served two separate functions. In the words of Hans Belting, its official task was to "represent a personal or natural face. Secretly, however, the portrait sought "to create a *role-face* (*Rollengesicht*) that was attached to an individual person and carried a specific name." Thus, "individual and collective traits merged together," most obviously in August Sander's *The Face of Our Time* from 1929.[49]

However, this dynamic is impossible to maintain today, which is why there has been an undeniable crisis of portrait photography particularly after the 1960s. This crisis reflects both the waning authority of traditional concepts of "subjectivity," on the one hand, and the increasing social fragmentation of postmodern Western societies, on the other. As the dualist split between individual and society, surface and depth, semblance and truth continues to break down, the portrait of the human face loses its sociomythical dimension and becomes a plain surface instead: "My face is my outside," Giorgio Agamben insists, "a point of indifference with respect to all of my properties, with respect to what is properly one's own and what is common, to what is internal and what is external."[50] This indifferent face signifies nothing other than the mere fact that its carrier is human.

Although the genre has shown a surprising resilience over the years, the recent portrait photographs by Thomas Struth or Thomas Ruff no longer contain the same sociohistorical dimension or ethical charge of their predecessors. Commenting on Struth's *Portraits* from 1997, Benjamin Buchloh suggests that Struth's work operates on a "transhistorical and meta-social" level insofar as his portraits seem to "ontologize the subject and its conventional modes of representation."[51] Put differently, we might say that the subject's gaze into the camera does not "speak" to us anymore with the same urgency and authenticity as before. Its individuality has been lost. Instead, the portrait's narrative power remains subordinated to "an overall system based on the principles of systematicity, taxonomy, and the series," as Norman Bryson puts it.[52] The increasing emptiness of the gaze is most evident in Thomas Ruff's series of portraits from 1988. His anonymous, passport-like photographs make clear how today, the mask has survived, but the individual is gone. Belting even points to the popular use of avatars and "cyber-faces" in contemporary computer games and digital photography as indicative of our total disassociation of mask and face.[53] "A digital portrait becomes paradoxical when it serves to undermine the analogy with a real face."[54] In other words, the human face along with the reciprocal gaze continues to lose its expressive power in an increasingly digitized Western society.

Depending on personal whim, critics may bemoan or welcome this sociocultural transformation. Humanists like Belting and Buchloh will certainly regard the phenomenon as evidence for the broken dream of total reconciliation, while others will promote the possibility of a "posthuman" history able to operate without such antiquated metaphysical hopes.[55] But, in any case, it should be clear that this development renders the picture of Junta's gaze anachronistic at best. In her efforts to give German fascism a distinct aesthetic face, Riefenstahl satisfied our need to represent fascism as an object of inquiry, a clearly defined reference point on which to hitch our analysis. Then and now, people could look at her (work) and proclaim: "This is what fascism looks like."

I have argued throughout this essay that this face of fascism has been a chimera all along—not because Riefenstahl was just an innocent bystander, but because her work was just one of many historical reflections whose meaning and significance varies over time. The images of Riefenstahl—both those she took and those taken of her—belong to the bygone era of a distinctly modern sensibility. Today, when hooded gunmen decapitate their prisoners in front of an Internet-connected camera, or when satellite-guided missiles send pictures of their targets seconds prior to impact, nobody signs off on these images. Most of them are anonymous, raw, ungroomed—like the anonymous picture of the American soldiers returning home in coffins. Coming to terms with Riefenstahl means above all to recognize this historical distance between her well-defined, choreographed representation of Nazi Germany and the diffuse proliferation of today's highly standardized techno-images of the Iraq war. In other words, a politically relevant aesthetics today must develop an ethico-political vocabulary for the critique of techno-images and digital media in absence of a proper name or an individual face that could be assigned to them. Riefenstahl's major contribution in this regard is a negative one. Both her work and much of its institutionalized critique epitomize what needs to be left behind in order to move ahead.

NOTES

1. Robert von Dassanowsky, for example, likens Riefenstahl to the protagonist Martha in *Tiefland* (played, like Junta in *The Blue Light*, by Riefenstahl herself). See Robert von Dassanowsky, "'Wherever you may run, you cannot escape him': Leni Riefenstahl's Self-Reflection and Romantic Transcendence in *Tiefland*." *camera obscura* 35 (1997): 107–130.
2. Quoted in Eric Rentschler, *The Ministry of Illusion: Nazi Cinema and Its Afterlife* (Cambridge, MA, and London: Harvard University Press, 1996), 154.
3. By *Ideologiekritik*, I mean a politically charged form of cultural critique whose goal is to unveil some hidden motif that allegedly determines a particular work of art or cultural production at large. Much of the classical work done by the Frankfurt School or contemporary Marxists critics can be subsumed under this category. As will become increasingly clear in the remainder of this essay, I am dubious of any such attempts to discover the "true" meaning of culture by reference to various socioeconomic factors or the proverbial false consciousness of the artist. My skepticism stems not from some conservative (and impossible!) effort to separate art and politics, but from the reductionism of traditional *Ideologiekritik*, which generally disallows for plural or contradictory readings of art and culture.
4. See, for example, Christof Wulf, Dietmar Kamper, and Hans Ulrich Gumbrecht, "Einleitung," in *Ethik der Ästhetik*, ed. Christof Wulf, Dietmar Kamper, and Hans Ulrich Gumbrecht (Berlin: Akademie Verlag, 1994), vii–ix.
5. Vilém Flusser, *Kommunikologie*, ed. Stefan Bollmann und Edith Flusser, 3rd ed. (Frankfurt: Fischer, 2003).
6. Guy Debord, *Society of the Spectacle*, trans. Fredy Perlman et al. (Detroit: Black and Red, 1983); Neil Postman, *Amusing Ourselves to Death: Public Discourse in the Age of Show Business* (New York: Penguin, 1985); Jean Baudrillard, *Fatal Strategies*, trans. Philip Beitchmann et al. (New York: Semiotext(e), 1990).
7. In light of this brief list of (male) names, one might consider a third attribute that renders Riefenstahl's case special, namely that she was a woman and ranked among the best-known *female* directors of all times. To what degree the lavish praise and

harsh critique of Riefenstahl's work is gender related remains a question beyond the scope of this study.

8. Walter Benjamin, "The Work of Art in the Age of Mechanical Reproduction," in *Illuminations. Essays and Reflections* (New York: Schocken, 1969), 217–252.
9. I disagree with Ruth Starkman's claim that "Müller's absorption in Riefenstahl's person and personal achievement as a filmmaker disables his critique of her aesthetics" (27). In my view, Müller's documentary technique literally renders that critique visible *on screen* in a way that would not be possible if it remained purely verbal. Ruth Starkman, "Mother of all Spectacles: Ray Müller's *The Wonderful, Horrible Life of Leni Riefenstahl*,"*Film Quarterly* 51, no. 2 (winter 1997–1998): 21–31.
10. See David Bordwell, Kristin Thompson, and Janet Staiger, *The Classical Hollywood Cinema. Film Style and Mode of Production to 1960* (New York: Columbia University Press, 1985).
11. For a comprehensive critique of this approach, see Judith Mayne, *Cinema and Spectatorship* (London: Routledge, 1993).
12. Karsten Witte, "The Indivisible Legacy of Nazi Cinema," *New German Critique* 74 (spring 1998): 23–30 (23).
13. Wolfgang Fritz Haug, "Ästhetik der Normalität—Vor-Stellung und Vorbild," in *Inszenierung der Macht: Ästhetische Faszination im Faschismus*, ed. NGBK (Berlin: Nishen, 1987), 79–102 (98).
14. Bertolt Hinz, "'Degenerate' and 'Authentic': Aspects of Art and Power in the Third Reich," in *Art and Power. Europe under the dictators 1930–45*, compiled and selected by Dawn Ades et al. (London: Thames and Hudson Ltd, 1995), 330–333.
15. For further documentation, see Joseph Wulf, *Die Bildenden Künste im Dritten Reich* (Frankfurt: Fischer, 1966).
16. Bertolt Hinz, "'Degenerate' and 'Authentic,'" 333.
17. Martin Loiperdinger, *Rituale der Mobilmachung: Der Parteitagsfilm "Triumph des Willens" von Leni Riefenstahl* (Opladen: Verlag Leske und Budrich, 1987), 52.
18. Philippe Lacoue-Labarthe and Jean-Luc Nancy, "The Nazi Myth," *Critical Inquiry* 16, no. 2 (1990): 291–312 (308; 311).
19. Sabine Hake, *Popular Cinema of the Third Reich* (Austin: University of Texas Press, 2002), 188.
20. Deleuze and Guattari, quoted in John Rajchman, *The Deleuze Connections* (Cambridge: MIT Press, 2000), 134.
21. Brian Massumi, *Parables of the Virtual. Movement, Affect, Sensation* (Durham, NC: Duke University Press, 2002), 13.
22. Heinz von Förster, *KybernEthik*, trans. Birger Ollrogge (Berlin: Merve, 1993), 78; my translation.
23. Roland Barthes, "The Third Meaning" in *Image. Music. Text* (New York: Hill & Wang, 1977), 61; 62.
24. Georg Friedrich Wilhelm Hegel, *Wissenschaft der Logik*, in *Hauptwerke in Bänden*, vol III (Darmstadt: Wissenschaftliche Buchgesellschaft, 1999), 50; my translation.
25. A good example in this regard is Thomas Elsaesser's essay on Riefenstahl from 1993. Having summarized "a number of key points . . . from the decades of debate" on the first few pages, Elsaesser proceeds with a careful and well-balanced account of Riefenstahl's work (187). But it is precisely because of his thorough investigation that Elsaesser is left, in the end, with the acknowledgment of "an impasse" he, and film criticism in general, is unable to get "out of" (197). Thomas Elsaesser, "Leni

Riefenstahl: The Body Beautiful, Art Cinema and Fascist Aesthetics," in *Women and Film. A Sight and Sound Reader*, ed. Pam Cook and Philip Dodd (New York: Scarlet Press, 1993), 186–197. Further references to this essay will appear in the text.

26. For an intriguing discussion of this relationship, see Georg Seesslen, "Blut und Glamour," in *Leni Riefenstahl*, ed. Filmmuseum Potsdam (Berlin: Henschel, 1999), 192–212. Seesslen rightly points out that "fascist aesthetics is a peculiar kind of pop" (193). See also the translation of this essay in the present volume.
27. Alain Badiou, "The Subject of Art" (lecture from 1 April 2005). http://www.lacan.com/badioulecture.html
28. Jacques Rancière, *The Politics of Aesthetics. The Distribution of the Sensible*, trans. Gabriel Rockhill (London: Continuum, 2004).
29. Michel Foucault, *The Archaeology of Knowledge*, trans. A. M. Sheridan Smith (New York: Pantheon, 1972).
30. Rancière, *The Politics of Aesthetics*, 4.
31. John Dewey, *Art as Experience* (New York: Perigee Books, 1980), 95.
32. John D. Caputo, ed., *Deconstruction in a Nutshell. A Conversation with Jacques Derrida* (New York: Fordham University Press, 1997), 132.
33. Boris Groys, *Über das Neue. Versuch einer Kulturökonomie* (Frankfurt: Fischer, 1999), 41; my translation.
34. Ibid., 19; my translation.
35. Laura Mulvey, *Death 24 x a Second: Stillness and the Moving Image* (London: Reaction Books, 2006), 160. Further references to this book will appear in the text.
36. "Cinema does not give us an image to which movement is added, it immediately gives us a movement-image," Deleuze famously claimed, because the "essence of the movement-image lies in extracting from vehicles or moving bodies the movement which is their common substance." Gilles Deleuze, *Cinema 1: The Movement-Image* (Minneapolis: University of Minnesota Press, 1986), 2; 23. Deleuze makes these claims with explicit reference to the philosophy of Henri Bergson, in spite of the fact that Bergson repeatedly denounced "the cinematographical method" as a fake and mechanical movement that freezes the duration of time into single, spatialized images. Deleuze's claim that Bergson had somehow misunderstood the theoretical implications of his earlier *Matter and Memory* (1888) remains unconvincing, in my view. Instead, I agree with Peter Wollen's conclusion that "movement is not a necessary feature of film" since "the impression of movement can be created by the jump-cutting of still images." Peter Wollen, quoted in Raymond Bellour, "The Film Stilled," in *camera obscura* 24 (1990): 99–123 (100).
37. I use the term "still image" to denote not only a single photograph, but also the "photogram" (the single film image separated from the film) and the "freeze-frame" (understood as the continuous projection of a single frame within the film). Since, in my view, there is no "movement-image" as such in cinema, the distinction between these terms is unnecessary. They are, in fact, one and the same (non-projected versus projected) image. Raymond Bellour admits as much when he suggests that it is "the unique privilege of the freeze-frame to make reappear, in the film's movement ... the photographic, the photogrammic." Bellour, "The Film Stilled,"105.
38. Some of her later underwater photography of corals and fish-life almost appear as "portraits" of the various species involved. See Leni Riefenstahl, *Wonders under Water* (London: Quartet Books, 1991).

39. Brigitte Peucker, "The Fascist Choreography: Riefenstahl's Tableaux," *Modernism/Modernity* 11, no. 2 (2004): 279–297 (280; 283). Further references to this essay will appear in the text.
40. Thomas Elsaesser, "Leni Riefenstahl: The Body Beautiful, Art Cinema and Fascist Aesthetics," in *Women and Film. A Sight and Sound Reader*, ed. Pam Cook and Philip Dodd (New York: Scarlet Press, 1993), 186–197 (190; my emphasis).
41. Lutz Koepnick, unpublished paper at the GSA conference 2006.
42. In Kracauer's words: "*Triumph of the Will* indulges in emphasizing endless movement . . . so that spectators not only see passing a feverish world, but feel themselves uprooted in it. The ubiquitous camera forces them to go by way of the most fantastic routes, and editing helps drive them on." Siegfried Kracauer, *From Caligari to Hitler* (Princeton: Princeton University Press, 1947), 302.
43. By contrast, Peucker argues that by "pitting expressive dynamism against formal containment and stasis, Riefenstahl pits eros and thanatos even in this early film" (292).
44. There is a particular sequence that I have in mind showing her quarreling with Müller in one of the Babelsberg studios. It ends with Riefenstahl's exasperated exclamation: "But I would look directly into the camera!"
45. Susan Sontag, "Fascinating Fascism," in *Under the Sign of Saturn* (New York: Farrar, 1976), 71–105.
46. For Sartre, Lacan, Merleau-Ponty, and Levinas, the "face of the Other" and the "Other's look" decenter human vision and subvert its inherent power structure. No longer the sole bearer of the look, the subject becomes the object of a gaze that relegates it to the periphery of a visual network it does not control. Cf. Jacques Lacan, *The Four Fundamental Concepts of Psychoanalysis*, ed. Jacques-Alan Miller, trans. Alan Sheridan (New York: Norton, 1978), 106; Jean Paul Sartre, *Being and Nothingness*, trans. Hazel E. Barnes (New York: Simon & Schuster, 1992), 340–400; Maurice Merleau-Ponty, *The Visible and the Invisible*, ed. Claude Lefort, trans. Alphonso Lingis (Evanston: Northwestern University Press, 1968), 134–135; Emmanuel Levinas, *Totality and Infinity: An Essay on Exteriority*, translated by Alphonso Lingis (Pittsburgh: Duquesne University Press, 1969).
47. Theodor W. Adorno, "Rede zur Lyrik und Gesellschaft," in *Noten zur Literatur. Gesammelte Schriften*, ed. Rolf Tiedemann. 20 vols. (Frankfurt: Suhrkamp, 1973), XI, 48–68 (52); my translation.
48. Graham Clarke, "Introduction," in *The Portrait in Photography*, ed. Graham Clarke (London: Reaction Books, 1992), 1–5 (4). This inherent ambiguity of portrait-photography existed from its very beginnings. On the one hand, nineteenth-and early-twentieth-century photography democratized representation and fulfilled the legitimate wish of the lower social classes to have themselves represented. On the other, it served the police to increase surveillance of the "masses" through passport photos and mock-shots. See Suren Lalvani, *Photography, Vision, and the Production of Modern Bodies* (Albany: State University of New York Press, 1996).
49. Hans Belting, "Das Portrait als Maske." Unpublished manuscript, 53 pages. 5.
50. Giorgio Agamben, *Means Without Ends*, 99.
51. Benjamin H. D. Buchloh, "Portraits/Genre: Thomas Struth," in *Thomas Struth. Portraits* (Munich: Schirmer/Mosel, 1997), 151–161 (159; my translation).
52. Norman Bryson, "Das Nicht-Wissen in der Portraitfotografie von Thomas Struth," in *Thomas Struth. Portraits* (Munich: Schirmer/Mosel, 1997), 127–134 (131).

53. See, for example, Hubertus v. Amelunxen et al., eds, *Photography After Photography: Memory and Representation in the Digital Age* (Amsterdam: G+B Arts, 1996).
54. Belting, "Das Portrait als Maske," 43; my translation.
55. N. Kathleen Hayles, *How We Became Posthuman. Virtual Bodies in Cybernetics, Literature, and Informatics* (Chicago: University of Chicago Press, 1999).

Chapter 3

0–1: Riefenstahl and the Beauty of Soccer

Lutz Koepnick

I.

International soccer has witnessed tremendous transformations since the 1970s. Gone are the days of dominant midfielders who organize the movements of their entire teams according to their individual ingenuity and who serve forward players with breathtaking passes across the entire field. Gone are the days of consummate dribble artists freely wheeling the ball around their designated defenders and thus upsetting the opponent's entire defensive formation. Mostly gone are also the days of agile *liberos* who would quickly move the ball from behind their own defensive lines so as to bridge the game's different regions. In today's age of zone defense, of forward and defensive pressing, the size of the playable field has shrunk dramatically, the result of which is a stronger emphasis on short-pass play, a much more flexible dispersal of individual players across the field, and a remarkable acceleration of the game even if the ball may often take much longer to arrive in the field's potential scoring areas. Similar to our contemporary culture of networked globalization, soccer today heavily relies on a team's ability to spread out variable nodes of action and interconnectivity across the playable field; to move shifting constellations of players up and down the pitch; to consider the field's space as a product of dynamic vectors and open-ended trajectories rather than as a bounded territory requiring individual players to inhabit predefined scripts and positions.

It is perhaps this intense acceleration of soccer over the past decades that leads us to enjoy the beauty of so-called standard situations like never before. Think of the execution of a free kick, to be shot from about twenty to twenty-five meters from the goal, the ball's initial position somewhere to the left or to the right of the penalty box arc. We see five or six players of the opposite team trying to form a defensive wall as their goalie—like a land surveyor—assesses the situation and directs his mates to position themselves effectively. We witness two or three players of the offensive team huddling around the ball as they decide who will take the shot and where it should go. We see at least ten players of both teams swarming around in the penalty box, offensive players trying to break lose from defensive coverage, defenders seeking to secure open spaces, all of them hoping to somehow interfere with what will unfold within a few seconds. The closer we come to the kick, the more we come to realize that everything is up in the air. There is nothing that allows us to predict at this point whether the free kick will aim directly at the goal or search for the head of a well-positioned forward. Whether the ball will come in low or high. Whether it will fly above or spin around the wall. Whether the kicker will seek a hole in the defensive wall or, through the sheer might of his shot, force a breach into it. Finally, we see the designated kicker run toward the ball. Once again we quickly scan the various activities in the penalty box. Our breath comes to a halt. The kicker kicks. The ball sails through the air. Our eyes follow its stunning curve over the edge of the wall. We do somewhere notice the figure of the goalie as he leaps toward the corner of his goal, his body as extended as it might ever get. We do somewhere notice the continued swarming of other players in the penalty box. But our gaze nevertheless remains entirely focused on the ball as it elegantly spins forward, arcs dramatically, and hits the goal—without having ever been touched by anyone but the kicker—in the goal's uppermost possible corner. Time to cheer. Time to breathe.

The velocity of skillful soccer kicks can easily reach up to 120 km/h.[1] The display screens of modern stadiums therefore increasingly offer what is standard fare for television audiences: instant replays of game-decisive shots in slow motion. And yet, decelerated repetition seems to do little to intensify the experience of plays like the one just described. The ball may have soared through the air with incredible speed, but as we followed its curve, and as we replay its trajectory in our mind long after the game, didn't the ball, for a seemingly timeless period, appear entirely suspended from the laws of gravity and chronological time? Didn't it just hang and hover there for a decisive second? Wasn't it much slower than any slow-motion photography could ever present it, slowness here being understood as an intensification of our temporal and spatial experience, a special receptiveness to perceive our present as one structured by multiple durations, rhythms, and trajectories?

Athletic beauty, in such ball sports as soccer, is a product, not so much of individualized physical performances (though it of course cannot do without these either), but of how entire teams succeed in establishing fleeting spatial figures and transitory constellations.[2] The game's beauty, far from ever achieving classical aesthetic conceptions of the eternal, infinite, and universal, is ephemeral and particular through and through, a passing instantiation of something that exceeds one central and predictable plan, will, and consciousness. Gorgeous free kicks remind us of the game's transient and performative beauty. What fascinates us about them is less the kicker's sheer determination and skill than the fact that these shots crystallize the game's spatial dynamic into what Walter Benjamin would call a dialectical image—a flash-like image pregnant with tensions.[3] No matter how long the actual kick might last, suddenly we see what this game is all about: the ongoing articulation and disarticulation of temporary constellations across the field; the actualization of variable nodes and networks of interaction. No matter how fast the ball, what constitutes the beauty of successful free kicks is the fact that they intensify our perception for what is at the core of every good ball game, namely a team's ability to explore time and space not as neutral containers of collective action, but as something to be shaped through ever-shifting interrelations of discrete elements. As something at times to be condensed and tightened, at other times to be stretched and extended. As a simultaneity of competing possibilities that may, or may not, result in what audiences, of course, desire most: a goal. No matter how high the kick's velocity, then, what defines the beauty of the shot is the fact that it sways us to see slowness—the intensified perception of time as an open space for the articulation of multiple possible actions and durations—as key to a successful mastery of the entire game. Soccer may have gotten astonishingly fast over the course of the past decades, but the faster the ball the more we come to realize that this game, at heart, is one of slowness; that what we call its beauty involves flow and swarming and resists a certain desire to reduce time and space to one unified vector or thrust.

Leni Riefenstahl's film *Olympia* (1938) continues to be seen as an essential moment in the definition and cinematic recording of athletic beauty. Riefenstahl's cinematography and editing no doubt revolutionized the capturing of athletic competitions and set commanding standards for many years to come. Her images famously celebrated athletic prowess and agility, the integration of body and mind through physical exertion. Over the last decades, the critical writing on *Olympia* has, understandably, focused on Riefenstahl's complicity with the Nazi regime when making this film, on the fact that Riefenstahl's praise of athletic beauty was not as politically innocent as the director claimed throughout her life. What has received much less attention, however, are the actual dimensions of Riefenstahl's aesthetic of athletic bodies, the way in which her camera and editing do justice to the logics of certain athletic performances—or not. Exactly what constitutes the beauty of different sports in Riefenstahl's eyes? To what extent does her camera, in its pursuit of beauty, draw our attention to the particularity of certain athletic disciplines? Does her camera treat different sports differently or does she impose universalizing ideas of corporeal beauty onto diverse physical practices, their struggle against time as much as their structuring of space?

When shooting and editing her monumental documentary, Riefenstahl—according to Taylor Downing—"led and inspired a creative team to achieve standards for Olympic film-making which have set the agenda for sports films ever since. Rarely, if ever, with all the advances in film technology since 1936, have these standards been surpassed."[4] The following pages, by examining the representation of soccer in *Olympia*, present Riefenstahl in much less command over her material than Downing and many others assume. For in stark contrast to the groundbreaking documentation of track and field events, of diving and gymnastic competitions, and of marathon and bicycling races, Riefenstahl's team clearly fell short of its pioneering role when it came to the filming and editing of the soccer final between Italy and Austria, a dramatic match the Italian squad won in overtime 2–1. Riefenstahl's film, I argue, not only obscures soccer's inherent spatial dynamic and slowness, that is, the game's definition of athletic beauty as a performative crystallization of transient and heterogeneous spatial figures. It also imposes on us an alternate regime of slowness, one which views the present—unlike a true soccer fan—as a mere replay of a seemingly timeless past, and one which erases the discrete, multiple, and particular in the name of homogenous time and space, of spatial containment and linear motion.

Riefenstahl's failure to accommodate the beauty and spatial dynamic of soccer is both systematic and symptomatic: It reflects a coherent set of preferences about the representation of moving bodies with the time-based art of film as much as it brings to light what is repressive about the overall aesthetic of *Olympia* and its quite excessive use of slow-motion photography.

II.

The first part of Riefenstahl's Olympia film, *Festival of the People*, famously starts out with images of ancient Greek ruins bathed in soft morning light. The camera gently travels along and across a field of crumbled stones, columns, temples, and statues. Extended dissolves endow these images with a sense of poetic otherworldliness. After a few minutes the camera comes to rest on a replica of Myron's *Discobulus*, a sculpture created around 450 BC and displaying the body of a discus thrower in midthrow. First the camera smoothly circles around the sculpture's head and neck; next it slightly moves away from the statue so as to allow us a full view of how both artist and athlete manage to synthesize utter attentiveness and admirable repose. Then we witness how this image of serene simplicity and controlled stillness dissolves into the image of a real discus thrower who will start his routine from where Myron broke off. Slow-motion images picture the athlete—Riefenstahl used the German decathlon champion Erwin Huber for this sequence—as he smoothly rotates his upper body twice around its vertical axis before we finally cut to a close-up of his arm as it tosses the discus forcefully into the sky.

As Crispin Sartwell has reminded us recently, the Greek words for beauty and the beautiful (*kalos*, *to kalon*) amalgamate the moral, the aesthetic, and the epistemic. Beauty entails a sense of nobility as much as it refers to visible principles of unity, simplicity, clarity, and rationality. As importantly, the Greek concept of beauty is connected to the idea of knowledge, of truth and unequivocal articulation. Sartwell concludes: "All of these meanings might be brought together in a notion of 'illumination': the kalos is above all, we might say, what is drenched in light. The noble soul is the clearly illuminated soul, and such a soul will be beautiful."[5] With the opening sequence of *Festival of the People*, Riefenstahl seeks to recuperate the various dimensions of the Greek *kalos* for the twentieth century. Situated amid northern beach grass and in front of a wide-open horizon, Riefenstahl's modern-day discus thrower is drenched in light indeed. The ease and supple balance of his motion here is to express the nobility of his soul, a prototype of psychophysical unity in which all traces of the unknowable, the dark, the mysterious, and the messy are extinguished. As captured by Riefenstahl's camera, the discus thrower lends physical reality to the principle of illumination; the smooth, albeit powerful, rotation of his body exemplifies a profound simplification of the world to its most basic elements. Viewers might find themselves desiring this beautiful body, but beauty here also designates the end of desire, the end of the erotic, because the purity of this perfectly illuminated physique leaves us with almost nothing to which we could attach our longing, our fantasy, or our hope for something that could make us tremble with surprise. Illuminated through and through, Riefenstahl's discus thrower personifies his director's notion of the beautiful, not because he causes us to long for transcendent realities, but because his flawless composure simultaneously embodies and consummates the viewer's desire.

But we should, of course, not think that the athlete's beauty—his being drenched in light; his achievement of unhampered visibility—is merely an achievement of his own. On the contrary, whatever we are intended to perceive as the discus thrower's *kalos* is a product of the athlete's graceful posture as much as it is an effect of Riefenstahl's skillful manipulation of cinematic lighting and framing, her expert handling of editing rhythms, and most of all her calculated management of recording and projection speeds. I will have more to say later about how Riefenstahl's use of slow motion is essential to her peculiar construction of athletic beauty and embodiment in her *Olympia* film in general.

For now let it simply be noted that Riefenstahl's deliberate deceleration of physical motion on the one hand actively displays the athlete's body as one open to the seemingly extra-temporal and transcendental power of illumination, while on the other hand the use of slow-motion photography is to demonstrate the extraordinary power of the apparatus itself to animate the world and shape the itineraries of physical reality. Rather than merely authenticating Riefenstahl's camera as a supreme instrument for the capturing of athletic speed and motion, the dissolve from statue to athlete, from stillness to movement, from no to slow motion, stresses the apparatus's godlike force to call things to life and light, make images move, and remain in full control over the velocity of pro-filmic events. Slow motion, in this opening scene, produces and celebrates the *kalos* of the athletic body as an effect of the machinic time of cinema. By decelerating the appearance of corporeal motion, Riefenstahl wants us to marvel, not merely at the skill of the athlete, but at the camera's ability to imbue bodies with light; to illuminate the physical world rather than merely to show this world as being illuminated; to eclipse the murky, messy, and mysterious and thus fuse the ethical, the epistemic, and the aesthetic into one single dynamic.

The use of slow motion, then, already in the prologue of *Olympia*, defines the cinematic frame not as a transparent window on to the world but as an artistic mechanism that engenders the world as being beautiful in the first place, as adhering to classical principles of clarity, simplicity, and balance—of illumination. Supervised by Kurt Neubert, the most eminent slow-motion expert in Europe in the mid-1930s, slow motion also dominates the pace and mood of *Olympia*'s entire two parts, its more essay-like openings (the Greek prologue of part I, the Olympic village and sauna opening of part II) as much as the recounting of individual sporting events. Neubert had worked for Riefenstahl's former director Dr. Arnold Fanck, shooting some of the latter's most stunning mountain sequences. Riefenstahl had approached Neubert about this new project nearly a year before the actual event, eager to employ his technical skill in running gigantic DeBerie cameras with camera speeds up to ninety-six frames per second for her peculiar aesthetic vision. Though principal photographers such as Hans Ertl, Walter Frentz, Gustav Lantschner, Heinz von Jaworsky, and Willy Zielke were equally responsible for the film's innovative strategies of picturing athletic efforts, the signature of Neubert's expertise is visible throughout the entire film: Not one sequence seems to pass by during the epic's combined running time of 205 minutes that does not rely on visual strategies of deceleration, of stretching time and movement, of expanding the now, so as to drench the athletes' struggle in light and to evidence the camera's own athletic efforts of maintaining control over the viewer's perceptual registers. In spite of Riefenstahl's own and many other critics' repeated comments about the pioneering positioning of the camera equipment, it is in *Olympia*'s use of slow-motion photography that some of the film's most remarkable aesthetic agendas become the clearest. And it is in these few sequences when Riefenstahl decides *not* to take the speed out of individual physical exertions such as the soccer final that the costs and burdens of these aesthetic agendas tend to bubble to the film's surface and expose to light what her neoclassicist pursuit of beauty and illumination cannot tolerate.

III.

What is immediately striking about the three minutes and ten seconds dedicated to the soccer final between Austria and Italy is the fact that they completely shun the otherwise dominant use of slow motion; that Riefenstahl's editing, in contrast to the breathtaking coverage of other sporting events, often misses decisive parts of the game; and that Riefenstahl neither has any patience for the buildup of crucial game situations nor seeks to capture the way in which successful soccer teams understand how to dominate the field with dispersed lines and flexible groupings of players. Unlike anything else in *Olympia*'s more than three hours, the presentation of the soccer final astounds the viewer as quite arbitrary, choppy, and inconclusive, not because individual shots do not communicate with one another, but on the contrary because Riefenstahl valorizes the framing of continuous and self-centered motion—the ball's and the shooters' thrust—over images that would picture the swarming of discrete bodies across the playable range of the field. Let us take a detailed look first, though, so as not to jump to conclusions.

The sequence commences with a shot showing both teams as they diagonally cross the screen in order to enter the field. We quickly cut to an image of some ecstatic onlookers before Riefenstahl presents us with the game's kick-off. Most of what follows is shot with a camera situated somewhere in the middle of the side stands, prompting a relatively severe and close viewing angle and causing the cinematographer to pan his camera frequently in order to catch up with shifting positions of the ball and the players. A few other shots, in particular the coverage of Italy's two goals and Austrian's one score, are taken from behind the respective goalposts, supplemented by a few additional shots that are captured from a camera located at playing field level somewhere at the height of the penalty box. All in all, Riefenstahl must have used about six to eight cameras in order to record this final, clearly fewer than what she was able to marshal for track and field events in the same stadium, but nevertheless more than enough to allow for a multiplicity of perspectives and thus for potentially converting the game's drama into a visual cinematic feast.

That, in spite of both the commentator's energetic invocations and Riefenstahl's legendary editing skills, this feast never really transpires on screen has several interrelated reasons. First, Riefenstahl's camera in most of the pivotal play scenes is simply too close to the action to give us an adequate picture of the game's dynamic. Her focus is on how particular players make the ball move, not on how they jointly use the depth and width of the field in order to circumvent and hence outplay the other team's defensive system. Repeatedly, when presenting the Italians' or the Austrians' offensive moves, Riefenstahl cuts from one image to another without securing any sense of spatial continuity, of how one shot relates to the other. Though the commentator tells us that what we are seeing is one team pressing toward the other team's goal, the editing is purely motivated by the visual direction of the rolling ball, not by how both teams, or parts thereof, move their tactical formations down and across the field. As result, we often find ourselves doing a lot of guesswork in order to comprehend the development of certain game situations; questioning the proper temporal sequencing of things; or simply getting frustrated because we do not see what we need to see in order to understand why the ball ended up where it is or how certain players could assume positions that enable them to score a goal. In spite of her many cameras, Riefenstahl's editorial choices during the soccer sequence fail to provide adequate coverage of action and field. The longer and more critical the game, the closer Riefenstahl zooms in on individual athletic efforts and enthusiastic fan behavior, thus shutting out the film's viewer from grasping the larger constellations on the field. Put simply, in order to infuse the soccer sequence with drama, Riefenstahl's editing increasingly detaches ball and players from their spatial surroundings; her interest is in isolating the sight of ongoing movement and activity, not in establishing a sense for how both teams succeeded (or failed) in dominating the field.

Second, what is striking about Riefenstahl's treatment of the soccer final is that it entirely refuses to communicate any sense for the ebb and flow of the game, the way in which one team might control the pace and field over certain stretches of time, while the other team might have the upper hand during other periods. Eager to present the final as a symphony of ongoing motion, as a beautiful performance of skillful athletes incessantly driving the ball from left to right and right to left, Riefenstahl's editing and narrative provide no information whatsoever about the actual course of the game. Neither does she inform us about exactly when certain goals were shot, nor does she draw our awareness to the fact that this game had to go into overtime. The sizzle of soccer, writes Dirk Schümer, relies on a proficient management of chance and unpredictability within an entirely nonaccidental and knowable set of elements. Equally as important is the fact that it also emerges from the uneven distribution of peaks and valleys of athletic successes across the allotted play time, the often fickle rhythm by which the game alternates between newness and redundancy, the difference between brief moments of triumph and extended periods of failure and stoppage. Like film itself, soccer is a temporal art form. For us to recognize the virtuosity or brilliance of certain moves, there needs to be countless moments of relative inaction, of dullness, of frustration, of anticlimax.[6] Riefenstahl clearly has no patience for the inconsistency and instability of the game, not because she only designates three minutes of screen time to present the final, but because the pace and measure of her editing surreptitiously treat these three minutes as if they were the entire game. Rather than sharpening our eyes for the uncertainty of the game, Riefenstahl tries to condense the actions of both teams into one focused expression of athletic resolve. Rather than exploring the game's aleatoric configurations of intensity and languor, Riefenstahl seeks to portray soccer as if the game consisted of one unmitigated climax, one consistent, coherent, self-enclosed, and hence predictable actualization of physical power.

That still leaves us with the question as to why Riefenstahl decided not to resort to slow-motion photography in presenting the soccer final; whether aesthetic strategies of deceleration would have been useful in order to provide a more ingenious solution to screen team sports such as soccer; and how the complete absence of slow motion in this particular sequence reflects on Riefenstahl's obsessive use of this technique throughout the rest of the film. In the remainder of this essay I will seek to find a comprehensive answer to these questions, not simply by focusing on the film's formal features, but by reading its aesthetic shapes and energies against the backdrop of the general state of slow-motion photography in the 1930s; its subsequent codification as a means of evoking psycho-physical transition and enabling perceptual intensification; the ideological construction of athletic beauty in Nazi society; and last but not least, the tactical innovations that affected soccer in the 1920s and 1930s and triggered an acute modernization of the game, one to which Riefenstahl's camera remained entirely blind. Riefenstahl discovers beauty in controlled and choreographed scenarios of symmetry, balance, volatility, and linear motion. While the choppy nature of *Olympia*'s coverage of the soccer final testifies to the extent to which Riefenstahl's pursuit of timeless beauty neglects soccer's essential slowness, the game's reliance on continued mobility, flow, swarming, and dispersal, Riefenstahl's refusal to employ slow-motion photography for the presentation of the soccer final sheds light on how deceleration in Riefenstahl's film in general serves a rather repressive project of fusing the intensive time of cinematic recording with the affective temporality of human experience, of integrating machine and human time into the unity of one single mechanism.

IV.

Prior to the arrival of sound cinema in the late 1920s, cinematic recording and projection speeds were extremely variable. They ranged anywhere between eighteen to twenty-four frames per second, and little could be done in order to warrant that projectionists would screen films at the same speed at which cinematographers initially had captured and editors had spliced them.[7] Due to this contingency of projection speeds and hence a profound lack of artistic control over the final product, filmmakers largely stayed away from utilizing the differential between recording and projection speeds as a means of aesthetic expression. The coming of synchronized sound in 1927 led to a momentous standardization of recording and exhibition practices. Yet with virtually all technological innovations and formal experiments dedicated to the coordination of the visual and the acoustic, and with camera and recording practices undergoing a temporary loss of mobility and flexibility, the first years of sound film did not yield a surge of films investigating the expressive uses of film speed. Moreover, to the extent that the 1930s, in North America as much as in Europe, witnessed a considerable waning of avant-garde sensibilities and the parallel rise of so-called classical realist codes of filmmaking, the space for developing a coherent aesthetics of slow-motion photography, of using temporal manipulations so as to displace the seemingly "normal" perception of time and space in cinema, became rather slim. It is therefore no exaggeration to say that the extensive use of slow-motion effects in Riefenstahl's two *Olympia* films set out to occupy rather pristine and uncodified territories. Neubert's contribution to the project did not simply consist in making available his well-known technical and professional skills as a cinematographer. Neubert's essential importance was to help define viable codes and meanings for the use of cinematic deceleration, present and future; his task was no less than to establish an aesthetic of slow motion in which the formal language of film would come to serve as a direct conduit to Riefenstahl's idea of athletic beauty, her valorization of physical self-absorption, and the production of psychophysical affect in the viewer.

Slow-motion photography today is of course no longer what it used to be. In the age of digital editing, there is no more need to record—like Neubert—certain events with accelerated frame speeds so as to produce, when later projecting the film at regular speed, impressions of temporal stretching, of deceleration. Instead, the manipulation of cinematic temporality can be directly accomplished with the help of editing software, independent of how the material was originally recorded. The aesthetic conventions for the use of slow motion today, however, in spite of its enormous profusion during the 1990s, still seem to follow most of the codes developed during the predigital era, less in the immediate wake of Riefenstahl's work of the 1930s than after the demise of classical narrative cinema during the 1950s and during the emergence of "young cinemas" in the late 1960s. Slow motion, during this period, became increasingly employed to suggest the dreamlike quality of certain experiences, to signify supernatural power or extraordinary violence, and to emphasize the lyrical quality of particular story elements. Strategies of deceleration temporarily suspended the drive of narrative progression in order to allow for moments of intensified visual perception, of amplified affect, of either dazzling spectacle or didactic exposition. The work of Sam Peckinpah circa 1970, as it intercut regular-speed with slow-motion footage, played the perhaps single most important role in this codification of slow-motion photography. Contrary to conventional wisdom, Peckinpah's use of slow motion was not to bring greater realism to the presentation of intense and violent action, but to explore temporal suspension and stylization as means to question the violent undercurrents of modern society. Whether Peckinpah's moral and political agendas really bore fruit is not for me to answer in this context. What needs to be pointed out, however, is the fact that Peckinpah's use of slow motion was especially compelling when, as Stephen Prince argues, its purpose was to signify a character's loss of physical volition, that is, to express "the metaphysical paradox of the body's continued animate reactions during a moment of diminished or extinguished consciousness."[8]

Riefenstahl's decelerated images of individual athletes in both parts of her film, in one sense, clearly anticipate the kind of metaphysics of slowness that was to energize the work of later directors like Peckinpah and that, after the explosive proliferation of East Asian martial arts films in the 1990s, serves as a major staple of dominant filmmaking today. Whenever Riefenstahl resorts to slow motion in order to document the efforts of her discus, javelin, and hammer throwers, her wide and high jumpers, her gymnasts and high divers, the director's aspiration is to stress acute shifts in human volition. Slow-motion photography in Riefenstahl is a technique encoding—and celebrating—profound moments of psychophysical transformation and transcendence: from a body merely willing and determined to win to one whose will and determination is entirely to triumph over this body's physical contingencies; from corporeality to the spiritual; from goal-oriented ambition to states of complete self-absorption and hence self-denial; from the banality of an unpredictable, unfocused, and mundane existence to the ecstasy of utter concentration and dedication.

In another sense, however, Riefenstahl's work with slow motion could not be more different from what later directors made of it. For unlike Peckinpah, Riefenstahl's metaphysics of deceleration does not aim at tracking the cessation of human volition and consciousness due to a violent mutilation of the body. On the contrary, Riefenstahl uses slow motion whenever she seeks to define and venerate athletic beauty as a self-enclosed unity of the virile and the spiritual, one which guards the human body and mind against the vagaries of time, against finitude. In stark contrast to Peckinpah and the slow-motion experts of contemporary action cinema, Riefenstahl's metaphysics of deceleration pursues nothing less than the emancipation of the human body from its own temporal existence, to showcase what is universal, paradigmatic, and therefore timeless about this body and its athletic efforts. What drives Riefenstahl's use of slow motion is not Peckinpah's (at once moralistic and gloomy) recognition of the passing of time, of the violence of temporal closure, but her desire to orchestrate universal types, models, and paradigms of bodily action so as to protect our bodily existence against its very intractability, against what is erratic, coincidental, unfinished, and capricious about any form of human embodiment. Slow motion in Riefenstahl redeems the body from its own ephemerality; it guards this body against possible penetrations from the outside as much as against the inevitability of death, against its own fleetingness and fragility. Failure, for Riefenstahl's decelerated bodies, is not an option. Nor can these bodies tolerate lack and ambiguity, the unexpected and incommensurable, the messy and unresolved. In radical contradistinction to the use of slow motion in contemporary action cinema, then, Riefenstahl employs it to stage transitory states in which athletes move on to triumph over their own transitoriness and mortality. Slow motion here masters the arbitrary and erases the untidy possibility of chance. It suspends the entropy of the living and thus, seemingly, provides the key for moving through time beyond it—to beat death and nonbeing at their own game.

V.

"The ball is round," says one of the most famous proverbs about soccer, coined by Sepp Herberger. It nicely addresses this sport's principal unpredictability, namely its flux and fickleness, the instantaneity and ephemerality of brilliance in this game, the way in which success and mastery can never be programmed and moments of highest intensity alternate with extended stretches of apparent standstill, of athletic nonbeing. Riefenstahl's decision not to capture the game in slow motion, and thus forfeit what she employs to showcase the beauty of other sporting events, was certainly a wise one. The tendency of slow-motion footage is toward inertia, unless alternating points of view and cunning editing strategies infuse these images with some rhythm and hence dynamic movement. Nothing would be more stale than to watch the essential highlights of a soccer game, let alone the whole thing, exclusively in slow motion, no matter how actively editors would splice together ever-shifting perspectives.

Yet nothing, at the same time, would be more wrong than to understand Riefenstahl's choice not to decelerate the presentation of the soccer final as a sign of the director's active recognition of the game's logic after all. Beauty, as defined by the opening scene of Riefenstahl's film, designates the rather miraculous appearance of strength and power within the realm of ordinary life; slow-motion photography is her privileged means in the *Olympia* films to evoke and document such an appearance, to illuminate the extraordinary, the underlying logic of things. Slow motion, in Riefenstahl, takes on the function of the long take as analyzed by André Bazin: It "strives to bring out the deeper structure of reality, to reveal preexistent relationships."[9] That is, the dynamic, albeit self-enclosed, architecture of the human body, the autopoetic interaction between the body's muscles and tendons, its shapes and volumes, its flesh and mind. Soccer, as seen through Riefenstahl's eyes and cameras, has no such pleasurable sights to offer. Riefenstahl's film abstains from using slow motion, not because she rightly fears that extended strategies of deceleration would take the drama out of the presentation of ball sports, but because she fails to find in soccer what in her view qualifies sports as sites at which athletic beauty can come into being. What is choppy about the editing of the soccer final symptomatically expresses the extent to which Riefenstahl got stuck in between her own ideal of physical beauty and her inability to come to terms with the spatial dynamic and unpredictability of team sports such as soccer.

What is remarkable about Riefenstahl's coverage of soccer is not only that she misreads the game's inherent logic, but that the game's logic here so adamantly presses against Riefenstahl's aesthetic preference, such that it enables us to see the film's otherwise dominant use of slow motion in a critical light.

Slow motion is what allows Riefenstahl to illuminate her ideal of athletic beauty as a structural relationship played out at the level of the individual body. While individual bodily skills no doubt are of crucial importance in soccer as well—think of the very different, yet similarly effective physical performances of David Beckham, Luis Figo, Ronaldinho, and Zinedine Zidane—the game's decisive deeper structure (and hence, its beauty) is defined by the aleatory and ever-shifting constellations of players across the entire field, by something that refuses to be captured in one single take and image. Slow motion, in Riefenstahl, underscores the power, skill, and determination that resides in the athletic body and waits to be awakened in the moment of competition. Though Riefenstahl tries hard to construct soccer along the lines of her ideal of athletic beauty, she desists from using slow motion because she has no sense for the open-ended, transient, messy, and collective structures that define this game and its beauty in the first place. In spite of the fact that Herberger was in many ways as much of a partisan of Nazi society as Leni Riefenstahl, nothing is more different than their respective approaches to soccer. The ball ideally used in Riefenstahl's conception of the game, and in sports in general, is everything but round. It does not roll into unexpected corners of the field. It does not force the cameraman to pan, dolly, or tilt his camera without being able to anticipate what comes next and hence to feel in relative control over the process. It knows of no moments of standstill and it always travels in straight lines to the opponent's goals. Its trajectory can be calculated (and therefore, securely framed) like the arc of a discus or a high diver sailing through the air. Slow motion in Riefenstahl defines athletic presence as a replay of a timeless and unchanging past, as a reiteration of a classical conception of corporeal balance, harmony, and absorption. There is no place for slow motion in presenting soccer because, for Riefenstahl, the ball's roundness—the unpredictability of the game—violates the very idea of beauty, her ideology of the aesthetic. If she had had her way, the ball would have been as square and cubic as could be.

VI.

The game of soccer, which arrived in Germany in the 1870s as a sport mostly played by members of the educated bourgeoisie, underwent a critical modernization in the course of the 1920s and 1930s. Initially developed by Herbert Chapman during his tenure as coach of both Huddersfield and Arsenal London, and then imported to the Continent, the breakthrough of the so-called "WM system" completely reorganized the tactical distribution, spatial range, and possible tasks of all players on the field.[10] What was most important about his scheme was to assign more flexible tasks to everyone: Midfielders had to take on more pronounced offensive or defensive roles, depending on the other team's tactical formation; half- and fullbacks had to help organize midfield operations and ensure effective transitions from defense to offense. Instead of simply asking individual players to stick to their positions and dominate their assigned spaces, Chapman's WM system turned the space of the field into an event, a dynamic simultaneity of different tasks and trajectories which defined movement, not through isolated action, but through flexible practices of interaction. Space, for Chapman, was multiple and relational. In spite of the field's basic limitations, his tactical formations considered it as essentially open and always becoming, even when defensive situations called for a tightening of the play zone and the systematic undoing of the other team's forward orientation. The success and pleasure of soccer was not in how individual players simply maneuvered the ball, but rather in how one's team sought to contract or expand its network of players across the different zones of the field, that is, to temporalize space with the intention to establish shifting nodes of intensity and interaction across the ever-fluctuating depth of the field.

German soccer made great strides in the mid-1930s in order to live up to the remarkable modernization European soccer had experienced around 1930.[11] Coached by Otto Nerz, the German national team in the early 1930s could, at best, be considered a second-tier organization, neither on par with the best international squads such as the ones from England and Uruguay, nor really drawing as much attention and enthusiasm as domestic club teams such as the lineups of the 1. FC Nuremberg and of Schalke 04. German soccer was internationally known for its disciplined players, its hardworking defenders, and the excellent stamina and strength of its players. What it was not able to do, however, was to translate individual robustness—its Protestant work ethic—into successful team action, thus lagging far behind the achievements of other international soccer organizations. Much of this was set to change during the early years of the 1930s when Nerz sought to infuse the hardiness of German national soccer with the flexibility of Chapman's WM system. By the mid-1930s, Nerz's tactical interventions began to prove successful, with the German team winning ever more important international games and thus emerging as one of the favorites of the 1936 Olympic soccer tournament in Berlin. The German squad won its first round game against Luxembourg on August 4 with an impressive 9–0, yet apparently this spectacular victory emboldened Nerz to such an extent that he decided to experiment with different players and formations in the second game against the rather negligible Norwegians. The encounter with Norway on August 7 turned out to be one of the darkest moments of early German soccer history. The German players quickly trailed the Norwegians with 0–2 and Hitler—noticeably upset about his team's failure to turn things around—left the stadium before the game's end. While Germany, due to its tactical negligence and much to the dismay of Nazi authorities, was thus eliminated from the competition, the equally favored Italians and Austrians moved on to the final and were thus able to showcase the tactical pleasures of modern soccer on August 15, 1936, in front of 80,000 spectators and Riefenstahl's many cameras.

Riefenstahl's cinematography and editing of the final, I have argued, was centered on presenting the ongoing movement of the ball toward the opponent's goal. I am now in a position to state more precisely the consequences of Riefenstahl's editorial choices, not only in terms of purely formal properties, but also in terms of the historical advances of soccer. Entirely focused on the movement of the ball, Riefenstahl's presentation of the final between Austria and Italy takes no notice of what makes modern soccer modern. The field's space, for her, is something solely to be traversed by the actions of individual players and the undisturbed trajectory of the ball. Instead of seeing the field—as Chapman did—as a dynamic space constituted through shifting nodes of player interactions, as a variable ground of ceaseless becoming and transformation, Riefenstahl's editing considers the field as a stable entity entirely subordinated to the ball's speed and forward motion. And instead of mapping the field as a simultaneity of interrelated, albeit not physically joined, itineraries, as a zone of flexible relations and interactions between different players, Riefenstahl's camera reduces the field's space to the mere status of a neutral container whose sole purpose is to foreground the sight of unidirectional physical motion, of unifying different human temporalities. Nothing could have been more oblivious to the modernization of soccer during the 1920s and 1930s than Riefenstahl's decision to present the field as a static frame, a preexisting backdrop, an unchangeable topography whose sole function was to bring to light the fusion of ball, body, and time into self-contained unity. Nothing could have been more blind to Chapman's groundbreaking temporalization of space, and nothing could have visualized more candidly the essential failure of German soccer in the 1936 tournament than Riefenstahl's overdetermined effort to present soccer as a game annihilating space and homogenizing time into one single trajectory, one unified thrust relentlessly moving forward so as to showcase the timeless beauty of motion.

And nothing, in the end, could have been more in line with the Nazis' ideological valorization of gymnastics, car racing, and boxing over soccer than Riefenstahl's inability to capture the flexible and dynamic spatiality of what even in the 1930s—in spite of all political dogma—was the most popular spectator sport in Germany. Though once a powerful means of both psychophysical and communal integration, modern sport culture—according to Nazi philosophers such as Alfred Baeumler—no longer served as a viable interface between the individual and the body politic. Unlike that of the ancient Greeks, nineteenth- and early-twentieth-century bourgeois society had unfortunately come to prefer spectatorship over athletic exertion. In the view of Nazi sports theorists, bourgeois culture considered the individual body not only as something separated from the human soul, but also as private property. It favored abstract competitions against clocks or marks—the abstract principle of achievements—over public celebrations of physical prowess and communality. "In competition," Baeumler noted, "abilities compete against each other, seek to outdo each other. Man doesn't compete with man, but rather achievement versus achievement, number versus number."[12] The state-managing of physical education in Nazi society was designed to overcome these deficiencies. According to Nazi ideologues, the role of sports again was to promote physical strength and mental decontamination, to overcome bourgeois rationalism and individualism, to interconnect the public and the private, in the hope of enlisting the individual body for the future tasks of the *Volk*, the national collective, the state. The decisive location to make all this happen was neither the bourgeois athletic club nor the bleachers of the modern mass stadium, but the circumscribed field of the *Turnplatz* (gymnastics field)—a site at which communities could emerge as living organisms due to the people's joint caring of their bodies.[13] The Nazi *Turnplatz*, as theorized by Baeumler, was a clearing at which the German body politic could enter the light of public visibility. It provided a space in which collective physical motion moved alienated individuals beyond the abstract constitution of industrial society; a frame in whose boundaries the modern subject could reconnect with the ahistorical, timeless, mythical, and affective grounds of race and nation.

Though I am not aware that Riefenstahl spent much time reading the influential works of Baeumler, I suggest we understand the crucial shortcomings of her presentation of soccer as a symptom of her desire to consider the soccer field as a *Turnplatz* in Baeumler's sense: not as a site of flux and becoming, a space actively produced by the flexible interactions of discrete players, but as a location of unchanging and graceful being; a place bonding individuals to the steady rhythms of an organic collective and the present moment to the archaic myths of the past; a ground mobilizing the individual precisely because it is seen as something devoid of time, devoid of conflicting trajectories, devoid of the possibility of allowing open-ended configurations and uncontained multiplicities.

VII.

In recent years much has been written to refocus our attention on the aesthetic and to overturn what, with some paranoia, has been considered the denigration of beauty at the hands of classical modernism, the historical avant-garde, postwar postmodernism, and/or the academic culturalism of the 1990s. Think of Elaine Scarry's plea to reassess the role of beauty and her attempt to promote the sight of symmetry and balance as a sensory training ground for articulating concepts of social justice.[14] Think of Arthur Danto's work, at once acknowledging the elimination of beauty through modernist artists such as Marcel Duchamp and arguing for a relegitimation of beauty as a source of meaning and vitality for our disenchanted postmodern lives.[15] It would be intriguing to contemplate the ongoing interest in Riefenstahl's work against the backdrop of this recent reinscription of beauty, not only to place Riefenstahl's cinematic work in a larger historical context, but also to expose some of the failings of our contemporary desire for a return of the aesthetic. In closing, let me nevertheless take another turn, reaching back rather than forward in time, so as to recap both the curious relationship of athletic grace and slow motion in Riefenstahl's *Olympia* films and their far from compelling representation of team sports such as soccer. Remember Schiller?

In his attempt to wrest discussions of the aesthetic from the Enlightenment focus on expressive creativity and individual artistic genius, Friedrich Schiller famously defined grace as "the beauty of form under the influence of freedom."[16] Grace, for Schiller, was a feature of bodies in motion; it designated a playful harmony of body and mind, one in which the soul would express itself through and to our senses without force, willful intentionality, strategic reason, and hence necessity. To be graceful is to perform gestures and movements as if no knowledge, routine, custom, effort, practice, determination, and thought were required in order to embody them. Grace renders visible the interiority of the human soul; graceful movements allow that which seems to resist appearance to appear in front of our eyes. Remember Kleist?

Gloomy and unyielding as ever, Kleist radicalized Schiller's notion of grace by claiming that either only the divine or a lifeless automaton could perfectly embody grace's union of body and mind, of absorption and self-transcendence: "Grace," Kleist wrote in his 1810 essay on the Marionette Theater, "appears purest simultaneously in the human body that has either none at all or else infinite consciousness—that is, in the puppet or god."[17] Grace signifies movements or gestures carried out without reflexivity, self-awareness, or self-perception. For Kleist, a puppet's remotely controlled lifting as much as the idea of God's all-encompassing universality was much more graceful than any human motion simply because both—the puppet's unbridled exteriority; God's all-inclusive interiority—defied what caused humans to thirst for grace in the first place: the mundane disparity of essence and appearance, body and mind.

Slow-motion photography is Leni Riefenstahl's principal means in her two *Olympia* films by which to encode athletic grace and communicate it directly to the viewer's sensory perception. Grace, for Riefenstahl, is a phenomenon of slowness, however rapid an athlete's body might move. Graceful movements, like slow-motion photography, allow us to view the present as an enactment of timeless forms and intensities; they cause us to perceive the fleeting as a replay, an instantiation, of the eternal. Riefenstahl's decision not to use slow-motion photography in her presentation of soccer, on the other hand, permits us to understand her distance from Schiller's conception of grace as much as it lets us fully understand the political index of her aesthetic, her valorization of form, linearity, symmetry, and illumination as the main constituents of the beautiful. No matter how much Riefenstahl's various cameras want to celebrate an athlete's harmonic union of body and soul, what is entirely missing in her slow-motion images of running, jumping, and gyrating competitors is Schiller's crucial notion of play. Grace, as captured with the help of Riefenstahl's slow-motion cameras, is devoid of what makes both Schiller and soccer tick: the aleatory, unpredictable, relational, flexible, and forceless force of playfulness. Contrary to her self-conception as a classical aesthete, then, Riefenstahl's aesthetic of corporeal beauty comes much closer to Kleist's darkly romantic vision of grace than to Schiller's post-Kantian classicism. Athletic beauty and grace, for Riefenstahl, appear the purest whenever the director's divine camera and will severs the represented body from its own intentionality and volition; they come into being whenever the cinematic frame produces the world as one beyond former boundaries between interiority and exteriority, one which knows neither of self-reflexivity nor of the autonomy of individual sensory perception and expressiveness.

While Riefenstahl completely elides the inherent slowness of soccer itself—the game's variable articulation of multiple temporal and spatial trajectories—she embraces the special effect of slow motion as a tool in order to cast the present as a mere replay of archaic and seemingly eternal forms of beauty.

Rather than keeping alive our hope for a different future, Riefenstahl's aesthetic of slowness and grace pictures the present as a spectacular iteration of the past. Precisely because deceleration, in Riefenstahl's work, is meant to consecrate each and every moment as one of historical weight and import, precisely because Riefenstahl's slow-motion cameras eliminate playfulness from the picture, history here emerges as a mere succession of deanimated and hence disempowering images. In spite of all commotion, agility, and mobility, Riefenstahl's present will and shall never produce what soccer engenders all the time: something new, different, and unforeseen. Riefenstahl's slow-motion cameras engineer the graceful with the intention to erase any notion of historical time as a fleeting series of open-ended configurations. Pictured as a monumental parade of the triumphant, history for Riefenstahl has no meaning unless it can be framed by the camera and mirrored in the timeless forms of the past.[18] Which is just another way of saying that Riefenstahl cannot imagine history as something open to intervention, change, and multiplicity. As something whose ball is as round as the one of soccer.

Notes

Special thanks to Suzuko Mousel Knott, Andy Markovits, Claudia Mohr, and Stephan Schindler for energizing discussions about the aesthetics and politics of soccer.

1. See the study on "Kicking" by Pekka Luhtanen, Senior Researcher, KIHU Research Institute for Olympic Sports, http://www.coachesinfo.com/article/106/ (accessed June 5, 2006).
2. For more on different conceptions of the aesthetics of modern sport, see Hans Ulrich Gumbrecht, *In Praise of Athletic Beauty* (Cambridge, MA: Belknap Press, 2006).
3. Walter Benjamin, *The Arcades Project*, trans. Howard Eiland and Kevin McLaughlin (Cambridge: Harvard University Press, 1999), 462–463.
4. Taylor Downing, *Olympia* (London: BFI, 1992), 91.
5. Crispin Sartwell, *Six Names of Beauty* (New York: Routledge, 2004), 88.
6. Dirk Schümer, *Gott ist rund: Die Kultur des Fußballs* (Frankfurt a. M.: Suhrkamp, 1998), 253–257.
7. Barry Salt, *Film Style and Technology: History and Analysis* (London: Starword, 1983), 203–204.
8. Stephen Prince, "The Aesthetics of Slow-Motion: Violence in the Films of Sam Peckinpah," in *Screening Violence*, ed. Stephen Prince (New Brunswick, NJ: Rutgers University Press, 2000), 185.
9. Quoted in Brian Henderson, "The Long Take," in *Movies and Methods*, ed. Bill Nicholas (Berkeley: University of California Press, 1976), 315.
10. For a detailed analysis of Chapman's WM system, see Christoph Biermann and Ulrich Fuchs, *Der Ball ist rund, damit das Spiel die Richtung ändern kann: Wie moderner Fußball funktioniert* (Cologne: Kiepenheuer & Witsch, 2004), 63–71.
11. For more on the history of German soccer during the 1930s, as well as its institutional entanglement with Nazi power, see in particular Gerhard Fischer and Ulrich Lindner, *Stürmer für Hitler: Vom Zusammenspiel zwischen Fußball und Nationalsozialismus*

(Göttingen: Verlag Die Werkstatt, 1999); and Nils Havemann, *Fussball unterm Hakenkreuz: Der DFB zwischen Sport, Politik und Kommerz* (Frankfurt a. M.: Campus Verlag, 2005).

12. Alfred Baeumler, "Sinn und Aufbau der deutschen Leibesübungen," in *Männerbund und Wissenschaft*, ed. Alfred Baeumler (Berlin: Junker und Dünnhaupt, 1934), 55.
13. Alfred Baeumler, "Die weltanschaulichen Grundlagen der deutschen Leibesübungen," in *Sport und Staat*, ed. Arno Breitmeyer and P. G. Hoffmann (Hamburg: Hilfsfond für den deutschen Sport, 1934), 33.
14. Elaine Scarry, *On Beauty and Being Just* (Princeton: Princeton University Press, 1999).
15. Arthur C. Danto, *The Abuse of Beauty: Aesthetics and the Concept of Art* (Chicago: Open Court, 2003).
16. Friedrich Schiller, "Über Anmut und Würde," in *Über das Schöne und die Kunst: Schriften zur Ästhetik* (Munich: DTV, 1984), 55.
17. Heinrich von Kleist, "On the Marionette Theater," trans. Roman Paska, in *Fragments for a History of the Human Body*, ed. Michael Feher (Cambridge, MA: Zone Books, 1989), 420.
18. For a similar juxtaposition of the temporality of Riefenstahl's and Eisenstein's aesthetic, see Oksana Bulgakowa, "'Riefenstein'—Demontage eines Klischees," in *Leni Riefenstahl*, ed. Filmmuseum Potsdam (Berlin: Henschel Verlag, 1999), 133–143.

Part Two

Afterlife

Chapter 4

The Afterlife of *Triumph of the Will*: The First Twenty-five Years

David Bathrick

> *Triumph of the Will* is probably the most quoted work of film history. Today there is not a documentary about National Socialism that can get by without using images from this film and no other film has defined as deeply our visual notion as to what National Socialism actually was.[1]
> —Jürgen Trimborn

I.

Jürgen Trimborn was not the first to stress the extraordinarily pervasive quoting of Leni Riefenstahl's 1934 Nazi Party Convention film *Triumph of the Will.* Nor has it seemed to have made much difference whether these borrowers were for or against the cause being propagated in the film. Regardless of their varying political predilections, most seem in solid agreement that what they were seeing represented was the very "essence of fascism."[2] Within the Reich itself, already in the late 1930s and soon thereafter in other European countries, clips from Riefenstahl's film were used in newsreel, documentary, and propaganda footage to inform, persuade, and even convert those beguiled by the rapid changes occurring in Germany's "awakening." On the other side of the political ledger, starting already in 1940, three anti-Nazi propaganda films were produced in England: Frank Watts, *The Curse of the Swastika* (1940); Len Lyes, *Swinging the Lambeth Walk* (1940); and Donald Taylor, *These Are the Men* (1943). All of these filmmakers drew heavily on clips from *Triumph,* as did the Hollywood directors Charlie Chaplin in *The Great Dictator* (1940) and Frank Capra for his seven-part anti-Nazi series *Why We Fight* (1943–1944).

If some postwar observers might have believed that the defeat of Hitler and the discovery of the camps would bring the interdiction of a film so clearly enabling of the Hitler myth, they were soon to be disabused of such expectations. What emerged in the place of censure was a look to *Triumph* by the victorious Allies as a chosen medium by which to comprehend, elucidate, adjudicate, denazify, or reeducate the defeated German nation. Beyond the parameters of World War II, even more astonishing is the extent to which clips from *Triumph* continue to provide, unabatedly it would seem, an iconic language to connote some form of absolute political evil framed as the now universal legacy of Hitlerian fascism.[3]

The purpose of my present endeavor will be to limit the scope and deepen the focus through an analysis of a select number of documentary and feature films from the period between 1940 and 1960 that drew on *Triumph* for radically differing political, philosophical, or aesthetic objectives.[4] In so doing, I shall demonstrate how the evolution of a cinematic language in this work was made possible by the fluidity of its representational patterns, permitting it to function both as index and as icon in relation to the material it was treating. Thus I begin my exploration with a contextual reading of *Triumph* as a film devoted to effacing the recent slaughter of the SA and rewriting the image of the Führer as Storm Trooper and street rowdy into that of a *Landesvater* and mythic icon. The word *icon* in this context might seem from one perspective inadequate. Emerging as it does from the world of graven pictura, an iconic image is thought at once to arrest and thereby transform something. Set in the era of mechanical reproduction, the indexical photograph is transmuted into a still photo: the logo-like graphic of Chaplin's Charcot with bowler hat, mustache, and cane; or the little boy in the Warsaw ghetto with his hands raised whose congealed synchronic form communicates *in nuce* the spatial and implied diachronic totality of a larger truth. What Riefenstahl gives us is an iconic language, the imagistic patois by which the legend of the Führer is instantiated visually.

II.

Until his assumption of power on January 30, 1933, Hitler had only been seen cinematically on rare occasions. Little documentary footage remains from this earlier period. There are, to be sure, occasional shots of his arriving or leaving a rally, or of other brief cameo appearances in the rapidly growing deployment of the *Wochenschau* during the late 1920s and early 1930s.[5] Also extant is a sequence focusing on the leadership of the NSDAP in a filming of *The German Day in Nuremberg (Der deutsche Tag in Nürnberg)* in September 1923 in which Hitler played second fiddle visually and performatively to the much more prominent General von Ludendorff. A copy of the first (silent) filming of a Nazi Party Convention in 1927 reveals a crude command of camera and editing techniques that proved notably ineffective in the party's efforts to showcase its rising star. A similar print of the 1929 party convention two years later demonstrates improved technical proficiency, but as propaganda it would also remain of interest only to the already converted ranks of the NSDAP. The same could be said for the few talkies made in 1932 of campaign speeches prior to Hitler's coming to power.[6] Thus despite myths about the powerful role of "the media" in the rise of Nazism in Germany, it is safe to say that prior to 1933, Hitler's reputed charisma as a public speaker was the result of being in his presence and hearing his voice, rather than of any direct form of mass mediation. The party did not produce radio, film, or phonograph recordings to any significant extent; nor did Hitler even avail himself of a microphone until 1928.[7] What this initial cinematic absence means for a treatment of documentary representations of Hitler on film is that we are largely limited to footage garnered over roughly a ten-year period between January 1933, when he came to power, to the end of 1942, when defeats on the eastern front and Hitler's own deterioration physically due to Parkinson's syndrome forced the Nazi leader increasingly to withdraw from public view and even hearing.

Yet significant for the question of image creation is also the fact that even the official documentary footage produced within the period of his greatest political successes, both domestic and foreign, reveal an effort both to contain the variety of Hitler's medial visualization, as well as a tendency toward repeated showings of the very same clips. This very conscious narrowing and controlling over the years of his official pictorial archive[8]—cinematic and photographic—has contributed to a transformation of its status from *indexical* witness into universal *icon*. Being limited in number and increasingly legible to larger numbers of viewers, these icons achieved already in the 1930s the status of a semiotic language. Iconic images express an aura of timelessness and a dearth of spatial and historical specificity. They claim implicitly to "speak" the truth, often "louder than words," to tell the entire story with the flick of a frame.

This move toward iconic status is important for understanding the film stagings of Hitler inside and outside the Third Reich in the 1930s, as well as the ever evolving cinematic reception of his image after 1945. Goebbels's organized filming—with the help of the official *Wochenschau* camera team—of Hitler's first major address to the German people as Chancellor on February 10, 1933, was considered by the Minister of Propaganda himself to have been a flop. Unsatisfactory for use as political propaganda, this thirty-three-minute recording remains the longest document of a single Hitler speech. In contrast, three documents that were to achieve canonical status as Hitler films from the period were Riefenstahl's filmings of the 1933 and 1934 party conventions, as well the famous twenty-minute section of the *Wochenschau* honoring Hitler's fiftieth birthday on April 20, 1939. In addition to their success as propaganda for the Nazi Party within Germany, this same footage also provoked anti-Nazi cinematic responses outside of the Reich as early as the end of the 1930s.

Goebbels attributed the perceived cinematic failure of the Hitler speech of February 10, 1933, to a lack of party control of the entire operation. The film opens with a stunning sequence depicting the growing anticipation among the waiting audience at the Berliner Sportpalast, one that segues effectively into the initially subdued and then ever expanding voice of Hitler as he reaches his first crescendo. But the newsreel soon begins to lose its sense of rhythm, focus, and editorial coordination. Whether this occurred intentionally, or just for lack of experience and organization on the part of the *Wochenschau* camera crew, remains uncertain. What it nevertheless led to was a decision by Goebbels and Hitler to turn to professionals and artists working outside existing political and bureaucratic agencies for purposes of shaping the Hitler image.

The first such selection was that of Riefenstahl, who already in May of 1933 was asked by Goebbels to make a "Hitler film" focusing on the upcoming party convention in Nuremberg in September of that year.[9] Riefenstahl was in many ways a strange and even risky choice. Here were Hitler and Goebbels willing to turn this important showcase opportunity with virtually no strings attached over to a woman with relatively little experience in the area of feature film directing, none whatsoever in documentary filmmaking, and who, in addition, had no deep connection to, or even real knowledge of, National Socialism. Both leaders had seen and been deeply impressed by her mountain film *The Blue Light (Das blaue Licht)* of 1932 and their instincts proved propitious beyond all expectations. The film, entitled *Victory of Faith (Sieg des Glaubens),* was a success cinematically as well as from a propaganda point of view. It was followed by its considerably more renowned sequel of the 1934 convention entitled *Triumph of the Will,* which was awarded several gold medals at the Venice Film Festival in 1935 as well as the Grand Prix of the Paris World Fair in 1937.

Goebbels and Hitler were not interested merely in the creation of an overtly ideological film made by an acolytic member of the NSDAP, nor were they seeking a newsreel masterpiece à la the style of the *Wochenschau*. Indeed, it was precisely Riefenstahl's mastery of figurative dramatization—the choreography of natural spectacle and her sense of narrative rhythms as a feature filmmaker—that drew them to her in the first place. As Goebbels was to emphasize throughout in his function as Filmminister, innovative, state-of-the-art production values, particularly as found in the entertainment film industry, were infinitely more effective than any crude compilation film in the service of *Kulturpolitik* or with a focus on more specific Nazi themes, such as "Aryan" purity, *Heimat* idylls, anti-Semitic diatribe, or national hegemony.[10] Conversely, and one might say ironically, what drew artists like Riefenstahl and Albert Speer into service for the party had more to do with artistic freedom and personal careerism than with any commitment to a political doctrine: freedom financially, due to unlimited state resources, to do what they knew they could do best; freedom aesthetically to lend inherent form and beauty to ideas and values that they viewed as far beyond and even unsullied by any narrow, instrumental notion of party or politics.[11]

Thus, the iconization of Hitler in both Riefenstahl films was enacted by virtue of bestowing eternal verity through art to the values of "belief" and "will" as configured in the dramaturgy of a six-day convention. What these texts produced at the same time, beyond any necessary intention or even awareness on the part of the filmmaker—and here begins my deconstructive, indexical reading—is a legitimation of Hitler's first two years in power as the story of a seamless transition from storm trooper to statesman. Central to this two-volume tale is the omnipresence in the first film and the total absence in *Triumph* of Hitler's longtime fighting comrade and head of the SA, Ernst Röhm. In *Victory of Faith*, it is the ruddy, pug-faced Röhm who ubiquitously and metonymically stands, indeed hovers, as a reminder of past acts of terror on the brutal road to "victory" as well as of present claims to power as the second in command. Footage of Hitler reviewing the parading SA and SS as well as paying homage to the fallen include Röhm situated as part of a duo; one of the film's highlights focuses on the two shaking hands, a shot that seems to cement the relationship between the state under Hitler and the state within the state represented by the brownshirts.

If the initial party rally film necessarily looks back and sums up visually the "victory of belief" by the margin over the center, *Triumph* is primarily about the domestication of Adolf Hitler as statesman and *Landesvater*. Lying between these party conventions historically are two deaths of enormous political and symbolic significance: the violent murder, organized by Hitler himself, of Ernst Röhm and the entire leadership of the SA on June 30, 1934, ten weeks before the party convention; and the death of President Paul von Hindenburg on August 2, 1934, which left Hitler in sole command. While neither of these events are mentioned explicitly in the film,[12] the title of the rally, "Reich's Convention of Unity and Strength" (*Reichsparteitag der Einheit und Stärke*), and the incessant cinematic and verbal articulations of resolution, harmony, oneness, forgiveness, death, posterity, and mourning all give voice to inchoate, unexplicated trauma.

Riefenstahl's cinematic stylization of Hitler in *Triumph* registers that trauma, through rituals of mourning pictorially and even in speech, and at the same time disavows it through the cinematic narrative of triumph by the one chosen leader it will construct for the future grounding of the state.[13] Although commemorations celebrating the fallen heroes of the failed Munich Putsch were a central ingredient of every party convention after 1923, *Triumph* represents a shift of dramatic significance. What binds the two volumes of Riefenstahl's party films into a myth of Shakespearean proportion is the missing body of Ernst Röhm in *Triumph*. His absent presence signals semiotically the end of any hope on the part of the SA for a second, Socialist revolution. Missing as well is the once rowdy image of Hitler as storm trooper. Both will be buried now—within the mise-en-scene, by the lone figure of the grieving, now hegemonic leader paying homage to the once-bloodied flag; imagistically by the Führer transformed into an ideogeme for all the people. It is with *Triumph,* and not *Victory,* that Riefenstahl delivers to Goebbels her once promised, henceforth canonical, "Hitler film."

I have said that Riefenstahl's film both domesticates Hitler, and legitimates him as a statesman. In some ways those two cinematic strategies might seem to be in aesthetic conflict with each other. On the one hand, we have the orator, seen at a distance, filmed at low and high angle, speaking stentorially to the "masses" of every conceivable constitutive making: Hitler youth, Labor Service, the SS, the SA, and the party activists. At the ceremony of the dead in the Luitpoldhain arena, where 200,000 were gathered, Hitler, the new SA leader Viktor Lutze, and Heinrich Himmler of the SS are viewed from above by means of a vertically dollying camera as they walk in religious gravity, Hitler in the lead, through the perfectly ordered columns of the now seemingly united warriors. It has been argued that this latter sequence, crowning Hitler visually (and in absence of speech) as the one who will embody the grievance of all those who have suffered, represents the cinematic high point of the Hitler cult.[14] Here Hitler functions as icon of forgiveness and forgetting, his own already unseemly crimes included, made iconic as well by the summarily perfect cinematic magic of Riefenstahl.

Opposed to such mass ornamental design, *Triumph* was also, in Martin Loiperdinger's words, "the first and only film, that offered an extraordinary abundance of medium and close-up shots of Adolf Hitler."[15] UFA's advertising campaign proclaimed that it was the close-ups in particular that offered the promise that the German people "would finally be able to see and experience the *Führer* as up to now only a few have been able to do"[16] The film framed Hitler in direct physical and shot-reverse-shot eye contact with specific individuals: babies, mothers, boys, girls, peasants, and individual soldiers; Hitler is caught also in occasional off-guard moments in telling close-up shots. Cameraman Sepp Allgeier offers a brief, almost intimate focus on Hitler's left earlobe as we the spectators join him in close proximity, speeding by car through the streets lined by the ecstatic crowd. Other shots reveal occasional close-up glimpses of a gentle, smiling Hitler. In the opening of the film, a camera perspective suggests Hitler's view from the cockpit of the arriving plane as he looks down upon the gentle medieval town of Nuremberg. In both these roles, as intimidating statesman and intimate *Landesvater*, Riefenstahl's Hitler is made respectable, even *salonfähig*. And it is the rhythmic editing patterns that ultimately suture it together. As is known, the filmmaker spent six months cutting 130,000 meters of film down to 3,000, a ratio of forty to one: Both the labor involved and "waste" of film stock would be simply prohibitive as part of a normal production process. Riefenstahl herself has described the strategy behind her work in musicological terms: counterpoint; dissonance, resolving into harmony; proliferation of melody giving way to leitmotif; and nights of turmoil dissolving into awakening dawn. The chaos of a six-day party convention is condensed and etherealized cinematically into the flow of an inexorable movement.[17] "Riefenstahl's formal language is inventive and functional," writes Rainer Rother, "her particularly powerful images . . . illustrate the ritual of the party rally with consummate sensitivity, patently intent on overwhelming her audience and achieving a 'classical' unity."[18] It will be the task now to explore the invocation of that "language" as its images are quoted as a part of that film's afterlife.

III.

We turn now to Goebbels's war against the Jews and Hollywood's war against the Führer between1940 and 1945. Based on its large number of "powerful images," *Triumph* soon came to offer an archival treasure trove for all those wishing to cannibalize it for purposes of Hitler representation, whether for compilation or *Wochenschau* filmings within the Third Reich, or in compilation and feature films being made by the Allies during and after the war. Certainly one of the earliest cinematic attempts to employ the Riefenstahl image archive in a feature film can be found in Charlie Chaplin's *The Great Dictator*, which had its initial screening on October 15, 1940, in New York City. Much has been written about Chaplin's preparation for the characterization of Hitler—that he studied every newsreel he could get his hands on, focusing with particular fascination on speaking poses, but also on the off moments. The revealing segments that Chaplin will employ to crack open what Heinrich Mann has referred to as the "*Führer* Face"[19] include Hitler doing his famous little jig after leaving the railway car following the French surrender; Hitler ranting, Hitler talking with children, greeting women, stroking babies, visiting patients in a hospital. Luis Buñuel, who was asked to cut a shorter version of *Triumph* for the Museum of Modern Art in the late 1930s, describes a special screening of the film for Chaplin and the latter's strong reactions to it—mostly hysterical laughter.[20] Finally, on more than one occasion Chaplin was described as being fascinated with Hitler's abilities as a performer: "this guy was one of the greatest actors I have ever seen."[21]

Clearly, Chaplin—playing Hynkel—was not interested in simply imitating Hitler, in a replication of recognizable expressions or gestures, but rather in de-centering the moments of what he had already grasped as an iconic image. As suggested above, iconography helps create hegemonic unity, the oneness and universality of an identity. What Chaplin employs aesthetically to achieve iconoclastic distortion or destruction of the unitary image is at once montage and collage: montage as the serial clashing temporally of heterogeneous cuts, scenes, and sequences; collage in the way objects within the same frame co-exist spatially and are in tension with one another. Both involve the pasting together of a not very tightly woven tapestry of slapstick, satire, invective, clowning, emotional hyperbole, vaudeville, even gentle irony, resulting in a Hynkel who is by turns brutal, weaning, pompous, vulnerable, ludicrous—sometimes even tender. Let us explore as one dimension of Chaplin's Hitler portrayal: the famous scene in which Hynkel dances a ballet with the globe of the world as a balloon. At some distant reach, this sequence is linked to Hitler's famous jig, just as at another level it references the whole cultural dimension of the Nazi imagery that starts with Hitler's Wagner obsessions in Vienna. The beauty and precision of Chaplin's choreography is at once haunting, moving, ridiculous, and grotesque. A look at the screenplay reveals this two-and-one-half-minute sequence to have been broken down into ten sections, which

Chaplin wrote out in detailed descriptions of the desired mood, and the gestures and facial expressions. The sequence was minutely rehearsed, shot, and reshot over a period of nine full working days. Section seven, for example, reads: "Gracefully he leans back over the desk and gets very Greek about the whole thing. He bounces the globe from toe to head to rear. He's carried away with the beauty of it."[22] Accompanied by nondiegetic strains from the prelude to Richard Wagner's *Lohengrin*, framed between hideous initial laughter, growing paranoia, and final mournful weeping, Chaplin's Hitler converges in a kind of aesthetic double-bind of auratic Wagnerian ecstasy and Brechtian distanciation.

In Hynkel we are given a figure as labile in his mood swings as he is variegated in his expression of the will to dominate: Hynkel/Hitler the artist, familiar enough from the writings of George Mosse, Joachim Fest, Brigitte Hamann, Albert Speer, and Thomas Mann, whose longing for beauty and possession will self-destruct in his own hate; Hynkel in gender trouble, whether in physical assault upon his "Aryan" secretary, a scene which is first erotically charged and then ends up in failed impotence; or in endless compensatory, often feckless, posturing as he competes with Benzino Napaloni; or in his allusion in the balloon scene to a possible gay Hitler, where, to quote Chaplin himself, Hynkel will lean over the desk and "get very Greek about the whole thing," as he bumps the balloon into the air with his rear end. But the ballet scene is more than just satire. As performance it stands in contrast to, for instance, Chaplin's vicious ridicule of Hitler/Hynkel's speaking style—a brilliant linguistic montage of nonsense Germanisms familiar from American mass culture, spewing forth in hideous guttural caricature, the very hyperbole of the Führer rant. Yet in the ballet sequence, the artist Chaplin plays out his own tenuous relationship to this perverted "actor" manqué, with whom he has so often been compared, by opening up Hynkel from the inside; by establishing through the grace of the dance, as only the body can do, a perilous moment of affiliation and extreme repulsion.

Am I suggesting a symbiosis here similar to the one that Thomas Mann confesses to in his famous 1940 essay "Bruder Hitler"? Yes and no. No in the sense that unlike Mann, Chaplin's whole aesthetic of slapstick and mocking satire was fundamentally at odds with the traditions of *Lebensphilosophie* and reactionary *Kulturkritik* that Mann was trying to recognize and thereby overcome in acknowledging *his* fraternal affiliation to some of the ideational roots of fascism. Yes, on the other hand, in that Chaplin was seeking to play out and thereby unveil a kind of actor's complicity with the forces of the auratic that left him linked, beyond the stupid little mustache, to the powers of corporeal manipulation. Chaplin takes us there through a reenactment of that quality in Hitler's repertoire that Mann himself described as "Wagnerisch—auf der Stufe der Verhunzung" (Wagnerian—at the level of the gutter) and then drops us with the pop of the balloon.[23] In this mimed dance Chaplin acts through subtleties of sensibility unreachable by human speech.

But what has all this got to with Riefenstahl? Clearly articulated visual citations of *Triumph* in *The Great Dictator* are few in number but obvious when they appear. For example, when Hynkel and his propaganda minister, Garbitsch, are about to be driven through the city in the backseat of an automobile, they are suddenly approached by a little girl offering Hynkel flowers, followed by a mother bearing a child who offers him first flowers and then her somewhat flatulent baby. Hynkel holds it for a moment, than hands it back and wipes off his hands. The citation is clearly an inversion of a sequence in *Triumph* in which a similarly adoring mother with child approaches Hitler's cavalcade as he drives from the airport to the hotel. Whereas the Riefenstahl version shoots the scene as a point-of-view Hitler high-angle shot, emphasizing the adoration of the viewee with no reverse reference to the gazing Führer, Chaplin's frontal eye line shots play out the unmasking of a bumbling, shat-upon Hynkel. Similarly, we are given throughout almost familiar hyperbolic low-angle shots of flags, high rear-angle looks over the orating Hynkel's shoulders at crowds, etc., which suggest but do not replicate an "original," deflect rather than deify a being in the presence of the legendary leader.

Yet as is obvious in the dance scene, Chaplin's representational *pas de deux*—between self and other, actor and Führer—dares to admit credence, with the aid of the nondiegetic majestic strains from the *Meistersänger*, to the aura that Riefenstahl's iconic reconstruction has bought into regarding the power of the image. When Chaplin wrote years later that "had I known of the actual horrors of the German concentration camps, I could not have made *The Great Dictator*; I could not have made fun of the homicidal insanity of the Nazis,"[24] it perhaps could have alluded as well, beyond the dangers of "making fun" of consummate evil, precisely to an affiliation at the level of bodily mimesis that might well bring one too close for comfort.

IV.

On October 2, 1939, one month after the German invasion of Poland, Goebbels dispatched the head of the *Reichsfilmkammer* (Reich Film Department) Fritz Hippler, and his *Wochenschau* camera team to the Jewish ghetto in Lodz with the order to film "Jews of all types, by which is meant character studies as well as in the workplace."[25] The express purpose sounded ominous: "We must photograph as much as we can in these places of Jewish origin, since soon there won't be any more Jews. The Führer plans to relocate them to Madagascar or other areas, and for that reason we need these film documents for our archives."[26] While some of this footage was used for newsreels and other documentaries, most of it ended up in an anti-Semitic propaganda film called *The Eternal Jew*, where it served as visual evidence for the apocryphal claim that these "character studies" represented everyday Jewish life in a large Eastern European city. What the viewers would not know is that the deplorable living conditions of this Polish ghetto thus documented were the direct result of the deteriorating social order under German occupation.[27]

Basic to the film's script was a system of photographs, narrative reenactments, camera positioning, and editorial crosscutting in support of the thesis that is spelled out explicitly, in ominous printed words, in the opening credits of the film:

> The civilized Jews that we know from Germany give us only an incomplete picture of their true racial nature. This film will show original footage from Polish Ghettos, it will show us the Jews as they really look, before they hide themselves behind the mask of the civilized European.[28]

While the dollying shots through the busy streets of the ghetto are designed as establishing shots to illustrate from a distance the chaotic everyday life of this "commercially indulgent" peddler's culture, a series of close-ups of the "Jewish physiognomy" focusing on the dress, gestures, face, caftan, and hair are clearly meant to underscore the threatening demeanor of a culture constitutively at odds with "Aryan" norms. What lends this "Symphonie des Ekels und Grauens" (symphony of horror and disgust)[29] a coherent anti-Semitic message is its verbal and visual reduction of all Jewry to a set of metaphors communicating a community infested with forms of disease, parasitism, and rodentlike behavior. A visit to a "typical" Jewish family home finds the camera focusing on the filth, the flies, the food, the disorder, and the family members eating with their hands. "They bring disease," we are told by a voiceover that concludes by eliding Jews and rats: "They are sneaky, cowardly, and move only in packs."[30] As an antidote to the egotistical, materialist, and degenerated notions of culture and work among the "eternal" Jews, the film offers three counter-clips exemplifying "Aryan" (not German) norms and values. The first two come relatively early in the film and focus on work and commerce. "That which for the creative Aryan people are genuine values," intones the voiceover, "the Jew has denigrated into a commodity, that he sells and buys again but that he himself cannot creatively produce."[31] The images that accompany these relatively short sequences, drawn from two well-known propaganda films, *Beauty of Labor (Schönheit der Arbeit*, 1934) and *Hands at Work—A Song about German Work (Hände am Werk—Ein Lied von deutscher Arbeit*, 1935), are, quite strikingly, of another visual register: beautifully ordered landscapes with long rows of plowed ground and tilled soil, the neatly piled pails with their ordered covers. Camera angle, editing sequences, and the harmonious music clearly articulate an absolute contrast to the seeming breakdown of order in the ghetto sequences.

The third such "Aryan" counter-sequence comes at the very end of the film and sutures together a series of shots showing ecstatic "German" bodies—most of them taken from *Triumph*—marching and saluting their way into an exuberant future Germany. In order to delineate that future, and its meaning for the film as a whole, it is important to describe carefully the two sequences that immediately precede the clip from *Triumph*. The first brings to conclusion the film's blistering barrage of abuse hurled at the uncivilized values of the eastern, i.e., "eternal," Jew with an unending, unbearable display of the brutal slaughter of cattle for the procuring of kosher beef by Jewish butchers. This, in turn, segues into Hitler's famous Reichstag speech about the removal of the Jews of January 30, 1939, and marking the sixth anniversary of the seizure of power. His final words aim to sum up the anger of the German people toward this growing menace and the Führer's personal determination to do something about it: ". . . should the international finance Jews push people into another world war, the result will not be a victory of Jewry, but the destruction of the Jewish race in Europe."[32]

The jubilant parliamentary audience's response to these words flows seamlessly into low-angle close-ups of individual members of the Hitler Youth, League of German Girls (BdM), SA, SS, Labor Service, and other adoring participants of the 1934 Nuremberg Rally as they raise their arms serially in row upon unending row of the Hitler salute—all of which melds into the final marching configurations from *Triumph*. These familiar, now iconic images are intoned with a voiceover informing us—as if functioning as a final addendum to Hitler's menacing tirade—that "this law of nature, keeping one's race pure, is the legacy which the National Socialist movement leaves to the German nation forever. In this spirit the united German people march on into the future."[33] *The Eternal Jew* was premiered on November 28, 1940, six weeks after *The Great Dictator* opened, as the fourth openly anti-Semitic film with major billing to appear in the Third Reich since the *Kristallnacht* pogrom of November 9, 1938. Goebbels's propaganda war against the Jews had begun in deadly earnest, and Chaplin was to be the only Hollywood—or for that matter Allied—filmmaker until 1943 to confront through the film medium the rapidly escalating Jewish catastrophe *as Jewish catastrophe*. Despite their obvious generic, stylistic, aesthetic, and certainly cultural-political (ideological) differences, *The Eternal Jew* and *The Great Dictator* do have some things in common. At a deeper structural level, both build their systems of cinematic address by juxtaposing iconic representations of the Jew and the "Aryan." In addition, and particularly important for the present essay, in doing so both are deeply indebted to the visual language of Riefenstahl's *Triumph*.

Chaplin's plan to make a "Hitler film" entailed the notion that the Jewish question would have to be as central a concern thematically and representationally as that of the Führer. Indeed, it was clear to him from the outset that the mirroring of the two, the struggle of concatenating iconic representations—a deconstructed Riefenstahl-Hitler, on the one hand, and a now Jewified Charlot with a bowler hat on the other—would make his own body the terrain on which the film would either fail or succeed. Similarly, the deployment of Riefenstahl's unsullied visual beatification of the "Aryan" body as an antidote to (and perhaps unwittingly even a disavowal of) the unremitting visual and verbal onslaught of Jew hatred permeating *The Eternal Jew* was surely intended to provide a much needed deus ex machina as utopian resolution. I say disavowal because, as is well known, *The Eternal Jew* was not at all successful at the box office in part because by the time it opened, in late 1940, audiences were beginning to have enough of that kind of crude documentary anti-Semitism, and in part because the brutality of the slaughter scenes had them literally running from the theater. The clip from *Triumph* at the conclusion of such a gruesome film was clearly meant to lend uplift, precisely because its own production process was built on a disavowal of the bloody history of racism and purge lying beneath the surface of both the rally and its cinematic etherealization. What better film than a documentary devoted to "Aryan" beauty and joy in which not one (explicit!) mention of Jews is to be heard.

V.

> "*Triumph of the Will* was the classic powerhouse propaganda film of our times. It was at once the glorification of war, the deification of Hitler, and the canonization of his apostles. . . . That film paved the way for Blitzkrieg. . . . How could I mount a counterattack . . . keep alive *our* will to resist the master race?"[34]—Frank Capra

Frank Capra's work with the U.S. information agency as a propagandist dedicated to defeating the Nazi menace was born in part from the physical fear he claimed to have experienced while first watching *Triumph*.[35] Like his predecessor Charlie Chaplin, Capra was immediately struck by the power of its iconic visual language to "canonize" Hitler and his followers. Similar to both Chaplin and Riefenstahl, Capra had made his name prior to this period working in the entertainment film industry (mostly comedies). Although his style in the pathbreaking seven-part documentary series *Why We Fight* has been described by one critic as that of "practical 'factual' argument, of conscious defense and counterattack rather than emotion," Capra was nevertheless deeply devoted to the notion of cinematic political persuasion as a form of entertainment.[36] One might also add that his ability to generate audience identification with the values of American democracy in the "fight" against "militaristic imperialism" by no means eschewed the employment of affect, or even hyperbole, in its call to act.[37] Here is one example: "They say trouble always comes in threes. Take a close look at this trio [still photo of Hitler, Mussolini, and Hirohito]. Remember these faces. Remember them well. If you ever meet them, don't hesitate!"

What separated Capra's documentary style most from either *Triumph* or *The Eternal Jew* at the level of technique, however, was the fact that his seven-part *Why We Fight* series was made up almost entirely of compilation material. Whereas Riefenstahl footage of the 1934 rally became the base material for the 114-minute *Triumph*; and whereas Goebbels's and Hippler's film teams spent weeks shooting original footage of "eternal Jews" in the Lodz ghetto of Poland,

Capra remained almost entirely a scavenger of others' material, to be used to a large extent against the unwitting donor. Thus it is indeed appropriate that Capra refers to his method as rooted in counterattack. For the point was to decontextualize and in turn recontextualize the enemy's propagandistic delusions and thus claim purchase to a deeper, subsurface insight into, for example in his use of *Triumph*, the "inborn natural love of regimentation and harsh discipline" on the part of the entire German people.[38]

The tendency toward black-and-white stereotypes and the essentializing of national characteristics was inherent to Capra's style throughout *Why We Fight*. Moreover, he has often been referred to as "blatantly" propagandistic, a characterization with which he would most likely have felt quite comfortable. Certainly the opening of *Prelude to War* (1942) sets the tone for what is to come. World War II is introduced with a quote from Henry Wallace stating that "[t]his is a fight between a free world and a slave world" that in turn is visualized by an image of the "free world" of the Allies as a brightly illuminated planet and the "slave world" of the Axis powers as shrouded in darkness and desolation. The section devoted to the "slave world" offers a cursory history of the rise of fascism in the three Axis countries beginning in the period after World War I. While much of the focus entailed vilification and ridicule of the Axis elites for "killing freedom," for "putting out the lighthouses one by one," blame was also placed on the people in these countries for having "surrendered their liberty . . . [given] up their rights as individual human beings . . . [become] a part of a mass, a human herd." To underscore the theme of massification, Capra concludes the section on the "slave world" with five minutes of military marching, without voiceover, one-third of the material of which came from the final sections of *Triumph*. Here, interestingly enough, Hitler for the most part has been edited out of what was originally shot-reverse-shot footage between Führer and Volk. The message appears in this instance to be visual rather than oral. It is an indictment of those who would allow themselves (and their children) to be brainwashed into being marching automatons. As is clear from the voiceover in other parts of *Prelude to War* and part II of *Why We Fight* entitled *The Nazis Strike*, Capra was adamant in his assertion that the German people as a whole had a certain proclivity to "[throw] away their human dignity," which is one reason why, given the residual isolationism and reluctance to go to war among many Americans in the early 1940s, such overtly anti-German films were not initially widely distributed in the United States.[39]

In summing up Capra's counterpunch technique, it would seem that despite his indebtedness to the techniques of such renowned news professionals as Edward R. Murrow, as epitomized in Murrow's "London Is Burning" broadcasts, the actual practice of Capra's own propaganda work did not look much more objective than the material that he was drawing from to make his point. Whereas Riefenstahl's cinematic aesthetic was positive in its orientation, emotionally overwhelming its viewers through its assertion of transcendent power and beatific dream, Capra's negation of that assertion through black-white reversal of the fascist icon leaves us not with a proper sense of what is good or bad but with a notion that anything goes.

The following characteristics mark Capra's style in this regard.[40] In keeping with his experience as a Hollywood director, the *Why We Fight* films are for the most part technically superb, blending music, direct-address narration, production footage, newsreel footage, captured footage, and Disney-like animation. The triangulated crosscut editing and prolific use of dissolves, wipes, and fades bind the three Axis powers into a seamless web of totalitarian destruction of existing democratic institutions as they march forward inexorably in their quest to dominate the helpless "free" world. Rhetorically, the films tend toward sweeping generalizations and half-truths calculated to dramatize the binaries of right and wrong, good and evil, free world versus slave world, etc. The overall tone of the high decibel voiceover is bombastic when leveled at the "evil fanaticism of the enemy" and overbearingly patriotic and often saccharine when singing the praises of the homeland. As is the case with the classical Hollywood entertainment films of the 1930s from which it borrowed its folksy hometown morality, one is struck by a cinematic language that seen from the present seems profoundly dated.

All of which returns us to the problem of filmic afterlife. In her article "Military Propaganda: Defense Department Films from World War II and Vietnam," Claudia Springer tells us that in their planning to make indoctrination films for the Vietnam War, the United States Defense Department considered and then rejected the dramatic techniques introduced in World War II by Hollywood directors such as Capra and turned instead to "a new, subtler, more sophisticated style based on ethnographic imagery and a pseudo scientific approach."[41] To cite such is not to argue that the deployment of black-and-white iconic images is inherently wrong; or that American World War II propaganda à la Hollywood was *eo ipso* aesthetically flawed. After all, even Brecht spoke about the necessity of contingently changing one's language and one's aesthetic when attempting to launch resistance "in dark times." On the other hand, the question of historical context does force us in the present discussion to ask that we reflect upon the aftermath of Riefenstahl's *Triumph* as well. Does the unabated co-optation of her Hitler iconography, seemingly regardless of context, suggest that in contrast to, say, Capra's *Prelude to War* this film has transcended historical contingency? Has it achieved the status of a universal language?

VI.

If Riefenstahl's *Triumph* served as a valued imagistic resource for British and Hollywood antifascist filmmakers committed to waging propagandistic war against the Hitler icon while the Führer was still alive, the situation was not to change very much in the Allied postwar efforts to come to terms with German guilt after the war. At the Nuremberg Trials, which began on November 22,

1945, two documentary films came to play a pivotal role in the proceedings and even the outcome of the trial. The first was a film showing footage taken by Allied photographers of the atrocities that they found when liberating "Nazi concentration camps" (the eventual title of the film) in 1945. The second, entitled *The Nazi Plan*, was a compilation film commissioned by the United States Counsel for the Prosecution, produced by Twentieth Century Fox, researched and written by Budd Schulberg,[42] and devoted, in the words of prosecuting attorney Commander James Donovon, to providing evidence to show "in simple and dramatic form the story of how a nation forsook its liberty."[43]

Certainly the raw "documentary" power of the images in these films, framed within the juridical authority of an international trial for which they were intended, lent them an aura of verisimilitude concerning the enormity of the crimes portrayed. For Robert L. Jackson, the renowned American chief counsel for the prosecution, for example, *Nazi Concentration Camps* and *The Nazi Plan* would stand as proof that, in the words of his opening address to the court, "the wrongs which we seek to condemn and punish here have been so calculated, so malignant, and so devastating that civilization cannot tolerate their being ignored because it cannot survive their being repeated."[44] Yet a closer consideration of the films and their intended larger function—beyond the machinery of justice within the trial—points to a deeper antinomy lying at the heart of the prosecution strategy. On the one hand, as stated explicitly at the outset of the proceedings, the first Nuremberg trial was dedicated to *proving*, not *assuming*, that the twenty-four indicted prisoners from the party and military elite had engaged in "conspiratorial" criminal acts as defined by relevant law. This was considered important both as a vital lesson to the German people about the workings of jurisprudence in a democratic society and as a counterweight to claims that the Germans were being accused of collective guilt.

The Nazi Plan indeed lent itself at one level "to making the conspiracy charge more than a paper abstraction." Budd Schulberg had compiled this film exclusively, and with no voiceover added, from captured German newsreels and propaganda footage from the years 1918–1945 that included not only clips from *Triumph* but also long sections of *Wochenschau* footage. Among that footage were the tirades of the Nazi judge Roland Freisler as he browbeat helpless prisoners as part of the kangaroo court following the July 20, 1944, attempt to assassinate Hitler. But did this film meet the test of juridical specificity? It is my assessment, regardless of the outcome of the trial, in which twelve were executed and others given sentences from ten years to life imprisonment, that it did not meet and perhaps could not have met such a test. And that one of the reasons in this regard was the excessive use made of the material taken from *Triumph*.

One hundred ninety-four minutes in length, the four sections of *The Nazi Plan* were shown in their entirety on December 11, 1945, as part of the court proceedings.[45] Approximately one-quarter of the film (forty-four minutes) comprised clips from Riefenstahl's *Triumph*. The caption and original voiceover introducing the section on the "Sixth Party Rally" describe the footage as "the official German film" with no mention of Riefenstahl or *Triumph* as the source.

There are two noteworthy aspects about the American editing of Riefenstahl's film. The first has to do with the discrepancy between the *Triumph* material used in the edited clip that was identified as the "Sixth Party Rally" (approximately twenty-five minutes), on the one hand, and the use of other material from *Triumph* elsewhere in *The Nazi Plan*, where no such attribution is made. A particularly egregious example of this discrepancy can be found in the film's coverage of the Röhm purge of the leadership of 1934. Instead of visual evidence or even information about Hitler's ruthless assassination of an entire branch of his own organization, we are offered instead Hitler's (and Riefenstahl's!) orchestrated cover-up of those bloody deeds in the elegiac calls for harmony and unity in *Triumph*. A similar instance occurs in this prosecution film's treatment of Hitler's destruction of the labor unions, where we are given the famous section of *Triumph* in which members of the Labor Service perform a choral chant in which they identify their individual region with the larger Reich. While such ceremony certainly communicates the ideological power of Nazi ritual as binding cohesion, it offers little in the way of juridical evidence of a "conspiracy."

But more disturbing than just the elision of *Wochenschau*, documentary, and official party/state performance of celebratory power, without any attribution of source, was the sheer fetishism displayed in the choice of clips from *Triumph* and other similar "documentaries" from the Nazi *Filmkammer* archives. Whereas the initial section of *The Nazi Plan*, entitled "The Rise of the NSDAP: 1921–1933," seemed focused on the political events that led to the growth and increasing criminality of the Nazi move toward totalitarianism (seizure of power, book burning, attacks on Jewish stores, etc.), starting with the screening of the 1934 rally, the film's focus becomes increasingly centered on scenes of marching and celebration. Schulberg offers us not one but *six* different Nuremberg Party Conventions between 1933 and 1938, plus any number of newsreels of Hitler's birthday and similar rituals, all of which contribute to a kind of mutation of *The Nazi Plan* into one long celebratory love parade.

Given the explicit goal of presenting "photographic evidence" of how "the dignity of the individual in Germany [is] destroyed by men dedicated to perverted nationalism,"one might well see the increased obsession with highlighting Nuremberg and Nuremberg-like orchestrations as in part based on a projection of what an American might see as a loss of individual will and the triumph, as it were, of totalitarian brainwashing. This may or may not have been the response of American or even German viewers in 1945. Putting that aside, what does seem to emerge on the juridical side of the equation in this film is a gradual waning of hard-core evidence of a conspiracy. Virtually no mention is made of the *Kristallnacht* pogrom in November of 1938, nor is there any treatment of slave labor, the Wannsee conference, the Warsaw ghetto, or the deportations. Beyond the question of conspiracy, what is communicated in this circus of unbroken enthusiasm is a sense, not of criminality or of manipulation, but of a powerful collective bond between a leader and his people. And it is here where *The Nazi Plan* unwittingly finds itself making an argument that goes precisely against the supposed intention of the prosecution not to accuse the German public at large of collective guilt.

VII.

Budd Schulberg and Twentieth Century Fox were not the only Hollywood-connected propaganda team to draw on Riefenstahl's *Triumph* as cinematic evidence for German complicity in crimes of war and crimes against humanity. Subsequent to the screenings of *Nazi Concentration Camps* and *The Nazi Plan* at the Nuremberg Trials, a twenty-two-minute compilation documentary on the concentration camps, entitled *Death Mills*, produced by Hanus Burger and re-edited by Billy Wilder—a Silesian Jew by origin whose family perished in the Holocaust—was screened to German audiences throughout the American Zone and parts of Berlin during the first months of 1946. These highly publicized commercial showings were reportedly met with a mixture of horror, shock, guilt, revulsion, and a growing refusal to accept what was perceived as enemy propaganda and an accusation of collective guilt. Unlike *Nazi Concentration Camps*, the voiceover of *Death Mills* concludes with a verbal and visual finger-pointing that places the responsibility for this grisly program of murder unequivocally at the feet of a German people, large numbers of whom were said to be living in close proximity to the 300 or so concentration camps located in Germany alone. The voiceover was written and also read in the German version by Oskar Seidlin, an exiled German Jew who at the time of his induction into the United States Army in 1942 was professor of German literature at Smith College. The following excerpt comes toward the conclusion of *Death Mills*:

> The farmers received tons of human bones as fertilizer . . . but apparently never suspected it came from human beings. . . . Manufacturers received tons of human hair but apparently never dreamed it came from the heads of murdered women; no nightmares ever haunted those who lived near concentration camps . . . the cries and moans of the tortured were no doubt believed to be the wailing of wind.[46]

Shots of corpses segue into the final sequence of the film, which opens with a cut to the frenzied conclusion of the Hitler Youth gathering in *Triumph* and the now iconic tracking shot panning the exultant crowds waving their farewells to Hitler. Seidlin's voiceover continues its harangue and sets these very images in relation to the horrors of the camps and the assertions of those postwar citizens who claimed not to know:

> Yesterday, while millions were dying in German concentration camps Germans jammed into Nuremberg to cheer the Nazi Party and sing hymns of hate. Today these same Germans who cheered the destruction of humanity, in their own land, who cheered attacks on hapless neighbors, who cheered the enslavement of Europe beg for your sympathy. They are the same Germans who heiled Hitler.[47]

Wilder encapsulates the disparity between once-exuberant adulation and now remorseless self-pity through a series of dissolves moving back and forth between blond and bleating figures at the rally and footage shown earlier in *Death Mills* of weary, now-ravaged citizens of Weimar being force marched to nearby Buchenwald to view the piles of emaciated corpses and shrunken heads left behind by the fleeing SS. Used in *The Eternal Jew* as an antidote to the threat posed by essentialized Jews from the Polish shtetl, this same clip is inverted now by the exile Wilder into a celluloid trope of dismembered memory. The exultant youthful participants of a party convention held one year after the Nazi takeover become frozen in time as the symbolic collective body of a nation implicated at every turn in the goals and actions of its leaders. What had appeared in *The Eternal Jew* as a world of lightness and joy juxtaposed to the rat-infested, darkened hovel of Jewish life in the ghetto now itself takes on the sinister form of pathological fanaticism.

We have seen how the visual language (and secondarily the sound track) of *Triumph* was used (and misused) by American authorities during the immediate postwar period to mete out justice under conditions that sometimes challenged the very boundaries of the law; or to denazify a larger German populace when the pedagogical and institutional means for such were inadequate to the task. A final task under the *Triumph* rubric in Nuremberg will be to consider a brief citation of it in one of the very earliest Hollywood feature films to deal with the Holocaust and German guilt—namely Stanley Kramer's *Judgment at Nuremberg* (1961). Like Wilder's *Death Mills*, Kramer draws on both the camp films and *Triumph*, tethered together again as the inevitable iconic before and after, to help map out his meditation on the dialectic of cause and effect leading to the catastrophe of the Nazi takeover and resulting Holocaust. The diegetic year is 1948; the tribunal in question is the trial of four Nazi judges before a panel of three American judges.[48]

The chief trial judge is named Dan Hayward (Spencer Tracy), a self-deprecating, folksy American circuit court judge, with no ax to grind, who has set himself the task of understanding the complicated issue of German culpability in the general populace, at the very same time that he is obliged to cast legal judgments upon four of its elites. His efforts to grasp the larger postwar picture bring him into contact with a number of citizens of Nuremberg, none more interesting than Frau Bertold (Marlene Dietrich), the enigmatic widow of a high-ranking military officer convicted and executed by an earlier tribunal. In her on-again off-again relationship with Hayward she becomes ever more determined to persuade him that Germany is not a nation of monsters, and that most who cooperated with Nazis had no idea about the death camps.

While for the most part we are not made privy to Hayward's inner thoughts or feelings about what he is learning in the court or in his leisure time spent in the Nuremberg community, an early scene in the film can best be described as epiphanal. It occurs during a break in the proceedings after the opening presentations by the prosecuting attorney, Colonel Tad Lawson (Richard Widmark), and the German attorney for the defense, Hans Rolfe (Maximilian Schell). At this juncture, Hayward's initial foray into the bombed-out city finds him walking through the ruins of the Luitpold Arena, where political gatherings of the SS and SA were held during various Nuremberg party rallies. As the lone figure of the American judge strolls along the edge of the field framed by imitation Greek columns and rows of empty seats in the background, the sound track is gradually filled with nondiegetic military march music sung by hearty male voices, all of which reaches closure just as Hayward himself stops to gaze up at an empty speaker's tribunal. After a moment of silence, during which we are given shot-reverse-shot close-ups—first a low-angle zoom to his face staring up at the speaker's stand; followed by a low-angle zoom from behind Hayward to the empty tribunal; and finally back to his face—at which point Hitler's unmistakable voice sounds forth the following lines of a speech: "Before us lies Germany, in us marches Germany, behind us comes Germany."[49] The sound of cheering crowds and the upsurge of march music link this sixty-five-second clip to the final lines of the Führer's address to the Hitler Youth in the soccer stadium as filmed in *Triumph*.

Where, we ask ourselves, is this now diegetic, initially nondiegetic sound coming from? And what does it mean? Clearly, at one level, it is linked figurally and thus narratively to the judge's struggle to understand the German past. Seen in that way, one might speak indeed of an epiphany, if by that we mean a sudden realization or comprehension of the essence or meaning of something. In either a philosophical, religious, or literal sense the term is often used to signify that one has access to new information or experience that illuminates a deeper frame of reference. Dan Haywood's final indictment of all the defendants is characterized in the film as incompatible with changing postwar alignments. By the time of the trial, the emerging cold war put pressure on Haywood to go easy on the defendants. The Berlin Blockade was underway, and foreign policy concerns suggested that the Germans were now allies rather than enemies. So what were the circumstances, beyond legal arguments, that led Hayward to resist those political pressures and find the German judges guilty? Certainly one important factor, as staged dramatically in the film, was the showing of the atrocity film *Nazi Concentration Camps* by the condemnatory prosecutor Colonel Lawson. Yet while such a film clearly has an impact on the entire court, including Hayward, it is the function of the earlier sound flashback of Hitler's voice in *Triumph* as a kind of imageless memory trace that appears to have initially motivated him to consider more deeply possible causes that might be seen to have led to the Holocaust. Precisely because the sounds of the rally and speeches conjure up a truly mediated, suggestively collective screen memory could the ghostly non-presence of Nuremberg's own prehistory be played/acted out diegetically and for the cinematic spectator as well. The power of this Hollywood film lies in the complexity of its representations and the impossibility of final answers. The disembodied voice of Riefenstahl's Adolf Hitler acts as both a cipher for what once was and a challenge to go still deeper in seeking the larger juridical truth.

VIII.

Judgment at Nuremberg was not the only or even the first post-1940s "Holocaust Film" to employ the visual dialectic of camp films and *Triumph* to wrestle with issues of perpetrators, victims, genocide, and the silence about this event on a global scale in much of the 1950s. In 1955, the French director Alain Resnais made what has come to be seen as the *opus classicus* of the genre called *Night and Fog*, a thirty-five-minute part compilation documentary combining color footage of the camps filmed by Resnais and historical black-and-white footage and photos selected by him. This pairing of black and white and color is just one of a number of aesthetic juxtapositions (sound and silence, dark and light, movement and stasis, poetry and prose, montage visuals and montage music, etc.) that serve to structure the film and imbue it with sets of competing, often conflicting, meanings that went well beyond established narrative or rhetorical patterns. Central in this regard thematically and structurally were questions about past and present—the extent to which one could talk about a separation between the two, and if so under what conditions.

The film starts off in a seemingly harmless present—a gentle color pan, left to right, of a lazy sunny afternoon gaze across a summer field. The scene is suddenly violated by the entrance into the bottom right corner of the frame of the top rung of a barbed wire fence, a disturbance in turn picked up by the voiceover to be slowly developed, orally and pictorially, into the mise-en-scène of an abandoned concentration camp. Here we have a past still within the present to be sure, until the next jarring break in the form of a black-and-white clip from *Triumph*, loaded imagistically with counter-meaning: goose-stepping black-uniformed SS soldiers on a city street moving from right to left; Hitler surveying an SS parade with arm stretched straight and Himmler standing to the right and below him. All this is countered in turn by nondiegetic wispy and playfully plucked violin-and-flute atonal music composed by Hanns Eisler. The voiceover commentary written by Jean Cayrol confirms our momentary displacement into the past: "1933, the machine has been set into motion, one needs a people without discord, one is settling down to work."[50]

The *Triumph* clip lasts thirty-eight seconds, but its contribution to the basic patterns of the film are in one sense foundational. The first pattern to emerge from this "break" is the switch from color to black and white, which, as Andre Colombat points out, is "legitimized by the metamorphosis of the rows of barbed wires into rows of parading soldiers and how the angles and movements of the camera are similar in both cases. In so doing, Resnais has turned Riefenstahl's images, filmed by order of Hitler to symbolize the growing power of the Nazi Party, into symbols of the crush of Europe by Nazi troops and the beginning of the Holocaust."[51]

The matching here is occurring on a number of negative and positive levels. The linking of a benign and peaceful present through a montage cut to the forceful countermovement (this time from right to left) of the SS goose stepping suggests a past that is not very far removed spatially from the banality of the quotidian, a proximity that also goes against the grain of a postwar silence that heretofore had refused to see any connection between the politics surrounding the seizure of power and what was found twelve years later in Bergen-Belsen. Yet those connections are not made explicit in Cayrol's poetic commentary. Rather they get enunciated, for instance, in the sometimes violent frictional montage of word, image, music, and camera movement. This reluctance to articulate with specificity, verbally and visually, emerges as part of a modernist aesthetic that will refrain from overbearing indoctrination while at the same time seeking to provoke and activate a viewer in a shared process of reception. That is the innovative, even provocative aspect of this very important film. But there is also an absence that emerges in part as a result of this refrain, namely the failure to present the genocidal assault against the Jews as "the essential pillar of the Nazi phenomenon."[52] There is to be sure much visual material that alludes to Jewish victimage in the camp system as well as the policies and policy makers that were responsible for its existence. The clip from *Triumph* includes, but does not identify, shots of Julius Streicher, notorious editor of the poisonously anti-Semitic journal *Der Stürmer*, as well as Heinrich Himmler, head of the SS and chief engineer of the concentration camp system. Fleeting pictures of Jewish prisoners with stars on their clothing; the now-iconic still photo of the Jewish child in the Warsaw ghetto with raised hands; a passing mention of the "Jewish student named Stern" may also be seen and heard. Yet few of these fractured images are elaborated on or put into a hierarchy of context. All feed into a concatenating representation of allegorical evil shorn of any contingency. To be fair, it was precisely the film's lack of specificity that enabled it historically to come into existence. *Night and Fog* was the first film of its kind to impress upon a Europe in denial the enormity of the "crimes against humanity" committed, not only by the Germans. At the same time, little or no mention is made of either Vichy France or the Nazi Holocaust as a Jewish Holocaust. As Nelly Furman sums it up:

> The film's unquestionable achievement is to have revealed for the first time to a large public the existence of the concentration camps. However, in its visual narrative, by fusing Buchenwald with Auschwitz-Bierkenau, in blending the French deportees with those marked for Jewish genocide, Resnais' film appears today as a documentary of the 1950s.[53]

The point is not to belittle the achievements of *Night and Fog*, but rather to indicate the extent to which even this extraordinary pathbreaking film participated in purely iconographical rather than indexical use of a clip from *Triumph*. Rather than reading against the grain of Riefenstahl's 1935 beatific transformation of Nazi thuggery, Resnais, like Hollywood's Frank Capra in *Prelude to War* or Budd Schulberg in *The Nazi Plan*, quoted verbatim from *Triumph*'s celebration of party sound bites as the self-evident truth of Nazi reality. As was the case with the film's original universalization (of the "Aryan," of the *Landesvater*, of the adoring masses, etc.), in many of the aftermath's re-invocations we are left with little indication of the specifically venal causes that led to the path of Jewish destruction. The impoverished dialectic of a party convention as icon for "Nazism," "totalitarianism," "massification," and the equally iconic images of unidentified corpses from the concentration and death camps in April 1945 often came to stand, on both sides of the equation, for an erasure rather than a deconstruction of our medial memory of that time.

NOTES

1. Jürgen Trimborn, *Riefenstahl. Eine deutsche Karriere* (Berlin: Aufbau, 2002), 200.
2. Martin Loiperdinger, *Rituale der Mobilmachung: Der Parteitagsfilm Triumph des Willens von Leni Riefenstahl* (Opladen: Leske + Budrich, 1987), 9–10.
3. More recent films to use either *Triumph*-like imagery or clips from the film include *Star Wars Episode IV, A Clockwork Orange, Gladiator, Hero,* the Lord of the Rings film trilogy, *The Lion King, Richard III, Red Dawn, Spartakus, Pink Floyd The Wall, Starship Troopers*.
4. Other films discussed below include *The Eternal Jew, The Nazi Plan, Death Mills, Judgment at Nuremberg,* and *Night and Fog*.
5. Joachim Fest and Christian Herrendorfer's film *Hitler, eine Karriere* (1977) offers a wealth of such cameo appearances, as does the compilation film by the Swedish director Peter Cohen entitled *The Architecture of Doom* (1991).
6. See Stephan Dolezel and Martin Loiperdinger, "Adolf Hitler in Parteitagsfilm und Wochenschau," in *Führerbilder: Hitler, Mussolini, Roosevelt, Stalin,* ed. Martin Loiperdinger, Rudolf Herz, and Ulrich Pohlmann (Munich: R. Piper, 1995) for an excellent discussion of the Hitler documentaries from the mid-1920s through the Third Reich.
7. Claudia Schmölders, *Hitlers Gesicht: Eine physiognomische Biographie* (München: C. H. Beck, 2000), 50.
8. Rudolf Herz, "Vom Medienstar zum propagandistischen Problemfall: Zu den Hitlerbildern Heinrich Hoffmanns," in *Führerbilder*, Loiperdinger, et. al., 51–64.

9. See the May 17, 1933, entry in Joseph Goebbels, *Die Tagebücher. Sämtliche Fragmente*, ed. Elke Fröhlich (Munich, 1987). In *Riefenstahl, eine Karriere*, Jürgen Trimborn argues that Riefenstahl's postwar claim that she never knew about her proposed filming of the 1933 party convention until two days before its opening when Hitler forced it upon her is clearly refuted by the numerous entries in Goebbels's diary mentioning their discussions about the project (177–178).
10. See David Bathrick, "Modernity Writ German: State of the Art as Art of the State," in *Cultural History Through a National Socialist Lens: Essays on the Cinema in the Third Reich*, ed. Robert Reimer (New York: Camden House, 2000), 1–10.
11. In her diaries, Leni Riefenstahl recalls Hitler saying the following to her in his efforts to persuade her to make the film: "I do not want a boring Party film, nor do I want Wochenschau footage, but rather a document of artistic images (*ein künstlerisches Bilddokument*). The official Party photographers have no understanding for such things. In your *Blue Light* you have proved that you can do that." Leni Riefenstahl, *Memoiren 1902–1945* (Frankfurt am Main: Ullstein, 1990), 220.
12. They are mentioned in speeches at the convention that do not appear in the film. In his address to the SA in the Luitpoldhain, Hitler makes the following oblique reference to the massacre of June 30: "A few months ago a black cloud hovered over our movement. The SA had as little as any other institution of the Party to do with this shadow. Anyone who believes that even the slightest tear in the fabric of our movement has occurred because of this is deceiving himself" (quoted in Loiperdinger, *Rituale der Mobilmachung*, 101).
13. Riefenstahl has denied that her making of *Triumph* contained "an orchestrated defense of Hitler's actions after the Röhm Putsch," as was asserted by Brian Winston, "Was Hitler there? *Triumph of the Will*: a puncturing reassessment," *Sight and Sound* 50, no. 2 (1981): 102–107. "When I have made *Triumph of the Will*, I have not one moment thought of Röhm. Not one moment in my mind," in: "Leni Riefenstahl interviewed by Gordon Hitchens," *Film Culture* (Spring 1973). While one can well imagine that Riefenstahl might have displaced any conscious effort to exonerate Hitler, her intuited understanding of the larger atonement strategy at the heart of the convention's rituals makes any discussion of direct intention on her part a moot point.
14. Loiperdinger, *Rituale der Mobilmachung*, 82.
15. Loiperdinger, *Rituale der Mobilmachung*, 69.
16. Ufa-Informationen, March 27, 1935. Cited in Loiperdinger, *Rituale der Mobilmachung*, 69.
17. Trimborn, *Riefenstahl. Eine deutsche Karriere*, 186.
18. Rainer Rother, *Leni Riefenstahl: Die Verführung des Talents* (Berlin: Henschel Verlag, 2000), 80.
19. Schmölders, *Hitlers Gesicht*, 165.
20. Luis Buñuel, *Mein letzter Seufzer* (Berlin: Ullstein, 1999).
21. David Robinson, *Chaplin: His Life and Art* (New York: Da Capo, 1994), 493.
22. Robinson, *Chaplin*, 500.
23. Thomas Mann, "Bruder Hitler," in *Politische Schriften und Reden*, V. 3 (Frankfurt/M: Fischer, 1968), 55.
24. Charles Chaplin, *My Autobiography* (New York: Simon & Schuster, 1964), 391.
25. Found in accompanying materials to the film, U. Sporman-Lorenz, Publ. Wiss. Film, Publiz. 4, Nr. 6/G 166 (1977), 32, footnote 4. Cited in Hornshøj-Møller, *"Der ewige Jude,"* 16.

26. Fritz Hippler, *Die Verstrickung* (Düsseldorf: Mehr Wissen, 1981), 187.
27. The city of Lodz fell to the Germans in the week after the invasion and was incorporated into the Reich on October 7, when it was renamed Litzmannstadt. Although occupation of Lodz meant the beginning of Heydrich's so-called "*Ghettoisierungspolitik*" within the existing Jewish ghettos, it was not until December 10 that Himmler issued orders to set up a special ghetto for all the Jews of Lodz (233,000 of a 700,000 populace) in the Balut slum district, which became in effect a massive prison and the largest of the ghettos in Poland. As the filming for *The Eternal Jew* was already completed by the third week in November, this final stage of ghettoization is not represented in the film. In addition to Lodz, there was also filming in the ghettos of Warsaw, Cracow, and Lublin.
28. Stig Hornshøj-Møller, "Der ewige Jude," in *Quellenkritische Analyse eines antisemitischen Propagandafilms* (Göttingen: Wissenschaftlicher Film, 1995), 309.
29. Fritz Hippler, "Wie *Der ewige Jude* verfilmt wurde—Dr. Hippler über seienen neuen großen Dokumentarfilm," in *Filmwelt* 49 (1940). Reprinted in Stig Hornshøj-Møller, "Der ewige Jude," 309.
30. Hornshøj-Møller, "Der ewige Jude," 85–86.
31. Ibid., 73.
32. Ibid., 181.
33. Ibid., 184–185.
34. Frank Capra, *The Name above the Title: An Autobiography* (New York: Da Capo, 1971), 328–331.
35. Capra, *The Name above the Title,* 329.
36. Jaqueline Austin, "A Battle of Wills: How Leni Riefenstahl and Frank Capra Fought a War with Film and Remade History," in *Artistic Strategy and the Rhetoric of Power: Political Uses of Art from Antiquity to the Present,* ed. David Castriota (Carbondale and Edwardsville: Southern Illinois University Press, 1986), 162.
37. Sound track from "The WWII Experience, Frank Capra's *Why We Fight,* Part I: *Prelude to War,*" 4 DVD set, [delta].
38. Capra, *Prelude to War.*
39. The series originally was mandatory viewing for all military personnel, but was not intended for screening to the general public. After General Marshall saw the rough cut of *Prelude to War* in August 1942, he told Capra the film should be shown to the public. President Franklin Delano Roosevelt strongly agreed and insisted as well that it be distributed in Great Britain.
40. See David Culbert, "'Why We Fight': Social Engineering for a Democratic Society at War," in *Film and Radio Propaganda in World War II,* ed. K.R.M. Short (Knoxville, TN: University of Tennessee Press, 1983).
41. Claudia Springer, "Military Propaganda: Defense Department from World War II and Vietnam," *Cultural Critique,* no. 3, American Representations of Vietnam (Spring 1986): 152.
42. During World War II, Schulberg served in the United States Navy, rising to the rank of Lieutenant Junior Grade. He was a member of John Ford's documentary unit, and wrote new narration with James Kevin McGuinness to Ford's picture *December 7th*, which won an Oscar in 1944 for Best Documentary Short Subject. Later he won another Oscar for his screenplay for *On the Waterfront* in 1955.
43. IMT, December 11, 1945, 286.
44. IMT, November 21, 1945, 220.

45. The four part divisions were entitled "The Rise of the NSDAP, 1921–1933"; "Acquiring Totalitarian Control of Germany, 1933–1935"; "Preparations for Wars of Aggression, 1935–1939"; and "Wars of Aggression, 1939–1944."
46. Hanus Burger, *Death Mills*, International Historic Films, Inc., Video.
47. Burger, *Death Mills.*
48. *Judgment at Nuremberg* is based historically on the third Nuremberg trial of 1947 (there were a total of thirteen), where charges were brought against sixteen functionaries in the Nazi legal system.
49. Stanley Kramer, *Judgment at Nuremberg*, Special Edition DVD.
50. Alain Resnais, *Night and Fog*, The Criterion Collection DVD.
51. Andre Colombat, *The Holocaust in French Film* (Metuchen, NJ, and London: Scarecrow Press, 1993), 130.
52. Ilan Avisar, *Screening the Holocaust: Cinema's Images of the Unimaginable* (Bloomington and Indianapolis: University of Indiana Press, 1988), 16.
53. Nelly Furman, "Viewing Memory through *Night and Fog*, *The Sorrow and the Pity*, and *Shoah*," *Journal of European Studies* 35 (2005): 72.

Chapter 5

Wonderful, Horrible Lies: Riefenstahl Memory and Riefenstahl History in Germany[1]

Wulf Kansteiner

I. *Tatort*

It was an obvious case. The murdered journalist had stockpiled evidence against Hamburg's most prominent business tycoon, Alexander Radu. The material proved how corrupt and criminal Hamburg's business elite really was. But Detective Casstorff and his team still faced a big problem. Their superiors in the justice department were in cahoots with Radu and obstructed the police investigation at every turn.

On June 11, 2007, almost six million viewers tuned their TV sets to the public television station ARD to watch the latest installment of Germany's longest running and most prestigious murder mystery series *Tatort* (crime scene).[2] In one of the key scenes of the show, Radu tries to convince a stalwart and beautiful public prosecutor that he is a victim of negative publicity. He launches into the following monologue:

> In 1999 my father organized a Riefenstahl exhibit here in Hamburg showcasing the fabulous photos of the African tribe of the Nuba. Ms. Riefenstahl had lived with the Nuba in Sudan for several years. But guess what topics were raised by the first three questions during the press conference at the opening of the exhibit: Hitler, Hitler, Goebbels. Do you understand what I am trying to tell you? For years I have been investing in culture, education, and social services. But the only thing that the public remembers is the fact that twenty years ago my father worked as a bouncer in Hamburg's red-light district. . . . It's a damned witch hunt.[3]

The passage of the script was certainly not written with the intention of justifying Riefenstahl's life choices. Since Radu is hardly depicted as an innocent victim, viewers are encouraged to entertain doubts about Riefenstahl's innocence as well. But it is remarkable that the scriptwriters developed this analogy at all. They must have assumed that, four years after her death and sixty-two years after her career as a Nazi filmmaker came to a crushing halt, Riefenstahl was still a household name.

II. 2007: Riefenstahl Is Everywhere

The scriptwriters of *Tatort* are not alone. Journalists drop Riefenstahl's name in all kinds of discursive contexts. References to her life and work appear in reports on new film projects and film history, contemporary pop and theater culture, National Socialist (NS) architecture and historical exhibits, alpine tourism, the Olympic Games of 2008, and even local soccer culture.[4] In all these contexts, Riefenstahl's name is mentioned without explanation; readers are expected to know the basics of Riefenstahl's life and understand the analogies.

There is another interesting aspect to contemporary Riefenstahl memory. As long as journalists are not concerned with the serious topic of NS history, they tend to use the term "Riefenstahl" as a playful rhetorical device of criticism and irony, for instance, to indicate their reservations about a specific project or person. But the irony cuts both ways. Since Riefenstahl memory is mobilized to poke fun at different mainstream artists, readers are led to believe that Riefenstahl was misguided and egocentric but that her films and actions were ultimately as harmless as those of Oliver Stone, Tom Cruise, or Steven Spielberg.[5] According to the symbolic code of the German feuilleton, "Riefenstahl" is short shrift for artists who like to play with fire, suffer from too much hubris, or have shown poor judgment but who otherwise conduct themselves within acceptable limits.

Riefenstahl memory is not only thriving in the feuilleton pages of the national press. Riefenstahl's life has also attracted considerable prime-time attention on television—in this case without ironic twist. In March 2007, Guido Knopp and his associates in the ZDF (*Zweites Deutsches Fernsehen*, a German broadcast television network) division for contemporary history dedicated forty-five prime-time minutes to the topic of Leni Riefenstahl. The program aired as the third installment of a series on *Hitler's Useful Idols (Hitlers nützliche Idole)* and featured a number of questionable strategies well known from ZDF documentaries and generally rationalized as adjustments to the alleged taste of prime-time audiences. The viewers could enjoy scenes depicting Riefenstahl dancing, Riefenstahl writing a letter to Hitler (Hitler paraphernalia on her desk), and Riefenstahl meeting the Führer in Horumersiel at the North Sea in 1932.

These reenactments provide little information—most historians consider them terribly inauthentic—but they constitute some of the visual highlights of the program. The fast-cut film also presents Hitler in Technicolor, Riefenstahl in nude scenes from the early days of Weimar cinema, and the occasional pseudo-eyewitness who has no firsthand knowledge of any of the events under examination but who is related to a contemporary of Riefenstahl who died many years ago.[6] In *Hitlers nützliche Idole*, Matthias Fanck, the grandson of the famous Alpine film director Arnold Fanck, pseudo-testifies in this vein about Riefenstahl's and his grandfather's attraction for each other although he is upstaged by an authentic eyewitness. For the benefit of the historical imagination of the prime-time audience, Riefenstahl's former cameraman and lover Hans Ertl attests to Riefenstahl's "simply extraordinary control over her body."[7] The producers also dutifully inform the viewers about rumors of a Hitler-Riefenstahl–liaison, but Knopp and Co. sensibly shy away from developing this topic any further and refrain from including play scenes of their alleged sexual encounters.

Hitlers nützliche Idole was part of the tail end of an extraordinarily successful run of documentary programs that ZDF had launched since the early 1990s.[8] The legendary, for some infamous, Guido Knopp and his team had revolutionized the representation of Nazism on television by abandoning the conceptual foci and visual strategies of the historical programming of the previous decades. Instead of pursuing historiographical questions, for instance, about the causes of the collapse of the Weimar Republic or the lack of resistance to Hitler, Knopp and Co. gave the well-adjusted citizens of the Federal Republic an idea of what it might feel like to be as powerful, ruthless, and evil as Hitler and his henchmen.[9] The simulations of history were made possible—both in the sense of not provoking political protest and in the sense of rendering history sensually accessible—by a new set of nonfiction television aesthetics. On the cutting tables of ZDF, Knopp and his associates carefully spliced together old films and photos (preferably in color), eyewitness testimony, atmospheric shots, and restaged historical events to form a fast-paced, visually attractive *Gesamtkunstwerk*. The intellectual content of the programs remained rather traditional and banal; the commentary rarely strayed from the textbook certainties of contemporary history and the conventional anti-Nazi rhetoric repeated ad nauseam in Germany's official historical culture. But the images told a very different, seductive, and transgressive story that celebrated and mourned the rise and fall of the most powerful Germans ever to walk the face of the earth.[10]

When *Hitlers nützliche Idole* does not deal in sexual innuendo, the documentary offers a surprisingly precise and critical view of the famous filmmaker. At this advanced stage in the evolution of German memory politics, idolizing Nazi power no longer represents a taboo-breaking, innovative gesture.[11] Therefore, the last crop of Knopp associates appears to have returned to the traditional task of producing TV biographies. For that purpose, they assembled an extraordinary cast of experts before the ZDF cameras. With the help of well-informed nonfiction authors such as Jürgen Trimborn and Lutz Kinkel, ZDF filmmakers describe Riefenstahl as an exceptionally egocentric, unappealing person who used any means at her disposal, including Nazi anti-Semitism, to advance her own interests.[12] Riefenstahl sought the friendship of Nazi leaders and used her connections to Hitler and his inner circle to silence pesky critics and business partners. She also received unprecedented financial and professional support from the Nazi state and consistently lied about all these facts after 1945, even when confronted with irrefutable evidence.

Hitlers nützliche Idole clearly succeeds in its primary objective of providing a state-of-the-art biography of Riefenstahl. But the film does not successfully contextualize and assess Riefenstahl's aesthetic achievements because the Knopp paradigm is simply not well suited for the exploration and representation of ambivalences and nuances. The indictment of Riefenstahl's character and political persona is quickly followed by a similarly harsh yet unconvincing critique of her artwork—delivered by none other than the Oscar-winner and German film industry executive, Volker Schlöndorff. The German filmmaker solves the riddle of fascist art by defining fascist films as "brutality in images" and obsessed with symmetry.[13] For Schlöndorff, this symmetry is realized in exemplary fashion in the opening scenes of *Triumph of the Will* because the film advances with textbook precision from establishing shot to intermediate shot to close-up. It does not seem to bother Schlöndorff that he thus classifies most of mainstream cinema as fascist, including some of his own work.[14]

Knopp and Co. dealt with Leni Riefenstahl after hundreds of programs about World War II and Hitler and his so-called henchmen. Riefenstahl received Knopp's undivided attention, first in 2001 and then again in 2007, after the history revolution launched by ZDF had already passed its zenith.[15] One might assume that ZDF historians initially stayed away from Riefenstahl because they sensed an eerie parallel between Riefenstahl's and their own manipulations of images for ideological and commercial purposes. But that assumption is probably incorrect; Knopp is neither that cynical nor that self-reflective. Knopp might have been reluctant to broadcast a critical biography of Riefenstahl in the 1990s because Riefenstahl was unwilling to tolerate any media coverage that did not closely follow her own carefully edited version of her life story and frequently went to court to prevent what she considered misrepresentations of her experiences and actions in Nazi Germany. This type of litigation between ZDF and the quarrelsome filmmaker would have made headlines and possibly undermined Knopp's legitimacy in the eyes of his viewers.[16] Moreover and more importantly, Riefenstahl was hardly worth this risk; she was never an important figure in the type of popular imagination of Nazi power that the Knopp revolution had served and shaped so successfully since the early 1990s.

III. 1933–2006: From Nazi Professional to Feuilleton Star—Vectors of Riefenstahl Memory

The belated integration of Riefenstahl into the popular, colorful world of Knopp television represents the latest chapter in the long history of Riefenstahl exegesis. Although the famous filmmaker has been the subject of a wide range of texts, the multilayered tapestry of representations and opinions that accumulated over the decades has one overriding thematic focus and displays a peculiar diachronic pattern. Until the mid-1990s, media coverage and scholarly texts relate Riefenstahl to Nazism and occur in sequential clusters with each cluster highlighting a different aspect or presenting a different assessment of Riefenstahl's persona or work.[17]

The National Socialism–Riefenstahl link was first crafted in the media of the Third Reich. Riefenstahl was a prominent filmmaker and celebrity and Goebbels's acolytes eagerly reported about her latest film projects and public appearances. The media coverage mentioned Nazi leaders as sponsors of Riefenstahl's work or as people who mingled with her at cultural gatherings for the NS elite.[18] After 1945, Riefenstahl continued to play an important part in the popular imagination of the Third Reich. She was still treated as a celebrity but was represented in a decidedly negative light. Especially the yellow press aggressively pursued Riefenstahl in the late 1940s and 1950s and cast her in the roles of Nazi collaborator and Hitler confidante. The negative coverage both focused on and influenced Riefenstahl's many legal adventures: her denazification trials, the libel suits she brought against publishers, and her attempts to attain ownership of her Nazi-era films.[19]

The first postwar genre of Riefenstahl texts is noteworthy for three reasons. First, in hindsight it is easy to determine that some media professionals dabbled in outrageous slander while others managed to paint a very accurate picture of Riefenstahl's career in the Third Reich. The popular weeklies, which gleefully reported on and sometimes caused Riefenstahl's legal troubles, and the national press, which covered the legal skirmishes, reminded their readers of Riefenstahl's association with Hitler and Goebbels, her use of slave labor, and her knowledge of Nazi crimes.[20] But the press also conjured images of Riefenstahl visiting death camps and dancing naked for Hitler.[21] Unfortunately, the courts were not always able to differentiate fact from fiction and counteract the media fog of facts, lies, and innuendo. Second, as these examples indicate, sexual and sexist undertones were key components of the press coverage and established Riefenstahl as a case of *Vergangenheitsbewältigung* unlike any other because no other professional woman had been equally prominent and successful in Nazi Germany. Third, Riefenstahl, who played an important role in the construction of her postwar media persona, proved to be the very opposite of media savvy. She stubbornly embraced a false and, more important, unconvincing version of her life in the Third Reich, showed no contrition whatsoever, and thus failed to lay the foundation for the kind of successful self-denazification that other Hitler enthusiasts, most prominently Albert Speer, crafted with great dexterity.[22]

As a result of all these factors, Riefenstahl became a whipping girl for a national collective of perpetrators and fellow travelers of National Socialism who held the filmmaker to standards of moral conduct that they were unwilling to apply to their own pasts. Riefenstahl was set aside from her many male colleagues who had also eagerly served Hitler but who could now rebuild their lives and careers without being dragged into the national limelight as persistently as Riefenstahl.[23] But one should not make the mistake of concluding that Riefenstahl was the victim of a conspiracy and systematically prevented from reentering her profession. Riefenstahl had primarily herself to blame for her inability to launch a comeback as a filmmaker because she proved once more unable to budget films successfully and keep to her own deadlines.[24]

The Riefenstahl press coverage subsided in the 1960s as Riefenstahl sought refuge from German history in Africa. At the same time, academic and intellectual interest in Riefenstahl and her work increased markedly. Especially in the 1970s, film historians and film critics scrutinized Riefenstahl's work in the pages of international film journals such as *Film Comment*, *Filmkritik*, *Film Culture*, and *Frauen und Film*.[25] Riefenstahl scholarship profited from the fact that Riefenstahl began to publish a steady stream of new work starting in the late 1960s when her Nuba photos were for the first time presented to the public.[26] The academic concern with Riefenstahl's films and photographs laid the foundation for an intellectual collective memory of Riefenstahl that evolved independently of popular Riefenstahl memory and remained focused on film and art history rather than Nazi history. The critics were particularly interested in questions of theory and aesthetics, for instance fascist aesthetics. They occasionally involved Riefenstahl in their scholarly efforts, for example by conducting interviews with her, but they analyzed Riefenstahl's work independently of her personal history.[27]

The scholarly interest in Riefenstahl was also reflected in several attempts to enlist Riefenstahl for the cause of feminism[28] and in a first wave of foreign language biographies, whose authors painted a relatively positive picture of Riefenstahl.[29] The publications could not ignore the topic of Nazism or fascism, especially after Susan Sontag had rejected Riefenstahl's entire oeuvre as a picture-perfect example of fascist aesthetics.[30] But the critics of the 1970s were so much focused on theoretical concerns and political causes, be they fascism or feminism, that they often failed to consider Riefenstahl's biography even when the person Riefenstahl was sitting right in front of them, as, for example, in interview situations.[31]

Yet another genre of Riefenstahl texts emerged in the late 1970s and gradually turned into a ritualistic journalistic performance. Beginning in 1977 on the occasion of Riefenstahl's seventy-fifth birthday and repeating the effort every five years, the press corps in Germany and abroad celebrated

Riefenstahl's passage into old age. Over the decades, journalists marveled more and more at her vitality and toned down their critical remarks about her work and life.[32] Moreover, the anniversary coverage hardly remained the only idolatrous type of Riefenstahl text. Riefenstahl published her self-indulgent memoirs in 1987 and became a permanent presence in the feuilleton in the 1990s.[33] A seemingly endless series of exhibits, retrospectives, and theater events showcased her work and life, accompanied by a flood of mostly laudatory news stories.[34] On top of that, all newspapers and major news outlets now featured interviews with Riefenstahl, which always followed the same protocol and produced almost identical results. Since Riefenstahl insisted on seeing the questions in advance and receiving a copy of the proofs before publication, the published interviews invariably confirmed Riefenstahl's own version of her life.[35]

The Riefenstahl texts of the 1980s and 1990s did not paint a universally positive picture of Riefenstahl the filmmaker. Some news stories contained the type of ironic remarks about Riefenstahl that we have already observed in the coverage from 2007. Moreover and more important, a number of scholars and journalists tried to set the record straight, although they were not always successful in their efforts. Many critics, for instance, highlighted the factual and stylistic shortcomings of Riefenstahl's memoirs without being able to prevent them from becoming a remarkable commercial success.[36] The single most determined critique of Riefenstahl was advanced in a 1982 TV documentary of the *Westdeutscher Rundfunk* (WDR). The freelance TV journalist Nina Gladitz repeated the charges made by the tabloid *Revue* in the immediate postwar years, although Gladitz had better sources than her predecessors. She argued convincingly on the basis of recently found documents that Riefenstahl had personally visited a concentration camp and selected Sinti and Roma inmates to appear as extras in her film *Tiefland (Lowlands).* Gladitz also maintained that, already in 1941, the Sinti informed Riefenstahl about the mass murder taking place in Auschwitz. Not surprisingly, Riefenstahl immediately took Gladitz and the WDR to court. After five years and several rounds of litigation, the judges ultimately confirmed the viability of Gladitz's first statement but asked her to desist from repeating the second claim. Since Gladitz was unable and unwilling to make the necessary cuts, the film disappeared in the WDR archives after the first broadcast in September 1982 and has never been screened in public again.[37]

The fate suffered by Gladitz and others explain the dearth of German-language biographies and monographs about Riefenstahl. Few authors and publishers were willing either to compromise their scholarly integrity or to meet Riefenstahl and her representatives in court. But Riefenstahl's upcoming one hundredth birthday proved too much of a temptation—combined perhaps with the hope that the centenarian had lost some of her litigious energy. Before and after Riefenstahl's death, at the same time that ZDF discovered Riefenstahl as topic for prime time, a string of excellent critical biographies set a precedent both in legal and moral terms.[38] It was always possible to get the facts on Riefenstahl without too much effort, but now there was no longer any excuse to tread lightly when media texts about Riefenstahl approached the topics of Hitler, slave labor, and war crimes.

This brief survey of Riefenstahl scholarship and press coverage explains why the facts of Riefenstahl's life lead such a precarious and fragile existence in the collective memories of the Federal Republic. With popular interest in Riefenstahl waxing and waning, academic interest focused on questions of aesthetics, and Riefenstahl herself tirelessly and aggressively distributing lies about her past, the basic parameters of Riefenstahl's Nazi career frequently disappeared behind a cloud of indifference and disinformation. In the course of Riefenstahl's long life, several generations of journalists faced the task of dealing with yet another Riefenstahl anniversary or Riefenstahl media event and several generations of scholars assessed her work and career from a number of different vantage points. Judging by the texts that resulted from these efforts, the journalists and scholars often found themselves unwilling or unable to retrieve the facts of Riefenstahl's life and integrate them into their publications. The disregard for factual knowledge seemed to have played a particularly important role in the academic and feuilleton discourse about Riefenstahl. Consequently and very ironically, the texts of popularizers like Knopp or the writers at *Revue* turned out to be more *historically* reliable than many of the texts crafted by film scholars and cultural journalists who chased the ghosts of fascist aesthetics, were enamored of Riefenstahl's star power, or simply frightened into submission by her litigious personality.

Memory habits are difficult to break; they give us a sense of security and help us maintain a positive self-image. Such habits might be particularly useful in the fast-moving business of journalism. In 2007, after the publication of the excellent Riefenstahl biography by Steven Bach (*Leni: The Life and Work of Leni Riefenstahl*), Johannes Willms of the *Süddeutsche Zeitung* published a very favorable review of the book. He celebrated the alleged fact that Bach had finally unraveled "the virtually impenetrable fabric of fiction and fact" that Riefenstahl had crafted and successfully defended over her lifetime.[39] Willms failed to mention that Riefenstahl was hardly the only culprit here. She had many useful accomplices among journalists in Germany and abroad who distributed her lies and, like Willms, quickly and conveniently forgot whenever the "fabric of fact and fiction" was penetrated. In fact, after reading Bach, if not beforehand, Willms should have known how often the fabric had been destroyed in Germany alone by Leiser, Kinkel, Rother, and Trimborn not to mention *Revue*, Gladitz, and Knopp. But the collective memory of his profession told Willms otherwise. It provided him with the convenient, contradictory message that he had been duped by Riefenstahl but that he was not at fault since her lies were "virtually impenetrable."

IV. 1993–1994: The Media Event *The Wonderful, Horrible Life of Leni Riefenstahl*

All the accomplishments and shortcomings of the intellectual Riefenstahl discourse are highlighted by the most important media event in the history of Riefenstahl memory, the 1993 documentary *The Wonderful, Horrible Life of Leni Riefenstahl.* The film illustrates how media professionals have used the case of Riefenstahl to ponder important questions concerning the limits of artistic ambition and political opportunism. But the film also demonstrates in exemplary fashion that journalists often found themselves unable to pursue these questions with historical rigor and intellectual honesty, especially if they involved Riefenstahl in their efforts.

The Wonderful, Horrible Life became a smash hit at film festivals in the U.S. and Canada in 1993 and 1994, was broadcast on many PBS stations, won an Emmy in November 1993, and was subsequently screened in theaters in many major U.S. cities. The documentary was less successful, yet equally widely distributed, in Europe. *Die Macht der Bilder,* as the film was called in Germany, was first screened on the French-German public cable TV station *arte* in October 1993. At that point in time, relatively few viewers had access to *arte,* which served as one of the co-producers of the film. But the documentary subsequently went into selective release in major cities in Germany and Europe and probably had its largest single audience in Europe in the spring of 1994. On March 27 and April 3, ZDF, another co-producer, broadcast *Die Macht der Bilder* in two installments as part of its late-night lineup and managed to keep over a million viewers awake until one o'clock in the morning.[40] The documentary was released on video in the U.S. in 1995 and in Germany in 2001, and is offered on DVD in several editions and packages on both sides of the Atlantic.[41] Anyone interested in the topic has had many opportunities to see the film; it has become the most widely used visual document on Riefenstahl and has played an important role in the evolution of the collective memories of the life and work of the infamous filmmaker. Steven Bach aptly calls *The Wonderful, Horrible Life* "the ultimate Riefenstahl spectacle," and the German film critic Rainer Rother describes it as "one of the most influential documentaries of the decade."[42]

Ray Müller, the director of *The Wonderful, Horrible Life,* has had a long and successful career in German public television. However, it has hardly been a career that reflects a particular expertise in interview films, or one that has earned Müller a lot of critical acclaim. First and foremost, Müller is a reliable director of travel documentaries.[43] In that capacity, he has informed German viewers about the everyday life of miners and cowboys in Australia and Latin America and frequently reported from Africa.[44] The latter continent seems to be Müller's favorite travel destination, perhaps because some of his ancestors tried their luck in Germany's colonial possessions in Africa in the decades before World War I.[45] Müller develops significant historical ambition in his travel documentaries, and it is therefore not surprising that he has also directed a number of historical documentaries for ZDF. The programs in question are typically prime-time fare dealing with spectacular aviation mishaps, maritime rescue operations, or most recently, the curious circumstances of the death of the Bavarian king Ludwig II.[46] Judging by the few available reviews and descriptions, the programs combine documentary footage with reenactments and appear quite compatible with the type of historical programming developed at ZDF under the aegis of Guido Knopp. Müller was hired to direct *The Wonderful, Horrible Life* by a consortium of European TV stations under the leadership of ZDF. But the idea for the documentary came initially from Riefenstahl herself who was also involved in finding an appropriate director. Müller was apparently the nineteenth candidate for the job, chosen after all others who had been approached before him either declined the job or were rejected by Riefenstahl.[47]

Müller begins *The Wonderful, Horrible Life* by cutting footage of Riefenstahl diving in tropical waters against excerpts from her work as a filmmaker, ranging from *Triumph of the Will* over *Olympia* all the way to her unpublished footage of the Nuba. The sequence only lasts two minutes but follows a clear logic. Initially, the five-second clips of Hitler and marching soldiers, underlaid with drum music, overpower the peaceful diving scenes; face-to-face with Hitler even the fish assume a vaguely threatening posture. But by the end of the fast-cut sequence, the fish, Riefenstahl, and the Nuba are perfectly in sync.

After this opening sequence, the title of the film appears in front of a black-and-white photo of Riefenstahl and the rehabilitation of the Nazi filmmaker continues. The camera slowly descends on Riefenstahl's beautiful modernist house. It is nighttime, the windows are lit, and the silhouette of Riefenstahl appears in the open patio door. The top-down camera movement approaching Riefenstahl at night turns her into the victim of our voyeuristic interest. The sequence is accompanied by pleasant, contemplative, and slightly melancholic piano and clarinet music. For those viewers who have not understood the fairly obvious visual and acoustic signs, Müller firmly positions the audience by having the commentator assume a posture of fake naiveté. With the pleasant music still in the background, a low-key, nicely balanced male voiceover sets the tone: "Approaching a legend. A name that is still a taboo for many in Germany today, Leni Riefenstahl, the infamous film director of the Third Reich. What could a film about Leni Riefenstahl be, the deconstruction of myth or the revision of prejudice? At the beginning I do not know what to expect. Therefore, I attempt to approach [Riefenstahl] without prejudice" (2:00).[48]

Obviously, anyone who has read anything about Riefenstahl knows what to expect. At age ninety-one she will most likely repeat the well-rehearsed, selective, at times invented, and utterly non-self-critical story of her life that she crafted shortly after the war and has never changed. But the posture of fake naiveté has interesting ideological effects. The film was probably not made with an American audience in mind, but Müller's rhetoric of neutrality corresponds very nicely to a widely held belief in the U.S. that the truth will miraculously emerge if all sides receive the chance to tell their story. In the case of Riefenstahl, the U.S. public also tends to believe that she rarely had a chance to tell her story and therefore deserves public attention. In Germany, where the rehabilitation of Riefenstahl has not advanced as quickly, Müller's gesture of fake naiveté and his subsequent wholesale endorsement of Riefenstahl's view of her life attracts attention precisely because he challenges some established perceptions of the filmmaker and calls into question some basic tenets of West Germany's historical culture. Müller seems to absolve Riefenstahl of the duty of having to self-critically reflect about her deeds and acknowledge her guilt and thus calls into question the liberal logic of *Vergangenheitsbewältigung*. By allowing Riefenstahl to peddle her self-serving lies in public, Müller inadvertently implies that the self-critical remembrance of Nazi crimes, which was hailed as one of the key West German accomplishments, has runs its course and should be replaced with a more relaxed and utilitarian approach to the burden of the past in unified Germany.

Considered from a historiographical point of view, *The Wonderful, Horrible Life of Leni Riefenstahl* is a terrible documentary. Müller fails to set the record straight about the many lies and inaccuracies that Riefenstahl tells in the course of their long conversations. One understands Müller's reluctance to challenge Riefenstahl directly and consistently whenever she strayed from the truth. Such persistence might have aborted the interview before it even began, or worse, caused the ninety-one-year-old serious harm. But there is simply no acceptable explanation for Müller's decision to let most of Riefenstahl's mistakes stand uncorrected and withhold from viewers pertinent details about her life and career. As a result, *The Wonderful, Horrible Life* does not paint an accurate picture of Riefenstahl's position in the Third Reich and her relationship to the Nazi leadership.

The first statement of Riefenstahl's that needed to be challenged or corrected occurs about thirty minutes into the film. Relating her version of the production history of *The Blue Light (Das blaue Licht),* Riefenstahl waxes about the "ideal collaboration" between her and her scriptwriter Béla Balázs in 1932 (33:00). Riefenstahl fondly recalls the latter's willingness to work on the movie script without compensation, and Müller sees no reason to inform the audience that this recollection is very problematic. *The Blue Light* was made on a shoestring budget and Riefenstahl could not afford to pay most members of her crew at the time of production. But she promised to pay her collaborators when the movie turned a profit and seems to have followed through on those promises with at least one important exception. Balázs, a Communist of Jewish descent, who fled Nazi Germany and lived in relative poverty in exile in Moscow, tried repeatedly to get paid for his work and, after waiting for more than a year, filed a lawsuit. Riefenstahl settled the legal dispute by turning the matter over to Julius Streicher, editor of the anti-semitic journal *Der Stürmer*. Balázs died in 1949 without having seen a dime.[49]

Riefenstahl used Nazi racial policies to her advantage on other occasions, for instance, when she exploited Sinti and Roma slave laborers during the production of *Tiefland* (*Lowlands*). Müller and Riefenstahl refer to this incident and the postwar litigation about its representation. Unfortunately, however, *The Wonderful, Horrible Life* systematically misrepresents the events of 1940–1941 and provides incomplete information about the postwar trials. In the last hour of the documentary Müller combines historical photographs of the Sinti and Roma with the following commentary: "Later, while shooting in Bavaria, there is a need for Spanish extras. Therefore, the production enlists the help of the employment office to obtain gypsies. They come from the camp of Leopoldskron near Salzburg. The director (i.e., Riefenstahl) has been fiercely criticized for hiring these people at a point in time when all non-Aryans were already brutally persecuted. There has been litigation about this incident until quite recently."[50] The phrase "the production" obscures the question of Riefenstahl's personal responsibility and the terms *employment office* and *hiring* falsely imply that a banal labor transaction took place and that the extras were paid for their services. Müller does not use the less benign but more accurate terms *labor camp* and *slave labor* and fails to inform the viewers about the fact that most of the extras who appear in *Lowlands* were murdered in Auschwitz. He also never mentions the substance of the postwar litigation and the judges' conclusion that Riefenstahl probably personally visited the camp and selected the Sinti and Roma for her movie.[51]

The Wonderful, Horrible Life contains other dubious statements about Nazi crimes. Müller accurately reports that Riefenstahl volunteered as a war correspondent in 1939 and asserts that she quickly aborted her mission after she witnessed the brutality of the German army's onslaught in Poland. Müller shows the famous photograph depicting Riefenstahl's horror-stricken face as she observes a massacre of Polish Jews committed by German army regulars. However, in the voiceover comment the incident is simply described as "a violent clash between the Wehrmacht and Polish civilians" and the commentator adds that Riefenstahl lodged a complaint with the army leadership and immediately left Poland (2:07). The word *clash* hardly describes what took place in Konskie. Müller does not tell his viewers that the victims were Jews, that the massacre was one of the first examples of racial warfare on the eastern front, and that none of the soldiers were ever disciplined for their crime.[52]

During the conversation about *Lowlands*, Müller misses an excellent opportunity to explore Riefenstahl's relationship to the Nazi state. Riefenstahl begins her discussion of the film by claiming that her *Olympia* films made so much money that she had sufficient funds for her second feature film (2:08). This is a false statement. *Lowlands* was almost completely funded by the Third Reich and to a large extent from Hitler's personal coffers. Riefenstahl spent the enormous sum of seven million *Reichsmark* at a time when feature films cost, on average, half a million *Reichsmark*, and she still did not manage to conclude the project by 1945.[53] By failing to follow the money trail, Müller remains silent about the extraordinarily privileged position that Riefenstahl enjoyed in the Third Reich. Unlike other filmmakers, she had personal access to Hitler and used him frequently to deal with skeptics within the Nazi bureaucracy and secure the very best production conditions for her own projects.[54]

On one occasion Müller does challenge Riefenstahl's faulty memory. Riefenstahl recalls rebuffing Goebbels's unwelcome advances, which caused them to have "the worst kind of relationship" and turned them "almost into enemies" (51:00). Müller finds it difficult to reconcile this statement with information gleaned from other sources, including Goebbels's diary.[55] In several entries from 1933, the propaganda minister describes spending time with Riefenstahl at his home, at Hitler's residence, and at the opera. When confronted with this evidence, Riefenstahl becomes increasingly agitated, alternately denies that the diaries contain these passages and calls them "pure fantasy," insisting that she never visited Goebbels at home. Müller ends the segment by showing three photographs of Goebbels that depict him in typical propaganda poses and combines the stills with two comments from offscreen. First the commentator intervenes, asking, "Who says the truth? The propaganda minister or the director? There are many contradictory statements," followed by Riefenstahl's voice emphasizing that "Goebbels was after all a master of lying" (54:00).[56] In the end, it does not matter if one reads this segment as an endorsement of Riefenstahl's point of view—she has the last word—or an open-ended inquiry that presents the conflicting statements without taking sides. Either way, Müller calls into question what most historians and experts consider the truth, i.e., that Riefenstahl had extensive social ties to Goebbels and Hitler before and after the Nazis came to power.[57]

At one point in their conversations toward the end of *The Wonderful, Horrible Life,* Riefenstahl explains to Müller that "she only becomes productive, creative, and has good ideas when dealing with topics which enthuse or about which one could feel enthusiastic." She adds that this principle applies to all her films (2:39). We can therefore safely assume that Riefenstahl felt quite enthusiastic about Hitler, the subject of her second documentary. Riefenstahl is indeed surprisingly forthcoming with information about her adulation of Hitler but provides little concrete information about their relationship. She uses the disarmingly honest admission of her infatuation with the Führer as a rhetorical tool to thwart unwelcome inquiries about the role she played in the Nazi elite and the art scene of the Third Reich. That strategy certainly works with Müller, who is happy to let her reveal her feelings for Hitler without challenging her story or asking precise questions. One might wonder, for example, how her fascination with Hitler and her study of *Mein Kampf* influenced her relationship to her Jewish friends before and possibly after the war. But these are not the kind of questions that Müller pursues. Instead, he listens patiently to Riefenstahl's own version of the Hitler myth and generously distributes her contradictory statements about Hitler over large segments of the film in such a way that the contradictions only stand out after several viewings.

Talking about her first meeting with Hitler, Riefenstahl emphasizes his special demonic, hypnotic powers, which made her fear for her independence and compelled her to make two films about the Nazi party rallies (46:00). She also admits that in hindsight and with after-the-fact knowledge of his crimes her collaboration with Hitler amounted to "a pact with the devil." Nonetheless, she immediately adds that Hitler was both "the devil and its opposite" and that, at the time, one only saw the positive, not the terrible side of his personality (1:04:00). Yet she also claims to have detested Hitler's racial policies and to have challenged him in person about the boycott of Jewish businesses in April 1933 (50:00).[58] Moreover, Riefenstahl maintains that she abhorred Hitler's rejection of modern art and that his dubious aesthetic preferences made her listen to his speeches much more critically (2:05). Obviously, none of this adds up. Hitler's evil side was hardly invisible in the 1930s, and his demonic powers over Riefenstahl could not have been very pronounced if he was not even able to convince her of the superiority of Arno Breker's work, let alone the integrity of his racial policies. Rather than invoking the Hitler myth, we should consider the unpleasant conclusion that Riefenstahl simply did not care that much about the victims and was happy to put up with Hitler's bad taste in art as along as he provided her with fantastic career opportunities.[59]

Sometimes Müller inadvertently produces revealing footage by simply letting Riefenstahl talk and confirming her self-serving statements in his own words. We might not learn much about fascist aesthetics and the relation between art and politics here, but Riefenstahl and Müller take us on a trip down memory lane all the way to the 1950s, a period in which most Germans could not speak about the victims of Nazi persecution without quickly changing the topic and emphasizing the hardships they had personally endured during war and occupation. In the last thirty minutes of the film, Müller compiles his attempts to extract statements of contrition from Riefenstahl. She describes in cataclysmic terms the "terrible fall" she experienced at the end of the war, the "shock" of learning for the first time about the concentration camps and seeing footage of their liberation. From her perspective, there were only two options: "to live with the terrible burden and guilt that now rested on our shoulders or to die; it was a permanent fight between living and dying" (2:23).[60] Approximately every thirty seconds Müller interrupts this testimony to show silent footage of the liberation of the camps. On one occasion, however, precisely at the moment when Riefenstahl delivers her life and death metaphor, Müller adds a rare and revealing comment that illustrates how much he identifies with her point of view. We see footage of bulldozers pushing naked corpses into mass graves and hear the commentator picking up where Riefenstahl left off, thus reinforcing her self-serving usage of the word *fight*. In response to Riefenstahl's lamentations about her struggle between life and death, the voiceover adds that "sixty million in Europe had already lost this fight at the time."[61] Speaking almost with one voice, Müller and Riefenstahl equate the suffering of the victims of Nazi persecution and the Nazi war of aggression with the mental anguish many Germans, including possibly Riefenstahl, experienced as a result of the collapse of their empire and worldview. Some Germans obviously continued to fight for survival after 1945, especially the expellees from the eastern territories. But people in Riefenstahl's situation, easily the vast majority of the population, did not face any problems that could be honestly equated with the experiences of the sixty million dead, i.e., the death camp inmates, the soldiers, or the victims of air warfare (which Riefenstahl escaped in 1944 by relocating from Berlin to Kitzbühel in Austria[62]).

Riefenstahl reiterates this false analogy in the next segment of the documentary. Müller asks Riefenstahl if she saw her work in a different light after she learned about the Nazi atrocities (implying that she really did not know anything about the crimes beforehand). Riefenstahl answers that she did not see her work differently but that she felt desperate because she had to live in those times. On second thought she adds, however, that "putting myself in the place of the victims one [sic] could understand that it was difficult to see the swastikas and the SS and the SA—all these people of whom we thought that they were not criminals. The collapse lasted forever; I have never overcome the terror I experienced at the time" (2:24). Again she glides seamlessly from the displeasure of the victims who might not enjoy seeing the SS uniforms in *Triumph of the Will* to the terror that she herself allegedly experienced at the end of the war. She seems to have no awareness of the fact that this comparison is inappropriate, among other reasons, because what caused her pain, the collapse of the Reich, was the very factor that alleviated the suffering of the victims.

Instead of probing the historical record more rigorously and confronting Riefenstahl's testimony with the results of that analysis, Müller treats his viewers to a number of entertaining *faux* confrontations between himself and Riefenstahl. When filming on location in Babelsberg, where Riefenstahl reminisces about her early acting career and her work with different Weimar-era directors, Riefenstahl initially refuses to follow Müller's instructions. Müller had his crew put tracks on the floor and wanted to capture Riefenstahl's testimony as she walks across the historic production hall. One would think that Riefenstahl sympathized with the objective of rendering the footage a little more dynamic, but she first rejects this plan, declaring categorically "that she never walks and speaks at the same time" (14:00). In the Alps, Müller and Riefenstahl discuss the extreme physical challenges the actors had to overcome while shooting Fanck's Alpine films (*Bergfilme*). Riefenstahl takes this as an opportunity to give Müller a crash course in directing, telling him how to place his cameras and cut the scene to attain the most dramatic effect (18:00). In Nuremberg, Riefenstahl recalls how the Nazi functionaries sabotaged her work in 1933 when she filmed the first party rally. She becomes visibly upset and plays up her emotions to demonstrate how much she suffered at the hands of the Nazis. Riefenstahl begs Müller to let her explain the events of 1933 in greater detail, and in the next moment swears at him, yelling that she does not want to talk about these important things anymore (56:00–59:00). In some of these scenes, Riefenstahl becomes physical, grabbing Müller's lapel or swatting at a crew member who tries to convince her to change her mind.

With a good sense for docudrama, Müller had his crew capture these confrontations with a small handheld video camera and cut them into the final film. The scenes serve a number of purposes. They are clearly among the visual and emotional highlights of the documentary. They illustrate how much energy and vigor the ninety-one-year-old possesses and what an accomplished actress Riefenstahl still is. She can switch quickly from professional banter to delivering her lines with composure or emotional depth for the "real" camera. But the video footage also serves as an alibi for Müller. The scenes represent his way of telling the audience, "Look how tough I was with Riefenstahl; I made her walk the line." In reality, power relations between the two protagonists were severely tilted in favor of Riefenstahl. Müller was able to convince her to walk and talk in front of the camera and ignore her editing advice—unfortunately, one might want to add, because the film is hardly a visually ambitious or complex documentary. But Müller rarely challenges her version of events, chooses not to correct blatant factual errors in her account, and completely ignores some of the most interesting aspects of Riefenstahl's life in the Third Reich, for instance, her friendship with Julius Streicher or the fact that she repeatedly used her connections to help victims of the regime.[63] Despite appearances to the contrary, especially as a result of the *faux* confrontations that both played up for their own reasons, *The Wonderful, Horrible Life* is a wholesale endorsement of Riefenstahl's carefully and very selectively constructed self-image.

The film constantly alludes to the important problem of the interdependence between art and politics and the more specific question of the affinities between Riefenstahl's visual language and the political ideology of National Socialism. In fact, it seems that Müller ticks off a list of every important critique that has ever been leveled against Riefenstahl's oeuvre. He asks her about the proto-fascist tendencies of the mountain film genre (Krakauer, 23:00), the glorification of Hitler in *Triumph of the Will* (1:09), and the fascistic adulation of the human physique in her work (Sontag, 1:39). Riefenstahl's short answers are certainly worth considering—she rejects the first and third charge but agrees with the second. Unfortunately, however, Müller never asks Riefenstahl to explain the specificity of her visual language in detail and therefore has no opportunity to approach the problem of fascist art from a new vantage point or armed with new information. That is particularly unfortunate because, unlike some artists, Riefenstahl is an excellent source of information about her craftsmanship and aesthetic preferences. Even at age ninety-one, she remembered all the technical details of her productions and very much enjoyed discussing her filming techniques and cutting strategies. It seems, therefore, that conversations about technical details could have been developed into comparative reflections about alternative editing strategies, the visual languages of other filmmakers, and the possible ideological implications of different artistic styles. Following this inductive approach, Müller might have been able to turn Riefenstahl the filmmaker against Riefenstahl the self-promoter and call into question her altogether unconvincing assertion that her films lack propaganda value because she only filmed what others orchestrated and never added any explicit political messages to her films (1:17–1:18). Instead of listening to two filmmakers converse with precision about Riefenstahl's remarkable skills and their effects, we are informed in general terms about "the frightening intensity" of her visual language (60:00, see also 2:16) and her unprecedented technical know-how (1:38). In essence, Müller made the mistake of taking Riefenstahl too seriously as an autobiographer and political commentator—and not getting very far on either terrain because Riefenstahl lacked critical self-reflexivity and political acumen—while not taking her seriously enough as a filmmaker.

V. Müller's Will, Riefenstahl's Will, or Both?

Many factors may have contributed to Müller's capitulation before his famous colleague. Perhaps the project was simply out of his league; Müller had never made this kind of interview film before (and has never made another since) and might not have had the training or the presence of mind to intervene at the right moment and in the right form. Maybe Müller intended all along to forsake judgment of Riefenstahl and erect a clearly visible sign of her rehabilitation. It is also possible, however, that Riefenstahl, ever the PR-strategist, literally held the trump in her hand and played her cards very effectively. Riefenstahl received an official contract that obliged her to cooperate unconditionally with Müller and that gave her no right to screen and intervene in the final product before it was presented to the public.[64] But Riefenstahl did more than that: She opened her private archive and contributed exciting, never-before-seen footage of her diving adventures and her excursions to Africa. The material on the Nuba is especially impressive and enhances the film's value as a visual document. Riefenstahl might have held this material hostage, unofficially, and thus received a chance to have more of an input in the shaping of the documentary than was initially planned.[65] We might never find out what exactly happened. But many passages of the film's commentary are so close to Riefenstahl's own language that it is difficult to imagine that she was not consulted in one way or another.

Müller had at least two alternatives. He could have made a tough film about politics, challenging and interrogating Riefenstahl as much as possible and adding a lot of outside information that Riefenstahl was not willing to provide but that would have been needed to arrive at a penetrating, honest political portrait. For this project, Müller might not have been able to rely on Riefenstahl's postwar footage and the kind of long, collaborative interviews with the filmmaker that are featured in *The Wonderful, Horrible Life.* Such an honest political portrait would have been a tough choice, considering that the postwar footage and the vigorous, combative personality of the ancient Riefenstahl were the most attractive features of the whole undertaking. Alternatively, Müller could have abandoned the political arena altogether, focusing instead on Riefenstahl's aesthetic insights and legacy. Rather than providing her with a platform for her autobiographical lies he might have chosen to sit down with her and review her oeuvre in detail, asking her to explain how she prepared the sets, captured the footage, and edited the films that made her so famous. As a number of scenes in *The Wonderful, Horrible Life* indicate, Riefenstahl would have been an enthusiastic collaborator in that enterprise. She could have finally told the world about the things she was really good at instead of being forced to discuss topics again and again about which she knew very little, never thought about in any self-reflexive way, and for which she is therefore one of the worst discussants imaginable. The second strategy would have turned the documentary into a master class taught by Riefenstahl herself. It would have told us much more about Riefenstahl and fascist aesthetics than the documentary ultimately did. The film would have been especially important because Riefenstahl was rarely encouraged to explain her technique in detail and never had the chance to make a film in a post-fascist environment (and thus shed new light on the important question of whether or not photographs, films, or other art objects can be inherently fascist). However, this option would have frustrated many viewers and Müller's superiors at the TV stations because the interesting details of Riefenstahl's biography might have disappeared behind technical jargon and insider talk.

By not pursuing either option rigorously and consistently, Müller wasted two fabulous opportunities. But he also demonstrated his professional strengths, namely, the ability to finish a difficult assignment in such a way that it appeals to a relatively large audience, even if that means taking some ethical shortcuts. Müller produced an entertaining compromise that reflects all our prejudices, yet was just enough of a taboo breaker to capture our imagination and an Emmy. Consequently, *The Wonderful, Horrible Life* will live on in the collective memories of academics and intellectuals who continue to be fascinated by fascism.

Some reviewers thought that they could tell from Müller's appearances in the film how uncomfortable he felt about Riefenstahl's refusal to engage in any self-criticism.[66] Müller's discomfort, however, could not have been very pronounced or perhaps appeared negligible to him in hindsight once the film became an international success. Working with Riefenstahl certainly was not always easy, as Müller tried to tell viewers by including the production footage in the final version of *The Wonderful, Horrible Life.*[67] Riefenstahl also claimed that their collaboration was fraught with difficulty. For months after the release of the film, Riefenstahl refused to watch it and complained about not having had the opportunity to prepare herself for Müller's "often brutal questions."[68] But Müller's and Riefenstahl's public acknowledgments of their problems with each other appear primarily as an elegant way for both to save face and justify what they or their critics perceived as the shortcomings of the project. Müller and Riefenstahl remained on good terms. Müller emphasized repeatedly that the film and its refusal to pass judgment reflected his objectives and his personal assessment of Riefenstahl's life and moral responsibility. Müller stated unequivocally that he had no intentions of telling viewers what to think and emphasized that Riefenstahl's career in the Third Reich should not deflect attention from the remarkable work she had done since.[69] Moreover, he must have felt comfortable enough in Riefenstahl's presence since he agreed to make another film with and about her. In 1998, they flew together to Sudan to experience and document a reunion between Riefenstahl and "her" Nuba. The project ended in disaster when their helicopter crashed, but Müller walked away from that experience with his respect for Riefenstahl intact. The result of the trip was Müller's hour-long documentary *Leni Riefenstahl: Ihr Traum von Afrika (Leni Riefenstahl: Her Dream of Africa)* released in 2000. It depicts Riefenstahl in a very favorable light.[70] When Riefenstahl died in 2003, Müller considered himself the person who "came to know her better than anybody else."[71] In light of all this information, it is safe to assume that the favorable depiction of Riefenstahl in *The Wonderful, Horrible Life* is not the result of Riefenstahl's manipulative powers over Müller but rather the outcome of the collaboration between two individuals who, despite their differences, held, or gradually developed, compatible views of Riefenstahl's accomplishments.

At some point, Müller probably had to choose between making the film of a lifetime and compromising his integrity in the process or aborting the whole project and facing negative repercussions for his career. It is perfectly understandable that he chose the first option. As a result, however, he turned into "Riefenstahl," at least to a certain degree. Working under much more benign circumstances than Riefenstahl did and producing a much more harmless film than *Triumph of the Will*, Müller nevertheless cheated his audience. Müller let stand uncorrected and occasionally even supported statements by Riefenstahl that he knew to be false. He probably also knew that the statements and passages in question were important, that most viewers did not have easy access to the correct information, and that setting the record straight in his film would have caused at least some viewers to form a more critical opinion of Riefenstahl than they ultimately did. It does not help Müller's case—and provides additional echoes of Riefenstahl—that he vigorously defended his choices after the fact.[72]

Perhaps it is wrong to blame Müller personally. Maybe he has also become a victim of collective memories, like Willms and others before him. After all, just at the time when Müller was making his film, the *feuilletons* had begun to embrace Riefenstahl's version of her life wholeheartedly or declared the topic "Riefenstahl" ambivalent and impenetrable. Consequently, in the early 1990s, the collective wisdom of his profession rendered Müller's choice perfectly acceptable. It is only with hindsight, after the latest turn in professional Riefenstahl memory ushered in by Kinkel and other film historians, that Müller's choices appear far more problematic. Even in this regard though, Müller's fate can be compared to Riefenstahl's. In the 1930s, her choices seemed perfectly natural. They were only considered impenetrable, ambivalent, and occasionally flat-out wrong after 1945.

VI. The Reception of *The Wonderful, Horrible Life* in Germany and the U.S.

Since *The Wonderful, Horrible Life* has seen so many different screenings and editions, there have been plenty of opportunities for feuilleton journalists to assess Müller's interpretation of Riefenstahl's life. The impressive trail of reviews indicates that journalists are attracted to the film for two reasons: While informing their readers on important aspects of NS history, they also get a chance to reflect on their identity as media professionals. The ruthless opportunism and questionable moral behavior that Riefenstahl displayed in her dual career as celebrity and producer of important media texts raises questions that many journalists have to deal with in their professional life. How should journalists define and preserve their professional integrity? To what extent and under what circumstances is it legitimate to advance one's own career by crafting news stories that serve the interests of the political and economic elites? In this regard, it is a blessing that Müller decided to adopt a seemingly neutral attitude toward his subject matter. His apparent lack of commitment makes it possible to appreciate the film in different ways and from a number of different vantage points. *The Wonderful, Horrible Life* is an excellent projection screen for all kinds of collective memories of Nazism and an excellent catalyst for reflections about the ethical limits of professional opportunism.

Journalists in the United States deal with the challenge of having to make sense of Riefenstahl by embracing ambivalence. The reviews of the film published in the U.S. teem with rhetorical questions, highlight the many allegedly insoluble contradictions of Riefenstahl's life, and celebrate Müller's lack of persistence and precision as a particularly apt illustration of life's existential undecidability. Jimmy Fowler of the *Dallas Observer* expressed this attitude most succinctly when he wrote: "But craven opportunism and genocidal complicity are two vastly different charges. Or are they? Here the moral dilemma of Riefenstahl's life blossoms into a conundrum that encompasses the role of everyone in society."[73] That conundrum also blossoms in many other reviews, usually in the form of binary oppositions that are left unanswered and unresolved: Is Riefenstahl a "liar" or does she suffer from "an extraordinary case of artistic myopia"?;[74] is she best characterized as "feminist pioneer or woman of evil"?;[75] was she "a Nazi," "a Nazi collaborator," or "just a Nazi employee"?;[76] is she "a brilliant deluded fool? A misguided obsessive, so caught up in cinematic perfectionism she was blinded to harsh political realities?";[77] is she "an appallingly amoral artist" or did she spend "the entire war in a state of total innocence"?[78]

American reviewers occasionally note, but do not seem to be bothered by the fact that Riefenstahl wins the duel with Müller. In their assessment, the film always remains sufficiently ambivalent to express the "incredible contradictions and monumental ironies capable of residing in one proud and indomitable old woman."[79] Consequently, for the U.S. press corps, Müller has chosen the only honorable and truthful path. He refrains from explicit judgment, presents both sides of the debate, and allows the viewers to form their own opinions. Müller thus elegantly acknowledges the fundamental contradictions and ironies of history. In the eyes of most U.S. critics, *The Wonderful, Horrible Life* is simply a fair, authentic, and entertaining rendition of the biography of Leni Riefenstahl.

Müller and his reviewers in the United States certainly share a number of basic assumptions about history, assumptions that have more to do with taste and aesthetics than with facts. But the enthusiasm with which critics welcomed *The Wonderful Horrible Life* in the U.S. is also a reflection of ignorance. Although some reviewers sensed that the film was more of an "authorized biography" than a critical historical inquiry, they generally lacked a clear grasp of the relevant historical record.[80] None of the reviews I have seen point out the blatant lies and omissions in Riefenstahl's testimony that Müller fails to correct. In fact, at least one critic, our much appreciated Jimmy Fowler, offers an altogether new version of history when he claims that many factors "caused a majority of the German electorate to name Adolf Hitler as chancellor in 1932."[81] In all fairness, one should note that it is easier today for a busy journalist to get the relevant facts about Riefenstahl than it was in 1993–94. As mentioned above, shortly before and after Riefenstahl's death a whole string of solid biographies were published. In 1994, the U.S. critics did not have easy access to such texts. If they refer to any source besides Müller's film, they mention Riefenstahl's autobiography, which had just been published in the U.S. but which is hardly a useful source for developing a critical perspective on Müller's film and Riefenstahl's life.[82]

The reviewers of *Die Macht der Bilder* in Germany developed many of the same themes as their U.S. counterparts, although they often considered the film from a different moral vantage point. A few German journalists wholeheartedly endorsed the film; they considered it a successful balancing act between homage and critical biography.[83] But more critics noted with mild concern or serious alarm that Riefenstahl got the upper hand in the exchange with Müller both in terms of the drift of their conversation as well as in terms of the different cinematic visions they offered to viewers. The superiority of Riefenstahl's images did not surprise anyone considering her talent and the means at her disposal. But unlike their colleagues in the United States, many German critics felt uneasy about the way that Müller let Riefenstahl get away with murder (figuratively).[84] The discomfort at Müller's lackadaisical approach prompted some reviewers to develop elaborate psychological schemes that Müller had allegedly pursued. Thomas Klingenmaier from the *Stuttgarter Zeitung,* for example, suggested that Müller was willing to accommodate Riefenstahl and depict her as a misled genius in exchange for a clear statement of regret. Klingenmaier speculated further that Riefenstahl refused to take the gambit and that viewers therefore only experienced the first part of Müller's proposed symbolic exchange, the Riefenstahl rehabilitation, and never saw her attempt to make amends.[85]

Die Macht der Bilder encountered more vocal criticism when ZDF broadcast the film as part of its late-night lineup on March 27 and April 3, 1994. The newspaper reviews represented a balanced spectrum of favorable, neutral, and critical voices.[86] However, in an unusual show of force in the normally tranquil late-night environment, over fifty ZDF viewers picked up the phone during and after the broadcasts and accused ZDF executives of having failed to develop an appropriately critical perspective on Riefenstahl's career in the Third Reich. Many of these disappointed viewers also criticized ZDF for having thus glorified National Socialism and supported the neo-Nazi movement.[87] In the following days, the criticism continued in the national media. A commentator with the liberal weekly *Die Zeit* suggested that Müller's and ZDF's decision to provide Riefenstahl with a platform for her self-serving, exculpatory views of history had caused damage to Germany's democracy.[88] In addition, on March 27, the very day ZDF aired the second part of *Die Macht der Bilder,* the station's public service competitor ARD went on the offensive. In flagrant violation of public broadcasting etiquette, executives with the TV magazine *Kulturreport* rebroadcast scenes from Müller's documentary, which presented Riefenstahl in a favorable light, and combined them with critical statements from liberal media personalities such as Ralph Giordano and Erwin Leiser.[89]

The critical response to *The Wonderful, Horrible Life* in Germany stayed within the conventional limits of the journalistic genre of *Vergangenheitsbewältigung.* German journalists paid, for instance, no attention to the reception of the film in the United States. With few exceptions, they failed to inform their readers, for example, that the film had won an Emmy, a fact that ZDF had emphasized in its widely distributed PR material for Müller's documentary.[90] The disinterest in the U.S. reception was particularly remarkable since a much more powerful media event was already casting its shadow across the Atlantic. Beginning on December 15, 1993, *Schindler's List* was screened in theaters in the U.S., and the film was released in Germany on March 3, 1994. But German journalists never compared the two media events or tried to determine what information the belated acknowledgment of Schindler and the increasing appreciation of Riefenstahl revealed about memory politics in Germany and the U.S.[91] It is also noteworthy that the German press coverage of *Die Macht der Bilder* only very rarely contained references to the current political situation in Germany, which was first and foremost on the minds of many German viewers. Whereas the members of the audience who called ZDF on the nights of March 27 and April 3 immediately drew a connection between Riefenstahl's rehabilitation and the disturbing wave of neo-Nazi violence in unified Germany, the members of the press corps refrained from developing such parallels, probably because they considered them naïve and moralistic.

The gaps in the media discourse in Germany highlight specific habits of cultural production that distinguish German media professionals from other collectives. In some respects, *The Wonderful, Horrible Life* was a transnational media event, although German intellectuals considered it primarily from within national parameters. Moreover, the film invited general reflections about visual representations of Nazism and state of Nazi adulation in Germany, but German cultural critics generally confined their remarks to questions of biography, Nazi memory, and nonfiction film aesthetics. In this respect, mid-size, genre-specific media events like *The Wonderful, Horrible Life* demonstrate that the routine production of collective memories occurs within relatively stable professional and sociological boundaries. These are only rarely and temporarily overcome, for instance, in the context of major memory events like *Holocaust* or *Schindler's List*.

VII. Facts, Lies, and Collective Memories

The history of Riefenstahl memory in Germany seems to corroborate the pessimistic assessment that facts do not matter in collective memory processes. Time and again, the facts of Riefenstahl's life have disappeared behind a screen of aesthetic, political, and legal concerns that play a much more important role in the construction of individual and collective identities than do bare historical data. People identify with narratives, with poignant mental and physical images, not with isolated statements of fact. The tragic narrative of the rise, fall, and rebirth of an artistic genius; the vision of the self-confident woman caught in the chains of patriarchy; the juxtaposition of power and sex; or the illusion of miraculous strength and agility in old age—these are some of the themes surrounding Riefenstahl that fascinated people and made them write texts and produce films. Facts are mere garnish, one type of data among a wide variety of material to be arranged according to the logic of these narratives and images. It is particularly disillusioning that some scholars and academics share this disinterest in facts. Apparently, academic communication represents just another idiosyncratic, sociologically and politically irrelevant form of collective memory.

But if this assessment is accurate, then how do we explain the persistent resurfacing of facts and the many confrontations about them in the long history of Riefenstahl memory? How do we explain that some people cared, even if their insights did not make much of a difference in the evolution of collective memories of their profession? How do we explain the latest turn in the development of Riefenstahl memory, which seems to have brought about a new appreciation of historical data? Was it not precisely Riefenstahl's lying that got her into trouble again and again despite the fact that so many people were ready to forgive her?

Perhaps some counterfactuals might help here. Can we imagine a Riefenstahl autobiography full of gestures of apology and contrition but still containing all the lies that she produced with such consistency after 1945? Would she have gotten away with it? Not likely. She might have escaped close scrutiny in the postwar years but sooner rather than later the champions of *Vergangenheitsbewältigung* would have uncovered the evidence proving that most of the extras appearing in *Lowlands* were murdered in Auschwitz, that Riefenstahl stiffed Balázs by sending Streicher after him, and that she knew Hitler and Goebbels too well for comfort.

Now a different scenario: Let us imagine an autobiography in which Riefenstahl acknowledges all these facts, apologizes profusely, while also trying to explain her behavior as best as possible. The moment when Riefenstahl reemerged from Africa would have been an opportunity to present such an honest, self-reflective autobiography that some segments of the public craved. This counterfactual is more difficult to assess because we have to stretch our imaginations and produce in our minds an honest Riefenstahl who admits to her ruthless ambition and opportunism, acknowledges the people she had wronged, tries to make amends, and also modestly highlights her accomplishments, for instance the fact that she helped a number of victims of Nazi racial policies. If Riefenstahl had behaved in this way, her postwar career would probably have developed quite differently than it did. For one thing, Riefenstahl would have avoided the never-ending cycle of lies, revelations, and scandals that kept her name in the limelight. But, immediately, here is the problem: At some point, probably already in the 1970s when Riefenstahl started to mingle with celebrities like Mick Jagger, her lying and unappetizing memory politics became part of the attraction. If Riefenstahl had been properly remorseful, she would have attracted considerably less media attention. Her Nuba photos would have still made a splash, although not such a big one, but her underwater photos were primarily distinguished by the fact that they had been taken by an unrepentant Nazi. Riefenstahl was not just a dinosaur, she was a bad, fascist dinosaur. Therefore she became a particularly sought-after creature in the *feuilleton* petting zoo. So maybe Riefenstahl chose the best option after all: clam up, lie, and sue.

This brings us to the strange conclusion that facts simultaneously do and do not matter. In the context of German memory politics of the last six decades, Riefenstahl could not have prevented the ugly bits and pieces of her biography from surfacing sooner or later. These details would have emerged no matter what path she took. At the same time, regardless of her willingness or unwillingness to tell the truth, Riefenstahl had a good chance to remain a celebrity, since lying does not disqualify people from a successful career in show business or the arts.

Facts only matter when collectives think they should matter and when collectives institute sanctions for members of the collectives who lie. Few collectives adopt such rules and in most collectives sanctions are only triggered in cases of particularly egregious lying. Moreover, the way that the rules are interpreted and applied changes constantly. So while there is no natural, stable causal relation between facts and particular visions of the past, collectives can pretend that such connections exist and that visions and narratives that contain factual inaccuracies have been discredited. Under such admittedly rare circumstances, facts play an important strategic role, especially if different aesthetic-political visions of the past coexist and compete with one another. Put differently, in an act of collective make-believe, facts can be made to carry an aesthetic-political burden.

The historical profession is a strange collective; it cares more about facts than other groups do and occasionally even punishes people who get them wrong. That might explain why many of the people who cared about Riefenstahl's lies, including Kinkel, Rother, Trimborn, and, last but not least, Knopp and many of his associates, are trained historians. But the absence of stable factual knowledge in the collective memories of Riefenstahl, however frustrating to historians, is not a curse but a blessing, even a necessity. For Riefenstahl to serve as an icon of *Vergangenheitsbewältigung*, to afford several political generations and collectives the opportunity to use her as a projection screen for their ideas, interpretations, and visions of Nazism, she had to remain an ill-defined, contradictory, and mysterious figure. The unappetizing facts of her life had to disappear frequently to assure that the figure Riefenstahl assumed a degree of moral ambivalence that the person Riefenstahl never deserved. In this way, it was easy for different generations and collectives to keep reinventing Riefenstahl and Nazism according to their own political, psychological, and aesthetic interests (and sometimes rediscovering the facts in the process). Riefenstahl, with her complex past, her own disdain for facts, and her craving for publicity, was ideally suited for the role of ambivalent Nazi. All of this explains why *The Wonderful, Horrible Life* is such a fantastic and valuable memory product and, at the same time, a deeply flawed text, if considered from the idiosyncratic perspective of a historian who suffers from the collectively produced illusion that the difference between a fact and a lie is a useful basis for moral judgments.

NOTES

1. The research and writing of this essay has been generously supported by the Jena Center for Twentieth Century History at the Friedrich-Schiller-Universität Jena. I am especially indebted to the director of the center, Norbert Frei, and to Lars Velter, who provided invaluable research support. I am also very grateful to the editors for their helpful comments on an earlier draft of this essay.
2. *Tatort: Investigativ*, ARD, June 10, 2007; the program reached 5.75 million viewers with a market share of 18.7 percent, which is relatively low for *Tatort*. The commercial TV station RTL reached the highest market share of the evening with its live broadcast of the Montreal grand prix (7.24 million/27.8 percent), "Quotenhits," *Leipziger Volkszeitung*, June 12, 2007.

3. *Tatort: Investigativ*. The exhibit Radu is referring to is a fictitious event. But, as the scriptwriters certainly knew, a Hamburg gallery staged indeed one of the first postwar exhibits of Riefenstahl photos. The controversial, commercial show took place in August and September 1997 featuring stills of the 1936 Olympic Games, photos of the Nuba, and photographic exploits of Riefenstahl's diving adventures; see *Riefenstahl-Rezeption nach 1945: Ausstellungen* (http://ruhr-uni-bochum.de/riefenstahl/n_ausstellungen_einzelne_ausstellungen.shtml).
4. See the following representative texts, which were published between mid-April and mid-July 2007: Hans Marquardt, "Ist Oliver Stone die neue Riefenstahl?," *BZ*, 3 July 2007; Helen Hoffmann, "60 Jahre Cannes," *Spiegel-online*, May 16, 2007; Ulrike Ruppel, "Tom Cruise als Claus Graf Schenk von Stauffenberg," *BZ*, June 22, 2007; Jan Kedves, "Die Gruppe Tocotronic ist inzwischen Deutschlands wichtigste Intellektuellen-Band," *Welt am Sonntag*, July 1, 2007; Markus Hundt, "NSDAP Parteizentrale," *Welt am Sonntag*, June 24, 2007; Alexander Cammann, "Geniekult und Vereinsmeierei: Rückblicke auf die wilheminische Eventkultur," *tageszeitung*, June 14, 2007; Stefan Schickhaus, "Flachland: Die Wiesbadener Maifestspiele eröffnen mit *Tiefland*," *Frankfurter Rundschau*, April 30, 2007; Jonny Erling, "Olympischen Spiele 2008 in China," *Die Welt*, May 8, 2007; "Vor dem Länderspiel," *Stuttgarter Nachrichten*, April 21, 2007.
5. Marquardt, "Oliver Stone;" Ruppel, "Tom Cruise;" Erling, "Olympische Spiele 2008."
6. The ZDF division of contemporary history has perfected the use of pseudo-eyewitnesses to present viewers with faces and names (ideally well-known names) when discussing events for which no living witnesses exist. The three-part documentary series *Stalin* from 2003 is a great example for the extensive use of pseudo-eyewitnesses: *Stalin 1: Der Mythos*, ZDF, March 4, 2003, 20:15; *Stalin 2: Der Kriegsherr*, March 11, 2003, 20:15; *Stalin 3: Der Tyrann*, March 18, 2003, 20:15).
7. *Hitlers nützliche Idole: Leni Riefenstahl*, ZDF, March 20, 2007.
8. *Hitlers nützliche Idole: Leni Riefenstahl*. The other two programs in the series dealt with Heinz Rühmann and Max Schmeling and were broadcast on March 6 and 13, 2007, respectively.
9. The new documentary television occasionally dealt with the experiences of the victims of the regime and thus extended the inquiry into the history of Nazi persecution that had been the subject of many prime-time movies and TV plays, especially after the invention of Holocaust memory in the late 1970s. Knopp's most prominent Holocaust program was *Holokaust*, ZDF, October 17, 24, 31, and November 7 and 14, 2000. But much more frequently, the ZDF team entertained the children and grandchildren of the Nazi generation by exploring the lives of the Nazi leaders and presenting the Third Reich as a criminal and dangerous but also very exciting place.
10. The extraordinary string of Knopp programs that followed upon the pathbreaking *Der verdammte Krieg* from 1991 is discussed in some detail in Wulf Kansteiner, *In Pursuit of German Memory: History, Television, and Politics After Auschwitz* (Athens, OH: Ohio University Press, 2006), 154–180; and Kansteiner, "Keine Macht den Zeugen!: Zeitzeugenschaft und Vergangenheitspolitik in den Geschichtsdokumentationen der Ära Knopp," 46. Deutscher Historikertag, University of Konstanz, Germany, September 19–22, 2006.
11. The topic of Leni Riefenstahl also offers few opportunities to explore German suffering during World War II, which has become the latest self-serving turn in the endless

annals of *Vergangenheitsbewältigung*, see William Niven (ed.), *Germans as Victims: Remembering the Past in Contemporary Germany* (New York: Palgrave, 2006).

12. Trimborn's is probably the best German-language biography currently available on Riefenstahl, and Kinkel has also carefully researched Riefenstahl's career during National Socialism; Jürgen Trimborn, *Riefenstahl: Eine deutsche Karriere* (Berlin: Aufbau, 2003); Lutz Kinkel, *Die Scheinwerferin: Leni Riefenstahl und das "Dritte Reich"* (Hamburg: Europa Verlag, 2002).
13. *Hitlers nützliche Idole: Leni Riefenstahl.*
14. Compare Schlöndorff's remarks to the more convincing comparative explorations of geometry as a register of cultural identity in Frauke Göttsche, *Geometrie im Film: Fritz Langs "Dr. Mabuse, der Spieler" und Leni Riefenstahl's "Triumph des Willens"* (Münster: Lit, 2003). Göttsche illustrates how Hitler is constructed as the authoritarian center of *Triumph of the Will* and embedded in an invented, seemingly linear Nazi tradition, Göttsche, *Geometrie*, 146–148.
15. *Hitlers Frauen: Leni Riefenstahl*, ZDF, May 23, 2001. Judging by the book that accompanied the series, the 2001 Knopp documentary about Riefenstahl followed the same strategy as the 2007 production, combining sexual innuendo with a critical and relatively accurate assessment of Riefenstahl's career during the Nazi period. See for example Knopp, *Hitlers Frauen* (Munich: Bertelsmann, 2001), 160–162 and 201–202.
16. Knopp has always carefully and successfully avoided engaging in any public discussion about his vision of Nazism. His popularity as a TV star historian depends on the impression of objectivity.
17. Riefenstahl memory has been researched in some detail since the turn of the century, see especially the project on "Leni Riefenstahl-Rezeption nach 1945" at the Ruhr-Universität Bochum. General information on the project and many of its results can be consulted at http://www.ruhr-uni-bochum.de/riefenstahl/home.shtml and in Kerstin Gabauer, *Das Bild Leni Riefenstahls in den bundesdeutschen Printmedien*, Staatsexamenarbeit, Ruhr-Universität Bochum, 2002. See also the work of Antje Baumann, whose comparative studies show that the Riefenstahl-NS nexus persisted in the German media at least through the mid-1990s, Baumann, *Von Kopf bis Fuss auf Bilder eingestellt: Zur Darstellung von Marlene Dietrich und Leni Riefenstahl in deutschen Zeitungen von 1946 bis 2002* (Tönning: Der Andere Verlag, 2005), 5, 323.
18. The NS media reported, for example, about the production of Riefenstahl's films, the many prizes she received in Nazi Germany and abroad, and her efforts as cultural ambassador for the Third Reich; see Trimborn, *Riefenstahl*, 193, 216–217, 261, 267.
19. Riefenstahl's postwar trials and PR tribulations are summarized in Kinkel, *Die Scheinwerferin*, 265–278.
20. The most visible attacks of the postwar years were launched by the popular weekly *Revue* in the context of two of Riefenstahl's four denazification trials. In 1949, *Revue* ran an article claiming that Riefenstahl had personally visited concentration camps to select Roma and Sinti extras for her film *Tiefland*. In 1952, the same magazine claimed that Riefenstahl had witnessed a massacre of Polish civilians in Konskie in Poland during her brief career as a war reporter and was thus well informed about Nazi war crimes. Both claims were in essence accurate but the courts sided with Riefenstahl when she sued the magazine. The coverage also failed to influence the denazification proceedings. Riefenstahl was finally classified as a *Mitläufer* (fellow traveler) and faced no serious sanctions; see Rainer Rother, *Leni Riefenstahl: Die Verführung des*

Talents (Berlin: Henschel, 2000), 137–145; for the coverage of the *Revue* charges in the national press see for example "Streit: *Tiefland* mit Filmsklaven gedreht," *Der Spiegel* no. 49 (1949): 31–32; and "Prozess Leni Riefenstahl gegen *Revue*," *Abendzeitung*, March 10, 1952.

21. These revelations were based on the alleged diary of Eva Braun that Luis Trenker published in France, the U.K., and Germany in 1948. It was quickly revealed as a forgery and pulled out of circulation after Riefenstahl sued but the stories had nevertheless been widely circulated; Kinkel, *Die Scheinwerferin*, 266.
22. On Speer's own problems with the truth and his elegant and efficient self-promotion see for example Joachim Fest, *Speer: The Final Verdict* (New York: Harcourt, 2002).
23. That Riefenstahl was treated differently from her male colleagues in the film business becomes obvious when her case is compared to that of Veit Harlan, the director of *Jud Süss*, see Rother, *Riefenstahl*, 134–137.
24. Trimborn, *Riefenstahl*, 419; Bach, *Leni*, 349–351; Kinkel, *Die Scheinwerferin*, 279.
25. http://www.ruhr-uni-bochum.de/riefenstahl/n_zeitleiste_alle.shtml (accessed January 21, 2008).
26. Riefenstahl initially had problems finding publishing venues for her Nuba photography. The first of her Nuba photos appeared in 1964, but they only attracted considerable attention when they were featured in the *Sunday Times Magazine* and *Stern* in 1967 and 1969 respectively; see Bach, *Leni*, 266. Riefenstahl published her first volume of Nuba photography in 1973, Riefenstahl, *Die Nuba: Menschen wie von einem anderen Stern* (Munich: List, 1973).
27. See for example Herman Weigel, "Interview mit Leni Riefenstahl," *Filmkritik* 16 (1972): 395–410; and Gordon Hitchens, "Leni Riefenstahl interviewed by G. Hitchens," *Film Culture* 56–57 (1971): 94–121. The conscious effort to focus on Riefenstahl's films and avoid her personal history and the political context of her work also informs Renata Berg-Plan's *Leni Riefenstahl* (Boston: Twayne, 1980) and the particularly successful study by David Hinton, *The Films of Leni Riefenstahl* (Metuchen, NJ: Scarecrow Press, 1978, 3rd ed. 2000).
28. Riefenstahl was a guest of honor at the Colorado Film Festival in 1973 and, in the same year, literally became a poster girl for the 1973 New York Film Festival because she was featured on the festival's PR material together with Agnes Varda and Shirley Clarke. A similarly apologetic, feminist interpretation of Riefenstahl's work and persona was adopted in Germany in the 1980s and 1990s by the filmmaker Helma Sanders-Brahms and Alice Schwarzer; see Kinkel, *Die Scheinwerferin*, 282–283.
29. See Charles Ford, *Leni Riefenstahl* (Paris: La table ronde, 1978); and more critical of Riefenstahl, Glenn Infield, *Leni Riefenstahl: The Fallen Film Goddess* (New York: Crowell, 1976), 233–234.
30. Susan Sontag, "Fascinating Fascism," *New York Review of Books*, February 6, 1975; and Sontag, *Under the Sign of Saturn* (New York: Anchor, 1980).
31. In this respect, the scholarly Riefenstahl discourse reflects general trends of the 1970s. At the time, many forms of cultural and institutional memory emphasized professional, seemingly objective, and sometimes overly theoretical strategies of dealing with the NS past; see Wulf Kansteiner, "Losing the War, Winning the Memory Battle: The Legacy of Nazism, World War II, and the Holocaust in the Federal Republic of Germany," Ned Lebow, Wulf Kansteiner, Claudio Fogu, eds., *The Politics of Memory in Postwar Europe* (Durham, NC: Duke University Press, 2006), 102–146, 135–136.

32. http://www.ruhr-uni-bochum.de/riefenstahl/n_zeitleiste_alle.shtml; and Baumann, *Von Kopf bis Fuss,* 161–162; and see the following representative texts: Michael Graeter, "Glanzvolle Party für die Altfilmerin und Jung-Fotografin," *Abendzeitung*, August 24, 1977; Michael Schwarze, "Verführungen: Leni Riefenstahl wird 80," *Frankfurter Allgemeine Zeitung*, August 21, 1982; and "Das erfolgssüchtige Stehauf-Frauchen ist 85," *Süddeutsche Zeitung,* August 24, 1987.
33. Leni Riefenstahl, *Memoiren* (Munich: Knaus, 1987).
34. Trimborn, *Riefenstahl*, 499–495; http://www.ruhr-uni-bochum.de/riefenstahl/n_ausstellungen.shtml.
35. See for example Brigitte Fleischer, "'Ich habe nur sehr nette Nachbarn': Interview mit Leni Riefenstahl zu deren 95. Geburtstag," in *Süddeutsche Zeitung,* August 21, 1997; and Jörn Rohwer, "Wieviele Leben haben Sie gelebt, Frau Riefenstahl? Ein Gespräch," *Zeitmagazin,* August 29, 1997.
36. For a thorough contextualization and assessment of Riefenstahl's memoirs, see Kinkel, *Die Scheinwerferin,* 290–306; see also the reviews of the memoirs by Erwin Leiser, "Die Kunst des Verdrängens," *Israelitisches Wochenblatt für die Schweiz,* June 19, 1987; and Margarete Mitscherlich, "Triumph der Verdrängung," *Stern,* October 8, 1987.
37. Trimborn, *Riefenstahl,* 336–339. Riefenstahl maintained a very ambivalent relationship to the postwar media. She relied on newspapers and television to reflect her inflated sense of self-worth. At the same time, she was obsessed with controlling her public image by insisting on screening all material before publication. For the same reason she refused to appear on live television after a her frustrating appearance on the talk show of Hans-Jürgen Rosenbauer in 1976; see Rother, *Riefenstahl,* 177–180.
38. Trimborn, *Riefenstahl;* Rother, *Riefenstahl*; Kinkel, *Die Scheinwerferin*; Bach, *Leni.*
39. Johannes Wilms, "Ein weibliches Monster," *Süddeutsche Zeitung,* July 2, 2007.
40. *GFK - Fernsehforschung Nürnberg,* March 27 and April 3, 1994.
41. The latest release of *Die Macht der Bilder* occurred in June 2006 when Arthouse finally offered German consumers a DVD with Riefenstahl films about the 1936 Olympic Games in Berlin (*Fest der Völker* and *Fest der Schönheit*). Apparently, the distributors did not want to expose viewers completely unprotected to Riefenstahl's visual charms and included Müller's documentary in the package as a form of ideological prophylaxis; see "Zitiert, kopiert, parodiert: Leni Riefenstahls 'Olympia-Dokumentation' auf DVD," *Kölner Stadt-Anzeiger,* July 10, 2006.
42. Bach, *Leni,* 290. Rother, "Leni Riefenstahl wird heute 98 Jahre alt," *Der Tagespiegel,* August 22, 2000. All Riefenstahl biographies published in the last years refer extensively to Müller's film. In addition, the exceptional status of *The Wonderful, Horrible Life* in the collective memory of media professionals is nicely confirmed by the reviewers of *Hitlers nützliche Idole.* The few critics who still bothered to review Knopp's documentary in 2007 had nothing new to say about Knopp or Riefenstahl yet explicitly based their critique on Müller's documentary. By including an intertextual reference to a thirteen-year-old nonfiction film, a very unusual rhetorical gesture for a newspaper review of a TV program, the reviewers clearly indicated that they considered *A Wonderful, Horrible Life* a canonical text.
43. On occasion, Müller has also written and directed television plays including *Der unsichtbare Freund,* based on a text by Stanislaw Lem (Südwestdeutscher Rundfunk, November 16, 1992) and *Tödliche Dienstreise,* a murder mystery set in North Africa (ARD, January 24, 1996).

44. Müller's documentaries featuring Australia include *Maulwürfe des Glücks, Cowboys der Luft* (1982) and *Abenteuer und Legenden: Mit dem Big Mack durch Westaustralien* (1994), dealing respectively with opal mining, helimustering (herding animals by helicopter), and trucking culture. His nonfiction programs about Latin America address, for example, myth and reality of the lives of the gauchos (*Gauchos,* Bayrischer Rundfunk, March 12, 2005) and the inhumane working conditions of miners in Bolivia (*Mineros*). Müller's programs on Africa include *Wüste Wege: Ein Saharatrip* (Bayrischer Rundfunk, April 30, 1988); *Safari: Abenteuer in Afrika* (ZDF, August 15, 1999); and *Von Egglham nach Tanzania* (Bayrischer Rundfunk, December 27, 2003). Sometimes Müller accepted projects that did not take him to illustrious locales, for instance, *Das Wagnis mit der Phantasie* (1981, dealing with new architectural trends in the U.S.); and *Die Alpen 4: Gegensätze—Vom Mittelmeer zum Mont Blanc* (ORF2, January 15, 1993).
45. In 2007, Müller published a historical novel about a young German couple in Africa before World War I, which, according to Müller's publisher, is based on the authentic story of Müller's ancestors in Africa; see Ray Müller, *Im Herz der schwarzen Sonne* (Munich: Langen Müller, 2007).
46. *Höllenfahrten: Notlandung in der Krokodilsbucht* (ZDF, 1999); *Höllenfahrten: SOS im Polarmeer* (ZDF, March 14, 1999); and *Sphinx: Ludwig II—Tod des Märchenkönigs* (ZDF, January 9, 2005). The first two programs have been frequently rebroadcast on the public TV cable channel Phönix.
47. Bach, *Leni,* 287; see also Trimborn, *Riefenstahl,* 495.
48. This voyeuristic effect might even be stronger in *The Wonderful, Horrible Life* than in *Die Macht der Bilder* because the commentary in the English-language version of the film is spoken by a female voice.
49. Trimborn, *Riefenstahl,* 119–122.
50. Here is the German original: "Da später für die Dreharbeiten auch in Bayern spanische Komparsen benötigt werden, lässt die Produktion über das Arbeitsamt Zigeuner holen. Sie kommen aus dem Lager Leopoldskron bei Salzburg. Das Engagement dieser Leute zu einer Zeit als alle Nichtarier bereits brutal verfolgt wurden hat man der Regisseurin immer wieder erbittert vorgeworfen. Bis in jüngste Zeit kam es darüber zu Prozessen" (2:08).
51. Later in the documentary, Riefenstahl gives examples for particularly outrageous accusations she has been subjected to, including the claim that she was Hitler's mistress and personally selected gypsies in a camp (2:26). Again, Müller does not intervene in any way. For a critical review of the available documentation about Riefenstahl's use of slave labor, see Kinkel, *Die Scheinwerferin,* 230–232.
52. Bach, *Leni,* 187–192; Trimborn, *Riefenstahl,* 295–300.
53. Kinkel, *Die Scheinwerferin,* 246.
54. Trimborn, *Riefenstahl,* 207–208, 325.
55. Goebbels is hardly always a reliable source, but since he intended his diary for publication it is unlikely that he would simply invent meetings with public figures like Riefenstahl.
56. The German original runs as follows: "Wer sagt die Wahrheit? Der Propagandaminister oder die Regisseurin? Es gibt viele sich widersprechende Aussagen" and "Goebbels war ja ein Meister der Lüge" (53:00–54:00).
57. Bach, *Leni,* 108–111; Kinkel, *Die Scheinwerferin,* 184–186, 189–195.

58. The language in *The Wonderful, Horrible Life* concerning Riefenstahl's alleged personal intervention is very vague. Riefenstahl only says that she raised "the topic" and that Hitler was absolutely unwilling to talk about "it" with her. Müller combines her statements with footage of the April 1 boycott, but in the same context Riefenstahl also regretfully mentions the emigration of some of her friends and disapprovingly refers to the Nazi book-burning campaign (which she claims not to have heard anything about when it happened because she was on location in Switzerland and "television did not yet exist" [48:00]). It is not clear from the testimony what topic she precisely raised with the Führer.
59. Riefenstahl claims that she lost faith in Hitler when he mobilized the Volkssturm and refused to visit the burnt-out German cities (2:20). Neither decision sheds a positive light on the Führer but both pale in comparison to his previous crimes. Perhaps Riefenstahl felt less enthusiastic about Hitler when she realized that her extraordinarily privileged position as a filmmaker was rapidly coming to an end.
60. The German original: "mit dieser entsetzlichen Belastung und Schuld, die auf uns jetzt ruhte, zu leben oder zu sterben. Es war eine ständiger Kampf: Leben oder Sterben" (2:23).
61. "Diesen Kampf hatten in Europa bis dahin bereits 60 Millionen verloren" (2:23).
62. Bach, *Leni*, 215–216.
63. Riefenstahl's biographers believe that Riefenstahl refuses to talk about the people she saved because her humanitarian interventions call into question her image as an apolitical artist without knowledge of Nazi persecution; see for example Trimborn, *Riefenstahl*, 373–376.
64. Bach, *Leni*, 288.
65. Riefenstahl has repeatedly been able to make such deals, for instance on the occasion of the exhibit of her work in the Filmmuseum Potsdam in 1998–1999, because her archives contain by far the best material, especially visual material, on the topic Riefenstahl.
66. Michael Althen from the *FAZ*, who thought he noticed Müller's discomfort, was also convinced that Müller had to leave it up to the viewers to come to terms with his and possibly also their own feelings of moral unease because Riefenstahl simply gave him no other choice, Althen, "Katastrophe des Willens," *Frankfurter Allgemeine Zeitung*, September 11, 2003.
67. In the PR material that ZDF distributed to TV guides prior to the screening of *Die Macht der Bilder*, Müller refers to the film as the psychologically most demanding project he has ever undertaken; see *ZDF Programm* no. 13 (1994), 53.
68. Maurice Tszorf, "Wider das Vergessen," *Der Tagesspiegel*, July 17, 1994.
69. "Portrait einer Frau mit Vergangenheit," *Focus*, October 4, 1993.
70. See Müller's long report about the trip "Der Besuch der alten Dame," *Stern*, March 30, 2000.
71. "Avantgardistisch. Propagandistisch. Uneinsichtig," *Der Tagesspiegel*, August 22, 2002. Müller's assessment of his relationship to Riefenstahl seems a little strange considering that she had lived with Horst Kettner since the late 1960s; Asch, *Leni*, 265; see also Müller's dismissive statement about Kettner cited in Trimborn, *Riefenstahl*, 465.
72. In essence, the film is a perfect, albeit inadvertent, illustration of what I would call the Christopher Browning axiom of Nazi history: Faced with the same pressures and temptations experienced by the citizens of the Third Reich, we would act like the citizens of the Third Reich and, with few exceptions, thrive under the dictatorship and

show little regard for its victims: see Christopher Browning, *Ordinary Men: Reserve Police Battalion 101 and the Final Solution in Poland* (New York: Aaron Asher, 1992).
73. Jimmy Fowler, "A Brilliant Life in Compromised Art," *Dallas Observer*, February 16, 1995.
74. Frederic Biddle, "Turning the Camera on the Irredeemable Leni Riefenstahl," *Boston Globe*, July 5, 1995.
75. David Hunter, "Leni Riefenstahl,"*Hollywood Reporter*, April 14, 1994.
76. Walter Goodman, "Too Brilliant for the World's Good," *New York Times*, July 5, 1995.
77. Matt Rosh, "The Whole Picture of Paradox," *USA Today*, July 5, 1995.
78. Norman Wilner, "Wonderful, Horrible Riefenstahl," *Toronto Star*, April 1, 1995.
79. Hunter, "Riefenstahl."
80. Brian Johnson, "Hitler's Director," *Maclean's*, April 18, 1994.
81. Fowler, "A Brilliant Life."
82. Leni Riefenstahl, *Leni Riefenstahl: A Memoir* (New York: St. Martin's Press, 1993).
83. See for example Claudia Lenssen, "Die Mutter aller Sportschuhtester," *Der Tagesspiegel*, December 13, 1993; Rita Mohr, "Führers Filmerin," *Der Tagesspiegel*, March 27, 1994; and Wilfried Wiegand, "Kein Bündnis mit der Wahrheit, *FAZ*, October 19, 1993.
84. The range of critical voices after the film's initial release is nicely illustrated by the measured critique by Stefan Reinicke, "In Augenhöhe," *Süddeutsche Zeitung*, October 7, 1993; and the pronounced criticism by Mariam Niroumand, "Nazis mit Sexappeal im Dokumentarfilm und anderswo," *die tageszeitung*, December 30, 1993.
85. Thomas Klingenmaier, "Leni Riefenstahl: Triumph des Starrsinns," *Stuttgarter Zeitung*, March 24, 1994.
86. Of the eighteen reviews collected in the archives of ZDF, five emphasized Müller's accomplishments, five found the program wanting, especially on ethical grounds, and the rest either offered no assessment or identified minor points of criticism or praise. For representative texts see "Die Macht der Bilder," *Münchner Merkur*, March 28, 1994; "Der Faszination erlegen," *Badische Neueste Nachrichten*, March 30, 1994; and "Beschreibung des Phänomens," *Südkurier*, April 5, 1994.
87. Only very few callers thanked ZDF for what they considered an excellent report on the brilliant filmmaker Riefenstahl and a welcome corrective to the overly critical reports on the Nazi era that dominated in the German media; for the few positive as well as the many more negative assessments of the program, see the confidential phone logs for the evenings of March 27 and April 3, 1994, assembled by the members of ZDF division for public relations, Kurt Hammers, Ingrid Claus, Hans-J. Steinmetz, and Dieter Beilstein.
88. Ulrich Greiner, "Hitlers List," *Die Zeit*, April 8, 1994.
89. *Kulturreport*, ARD, March 27, 1994; see also the criticism of the ARD position in this unusual public skirmish between ARD and ZDF by Birgit Weidinger, "Die Macht ihrer Bilder: Wie die ARD auf Ray Müllers Riefenstahl-Film reagierte," *Süddeutsche Zeitung*, April 9, 1994; and Dieter Borkowski, "Fasziniert von der macht der Diktatur," *TM*, May 2, 1994.
90. Only Christian Schütze of the *Süddeutsche Zeitung* noted the Emmy in his review: Schütze, "Triumph ihres Willens," *Süddeutsche Zeitung*, March 29 1994.
91. One of the exceptions is the already mentioned piece by Ulrich Greiner in *Die Zeit* entitled "Hitler's List"(April 8, 1994), although he also does not develop any systematic comparisons in his short text.

Chapter 6

Reading Rammstein, Remembering Riefenstahl: "Fascist Aesthetics" and German Popular Culture

Valerie Weinstein

"Rammstein *sucks.* Everyone knows it. And it is linked to the aesthetically clueless and historically insane Leni Riefenstahl revivals in videos, Nike ads, or symposia and retrospectives in Potsdam."[1]—Diedrich Diederichsen, *Süddeutsche Zeitung,* May 12, 1999

I. Rammstein—Riefenstahl—Reception

In the 1990s and the early years of the new millennium, Leni Riefenstahl received significant media exposure.[2] In 1993, Ray Müller released the documentary *The Wonderful, Horrible Life of Leni Riefenstahl* (*Die Macht der Bilder*). Three additional biographical Riefenstahl films went into the planning stages in the decade that followed.[3] In 1996, the conservative publisher Verlag und Agentur Werner Symanek compiled a tribute to Riefenstahl in the form of two music CDs.[4] In 1998, the Filmmuseum Potsdam organized the first exhibit in Germany devoted solely to Riefenstahl's work and life.[5] Symposia, film screenings, and a comprehensive catalogue accompanied the show.[6] Riefenstahl's photographic work was also on view in commercial galleries in Hamburg in 1997 and in Berlin in 2000, and her final film, *Impressions under Water (Impressionen unter Wasser),* was released in 2002.[7] For many young Germans, however, exposure to Riefenstahl's images at the end of the twentieth century came via Rammstein, Germany's most internationally successful rock band. Its 1998 recording of "Stripped" reached number nineteen on the German singles charts in part because of the popularity of its music video, largely a montage of footage from Riefenstahl's *Olympia*. Another video, "Links 2-3-4," followed, this time featuring references to *Triumph of the Will.*

Rammstein's recourse to Riefenstahl and her films was the source of controversy in contemporary German culture at the time.[8] In the Berlin newspaper *die tageszeitung* (*taz*) Daniel Bax concluded: "Rammstein is to blame for the fact that you can buy Leni Riefenstahl picture books and calendars in every department store."[9] His accusation was part of a larger media reaction that heard and saw right-wing tendencies in Rammstein's music and videos, and that clearly still viewed Riefenstahl as a prototype and a representative of a nebulous and perhaps nonextant "fascist aesthetics." The stigma associated with this label affected what and how Riefenstahl's images signified for a German public. Indeed, the debates surrounding "Stripped" and the later "Links 2-3-4" that I will explore in this essay indicate that "Riefenstahl" functioned as a static political symbol in the late twentieth century while simultaneously undergoing intriguing adaptations in new artistic and cultural contexts.[10] Through a close reading of Rammstein's videos, I will show that the recycling of Riefenstahl's images produced meanings that exceed a simple reproduction of fascist fantasies, as the press contended at the time. In short, while the video "Stripped" does indeed express a desire to escape civilization, its focus is not the promotion of a right-wing ideology. Instead, critics missed the fact that the video exposes an uncomfortable closeness between contemporary pop culture and aspects of Riefenstahl's work that have been associated with fascism. The video "Links 2-3-4," which reacted to the accusations of neofascism that resulted from Rammstein's citation of Riefenstahl in "Stripped," appears to appropriate images for the contemporary political left that were previously assigned to the right. However, the juxtaposition of image and lyrics in the video significantly shifts and drains meaning from the original source. With "Stripped" and "Links 2-3-4," then, Rammstein does more than shock the public, sell records, and render Riefenstahl *salonfähig*; the band uses her work to comment on contemporary culture. In the process, the videos underscore Riefenstahl's vexed though established position in German popular culture at the turn of the millennium.

Rammstein's use of Riefenstahl's footage and the press reaction to it is best understood in the context of the band's background and reception. The rock group is composed of six men, all born in the German Democratic Republic between 1964 and 1971. They came together in the early 1990s to produce a popular sound that layers distinctive German vocals, heavy metal rhythms, and techno motifs with electronic, industrial, and Gothic influences. Rammstein sells its sound with provocative macho and militaristic images. This is the combination that pioneered a musical and marketing trend known as the *Neue Deutsche Härte* (New German Hard Rock). Rammstein has cut multiple platinum albums, earned numerous music industry awards and nominations, and, as of 2005, sold over ten million records worldwide.[11] Particularly as part of the ongoing debate on the politics of the *Neue Deutsche Härte*, Rammstein is often at the center of controversy. That fact also has to do with the group's deployment of what are perceived as "fascist aesthetics."

Such assessments of Rammstein's sound and style are common in the German media. In 1999, the Munich *Süddeutsche Zeitung* described Rammstein as the most prominent of "a series of German bands that trample away so Teutonically, as if they wanted to show that they never have had trouble with their German identity."[12] The newspaper noted further that a kind of "Walser debate" had coalesced around the group as part of the perception that Rammstein had trivialized Germany's past. Many music and culture critics see Rammstein's "Teutonic trampling" as somehow "fascistoid." That view is often drawn from particular characteristics of the band itself. These include lead singer Till Lindemann's guttural German and much commented upon rolling R's, his muscular physique, and the entire band's hypermasculine, aggressive, at times paramilitary, posturing.[13] The band's spectacular stage shows, designed by Gert Hof, contribute to this impression. Hof has been described as the male version of Riefenstahl, and his lighting design, known for its excess, provocation, and spectacular pyrotechnics, has been compared to the work of Albert Speer.[14] Culture critic Daniel Bartetzko summarized these aspects of the group's performances in the *Frankfurter Rundschau*: "[Rammstein's] show brings together everything that is in any way militaristic: flames and fireworks, 'Storm of Steel' and stormy seas. Between Leni Riefenstahl and *Blade Runner*, the impressions fall all over each other, but they can be reduced to the formula: sex and violence."[15] Even Rammstein's sound has been understood as reactionary. Hubert Mayer of the right-wing *Deutsche Stimme* notes that many Rammstein fans speak of a "Storm of Steel" sound, a reference to Ernst Jünger's reactionary *Meisterwerk*, which would also explain Rammstein's cult status in the right-wing youth movement.[16] Right-wing youth, however, are only part of Rammstein's broad fan base, and the group treats this cohort as inconsequential no matter the extent to which that fact disturbs the band's critics.[17]

These media reactions attest to the fact that Rammstein's flirtations with images from the Nazi period have led both to its becoming "Germany's most demonized band" and its commercial success.[18] Aram Lintzel concludes that Rammstein's "offensive and blatant references to the darkest German traditions" have a commercial motive, because for German bands success in the international music market requires that musicians exploit their German "difference" instead of copying existing international styles. For Rammstein, this marketing of its so-called Germanness produces a caricature of the "ugly German" that frequently crosses the boundaries of political correctness and good taste.[19] The views and reviews on Rammstein's style and image were summarized in the newsmagazine *Focus* as falling into four distinct takes on the music. These are positions held by the German press as well: Some think Rammstein's music is "merely harmless shock rock." Others consider it a "fascinating new development in [musical] style." Some listeners claim that the music is "artistically lacking," but that its provocations are allowable because they work against the "politically correct social worker rock" and the culture of the left-liberal bourgeoisie. Of course, this view implies that the German musical marketplace has become so saturated with unreflective, politically correct sentiment that the offensive gestures of the *Neue Deutsche Härte* function to shake up the status quo, which ignores the presence of other right-wing popular sounds such as Oi music or the Böhse Onkelz. Finally, some critics of Rammstein "hear the brown battalions marching or see, at a minimum, an irresponsible game with fascist aesthetics," as *Focus* magazine put it. In other words, critics believe that recalling a historically fascist look or sound has the potential to inspire contemporary neofascists.[20] These differing views of Rammstein's aesthetic are—in my view—all exaggerated and lacking in nuance, and so deeply entrenched as to be unshakable. This multilateral intransigence leads to the periodic reemergence of the same debates whenever Rammstein provokes the public anew. Frequent, yet insubstantial, protestations by the band members that their work is apolitical do little to silence critics. In fact, while such protests allow Rammstein to profit from its own notoriety, they do little to shed light on the significance of the band's style for an understanding of fascism or neofascism. The close readings of the videos that follow will locate more substantial and sustained engagement with the problems of so-called "fascist aesthetics" and their implications in late twentieth-century Germany in Rammstein's work.

II. "Stripped"

Rammstein drew the most and the harshest accusations of promoting neofascism when the band set Leni Riefenstahl's images to its music in the video "Stripped." For Rammstein, footage from *Olympia* served an important commercial function. One of the group's few English-language songs, "Stripped" is a cover of a 1986 number by the popular British New Wave band Depeche Mode. Rammstein recorded "Stripped" for the album *For the Masses* (1998), a compilation of Depeche Mode cover songs by various artists that was intended as a tribute to the British band. The single did not do particularly well before the production of the Rammstein video.[21] Designer Gert Hof decided to borrow footage from Riefenstahl's *Olympia* to sell the borrowed Depeche Mode song.[22] The use of Riefenstahl's footage was the latest example of the shock tactics and references to Nazism that had helped Rammstein to prominence. Such tactics capitalized on the band's commercially motivated penchant for scandal, and indeed, the press and cultural elite reacted strongly to the song and video. Typically, the band members claimed naiveté in regard to the video's political implications.[23]

The controversy around the "Stripped" video stems in part from widespread treatment of Riefenstahl's work in the context of fascism. In the seminal essay "Fascinating Fascism," Susan Sontag defined Riefenstahl as the best and, indeed, only definitive example of "fascist aesthetics," whose attributes include a glorification of the primitive, themes of domination and submission, the objectification and spectacularization of the masses, and the glamorization of death.[24] Expanding on Sontag's assertions, Georg Seesslen sees Riefenstahl as having abstracted these elements to such an extreme and removed them so far from their referent that her work is more fascist than fascism itself.[25] The link between Riefenstahl and "fascist aesthetics" is widespread in the popular press as well. Dirk Kurbjuweit's characterization of the two-part *Olympia* as a "major work of fascist aesthetics" is typical.[26] Regardless of the meanings of the slippery term "fascist aesthetics"—its self-referentiality, synonymity with "Riefenstahl," the political stigma it bears, and its interpretive limits—the term is prevalent in the discussions surrounding Rammstein. In fact, the band's citations of Riefenstahl are treated as "fascist" by definition.

There are some problems with these connections both in terms of the specific appropriation of Riefenstahl's images in this video and in terms of how "fascist" images have been used in pop culture more generally. The popular reception of the video for "Stripped" does not question Riefenstahl's auteurship of the opening sequences of the film or their presumed inherent "fascism." These assumptions are made despite the fact that Willy Zielke, not Riefenstahl, took the photographs of the "classical" nudes that begin the prologue to *Olympia*, which are used in the Rammstein video.[27] Of course, as is typical in music video production, the Riefenstahl footage was re-edited in this case to highlight dominant musical features of Rammstein's recording, a process that inevitably changes the meaning of the original images. Moreover, seen in the larger context of rock music, Rammstein's citation of Riefenstahl might not be so problematic. A number of music critics have claimed that other bands—the Sex Pistols, the New York Dolls, New Order, Kraftwerk, and Laibach, for example—have cited "fascist" imagery in a critical way.[28]

However, the case of Rammstein is different, at least in terms of its reception, because the music press found no critical potential in the group's appropriation of Riefenstahl. Critics like Wolf-Rüdiger Mühlmann describe Rammstein's appropriation of such iconography as egregious. He sees no thematic connection between the lyrics and Riefenstahl's images. Their use is, he claims, nothing more than the inspiration for extended debate and increased international sales.[29] Martin Büsser categorizes Rammstein's recourse to Riefenstahl as unambivalent and unproblematized, because it decontextualizes fascist images by removing obvious signs of Nazism (Hitler, the swastika). It fails to give these markers a new, apparently ambivalent context. He finds no irony in Rammstein's productions—they are merely empty, commercial products that trivialize Nazi art and provoke violence among right-wing youth.[30] Ulf Poschardt maintains that the members of Rammstein, because they are not intellectuals, lack the necessary control over their image and their images.[31] Predictably, the right-wing youth magazine *Sigill* praises Rammstein's video as "a symphony for eye and ear" that belongs to a "conservative cultural avant-garde."[32] Despite these differing impressions, the German press argued polemically that Riefenstahl was still an incendiary, polarizing figure who remained an emblem of the political right even in the contemporary setting.

As we can see, Rammstein's citation of Riefenstahl provoked a counterreaction, but not a critical engagement with the video itself. A closer analysis of the video, however, reveals that the juxtaposition of lyrics, music, and Riefenstahl images signifies in complex ways not acknowledged by its detractors and not readily apparent on the surface level of the images. The video lacks neither reflective meaning nor irony. However transparent and escapist its messages, "Stripped" is more than a simpleminded reproduction of Riefenstahl. The manner in which Rammstein modifies Depeche Mode's music and lyrics (originally composed and written by Martin Gore) and juxtaposes them with the re-edited Riefenstahl footage is evidence that "Stripped" does, in fact, have critical potential. It reproduces an antimodern desire to escape society as well as the ideological manipulations of the media. The video suggests that these influences, coupled with a desire to escape them, constitute a paradigm that was historically valid in Nazi Germany, but that also still applies in the context of contemporary, Anglo-American–dominated popular culture. Thus, the video draws uncomfortable parallels between Riefenstahl's "fascist" visions of the body—her antimodernist escapism—and the values of our contemporary media culture.

Specifically, in "Stripped" Rammstein expresses a desire to know a loved one in a manner that is unencumbered by the physical and ideological pollution of modern metropolitan life. Using the second person narrative voice, the vocalist (Lindemann) invites an unknown addressee into nature, repeatedly asking to see "you stripped." Addressing the listener as a beloved, he tells the "you" that he wants to see "you" naked and freed from the constraints of civilization. This undressing is construed as both a physical and a mental escape: The singer wants to leave the city and return to the "land," and to "see you make decisions without your television." His direct address to the listener invites "you" to join him and share his sexualized, escapist fantasy. In the original Depeche Mode song, in contrast, escape from civilization amounts to a stripping of flesh that renders the beloved wounded and vulnerable. It wants to "see you stripped down to the bone" and to "see you crying just for me." Rammstein, although known for violent imagery and lyrics, diminishes the threatening nature of Depeche Mode's escapist fantasy, emphasizing instead a more positively construed desire to see the human body in a supposedly natural state. The original lyrics are replaced with the simple "let me see you stripped." The vocalist wants to see a body that is physically and purportedly ideologically pure: When kissed, its breath would no longer taste of "fumes," and its thought and speech would be liberated from television and from all expectations except those of the singer. In the music video, Riefenstahl's strong and beautiful bodies, taken from *Olympia*, represent this new body as it is now envisioned by Rammstein.

The editing of shots from *Olympia* into and within "Stripped" implies that getting away from civilization leads to physical and spiritual rejuvenation. A montage of Greek ruins from the opening sequences of *Olympia* mentioned above—images of a dead civilization—accompanies the first two verses of "Stripped." In the first chorus, as Lindemann asks to see "you stripped," a frozen discus thrower replaces the statues. He then begins to move, emerging as a toned, live athlete freed from the marble (figure 1). Rapid cuts and the addition of an electric guitar to the rhythm follow, thus accentuating the excitement and the movement of the athlete. Other athletes and dancers join him and then take his place. The video suggests that abandoning civilization and its artifacts results in exuberance, strength, and beauty. In the second use of the chorus ("let me see you stripped") an image of the Olympic flame dissolves to a double exposure of the flame over the man lighting it, followed by a cut to the man carrying away the lighted torch. His control of the flames seems to be reborn out of the fire that previously consumed the screen. The beautiful body and the burning body—an overlap of "pure" Riefenstahl and "pure" Rammstein images—suggest fascist themes of physical perfection, self-sacrifice, and death.[33]

Figure 1

Thus, while Rammstein's insertion of Riefenstahl's footage renders visible the desires expressed in "Stripped," it also implies a link to fascist (Nazi) desires of the kind Seesslen locates in the kinship between pop and Riefenstahl's "aesthetic."[34] My reading of "Stripped" intends to show how Rammstein's references to Riefenstahl corroborate this critical point. Jan Raabe and Andreas Speit describe the glorification of Nazi ideals in Riefenstahl's images as the unification of a magical nature and heroic man in the transcendental ideal of purity and beauty.[35] They relate this move to the antimodernism shared by conservatives, reactionaries, and fascists in the early twentieth century.[36] Michael Mackenzie argues convincingly that while there may be points of intersection between Riefenstahl's aesthetics and fascist ideology, *Olympia* can in fact be read in the context of earlier conservative discourses of *Ausdruckstanz,* the discipline in which Riefenstahl began her career.[37] Seen in this context, *Olympia* adopts styles of movement and beauty that are consistent with an organic, mystical, authentic *Kultur.* These elements serve as an opposition to the mechanized, international *Zivilization* associated with modern sports.[38]

This early-twentieth-century conservative paradigm, which privileges the organic, mystical, and authentic over the mechanized and international, suits the message of "Stripped." Its glorification of the body, of the pure and primitive and the neoclassical contours of its images, which Sontag saw as components of "fascist aesthetics," reflect trends in pop that have historical roots not only in fascism but also in other conservative ideologies. Nevertheless, that lineage does not reverberate with contemporary German audiences, who connect Riefenstahl's cult of the body beautiful with fascism. Generally speaking, of course, Rammstein's arrangement fits pop culture conventions. This is so with respect to length, the predictable alternation between instrumentals, bridges, choruses, and verses, and the simple rhyme structure. In terms of style, Rammstein's singing about a flight from the civilized world and use of Riefenstahl to show how that escape liberates the strong, pure body, does appear to duplicate a presumed fascist ideology. If one looks more carefully at "Stripped," though, this supposedly fascist desire is revealed as an integral part of contemporary culture. Rammstein's lyrics experiment with the tension between structure and freedom and draw attention to an escapist desire produced by the very structure that contains it.

Like this complexity, some segments of the song seem less fettered by musical convention. Indeed, Rammstein's version of "Stripped," unlike the Depeche Mode original, begins not with clockwork but with atonal droning. Lacking in melody and strong rhythmic emphasis, Lindemann's vocals are a growl. To match this free form, initial shots in the video are open, with fluid camera movement, and organic and asymmetrical shapes. Frequent dissolves emphasize the loose structure. Initially, the desire to be stripped seems to come from outside the pop system. As the song progresses, however, its musical structure becomes more rigid and conventional. The wish articulated here is shaped by civilization. The first chorus introduces an electronic beat and is later joined by new layers of instrumentation and rhythm. The athletes' movements and the editing of the video emphasize the beat and Lindemann's vocals become more melodious, but do not fully shift from chant to song until around the fifth verse. The song's structure emerges more forcefully as its lyrics become more pointed—the desire is not simply for idyllic romance, but to escape "fumes." At the song's climax, the instrumentation is most intense. The single recurring refrain concerns how television dominates our decisions and utterances. The song becomes most musically pleasing at this point, and the electronic beat emphasized here is truly the "hook" that listeners remember.

Ironically, at the point at which Lindemann sings of the dominance of media-influenced cultural norms, "Stripped" conforms most obviously to them. Indeed, the wish to escape television becomes even more firmly imbedded in the commercial mass media of which it is a part. The electronic rhythm takes over, now accompanied by a rich layering of audio elements that include more conventional vocals. The desire to escape, then, becomes imbricated in a larger system that now receives visual support.

At the song's high point between the two repetitions of the chorus and final verse, a bridge of the electronic rhythm draws attention to the visuals, a section from Riefenstahl's footage of the rhythmic gymnastics exhibition. A field of women in identical tunics swing pins in unison at a speed that seems to have been altered to match Rammstein's beat. This image is a conspicuous, if unintended, quote of Kracauer's "mass ornament," in which mass entertainment reproduces the forms of industrial capitalism. It implies a representation of the concept that the rhythm of the mass media produces figures that all look alike. Yet the desire to strip oneself of that influence and to find the naked, pure, and free body comes from the same system. Thus, the video contains the very contradictions of mass culture—in its leveling function it creates the conditions for the wish for emancipation. The system that produces this desire is global, but it is associated most concretely with the English-speaking world. After all, the song is borrowed from a major British band. Lindemann's accent and apparent discomfort with the English he sings underscore what fans already know—that global culture is an Anglo-American culture. Directly following the climax of the song, with the women still performing in synch, Lindemann sings "let me see you stripped" as an American flag fills the screen. It then dissolves into the face of an athlete wearing a laurel wreath. The next athlete's face dissolves into the flag of Japan, a nation that shares with Germany both contemporary democracy and economic prosperity and a historical legacy of fascism and militarism. The singer wants to see these individual faces emerge from behind the flags. This move fantasizes escape from an international, capitalist culture that is dominated by the United States. It is, however, also associated—via recourse to Riefenstahl—with fascism. Particularly when placed alongside the Japanese flag, the U.S. flag, problematically, comes to stand in for the absent and taboo Nazi flag. Anglo-American culture, not German culture and the much-maligned band members themselves, becomes the representative of neofascism and a homogenization imposed by global popular culture, from which the singer, who is part of it, wants to escape.

This desire to flee from an international, mechanized civilization can be seen as reactionary, even fascist, particularly when it relies on images that have been branded with the term "fascist aesthetics." The editing of "Stripped" posits U.S.-dominated global culture as the homogenizing force from which the individual desires to escape. This may not sound so different from early-twentieth-century conservative disavowals of "Americanism," the view that American popular culture and modes of production were replacing traditional European culture and forms. Yet Rammstein, as a platinum rock band, is clearly implicated in and the beneficiary of the spread of such global culture, an irony that is unlikely to have escaped the makers of the video. Thus, I read Rammstein's ham-handed reproduction of this escapist fantasy and its use of Riefenstahl to present it not as neofascist, but as self-critical and self-conscious, precisely because of the irony and excess represented in the video. Accompanied by images that German discourse marks as "fascist," the reference to America, the expression of escapism through an English cover song whose borrowed, "foreign" nature is intensified by Lindemann's heavy accent, and the crescendo of pop structures that underscores that wish, the video's elements all locate a fascist desire in a contemporary Anglo-American–dominated pop culture. The song and lyrics construe the singer and the listener—"you"—as a part of the same system. Rather than simply selling fascism in "Stripped," Rammstein removes the veil from the connections between recognizable icons and fantasies of fascism, contemporary pop culture, and the viewers and listeners of today. Thus, the video's message was more culturally and self-critical than was acknowledged by the band's critics at the time. Their political and aesthetic judgments of Rammstein's use of Riefenstahl as a means to connect pop culture and fascism would find a retort in the band's video for the single "Links 2-3-4."

III. "Links 2-3-4"

Released in 2001, "Links 2-3-4" was seen as Rammstein's riposte to the "Stripped" scandal[39] and a declaration of leftist sympathies on the part of the group.[40] The following chorus supposedly provided evidence of that characterization: "*Sie wollen mein Herz am rechten Fleck. Doch seh ich dann nach unten weg, da schlägt es links, links 2-3-4*" ("You want my heart in the right spot. But then I look down and it beats on the left, left 2-3-4.") Many recognized this as a reference to contemporary German politics. In March 1999, Oskar Lafontaine had stepped down as head of the SPD (Social Democratic Party) and as Federal Minister of Finance with the words, "*Das Herz wird noch nicht an der Börse gehandelt, aber es hat einen Standort—es schlägt links*" ("The heart is not yet traded on the stock market. But it has a place of business: it beats on the left").[41] Lafontaine's words became the title of his book, *Das Herz schlägt links* (*The Heart Beats on the Left*). The slogan's next incarnation emerged in early 2001 as the title of Lafontaine's column in the widely read *Bild* newspaper. It appeared opposite a column by CSU (Christian Social Union) politician Peter Gauweiler entitled "*Mein Herz schlägt auf dem rechten Fleck*" ("My heart beats in the right spot").[42] By exploiting these phrases against a heavy-metal-influenced march rhythm in "Links 2-3-4," Rammstein perpetuated its hard German image at the same time as it was able to clear itself of charges of right-wing sympathies through reference to the words of an SPD politician.

This agenda received visual backing in the award-winning animated video for "Links 2-3-4" by Zoran Bihac. In the video, an ant colony fends off a hostile invasion in scenes that obviously cite Riefenstahl's *Triumph of the Will.* These overt visual references, however, are strangely absent from the German discussion of the video. That fact suggests that the citation of Lafontaine, as a more recent political-cultural memory, had trumped the citation of Riefenstahl and her infamous film. One other possible explanation is that the citation of Riefenstahl in Rammstein's video was not recognized because screenings of *Triumph of the Will* are strictly limited by German law. Rammstein's unremarked use of Riefenstahl in "Links 2-3-4," though, is of interest not only as a further example of the group's commercial use of Riefenstahl's aesthetic, but also as a nod to the filmmaker that forms a complex message about citation and reception. This message is constructed on lyric, aural, and visual levels. Indeed, with each repetition of the line, this song suggests, the meanings of the phrase are shifted or lost. This is a reminder that quotation does not equal endorsement of a political view, and it constitutes a subtle response to the noisy critique of Rammstein's adaptation of Riefenstahl's footage in "Stripped." That response proves far stronger in its impact than the primary message of the apparently direct lyric (the indirect citation of Lafontaine) that was understood as the band's declaration of leftist sympathies. Indeed, the lyrics, sounds, and imagery of "Links 2-3-4" complicate any reading of the video as simple evidence of a leftist orientation as understood in a contemporary German sense. The video's components exhibit a militarism that is, of course, rejected by the German left.

In an interview with the popular German magazine *Stern,* Rammstein drummer Christoph Schneider described "Links 2-3-4" as Rammstein's first artistic attempt to deal with the "eternal accusation" of being a right-wing band.[43] However, in the same interview he and Lindemann readily admit that their aim is to remain ambiguous in style, an approach that has to do with their past as punk rockers in the German Democratic Republic.[44] Schneider's statement implies that this East German punk experience, in which views contrary to official state ideology had to be expressed covertly, led to the band's habit of masking its beliefs in music. Therefore, as Schneider's words indicate, political viewpoints are tangled among the ambiguities in the songs.

Such is the case with "Links 2-3-4," whose contradictions reveal more about Rammstein's response to the "Stripped" controversy than does their apparent parroting of the Lafontaine quote. Accompanied by heavy metal drum, bass, and rhythm guitar, a driving 4/4 rhythm, and the sound of marching boots, the lyrics to "Links 2-3-4" are initially perplexing. Three key elements alternate: Questions are phrased in trite idioms about the heart, that ask, for example, whether hearts can be broken, or whether they can be made of stone. The refrain that cites Lafontaine returns repeatedly, and there is an ever- increasing number of military marching cadences as the song progresses ("left 2-3-4; left 2-3-4"). Both because the Lafontaine quote was so timely and because it appears to answer the perennial question about Rammstein's politics, many listeners understood the dominant message in the lyrics to be that "my heart beats on the left." However, such a surface interpretation ignores the framing of the quotation by the dominant marching cadence in the song's sound, and the repeated rhetorical questions concerning the heart in the verses, which are sung in a lyrical whisper. From this combination of themes we might conclude that Rammstein is trying to connect a leftist heart with sentimentality, militarism, and mass culture. The video's "fascist aesthetics," then, might come from the Riefenstahl-inspired visuals, which suggest that such elements are, surprisingly, not incompatible with leftist politics.

The video, of course, does represent such a position. Yet I would argue that this position is a component part of a more complex statement. In the reassignment of images and sounds to the left that are presumed to belong to the right wing, we find evidence of what I argue is the heart of Rammstein's response to the "Stripped" scandal in "Links 2-3-4," namely that citation in a new context alters the significance of a quotation substantially. The predominant cadence "left 2-3-4," for instance, commonly chanted so that soldiers march in step, begins (as it does in its military usage) on the left. This repeated "left" acquires new political meaning in its present context in the juxtaposition to the Lafontaine quote. More than merely calling out to foot soldiers to begin a march, the phrase becomes an expression shared between a social democratic heartbeat and a military, and presumably right-wing, march. As Rammstein shifts and combines the meanings of these well-known phrases, as the analysis below will show, the song uses its sentimental, rhetorical questioning to challenge whether words and citations mean what they initially seem to mean. In the process, the song problematizes the assumption that neofascist politics necessarily follow the recycling of "fascist aesthetics" in more popular forms of culture.

Figure 2

The visuals of the video highlight the military theme in the song with a clear narrative in which an army of ants repels beetle invaders. Although lyrics march left, visually the video drags the song farther back toward a kind of "fascist aesthetics." While the band chants about its leftist heartbeat, the militarism in the video assumes a pseudo-fascist look. After the invasion and the final variation on the refrain, a single ant takes a position on a high column far above the others within the cavernous anthill. Quivering, it raises its antennae in a salute that looks like an ant version of the Nazi salute. Beneath this saluting ant, the other ants respond in kind—all to the call "Links, Links." They stream out from the anthill to assume mass military formations that recall images of *Triumph of the Will.* Directed from above by the leader ant, the battalions of ants outnumber and overrun the much larger beetles during the many bars of cadence in the last minute of the song. These form shifting geometric shapes. In "Links 2-3-4" victorious mass movements conducted under the direction of a single charismatic leader illustrate the words of those whose hearts beat left.

The leader ant is not the only choreographer of the masses. Indeed, each time the refrain about the heart beating left is repeated, the ants follow a different leader. Militarism is not the only source of mass ornaments. Before the uprising, it is not the ants' military leader but mass culture that is depicted as a site of mass control: The first time the band chants "*da schlägt es links*" ("it beats on/to the left"), an ant DJ spins a Rammstein record, raising its arms in the air, leading the enthused ant "fans" below to groove to the song's marching beat. It is both this beat and the following imagery, however, that create a segue from mass culture to militarism.

Figure 3

Before the next iteration of the refrain, the ants pour into a movie palace to watch a Rammstein film. With the "*Doch*," the black-and-white film begins: Cross and sunlike symbols that are regularly used by Rammstein appear on the screen before we see Lindemann bellow, "Links." The suns evoke the black sun of the SS and the Greek cross suggests not only the swastika but also the use of similar symbols in other fictional representations of fascism in films like *The Great Dictator* (Charles Chaplin, 1940), *Pink Floyd The Wall* (Alan Parker, 1982), or *V for Vendetta* (James McTeigue, 2005). Shots of the instrumentalists and the ant spectators in the movie palace alternate with close-ups of Lindemann. The black-and-white, low-angle shots, the grainy stock, and particularly the close-ups of the passionately singing and gesticulating Lindemann—emphasized on each downbeat "Links"—resemble the Nazi orators in *Triumph of the Will.* As in the nightclub, the ants dance to the beat until beetles tear through the screen and chase them from the theater. Later, when the ants amass to conquer the beetles, they form some of the symbols from the film screen from the mass of their marching bodies. Mass culture (as music, choreography, and film), like the ant leader, influences and shapes the masses in pseudo-fascist form. Nevertheless, the lyrics tell us that the producers of these images are guided by a leftist heartbeat.

Of course, the juxtaposition of Lafontaine's words with fascist imagery seems to be contradictory. The addition of the verses about the heart renders the citations of word and image jarring and ambivalent and voids their initial political meaning. The slower, softer, and more melodious verses about the heart introduce a romantic element into this song. In general, though, neither romance nor militancy is particularly unusual for Rammstein's music. Here, however, the sudden jump from the one to the other in theme, vocal tone, rhythm, and accompaniment emphasizes the refrain, showing how incongruous it is. Ironically, leftist politics are jarring when placed alongside Rammstein's sentimental lyrics, but do indeed blend well with the military portion of the song. The verses about the heart that foreground the political refrain also turn it into an empty cliché. They do not tell a meaningful love story but rather insistently question romantic language. By running through platitudes about the heart as questions, "Links 2-3-4" suggests that these idioms are empty. Putting these banalities alongside the references to the "left" Lafontaine and the "right" Gauweiler weakens the assertion about the singer's own heart. The lyric voice—which fans and critics have taken as speaking for the band—is uncertain about the link between meaning and form. This uncertainty, expressed in the verses, infects the refrain.

The questioning of romantic, idiomatic, and political rhetoric is typical of the video images as well. If hackneyed phrases fail to hold their intended meanings, then borrowed images are likewise open to interpretation and debate. Although the video appears to be an allegory about militarism and the mobilization of the masses by the media, the question remains as to whether a video about ants that is stylized along the lines of *Triumph of the Will* refers to anything beyond itself, particularly if its citations are empty and metaphors suspect. As a response to the "Stripped" scandal, this video seems to say that Rammstein can sample any phrases and images it likes—Lafontaine, Gauweiler, Depeche Mode, popular banalities, or even Riefenstahl—since these symbols lose meaning in the repetition. In pointing to the meaninglessness of political rhetoric and imagery, then, Rammstein follows musical traditions of the 1980s, from Punk to New Wave, which Seesslen claims had emptied political language and political symbols of their force.[45] But the hook of "Links 2-3-4" is that a left-beating heart lies beneath those Riefenstahl-influenced "fascist aesthetics."

These layers of meaning serve Rammstein well. While taken by the mainstream press as a declaration of concrete political loyalties, the video does not shut down debate altogether. Questions about its ambiguities remain, and appear calculated not only to perpetuate the discussion—and the concomitant publicity around Rammstein—but also to avoid alienating the group's right-wing fans.[46] Tobias Wimbauer's commentary for the extreme right-wing *Junge Freiheit* says as much, that the seeming political message of

"Links 2-3-4" is undermined by "the quiet irony behind the militarism."[47] This is the same irony that shows how Riefenstahl citations signify differently in new contexts. It allows the right to view the Lafontaine quotes here as devoid of meaning. Thus, in the end, the ambiguity and irony of the juxtapositions in "Links 2-3-4" allow different publics to construe this number differently, thus marketing the song more widely, watering down any political message or self-defense, and demonstrating that words and images cannot be pinned to a single meaning.

Rammstein's adaptations of Riefenstahl's work and the immediacy of the reactions to them reflect the filmmaker's dual role as an influential part of German culture and as a lasting element in the memories that haunt it. In "Stripped" and "Links 2-3-4," Rammstein's use of Riefenstahl's image as a shock tactic and a marketing tool relies on her as a reliable symbol of a "fascist aesthetics" that will provoke controversy and garner publicity. As I have shown, however, Rammstein's videos treat her images not as inherently fascist, but rather as an element of a visual vocabulary. Through these idioms the band shows the power of the mass media in contemporary culture in a manner that is similar to the function of Ray Müller's film title, *Die Macht der Bilder* (literally, the power of images), which describes paradigmatically the power of the cinema in the context of Riefenstahl. A belief in the power of the media is shared by Rammstein's critics, who deem Riefenstahl's aesthetic so powerful as to be dangerous. This viewpoint is so strong that it obscures the other functions of Riefenstahl citations in Rammstein's videos. In "Stripped," the media shape fantasies of strength, freedom, and escape from civilization. Riefenstahl's images are edited and combined with Depeche Mode's lyrics in a way that posits the continued existence of similar fantasies and influences today. In "Links 2-3-4," the media make fans march to meaningless, hackneyed slogans, even as the unity created by a military and cultural leadership gives the masses the strength to overcome greater adversaries. Riefenstahl-like images in this video become just another recycled trope, fragmented, sampled, and voided of any reference to an original intent. Rammstein's use of Riefenstahl exposes pop culture and its critics, the former for the ideology it produces, the latter for attributing too much significance to it. Of course, Riefenstahl's work invokes the memory of fascism and, for some, threatens to revive it.

NOTES

1. "Rammstein sucks. Jeder weiss das. Und steht in einem Zusammenhang mit aesthetisch ahnungslosen und historisch wahnsinnigen Leni-Riefenstahl-Revivals in Videos, Nike-Werbung oder Symposien und Retrospektiven in Potsdam." Diedrich Diederichsen, "Die Boxen des Bösen," *Süddeutsche Zeitung*, May 12, 1999, http://0-web.lexis-nexis.com.innopac.library.unr.edu:80/universe/ (accessed July 20, 2007). All translations, unless otherwise noted, are my own.

2. Rainer Rother's biography of Riefenstahl provides a useful summary of her revival and publicity in this period: Rainer Rother, *Leni Riefenstahl: The Seduction of Genius*, trans. Martin H. Bott (London: Continuum, 2002), 173–176.
3. Dirk Kurbjuweit, "Wie Sexy dürfen Nazis sein?" *Spiegelreporter*, February 2000, 119–120, 124–125. Stephan Lindke, "Der Tabubruch von heute ist der Mainstream von morgen: Die 'Neue Deutsche Härte' als ästhetisches Spiegelbild der wiederstarkten Nation," in *Ästhetische Mobilmachung: Dark Wave, Neofolk und Industrial im Spannungsfeld rechter Ideologien*, ed. Andreas Speit (Hamburg: Unrast, 2002), 261.
4. Lindke, 284. Jan Raabe and Andreas Speit, "L'art du mal: Vom antibürgerlichen Gestus zur faschistoiden Ästhetik," in *Ästhetische Mobilmachung: Dark Wave, Neofolk und Industrial im Spannungsfeld rechter Ideologien*, ed. Andreas Speit (Hamburg: Unrast, 2002), 93–99. Martin Büsser, *Wie klingt die Neue Mitte? Rechte und reakationäre Tendenzen in der Popmusik* (Mainz: Ventil, 2001), 99.
5. See Brigitte Werneburg's discussion of the problems with assembling such a retrospective: Brigitte Werneburg, "Kraft durch Pose: Mehr De- als Remystifikation: Die erste deutsche monographische Werkschau zu Leni Riefenstahl in Potsdam," *die tageszeitung*, December 4, 1998, http://0-web.lexis-nexis.com.innopac.library.unr.edu:80/universe/ (accessed July 20, 2007). See also the essay by Ingeborg Majer-O'Sickey in this volume.
6. *Leni Riefenstahl*, ed. Filmmuseum Potsdam (Berlin: Henschel, 1999).
7. Lindke, 262.
8. Wolf-Rüdiger Mühlmann's chapter of *Letzte Ausfahrt: Germania*, "Riefenstahlgewitter und Presseschelte: Ein Videoclip und seine Folgen," provides a detailed account of the debate and press reactions to Rammstein's "Stripped." Wolf-Rüdiger Mühlmann, *Letzte Ausfahrt: Germania. Ein Phänomen namens Neue Deutsche Härte* (Berlin: I. P. Verlag Jeske/Mader, 1999), 26–35.
9. Daniel Bax, "Rammsteins neues Album 'Mutter': Herz am rechten Fleck," *die tageszeitung*, April 6, 2001, http://0-web.lexis-lexis.com.innopac.library.unr.edu:80/universe/ (accessed July 20, 2007).
10. "Stripped" is available as an extra, hidden feature on the Rammstein DVD *Live aus Berlin* (1999) and "Links 2-3-4," although released as a DVD single in Europe, is most easily purchased through iTunes.
11. " Timeline, 2005," Rammstein official Web site, http://www.rammstein.com/_LittleRose/Band/Timeline/T2005/ (accessed July 20, 2007).
12. "...eine[r] Reihe deutscher Bands, die so schwer teutonisch dahertrampeln, als wollten sie zeigen, dass es für sie noch nie eine Schwierigkeit mit dem deutschen Wesen gegeben habe." Hirsche Blickwechsel, *Süddeutsche Zeitung*, January 7, 1999, Lexis-Nexis, via Getchell Library, http://0-web.lexis-nexis.com.innopac.library.unr.edu:80/universe/ (accessed July 20, 2007). The "Walser debate" refers to the controversy unleashed in 1998 when author Martin Walser commented on the problems surrounding the "instrumentalization" of the Holocaust in contemporary Germany and its relation to German national feeling. Critics of Walser's stances, among them Ignatz Bubis, the head of the Central Council of Jews in Germany, accused this public intellectual of aiding the cause of historical revisionists and Holocaust deniers. By comparing the debates around the *Neue Deutsche Härte* to the Walser controversy, the newspaper highlights the way in which its unproblematized embrace of German national identity provokes questions about identity and history that Germans have faced as part of dealing with the Nazi past.

13. Daniel Bartetzko, "Der Duce kocht," *Frankfurter Rundschau*, December 13, 2004, http://0-web.lexis-nexis.com.innopac.library.unr.edu:80/universe/ (accessed July 20, 2007).
14. Margret Steffen, "Grössenwahn zur Jahrtausendwende," *die tageszeitung*, December 7, 1999, http://0-web.lexis-nexis.com.innopac.library.unr.edu:80/universe/ (accessed July 20, 2007). Henrike Thomsen and Peter Disch, "Der Blender," *Die Zeit*, May 25, 2005, http://www.zeit.de/2005/22/Gert_Hof?page=all (accessed July 20, 2007).
15. See Bartetzko.
16. Hubert Mayer, "Für den Grammy zu böse: Rammstein bringen es immer wieder fertig, festgelegte Tabugrenzen zu überschreiten," *Deutsche Stimme*, April 1999, 9.
17. Mühlmann, 32. Andreas Becker, "Der Motor allen Schlachtens," *die tageszeitung*, May 21, 2001, http://0-web.lexis-nexis.com.innopac.library.unr.edu:80/universe/ (accessed July 20, 2007).
18. Peter Richter, "Die einzige Alternative zum Nüßchen-Essen," *Süddeutsche Zeitung*, May 21, 2001, http://0-web.lexis-nexis.com.innopac.library.unr.edu:80/universe/ (accessed July 20, 2007).
19. Aram Lintzel, "Nur geschmacklos—oder schlimmer?" *Tages-Anzeiger*, September 11, 1999, http://0-web.lexis-nexis.com.innopac.library.unr.edu:80/universe/ (accessed July 20, 2007).
20. "Deutschrock: Im Banne der Teutonen," *Focus Magazin*, January 18, 1999, http://0-web.lexis-nexis.com.innopac.library.unr.edu:80/universe/ (accessed July 20, 2007).
21. Mühlmann, 25.
22. See Thomsen and Disch.
23. Mühlmann, 26–35.
24. Susan Sontag, "Fascinating Fascism," *Under the Sign of Saturn* (New York: Farrar, Straus, and Giroux, 1980), 90–91.
25. Georg Seesslen, *Tanz den Adolf Hitler: Faschismus in der populären Kultur* (Berlin: Tiamat, 1994), 85.
26. Kurbjuweit, 120.
27. Rother, 176. Michael Mackenzie, "From Athens to Berlin: The 1936 Olympics and Leni Riefenstahl's *Olympia*," *Critical Inquiry* 29 (2003): 319.
28. For such assessments, see Lindke, 235; Mühlmann, 27; Lintzel; also Jason Hanley, "'The Land of Rape and Honey': The Use of World War II Propaganda in the Music Videos of Ministry and Laibach," *American Music* 22, no. 1 (2004): 168–174. Marc Deckert, "Spiel mit dem Verdacht," *Süddeutsche Zeitung*, October 17, 1998, http://0-web.lexis-nexis.com.innopac.library.unr.edu:80/universe/ (accessed July 20, 2007). See also: Büsser 21–24. In his praise of bands like the Sex Pistols, the New York Dolls, and Laibach, Büsser lauds the "ambivalence" of the use of "fascist" symbols alongside other imagery (such as drag or Stars of David) by those who would clearly have been marginalized by the Nazis (22). See also Ulf Poschardt, "Stripped: Pop und Affirmation bei Kraftwerk, Laibach und Rammstein," *Jungle World*, May 12, 1999, http://www.nadir.org/nadir/periodika/jungle_world/_99/20/15a.htm (accessed July 20, 2007). Poschardt connects what he sees as rebellion, glorification of technology, and self-conscious play with German identity in Kraftwerk to the punk combination of self-deprecation and fascist imagery by the Sex Pistols and the New York Dolls. He interprets the music of the Slovenian band Laibach and its blending of fascist and communist aesthetics to show fascist ideology to be empty and inauthentic.

29. Mühlmann, 27. Deckert sees the use of *Olympia* for "Stripped" not as egregious but rather as banal—for the use of similar images, such as bodies, smoke, and fire, became fairly standard for music videos by the 1980s—but, like Mühlmann, he interprets its use as primarily aimed at controversy and sales.
30. Büsser, 23.
31. Poschardt. Daniel Bax also accuses Rammstein of emptying meaning from fascist signs and symbols. Stephan Lindke and Baenz Friedli as well fail to see irony or distance in Rammstein's "provocations." Lindke, 235. Baenz Friedli, "Heil Hitparade!" *Facts*, December 10, 1998, http://0-web.lexis-nexis.com.innopac.library.unr.edu:80/universe/ (accessed July 20, 2007).
32. Mühlmann, 29.
33. Rammstein shows feature elaborate pyrotechnics. During performances of the song "Rammstein" (with the opening line "Rammstein—ein Mensch brennt"/ "Rammstein—a man burns"), Lindemann appears in flaming robes, which *Stern* calls "the high point of every Rammstein show." Florian Gless and Hannes Ross, "'Wir sind mit dem Panzer losgefahren': Mit Tabubrüchen hat Rammstein weltweit Erfolg gehabt. Jetzt, sagt die Band, ist die Zeit der Provokation vorbei," *Stern*, April 14, 2001, 228.
34. Georg Seesslen, "Blut und Glamour," in *Leni Riefenstahl*, ed. Filmmuseum Potsdam (Berlin: Henschel, 1999), 198, 207. See also the translation of Seesslen's essay in this volume.
35. As "magische Natur und heroische Menschen vereint in Reinheit und Schönheit zum transzendenten Ideal," Raabe and Speit, 96.
36. Raabe and Speit, 67–71.
37. Mackenzie, 313. See also the essay by Mary Rhiel in this volume.
38. Mackenzie, 319–325.
39. For example, see: Bax, Richter.
40. Described in Lindke, 240–241. For examples, see: Bartetzko; Becker; also Michael Pilz, "Das Herz schlägt links, zwei drei vier. Marschmusik am Muttertag: Rammstein nimmt sich mit dem neuen Album der Klone an," *Die Welt*, April 2, 2001, http://www.welt.de/data/2001/04/02/483949.html (accessed July 20, 2007). Stefan Henseke, "Rammstein," *Berliner Kurier*, April 2, 2001, http://0-web.lexis-nexis.com.innopac.library.unr.edu:80/universe/ (accessed July 20, 2007). Thomas Winkler, "Mahnmal für den Aufbau Ost: Auf ihrer neuen Platte 'Reise Reise' rollen die Jungs von Rammstein das R wieder jeden Berg hinauf," *Frankfurter Rundschau*, September 21, 2004, http://0-web.lexis-nexis.com.innopac.library.unr.edu:80/universe/ (accessed July 20, 2007).
41. "Das Herz hat einen Standort: Es schlägt links," *Die Welt*, March 15, 1999, http://0-web.lexis-nexis.com.innopac.library.unr.edu:80/universe/ (accessed July 20, 2007).
42. "Lafontaine und Gauweiler schreiben für die 'Bild'-Zeitung—'Herz schlägt links' und 'Herz auf rechtem Fleck,'" *Agence France Presse—German*, January 19, 2001, http://0-web.lexis-nexis.com.innopac.library.unr.edu:80/universe/ (accessed July 20, 2007).
43. "['Links 2-3-4'] war der erste Versuch von Rammstein, sich künstlerisch mit dem ewigen Vorwurf auseinander zu setzen, wir seien eine rechte Band." Gless and Ross, 226.
44. Gless and Ross, 226.
45. Seesslen, *Tanz den Adolf Hitler*, 169–173.
46. Gless and Ross, 226; Bax; Pilz.

47. "Links 2 3 4. . . könnte fehlgehend politisch aufgefasst werden. . . . Die Band hat sich um Klischees politischer Art wie Rechts und Links noch nie gekümmert, abgesehen von bewußter Provokation mittels Symbolik. Das auf den ersten Blick manchem offensichtlich zu sein Scheinende wurde stets feinsinnig (das ist kein Widerspruch zu Text und Musik, wenn man die leise Ironie hinter der Martialität sehen kann) hintergangen und erfuhr so auf einer anderen Ebene die Wandlung ins Gegenteil." Tobias Wimbauer, "Feuer, das in Lust verbrennt: Nach vier Jahren ist ein neuesRammstein-Album erschienen," *Junge Freiheit* 17 (2001), http://www.jf-archiv.de/archiv01/171yy32.htm (accessed July 20, 2007).

Part Three

Continuities

Chapter 7

A Founding Myth and a Master Text: *The Blue Light* (1932)[1]

Eric Rentschler

On a drizzly afternoon in mid-September 2003, Leni Riefenstahl, who had passed away at the age of 101, was laid to rest in the Munich Ostfriedhof. The services were open to the public and hundreds of admirers arrived to pay their last respects.[2] In the first row of mourners sat Horst Kettner, Riefenstahl's partner for thirty-five years, and Gisela Jahn, her housekeeper. Behind them were Leo Kirch, the media mogul, and Hilmar Hoffmann, former president of the Goethe-Institut. Antje-Katrin Kühnemann, a personal friend and television celebrity, delivered the funeral oration and, at a poignant moment, quoted the closing lines of *Das blaue Licht (The Blue Light*): "Her memory however continues to live on in the village which has inflicted such terrible injustice on her."[3] It was most fitting that these last words derived from the director's first feature, the seminal work of 1932 that in time would crystallize as a career's founding myth and a life's master text.

I. Aesthetic Reveries and Political Realities

Debuting as a dancer, Leni Riefenstahl went on to gain initial acclaim as a screen star during the Weimar Republic. In the mid-1930s, she would become the Third Reich's most famous director and, after 1945, film history's most controversial filmmaker. Throughout the postwar and post-Wall eras, she remained ever present, long after she commandeered the cameras that recorded the 1934 Nuremberg rally. Stars and dignitaries from all over the world flocked to her ninetieth birthday party in 1992; among fashionable circles in Munich, the event was the talk of the town. Stephen Schiff's portrait and Helmut Newton's photographs of the remarkably vital senior citizen graced the pages of *Vanity Fair*.[4] John Simon's rave notice about her memoirs appeared on the cover of the *New York Times Book Review*.[5] *Time* magazine extolled "Riefenstahl's Last Triumph" and touted her autobiography as one of 1993's five best nonfiction books.[6] Ray Müller's three-hour documentary homage, *Die Macht der Bilder* (*The Wonderful, Horrible Life of Leni Riefenstahl*, 1993) played at the New York Film Festival and found wide release and an enthusiastic press response. Early in 1994, rumors circulated in Hollywood that Madonna intended to option Riefenstahl's memoirs; later that year, CNN announced Jodie Foster's plans for a Leni biopic, a project that, more than a decade later, finally seemed ready to enter production.[7] On March 3, 1998, Riefenstahl was invited to *Time*'s seventieth anniversary together with Bill Clinton, Mikhail Gorbachev, Norman Mailer, Elie Wiesel, Bill Gates, and other luminaries whose photograph had graced the cover of the news weekly.[8] Her centennial celebration in 2002 occasioned even more elaborate media coverage and renewed discussion about the celebrity's well-known past and her controversial notoriety. "Tabloid pages," as biographer Steven Bach relates, "cackled with gossip about the lavish birthday party for almost two hundred guests to be held on a terrace overlooking Lake Starnberg."[9]

The Führer's protégée and confidante, the woman who directed the definitive Nazi self-portrait, *Triumph des Willens* (*Triumph of the Will*, 1935), Riefenstahl remained for many decades the Third Reich's most visible survivor and a constant object of lurid speculation, be it as "Hitler's girlfriend,"[10] a "Nazi pinup girl,"[11] or a "fallen goddess."[12] The spectacle of Riefenstahl always made for good press. Championed in the thirties by Avery Brundage, Josef von Sternberg, Walt Disney, Douglas Fairbanks, and Charlie Chaplin, her subsequent admirers included Jean Cocteau, Dusan Makavejev, Mick and Bianca Jagger,[13] Siegfried and Roy, Andy Warhol, George Lucas, Steven Spielberg, Volker Schlöndorff, David Bowie, Bryan Ferry, and the heavy metal band Rammstein. Even Rainer Werner Fassbinder asked Riefenstahl to be his cinematographer for *Querelle*: "I think you might be able to develop a strong feeling for my work. And besides, this would make me very proud."[14] Riefenstahl had a large throng of enthusiasts, especially in the United States and Japan, partisans who disregarded her embattled past and celebrated her cinematic genius. For the British film historian Kevin Brownlow, she was a cause célèbre: "Art transcends the artist . . . politics and art must never be confused . . . these old adages are forgotten instantly the name of Riefenstahl is raised. And it is our fault. We have ourselves been the victims of insidious propaganda."[15] Her apologists endorsed the filmmaker's claim that she never was anything more than an artist compelled by an aesthetic calling.

Detractors, on the other hand, asserted that Riefenstahl's unquestionable artistic powers were put to nefarious purposes, that her pact with Hitler was tantamount to sympathy for the devil, that her hagiographical portraits legitimated the Nazi leadership and helped consolidate the new order.[16] Susan Sontag, in her influential essay of 1975, coined the term "fascinating fascism" in a larger discussion of Nazism's problematic continuing appeal. Nazism's substance, argued Sontag, has become neutralized in formalistic appreciations; its theatrical spectacles and ritualistic scenarios reappear in fetishized and sexualized appropriations. Esthetes and camp followers applaud the beauty of Riefenstahl's images and denude them of political meaning. "Without a historical perspective, such connoiseurship prepares the way for a curiously absentminded acceptance of propaganda for all sorts of destructive feelings—feelings whose implications people are refusing to take seriously."[17] Riefenstahl's documentaries of the 1930s demonstrated, in Sontag's assessment, a brute symmetry and an overwhelming choreography, "the massing of groups of people; the turning of people into things; and the grouping of people/things around an all-powerful, hypnotic leader-figure or force."[18] The fluid traveling shots in *Triumph of the Will,* elaborated Karsten Witte several years later, "work with induced movement intended to set inanimate matter into waving motion and make human masses freeze into stone blocks. The masses are allowed to enter the picture, but only their leaders are allowed to speak. Hitler himself is the main actor, here celebrating his wedding fantasies with the masses."[19]

Riefenstahl considered such assertions preposterous. She insisted her work was no party to Hitler. Asked by Ray Müller what fascist aesthetics might be, she said that for her the phrase had no meaning.[20] "What do I have to regret, where does my guilt lie?" inquired the unreconciled filmmaker in the closing moments of Müller's documentary. Clearly, the past plagued her like an albatross. Her life had a tragic dimension, according to a recent assessment, "for she seems to have borne the brunt of public shame more openly and more frequently than the real culprits of the regime."[21] To the end, the director saw herself as a person unfairly maligned, the object of witch-hunting and never-ending persecution.

In response to her assailants, Riefenstahl regularly employed her directorial debut of 1932, *The Blue Light,* as a character witness. *Sieg des Glaubens* (*Victory of Faith,* 1933) and *Triumph of the Will* might have glorified the Führer. *Olympia* (1938), financed by the government and overseen by the Ministry of Propaganda,[22] rendered Hitler as a modern Zeus who has an omnipotent gaze, an "*Übermensch*" with an "*Überblick.*" *Tag der Freiheit—Unsere Wehrmacht* (*Day of Freedom—Our Army,* 1935) celebrated a reconstructed army and a soon-to-be-remilitarized nation.[23] *The Blue Light,* however, did not lend itself so readily to political objections. Its young and inexperienced director had not met Hitler and knew nothing of *Mein Kampf.* The film's scriptwriter, Béla Balázs, was a Jewish intellectual and a prominent leftist.[24] Unlike the later documentaries, the mountain film appeared to be the work of a naïve artist.[25]

The Blue Light tells the legend of Junta, a strange woman living in the Alpine heights above a Tyrolean village, who has privileged access to a cave of crystals. On full-moon nights, a blue light emanates from her secret grotto, luring young men from the valley to seek out the radiant beam.[26] Their quest invariably ends in death and causes the townspeople to vilify Junta. A painter from Vienna, Vigo, befriends the outcast woman. He becomes her protector and falls in love with her. Following her one blue-lit night, he discovers the way to the cave. He draws a map, thinking that the safe passage to the grotto will serve the best interests of both Junta and the villagers. The townspeople arm themselves with tools and climb to the cave, plundering the valuable crystals and celebrating their newfound fortune. Finding her private sanctuary ravaged, Junta despairs and plunges to her death.

The impetus for *The Blue Light*, Riefenstahl recalled, came from personal reveries: "I began to dream and my dreams turned into images of a young girl who lived in the mountains, a creature of nature. I saw her climbing, saw her in the moonlight."[27] Gripped by this vision, Riefenstahl set out to make her own film, assuming the part of Junta and taking on the role of director and co-producer. In forming her own images, Riefenstahl created her life's fantasy. Speaking to *Cahiers du Cinéma* in 1965, she elaborated how *The Blue Light* forecast her future:

> Well, when her dream is destroyed Junta dies. I spoke of that as my destiny. For that is what was accomplished, much later, in me, after the war when everything collapsed on us, when I was deprived of all possibility of creating. For art, creation—this is my life, and I was deprived of it. My life became a tissue of rumors and accusations through which I had to beat a path.[28]

Riefenstahl's film sanctifies elemental nature and its enchanting powers. And the director identified herself as an artist whose true homeland resides in this sublime and special space. Many commentators have viewed Junta as an embodiment of her creator, an artist who, in the words of an American enthusiast, "had her own intuitive feelings about nature and was destroyed by her naive disregard of the real world around her, the world she set out to avoid."[29] As a projection of the director's desired self-image, Riefenstahl becomes a romantic poet-priestess whose vision transcends reality and history, someone whose films reflect a fascination with beauty, strength, and harmony.[30]

Riefenstahl, justifiably or not, came to embody a problematic legacy. Controversies about the filmmaker to this day invariably lead to a standoff between moral castigation and aesthetic vindication. Either she is an unrepetent Nazi propagandist or a misunderstood artistic genius. Borrowing Albert Einstein's soothing words as the epigraph for her *Memoir*, Riefenstahl went so far as to align herself with a Jew: "So many things have been written about me, masses of insolent lies and inventions, that I would have perished long ago, had I paid any attention. One must take comfort in the fact that time has a sieve, through which most trivia run off into the sea of oblivion." The filmmaker remains central to any consideration of Nazi aesthetics and its disputed place in history. And central to any discussion of Leni Riefenstahl is the relationship of film art to a larger general history, of romantic fantasies to German dreams, of aesthetic reveries to political realities.

II. A Vampire Film

Riefenstahl's career, like her debut film and its effective history, spanned many epochs, from the Weimar era and the reign of Hitler to the Bonn and Berlin Republic. Shot on location in Switzerland and South Tyrol during the summer of 1931, *The Blue Light* premiered in Berlin at the Ufa-Palast am Zoo on March 24, 1932.[31] In the wake of *Olympia*'s great success, it was reprised on September 27, 1938. After the war it was re-edited and newly scored for what Riefenstahl described as "a dazzling gala screening" in Rome on November 21, 1951.[32] The film reappeared a few months later in Austria (where it bore the title, *Die Hexe von Santa Maria/The Witch of Santa Maria*) as well as in the Federal Republic. *The Blue Light* assumed different countenances in its various incarnations. The National Verleih press booklet for the postwar version bills it as "a standard work in German film history," "a film of lasting quality . . . that must be numbered among the most unforgettable titles." In March 2005, an Arthaus DVD appeared that contained both the premiere version of 1932 (which, for a long while, had been up for lost) as well as the shorter postwar release.[33]

Critical discussions by and large have assumed similarly reverent tones. They suggest that the film, an example of canonical greatness, has remained unaffected by tradition or time's passage. Typically, commentators praise the director's immediacy and intuition, her atmospheric images and breathtaking panoramas. Her genius, so it would seem, flourished freely, breaking new ground while remaining unfettered by models or conventions.[34] Apart from the film's "romantic mysticism" and the title's deference to Novalis's "blue flower,"[35] Riefenstahl's sole authorship seems beyond question—until we start to look at the feature's original cast of players. In 1932, the opening sequence announced "*The Blue Light*, A Mountain Legend from the Dolomites, rendered in images by Leni Riefenstahl, Bela Balacz [sic], Hans Schneeberger." Although the director subsequently acknowledged Carl Mayer's important assistance with the script and Arnold Fanck's editorial counsel, neither name showed up in the original credits. Six years later, the titles proclaimed, "*The Blue Light*, a mountain legend told and shaped into images by Leni Riefenstahl." The first version of the film would list the Jewish scriptwriter Balázs as a co-author; the second one would not. (Nor is there any mention of co-producer Harry Sokal.) After World War II, *The Blue Light* simply became "a mountain legend by Leni Riefenstahl."

From its very first signs, already in the title credits, *The Blue Light* arose as the product of unacknowledged forces. "I wanted to make a film without the film industry, without a producer and without a director," Riefenstahl would later declare.[36] None of the release versions disclosed the book from which she gained her initial impetus, Gustav Renker's novel, *Bergkristall* (*Mountain Crystal*).[37] In early accounts, she averred that she had adapted a peasant legend of the Alps; later (as in her *Memoir*), she insisted that the narrative was derived from her own dream images. The filmmaker claimed a direct access to the story ("everything that happened came from my head"[38]), when it in fact had come to her in a much more mediated fashion. Renker, a well-known Swiss writer, published *Bergkristall* in 1930, a tale about an artist who flees the big city to an Alpine retreat and becomes enchanted by a huge mountain from which emanates a "blue light." "It really exists," swears one of the villagers. One can see it "around midnight when the moon is full."[39] In Renker's novel a rock formation and its mysterious quarry become a painter's obsession. Here, too, an artist from the city falls in love with a woman who herds sheep and lives in the wild with a young boy.

The film's title also recalls the blue flower from Novalis's *Heinrich von Ofterdingen*, the quintessential symbol of the romantic quest. One of Riefenstahl's early dance routines bore the name, "Die blaue Blume." Before becoming a dancer, she attended the State Academy of Arts and Crafts in Berlin and studied painting and drawing. Riefenstahl's output demonstrates considerable familiarity with nineteenth-century art history, notably with the work of Caspar David Friedrich.[40] *The Blue Light* abounds with images reminiscent of Friedrich, sweeping unpeopled mountainscapes in general, or compositions that explicitly defer to his work, for instance the shot where Vigo peers from a panoramic height like the "Wanderer Above the Sea of Fog" or where Junta stands before a precipice in the manner of "Woman on the Abyss."[41] *The Blue Light* infuses nature with an arousing power; like Friedrich, Riefenstahl transforms exterior landscapes into emotional spaces.[42] The physical world becomes irreal and fantastic, molded by an imagination whose highest goal is to represent invisible and ineffable forces. Friedrich's use of landscape, as Alice Kuzniar has argued, "turns the medium of perception into its object of depiction." His idealized topographies provide "the epitome of romantic self-reflexive art or the art, that, instead of referring to the natural world outside it, calls attention to the means, conditions, and operations of its being."[43] Riefenstahl likewise imparted a self-reflexive dimension to her debut film by introducing a romantic landscape painter, whose ultimate creation will be the map that brings modernity to the village and perdition to Junta.[44]

If the images and the artistic impetus went back to Friedrich's evocative landscape painting, the narrative proper came equally as a legacy of the nineteenth century. The earliest versions of the film, the 1932 and 1938 releases, contained a frame story redolent of many German *Novellen*. Confronted with trinkets bearing Junta's picture when they drive into Santa Maria, a dapper honeymooning couple from the city enter a hotel room to find a religious painting with the same votive image.[45] "Who really is this Junta?" asks the young woman. The proprietor, as if awaiting the question, sends for a leather-bound volume that bears Junta's countenance and legend. The film then dissolves from her image on the book to a shot of a mist-covered crystal, opening to a view of Junta clasping the mineral and yielding to an extended flashback. We move from the contemporary setting to 1866 and learn who Junta is and what her image has to do with the crystals proferred to the tourists.

The inscribed narrative serves a function similar to the story's point of orientation, the image- and mapmaker Vigo: Both resolve seeming enigmas, offering routes of access to terrains deemed mysterious and demonic.

The film's images may recall the high-flown language of nature worship and the "noble awe" of the sublime,[46] but the narrative as a whole stems from an intelligence able to fathom nature's mysteries and to transform superstition into knowledge. This undeniably modern impetus, as we know from German literary history, inheres in the *Novelle*, a genre often featuring frame stories whose apparent supernatural foundations give way to the more tangible loci of human agency, causality, and rationality, shifting from a naïve worldview to a sentimental one.[47] This legacy will find its way into the complex and self-conscious frame structures of many Weimar films.[48] The nested narrative of *The Blue Light* resolves the mystery of Junta. During the tale, Junta evolves from an agent of the uncanny, a witch and a curse, into a public martyr and a popular icon. The film's romantic images hallow nature's mystery and impart to the elemental a stirring resonance; the narrative, on the other hand, ultimately renders seemingly inexplicable phenomena both straightforward and transparent. Romantic images that accentuate nature's irrational potential take their place in a story logic governed by enlightened reason, indeed instrumental rationality.

A further crucial (and more widely acknowledged) generic legacy for Riefenstahl were the Weimar mountain films (*Bergfilme*), a popular vein in which she received her start as an actress.[49] These Alpine dramas, filmed on location amid majestic peaks, feature vigorous athletes confronting untamed elements. Bound by a hardy code, these feckless males stand above the pedestrian world of restriction and cultivation, viewing themselves as adventurers in touch with a mightier destiny, the call of the mountains. Sporting visual effects caught in glaciers, rocky peaks, and snowscapes, Arnold Fanck, the master of this form, built his *Bergfilme* around romantic melodramas, triangles involving two climbers, usually close companions, and a mutually shared loved interest who causes disturbance. Siegfried Kracauer appropriately dubbed the films "a mixture of sparkling ice-axes and inflated sentiments," indicting the *Bergfilme* for their immature male protagonists, without commenting on the conspicuous role played by women in these scenarios.[50]

Riefenstahl's feature film debut came in *Der heilige Berg* (*The Holy Mountain*, 1926). We first see the actress in a close-up portrait; her face is pale, her eyes are shut. Anticipating Junta's ultimate incarnation, this initial view of Riefenstahl appears to be a death mask. The face is that of Diotima, who comes to life in a dance by the sea. The editing renders the fluid choreography of her gestures and leaps at one with the natural forces that cause the waves to break. The dancer's image reappears on a poster announcing her evening performance in a resort hotel. Robert, the mountain climber, finds himself perplexed after Diotima's show. He flees into the Alpine peaks, as the intertitles put it, "to master the overwhelming impression." In the *Bergfilm*, men seek to master mountains and women with mixed success. Catastrophe ensues when Robert and his younger companion become rivals for Diotima's affection. They perish in a climbing accident. Remorseful and guilt-ridden, Diotima returns to the sea. The mourner is at once inhibited and inhabited; her sole obsession remains her memories of the dead admirers. In conceptualizing *The Blue Light*, Riefenstahl wanted to create a *Bergfilm* in which a woman figured more prominently than the mountains.[51] In so doing, she clearly recognized their paradigmatic equivalence in the generic economy.

Like many nineteenth-century *Novellen*, mountain films probe the mysteries of nature with the tools of modernity. Besides snowy scapes, billowing clouds, and unpeopled expanses, Fanck's films show us tourists, resort hotels, automobiles, airplanes, observatories, and weather stations. Contemporaries in the twenties frequently hailed the ability of Fanck's camera both to hallow and to penetrate nature, to sanctify its secrets and still disclose its uncanny properties.[52] Critics recognized the genre's synthesis of mountains and machines, of natural force and technological power, of bodily energy and spiritual endeavor, its impressive merger between the physical world and the sophisticated scientific devices that measure and elaborate it. For Fanck nature remains mute and unexpressive unless captured by a camera. His features in this regard offer a modern reiteration of Schelling's romantic transcendentalism, the belief that human awareness of oneself and the world around one brings "the unconscious life in nature to conscious expression."[53] In this way, mediated effects become natural presence, formal will imparts to raw material its true identity, manmade machines render the real authentic.[54] Riefenstahl, in a similar fashion, combined the callings of a romantic artist and a technical engineer. "With light you can turn the camera into a magic instrument," she reportedly boasted to Fanck, "and if you also use color filters to change the tonal values you can succeed in altering the outdoors and stylizing nature."[55]

Many critics have observed how Riefenstahl, like F. W. Murnau, sought to grant natural settings an eerie and ethereal aspect, something she accomplished through special effects, technical ploys involving time-lapse photography, filters, smoke machines, and modulated lighting.[56] Both directors recast the still lifes of romantic painting in moving images. Neither wanted to reflect physical reality, but instead to probe its hidden secrets and its subterranean reaches. "Too often," complained Murnau, "pictures have made the world banal instead of revealing new heights and depths in life."[57] He wanted to photograph thought, to make images that speak more strongly than words. *The Blue Light* exudes at times what Balázs termed the "chilly draft from doomsday" atmosphere of Murnau's silent classic, *Nosferatu* (1922).[58] Balázs was of course a great admirer of Murnau and one of his most eloquent supporters, so these similarities are hardly coincidental. Frieda Grafe has likewise pointed out the resemblance between Vigo's approach to the mountain village and Thomas Hutter's entry into the realm of the vampire.[59] *The Blue Light*'s reliance on *Nosferatu*, however, transcends the atmospherics of single scenes and technical touches. Both films dramatize a disparity between images attuned to primal emotions and unconscious desires and an intelligence that seeks to render the inexplicable and unsettling in terms of human generality. In *Nosferatu* the visual track often conflicts with written signs, producing a profoundly ironic tension. Murnau's tableaux show us things that the narrator, a city scribe, only partially understands and in some cases simply fails to comprehend.[60]

Like *Nosferatu*, *The Blue Light* uses the stylized image of a woman as a point of departure and a focus of attention. We first encounter both heroines enclosed by frames: the close-up of Ellen Hutter at the window, the picture of Junta on the cover of the village chronicle. Both women sleepwalk at night and commune with nature's primordial powers. The two films cast a woman in the role of martyr, whose sacrificed body ensures a community's future well-being. Ellen becomes the agent of civilization in its battle against the demonic side of nature it wishes to disavow, the repressed energies vested in Nosferatu.[61] She takes on this responsibility after reading *The Book of the Vampires* and making a conscious decision. Junta also becomes a martyr, but this role is not of her choice. She does not understand Vigo as he explains the advantages of mining the grotto and thus has no voice in the destruction of her most intimate space. In both films a community fortifies itself against outside threats. In *Nosferatu* this involves systemic repression, the sublimation of nature's underworld and the exorcism of its darker side. The price of civilization in *The Blue Light* similarly entails a processing of elemental forces and the exorcism of a dangerous sensuality. Both films culminate in scenes where a heroine lies supine and has all vitality sucked out of her. Ellen holds Nosferatu by her bedside until the creature dissolves in the rising sun; Vigo stands over Junta's corpse in the early morning light.[62]

Itself the product of considerable recourse to tradition, of recasting and recycling, *The Blue Light* offers a legend that reflects—and embodies—a distinctly modern process of appropriation. The narrative dramatizes the plundering of nature and the undoing of a woman, stylizing the double violation in the form of a village chronicle, the "Historia della Junta" offered for the amusement and edification of tourists. Riefenstahl's film sanctifies premodern landscapes and documents a village's entry into modernity. In so doing, it enacts a tension between the romantic worship of nature and the exercise of instrumental reason. Riefenstahl's sympathies and those of her film seem unquestionably aligned with Junta and the mountain girl's pristine world. Or at least so it would seem.

III. Histories of Horror

Junta's victimization at the hands of mercenary contemporaries, claimed Riefenstahl, presaged the filmmaker's own subsequent suffering. Her autobiographical reading set the tone for many discussions and still informs prominent appraisals today. *The Blue Light*, for Vincent Canby, is a "very significant film," "the fable-like story of a woman whose search for the ideal, not unlike Ms. Riefenstahl's search in a very different world, leads to disaster." The reviewer applauds the film and goes on to hallow the director as beyond good and evil: "She's too complex, too particular and too arrogant to be seen as either sympathetic or unsympathetic."[63] The special status of Riefenstahl's debut film has remained undiminished despite the interventions of her most vocal detractors. Siegfried Kracauer and Susan Sontag have offered compelling and controversial assessments of German mountain films. They see *The Blue Light* as escapist fare with regressive implications, a work whose high altitudes and lofty attitudes celebrate protofascist dispositions: fulsome antirationalism, blind enthusiasm, and overwrought pathos. For Kracauer, Junta "conforms to a political regime which relies on intuition, worships nature and cultivates myths."[64] Sontag, likewise, connects the cult of the mountains with the sanctification of the Führer, "the ultimate affirmation of and escape from the self—into the brotherhood of courage and into death."[65]

Both Kracauer and Sontag have come under frequent attack and been called ax-grinding ideologues or moralistic zealots. Resolute auteurists defend Riefenstahl's visual power, blithely dismissing these interventions: "And anyway," wisecracks Andrew Sarris, "she never claimed to be working for British intelligence while she was making *Triumph of the Will.*" Sontag, he argues, quotes from the very few film historians who support her position, and ignores or insults the rest. Siegfried Kracauer's very questionable *From Caligari to Hitler* is trotted out as if it were holy writ, its mandate for 20/20 hindsight renewed. Still, the problem with either a prosecution or a defense of Riefenstahl is that so much of the evidence has disappeared in the rubble of the Third Reich that we can never be quite sure whether Leni was Little Eva (as she claims) or Lucretia Borgia (as Sontag suggests) or (more likely) an opportunistic artist who has been both immortalized and imprisoned by the horror of history.[66]

Why Kracauer's book is "very questionable" does not receive further comment. Which missing evidence Sarris has in mind is equally open to speculation. And precisely what the critic means by "the horror of history" remains anyone's guess. Is it simply fate, one wonders, or does it involve human agency? Within much broader and far-reaching arguments, Kracauer and Sontag link *The Blue Light* to National Socialist sensibility, indeed, to a larger German history of horror. For them the film is less a romantic tale than a political allegory. Their comments about the film are brief and provocative, suggestive, but either too terse (Sontag) or schematic (Kracauer) to be conclusive. If one follows their lead, one can indeed go further.

In her discussion of *The Blue Light,* Sontag provides a noteworthy postmortem. The cause of Junta's death lies in "the materialist, prosaic spirit of envious villagers and the blind rationalism of her lover, a well-meaning visitor from the city."[67] Sontag goes on to make important general observations regarding Nazi art's celebration of death, its desire to contain physical desire—and to stifle female volition. "The fascist ideal," she claims, "is to transform sexual energy into a 'spiritual' force, for the benefit of the community. The erotic (that is, woman) is always present as a temptation, with the most admirable response being a heroic repression of the sexual impulse."[68] *The Blue Light* recodes Christian symbols in its secular religion of abandon and death. Early in the film, Vigo stumbles across figures etched onto a rocky mountainside, a martyr surrounded by mourners, a structure lingered over by the camera, a creation merging elemental nature and human sacrifice in an artistic construction. As he passes the faces carved in stone, Vigo asks, "What are those figures?" and echoes the tourist's initial question about the mountain girl. The connection is not fortuitous, for after her demise, Junta will reappear as a religious martyr and an aesthetic countenance.

As in *The Holy Mountain*, sexual energy will become a spiritual force. The outsider is the object of lascivious stares, her body linked by the editing with wild animals. Her attraction and that of the blue light cause suicidal frenzy among the village's young males. For this reason, she is the target of the imperiled community's anger and aggression. Junta's primal vitality and erotic magnetism pose a public menace, because the boys dying on the rocks are its future fathers. The energies vested in her and the alluring grotto will be harnessed and transformed in a way that brings collective relief and welcome prosperity to the community. Junta's face transmutes into a crystal-studded image as the frame dissolves into the portrait adorning a book with her story.[69] The same image will serve as a kitsch object offered by children to out-of-town visitors, the picture of someone whose afterlife as a legend, fetish, and commodity has a crucial bearing on the Alpine community's spiritual—and material—welfare.[70] Without a doubt, the citizens of Santa Maria act as consummate vendors of native tradition, hawking crystal images of the local hero and attracting tourists with their gripping village tale.

The mountain community we first see in the film's prologue lives in an age of automobiles and tourism, yet abides as a hardy *Gemeinschaft* and appears to live at one with elementary nature. On the whole the residents of Santa Maria do not seem avaricious or enterprising. Their stark and noble features, captured in affectionate close-ups, recall Dürer woodcuts. The intertitles of the original framing passage introduce the townspeople of the present as a healthy folk unsullied by modern malaise:

> We, the people of the Dolomites, far from the strife and turmoil of the outside world, dwell primarily in the rugged wilderness and magnificence of the Italian Tyrol. We are a simple peasant folk, and strange legends have come down to us through the centuries casting shadows on the peace of our lives. Above all do we cherish the legend of Junta, the mountain girl, whose story we have reverently engraved for future generations.[71]

Oskar Kalbus, an eminent film publicist in the Third Reich, praised the Alpine community's racial vitality, admiring physiognomies that recall the Visigoths.[72]

The village, effused a British commentator in the mid-sixties, appeared "to blend with all aspects of the past and present; time itself seemed petrified as the mute figures carved from rock; the faces of peasants appeared out of archaic time, touched by a stoic dignity."[73] Recent critics have lauded the film's ethnographic intensity and linked Riefenstahl's sympathetic handling of the Sarn Valley peasants with her affectionate treatment of the Nuba tribespeople.

The film may well recall blood-and-soil rhetoric, but it also shows a thriving nascent culture industry. The village reshapes memories from its past into a form of pseudo-eternity, making mountains and mountain girls into powerful images and spellbinding tales. The film puts this activity on display and positions the legend as an expression of collective regret and sincere sorrow. An acute formulation by Kracauer recognizes, though, how profoundly the village profits from the tragedy. "To be sure, at the end the village rejoices in its fortune and the myth seems defeated, but this rational solution is treated in such a summary way that it enhances rather than reduces Junta's significance."[74] The film pictures the celebration after the cavern's exploitation as an ecstatic moment with disquieting overtones, especially in the close-up of spilled wineglasses, whose traces on the table suggest the flow of blood. Greedy villagers, the shot suggests, have opportunistically plundered the mountain cavern, raping nature and robbing Junta. The scene as a whole, however, also amounts to a structural reversal of an earlier tableau that showed subdued townspeople mourning the deaths caused by the blue light.

The prologue acknowledges a village's injustice, but the act seems to bear no trace of human agency. "Strange legends" have come down to this peasant folk and "cast shadows" on the peace of their lives. (The "horror of history" once again seems to be up to its old tricks.) To be sure, the community continues to circulate the story, marketing a legend purchased at a bloody price. The chronicle both acknowledges and yet glosses over the fact of violence, rendering the act of expropriation as a necessary evil, in Kracauer's words, a "rational solution." The solution, to be sure, intimates another history of horror, a "final solution," which also involved a reckoning with people branded as outsiders as well as a communal act of violence.

The initial version of *The Blue Light* ends with a coda, a return to the framing episode. A honeymooning couple from the city have driven into Santa Maria, garbed in aviator glasses and long trenchcoats that obscure their gender. This would appear to be an indication of a modern world where traditional orientations no longer hold sway, where patriarchy has lost its grip. The telling of the tale makes a strong impression on the urban pair. For, when we segue back to the contemporary setting, the united and more conventionally attired couple walks to their hotel room window, looking out onto a waterfall and a mist-shrouded mountainside. The site of the blue light, despite the incursion of the villagers, appears no worse for the wear, retaining its evocative beauty. The legend of the blue light also has an undiminished power: In relating how domestic order was restored in the past, it serves to sustain the life of community.

At face value, *The Blue Light* seems marked by romantic sentimentality and an antimodern incentive. When we look more closely, we find the undeniable awareness of a sophisticated modern rationality, an elaborate ideological construction in the form of a legend that accompanies the exploitation of nature, a woman, the past. The final page of the story reads:

> This was the sad end of poor Junta from Santa Maria. Her memory, however, continues to live on in the village which has inflicted such terrible injustice on her. For without her such great riches would never have come to it from the wonderful "hell" of Mount Cristallo.

The text relates a village's wonderful, horrible life. It pays lip service to the mistreatment of Junta, but establishes a causality between a "terrible injustice" and the "great riches" that came from it. During the film, we do not see a single image of mourning—except for Vigo's tear and the aggrieved countenances of parents and relatives whose sons have plunged to their deaths in their quest for Junta and the blue light. The townspeople of Santa Maria mine the elemental and a female outsider, place them in lucrative ornamental shapes, and create a captivating story that glosses over their instrumental activities.

The elemental, the ornamental, and the instrumental thus come together in Santa Maria's cottage culture industry. Its offerings unite premodern sentiment and modern rationale in a manner that anticipates National Socialism's synthesis of romanticism and technology. The Nazis claimed to worship a world of nature and innocence. They devoted much effort, however, to recycling that nature and to molding it into new structures. The reshaping process accorded to larger agendas and reflected the workings of an instrumental rationality. It is precisely this third dimension, though, that often became mystified and disavowed. National Socialism, as we know from Ernst Bloch, recognized the mighty appeal of nonsynchronous sensibilities, thoughts out of keeping with modern vicissitudes, especially a romantic anticapitalism fueled by a discontent with contemporary civilization. One turned to an evocative past of simple peasants, pristine countrysides, and idyllic communities, utilizing "gothic dreams against proletarian realities," "needs and elements from past ages" of decisive value in the state's coordinated effort to capture the imaginations of its citizenry and to offer sustenance for their fantasy life.[75]

For all its idealized landscape painting and blood-and-soil fustian, German fascism pursued the domination over nature through a vast technology that stretched from the rationalized way in which an entire country was organized to an elaborate bureaucratic mechanism to a military machine, a world war, and ultimately the death camps, vast factories that recycled bodies, pressing out of human material every possible commercial gain. The Third Reich practiced a reactionary mode of modernism, an instrumentalism blending the cultural system of the romantic past with the rationality of modern technology.[76] Riefenstahl's debut remains both instructive and provocative for us today as a film made during the Weimar era that prefigures Nazi fantasy production, as a film shrouded in the jargon of authenticity, which, as a fictional text and a material object, enacts the dialectic of enlightenment.

Junta's metamorphosis both destroys and recasts a female image; it reassembles her dead body and person in new structures. Let me return briefly to the filmic production site and recall how Vigo leans over her limp shape in a translucent morning light. In a subjective shot that aligns the camera's perspective with that of the onscreen artist, Junta's physiognomy takes on a different appearance. The dead woman becomes a living legend, a popular memory and a gripping story as well as an alluring icon. The transformation divests her of independent life and forms what once was a constant source of anxiety into a less disruptive shape.[77] Vigo is a stand-in for the camera, an evil eye with a sympathetic countenance, an anti-Pygmalion who transforms the object of his erotic desire into an auratic image. If Riefenstahl resembles anyone in the film, it is the artist from Vienna who paints and pursues Junta, expropriating landscapes and physiognomies with a marked regard for the aesthetic worth and commercial value of these raw materials.

IV. Emanations of *The Blue Light*

Both the narrative and the reception history of Riefenstahl's debut feature reveal much about the dynamics behind the making and marketing of legends. *The Blue Light* was surely not made by Nazis. It was certainly seen by Nazis and applauded by Nazis. Indeed, Hitler was one of the film's earliest admirers. It also would play a seminal role in the Third Reich's most famous director's dealings with her Nazi past. Riefenstahl's reclamation of the film as a lifescript coincided with her concerted attempts over time to recast the film, from its production to its reception, in her own image. What began as the rendering of a local legend by a collective team, involving a director, scriptwriter, and cameraman, became the product of a single formative influence, of an artist who provided the vision, the story, the dialogue, the images—in short, the entire production.[78] Revision and erasure went hand in hand with this auteur's willful triumph, fostering a director's myth and the myth of a director while making for changing shades of meaning in the different emanations of *The Blue Light*.[79]

The reception history of *The Blue Light* follows twists and turns that boggle the mind. The film found mixed reviews and lackluster box office returns upon its initial German run in 1932. The *Film-Kurier* notice bore the headline "Zwei Legenden" and compared the film about Junta's legend unfavorably to a reprise of Chaplin's legendary feature *The Gold Rush*. In Chaplin's silent masterpiece "everything speaks despite the lack of sound." In Riefenstahl's debut one "misses an ordering hand and a visual word. This work's world is not seen filmically, but rather photographically." For all its impressive images, the film lacks substance; it is "sick at the core" and "misbegotten."[80] Riefenstahl reputedly blamed Jewish critics for the film's devastating failure and railed against their inability to understand German culture.[81] She felt vindicated by foreign responses, especially by the silver medal awarded her at the Venice Biennale in 1932. The film would also receive a gold medal at the Paris World Fair in 1937 and one in Venice in 1959 as a film classic.

In an effort to capitalize on *Olympia's* massive success, *The Blue Light* was revived in September 1938. An interviewer in *Film-Kurier* attributed the film's initial German failure to "non-Aryan sectors," seconding the director's wish that her work might now enjoy the enthusiastic response "denied it earlier because of bad will and incomprehension."[82] The Degeto Kulturfilm version purged the names of Jewish co-workers, including the producer Harry Sokal and the co-author Béla Balázs. Riefenstahl, in fact, had denied the latter any payment for his considerable work on the film, responding to Balázs's urgent inquiry with a note on Kaiserhof stationary: "I grant to Herr Gauleiter Julius Streicher of Nuremberg—publisher of *Der Stürmer*—power of attorney in matters of the claims of the Jew Béla Balázs on me."[83] The document signed in her hand belies the account we find in her *Memoir*, where Riefenstahl describes how her "friend" Balázs wrote about his flight to Moscow after Hitler's rise to power, how she wept as she held his letter in her hand. "An ardent Communist, he wanted to remain in Russia for the time being."[84] In the end, as Joseph Zsuffa points out, Balázs never received any compensation for his work on the film.[85]

In 1951, Riefenstahl reassembled outtakes of the film, added a new score, redubbed the voices, and later re-released *The Blue Light*, now without its framing passages.[86] This reshaping of the narrative changed Riefenstahl's story substantially. For without the prologue and coda, there remains no temporal distance nor ironic tension between the premodern and the contemporary world. Instead, we have a melancholy tale addressed to a timeless present. Any awareness of the power of images and the economic value of icons vanishes. A hallmark of Weimar cinema, whose illustrious collaborators included Balázs, Carl Mayer, Arnold Fanck, and Hans Schneeberger, becomes shorn of its ironic tension between past and present and now appears as the director's personal fantasy. We see no tourists, no tourist industry. If any flashback now determines how we view *The Blue Light*, it is the filmmaker's retrospective reading of the film as a paradise lost: "As if it were a premonition, *The Blue Light* told of my ultimate fate: Junta, the strange mountain girl, living in a dream world, persecuted and driven out of society, dies because her ideals are destroyed."[87] Riefenstahl, ever casting about in the postwar era for possible sources of income, would seek to return to paradise and remine *The Blue Light* in projected (but unrealized) recastings of the source as a ballet and a remake with Pier Angeli as Junta and Laurence Harvey as Vigo.[88]

In October 1963, the director's first feature played in the Nuremberg Meistersingerhallen to resounding applause. Carl Müller, prominent owner of the Studio für Filmkunst in Bremen, described the event: "Hundreds couldn't get in. . . . Rarely have I seen such an enthused audience. . . . How often I heard people say, 'What a film!'—Why don't they make films like this anymore?"[89] *The Blue Light* endures as a masterpiece, an important title in a celebrated career. Riefenstahl would undergo reevaluation by auteurists in the 1960s and 1970s, first in America, Great Britain, and France, then later in Germany.[90] The "Hitler-wave" in the Federal Republic of the mid- and late seventies also led to renewed public fascination with Riefenstahl, on television, radio, and in the print media. With the appearance of her memoirs and Ray Müller's directorial portrait in the early 1990s, the filmmaker and her myth yet again enthralled international audiences. *Time* magazine called *The Wonderful, Horrible Life* perhaps "the last great Riefenstahl film."[91]

The first feature and the director's recollections relate the myth of a "wonderful, horrible life," but let us not forget Leni Riefenstahl's considerable hand in the creation of these narratives that rendered her a victim of history and suggested an equivalence between her fate and that of the Jews. The mountain girl's tragic destiny is both the product of a script and a director's mise-en-scène, for Riefenstahl stood both in front of *and* behind the camera. She conceived Junta as an embodiment of purity, "a young girl, intact and innocent, whom fear made retract at any contact with reality, with matter, with sex."[92] Junta's cavern has a vaginal opening and its interior is a womblike space. The grotto will be violated, and so too will be Junta. The story, related the filmmaker, arose in a violent dream: "I watched her [Junta] being chased and pelted with stones, and finally I dreamed of this girl as she fell away from a wall of rock and slowly plunged into the depths."[93] The child of nature becomes the film's quarry. The camera constantly stalks Junta, exposing her figure, caressing her face, fetishizing her body with filters, soft-focus lighting, and striking compositions: It literally loves her to death. Riefenstahl assumed a double role, actress in a punitive fantasy in which she acts upon herself, at once victim and victimizer, masochist and sadist, both the object and agent of violence.

In her only other feature film, *Tiefland* (*Lowlands*), Riefenstahl also played the female lead role, focusing on the itinerant dancer Marta as the hapless object of erotic desire and repeated rape. Here, too, the director commingled voyeurism and exhibitionism, capturing the fascinated and lusty reactions of male audiences to Riefenstahl's onscreen presence and echoing their lecherous gaze with a camera that feasts on her own body's movements. Helma Sanders-Brahms maintained that *Lowlands* is best understood as Riefenstahl's sincere attempt to rehabilitate herself. In this reading, Don Sebastian is "the wolf" and, as such, an obvious Hitler-surrogate; the film shows how a woman makes herself available to the tyrant and comes to recognize the error of her ways and to resist her tormentor.[94] Even if this interpretation sounds plausible, one should bear in mind that the film, though shot during the war, was not completed until 1954. For all its putative resistant energy, *Lowlands* still relishes yet another Riefenstahl persona who is patently helpless, indeed subservient to male power. Marta submits to the Marquis "as though in a trance" and only can free herself from the malevolent lord through the intervention of her nature-boy lover.[95]

And it surely is of a piece with Riefenstahl's work, both onscreen and in writing, which abounds in moments where she makes a spectacle of her own suffering.[96]

A film about the sacrifice of a woman for the sake of a community, *The Blue Light* endeared Riefenstahl to the man who would become Führer. "Once we come to power," Hitler reputedly said to Riefenstahl when they first met in 1932, "you must make my films."[97] Her mountain girl was made to measure for soldier males. For here, as Gisela von Wysocki observes, one found

> . . . the beautiful soul, purity of desire, a self-effacing, purpose-free essence. Her body is yearning and image. In the connotations of the age it becomes a monstrous surface for fascist propaganda, erected against the equality of the sexes, against prostitution in the big cities, against the "degeneration" of the modern woman.[98]

Riefenstahl would put her person and her image at the disposal of the state leadership and the Nazi Party.[99] She focused on the new man marching in front of the camera while disavowing her own person behind the camera. Repeatedly she has claimed that she staged nothing and just let events speak for themselves. Even after 1945, Riefenstahl constantly would insist that she only documented the events of the Nuremberg Party Rally.[100]

The Führer's "perfect woman" was also Nazi Germany's most celebrated filmmaker.[101] (Thea von Harbou was one of the very few women who directed features during the Third Reich.) To describe Riefenstahl as the "most powerful woman in German fascism," however, is both accurate and misleading. For that status came at the price of servitude to a male order and a denigration of female volition.[102] Riefenstahl had little to do with other women; she resolutely steered clear of Nazi Germany's female organizations. Belonging to a woman's world, according to Margarete Mitscherlich, "would not have brought her sufficient glory or fame." Together with the *Herrenmenschen* of the Thousand-Year-Reich, "Femininity in its real physical materiality held no attraction for her."[103] Riefenstahl's fixation on phallic strength, then, coincided with her documentary images of women on the sidelines cheering the men who make history as well as her feature film enactments of female suffering. It stands to reason that the director's most important work celebrates the triumph of male will.

The same film that provided Riefenstahl a ticket of admission to the new order would be used, after the war, as a *Persilschein*, an identity card to clear her from charges of Nazi collaboration and to demonstrate that her art transcended the Hitler era. Riefenstahl maintained that she only served the cause of beauty, arguing for an artistry and an authorship outside of time and beyond any political or religious persuasion. Of course, strength and beauty are anything but immutable categories. For Béla Balázs, Riefenstahl's erstwhile collaborator, beauty is not an absolute, an unchanging, ahistorical, "objective reality." Rather, it represents "a subjective experience of human consciousness" and is a function of different "races, epochs, and cultures."[104] The Nazis knew this as well. During the Third Reich, beauty played a central role in the party's aesthetics as well as in its racial politics and medical policies. While Riefenstahl sat at an editing table reworking the sublime physiques from the Berlin games, the afflicted physiognomies of the sick and mentally ill from *Opfer der Vergangenheit* (*Victims of the Past*, 1937) confronted viewers in German cinemas. Nazism's ideals of physical strength and beauty were inextricably bound to its disdain for degenerate, diseased, and disabled bodies.[105]

Like many other artists who worked in Germany during the Hitler era, the director denied her role in history and declared that her endeavors stood outside of time. International auteurists, likewise, argued that her rightful place lay in the pantheon of cinema's immortals.[106] National Socialist leaders often spoke of art's eternal power and of film's timeless aesthetics while enlisting artists and filmmakers in political campaigns and historical missions. The task of the artist, Goebbels said in 1937, lies in capturing life, in shaping, concentrating, and compressing it in expressive forms:

> Art is nothing other than the shaper of emotion. It comes from emotion and not from the intellect; the artist is nothing other than the person who grants meaning to this emotion. He differs from normal human beings not because he has emotion, but because he has the power to impart form to feelings.[107]

Leni Riefenstahl's art fulfilled a timely service by imparting sublime form to *völkisch* feelings. It created beautiful images that fueled Nazi fantasies, images of heroic men and subservient women.

As a work of art and an artifact, *The Blue Light* anticipates and embodies the abuse of the cinematic machine under National Socialism. It illustrates the continuing attraction of that machine and its central movers to this very day. The feature film played a key role in Riefenstahl's revisionist fiction; the personal myth of an unknowing and innocent artist was configured as a multimedia event and a mass-market recollection. In this melodramatic spectacle, promulgated by Riefenstahl, supported by prominent artists and film directors, sustained by influential journalists and critics, and followed by audiences throughout the world, Hitler's most prominent image maker metamorphosed into a preeminent victim of the past.[108]

NOTES

1. This essay is an updated and revised version of a chapter that appeared in my *The Ministry of Illusion: Nazi Cinema and Its Afterlife* (Cambridge, MA: Harvard University Press, 1996), 27–51.
2. See Steven Bach, *Leni: The Life and Work of Leni Riefenstahl* (New York: Knopf, 2007), 298: Funeral guests placed "old star photographs on the bier, where Horst [Kettner],

visibly shattered, laid his own farewell bouquet next to a fan's Leni scrapbook, open to an autographed portrait of Junta."

3. As reported by Hanns-Georg Rodek, "Die Abschiedsszene," *Die Welt*, September 13, 2003.
4. Stephen Schiff, "Leni's *Olympia*," *Vanity Fair* (September 1992): 252–261, 291–296. The same issue also contains a short portrait of Riefenstahl's famous archenemy, likewise written by Schiff, "Prodigal Sontag."
5. John Simon, "The Führer's Movie Maker," *New York Times Book Review*, September 26, 1993, 1, 26–29.
6. Richard Corliss, "Riefenstahl's Last Triumph," *Time*, October 18, 1993, 91–92.
7. As reported in Paul Harris, "Hollywood Tackles Hitler's Leni," *The Guardian*, April 29, 2007. Foster is slated to play the role of Riefenstahl; the script is being written by Rupert Walters with a director still to be named: "The movie is part of a trend of seeing individual figures in a more morally complex light," surmises Harris; indeed, claims one of his sources, the project responds to "a desire on behalf of the audience to see 'good' Nazis."
8. For a comprehensive account of Riefenstahl's comeback, see Jürgen Trimborn, *Riefenstahl: Eine deutsche Karriere. Biographie* (Berlin: Aufbau, 2002), 475–505.
9. Bach, *Leni*, 293.
10. See Ernst Jaeger's lurid account, "How Leni Riefenstahl Became Hitler's Girlfriend," *Hollywood Tribune*, April 28, through July 17, 1939 (weekly installments). Jaeger, former editor in chief of *Film-Kurier*, defected to the United States while accompanying Riefenstahl on her ill-fated 1938 tour through America.
11. Budd Schulberg, "Nazi Pin-up Girl: Hitler's No. 1 Movie Actress," *Saturday Evening Post*, March 30, 1946, 11.
12. See Glenn B. Infield, *Leni Riefenstahl: The Fallen Film Goddess* (New York: Crowell, 1976).
13. Bianca Jagger, "Leni's Back & Bianca's Got Her," *Interview* 5 (January 1975): 35–37.
14. Quoted in Georg Seesslen, "Die Krieger, der Tanz, das Mädchen und der Führer," *Blimp* 22/23 (spring 1993): 23. See her response in *Leni Riefenstahl, A Memoir* (New York: St. Martin's, 1992), 650: "I would love to have met this unusually gifted as well as controversial director and to have worked with him—especially after he wrote to me how keenly he looked forward to our collaboration." Fragile health, it was claimed, prevented her from accepting Fassbinder's offer.
15. Kevin Brownlow, "Leni Reifenstahl [sic]," *Film* (London) 47 (winter 1966–1967): 15.
16. The secondary literature on Riefenstahl's career and films is massive and evergrowing. A useful, albeit outdated initial guide is Sandra Bernstein and Michael MacMillan, "Leni Riefenstahl: A Selected Bibliography," *Quarterly Review of Film Studies* 2, no. 4 (November 1977): 439–457. Recent career studies include David B. Hinton, *The Films of Leni Riefenstahl* (Metuchen, NJ/London: Scarecrow Press, 1978); Charles Ford, *Leni Riefenstahl* (Paris: La Table Rounde, 1978); Renata Berg-Pan, *Leni Riefenstahl* (Boston: Twayne, 1980); and Leonardo Quaresima, *Leni Riefenstahl* (Florence: La Nuova Italia, 1984). The most comprehensive account of the director's early films as actress and director remains Peggy Ann Wallace, "An Historical Study of the Career of Leni Riefenstahl from 1923 to 1933," Diss. University of Southern California, 1975. There has been a recent spate of biographical studies. Besides the previously cited books by Bach and Trimborn, see *Leni Riefenstahl*, ed. Filmmuseum Potsdam (Berlin: Henschel, 1999); Rainer Rother, *Leni Riefenstahl. Die Verführung des*

Talents (Berlin: Henschel, 2000); Diane Chauvelot, *La Passion de l'image: Leni Riefenstahl, entre le beau et le bien* (Paris: Editions de Janus, 2000); and Lutz Kinkel, *Die Scheinwerferin. Leni Riefenstahl und das "Dritte Reich"* (Hamburg: Europa, 2002).

17. "Fascinating Fascism," reprinted in Susan Sontag, *Under the Sign of Saturn* (New York: Vintage, 1981), 97.
18. Sontag, 91.
19. "Visual Pleasure Inhibited: Aspects of the German Revue Film," trans. J. D. Steakley and Gabriele Hoover, *New German Critique* 24–25 (fall/winter 1981–1982): 261.
20. Riefenstahl also produced two short films about prominent fascist artists, both of which were directed by Arnold Fanck: *Joseph Thorak, Werkstatt und Werk* (1943) and *Arno Breker* (1944).
21. Thomas Elsaesser, "Portrait of the Artist as a Young Woman," *Sight and Sound* 3, no. 2 (February 1993): 18.
22. Hans Barkhausen provides incontrovertible evidence regarding the Nazi government's support of the two *Olympia* films. See his article, "Footnote to the History of Riefenstahl's *Olympia*," *Film Quarterly* 28, no.1 (Fall 1974): 8–12.
23. Late in 2002, documentary filmmaker Maurice Philip Remy claimed that he had discovered a color *Kulturfilm* directed by Riefenstahl, *Das deutsche Erntedankfest auf dem Bückeberg*. Subsequent scrutiny by specialists, however, determined that the Ufa production was made by Kurt Waschnek. See the dpa press release, "Erntedankfest ohne Leni," *Frankfurter Allgemeine Zeitung*, November 20, 2002.
24. For a detailed account of Balázs's work on *The Blue Light*, see Joseph Zsuffa, *Béla Balázs: The Man and the Artist* (Berkeley/Los Angeles/London: University of California Press, 1987), esp. 203–206, 214–215. According to Zsuffa, Balázs's influence was central to the film's conception and ultimate shape. Carl Mayer assisted Balázs in the writing of the script as well as participating in the editing, clashing violently with Fanck, who also played a key role in the cutting of the film (219). Zsuffa's reconstruction of the production and division of labor provides a dynamic sense of collaboration, cooperation, and conflict. His discussion, though sympathetic to Balázs, is meticulously documented, drawing on private correspondence, archival materials, and contemporary reviews, rendering it more credible than Riefenstahl's self-serving and contradictory recollections. See also John Ralmon, "Béla Balázs in German Exile," *Film Quarterly* 30, no. 3 (spring 1977): 12–19; and, more recently, Hanno Loewy, *Béla Balázs—Märchen, Ritual und Film* (Berlin: Vorwerk 8, 2003), esp. 351–378.
25. During the mid-1980s, the German journalist and filmmaker Nina Gladitz engaged in a vigorous campaign against Riefenstahl, claiming the director willingly exploited gypsy inmates from a concentration camp during her wartime work on *Tiefland* (*Lowlands*), offering help if they cooperated, but in the end failing to make good on her promise, allegations denied by the filmmaker in an enusing court battle, a further occasion where Riefenstahl argued that she stood unfairly accused. See, for instance, Wolfgang Rumpf, "Infame Lügen," *Tip*, December 14, 1984, 56–57; and Ulrich Enzensberger, "KZ-Zigeuner tanz' mit mir," *Konkret* (February 1985): 12–17. Also see Gladitz's film about Riefenstahl and *Lowlands*, the WDR production that prompted the legal proceedings, *Zeit des Schweigens und der Dunkelheit* (*Time of Silence and Darkness*). For an analysis of the documentary, see Andreas Seltzer, "Bildbanditen," *Merkur* 39 (July 1985): 621–625. After Riefenstahl appealed the initial verdict, a second trial confirmed Gladitz's claims that the director had selected sixty gypsies from

a group of 250 concentration camp inmates and forced them to act in *Lowlands* without pay ("zwangsverpflichtet"). Among the many press accounts, see Hanno Kühnert's critical essay, "Wenn Juristen Vergangenheit klären," *Die Zeit*, March 27, 1987.

26. Siegfried Kracauer, in *From Caligari to Hitler: A Psychological History of the German Film* (Princeton, NJ: Princeton University Press, 1947), describes Junta "as a sort of gypsy girl," 258.
27. Riefenstahl, *A Memoir*, 89. An identical translation appeared in Great Britain under the title *The Sieve of Time* (London: Quartet, 1992). The German original edition, *Memoiren* (Munich/ Hamburg: Knaus, 1987), is more than 250 pages longer.
28. Michel Delahaye's exchange with the director appeared in the September 1965 number of *Cahiers du Cinéma*. The passage is quoted from the clumsy English translation by Rose Kaplin that appears in *Interviews with Film Directors*, ed. Andrew Sarris (New York: Avon, 1967), 468.
29. Barsam, *Filmguide to* Triumph of the Will, 9. See also John Simon, "The Führer's Movie Maker," 29: "Perhaps we should look to the character with whom Riefenstahl most closely identifies herself: Junta, the mountain girl in *The Blue Light*, who was willing to die for her aspirations. Riefenstahl, too, was ready to sacrifice all in pursuit of her obsessions."
30. See David Gunston, "Leni Riefenstahl," *Film Quarterly* 14, no. 1 (fall 1960): *The Blue Light* is "the one film above all others that was to settle her fate as a director" (12).
31. Invitations to the Ufa-sponsored gala premiere of 1932 announce a 6:45 p.m. curtain. The program began with Ufa sound newsreel, no. 81. Guiseppe Becce conducted the Ufa Symphony Orchestra in a live performance of Tchaikovsky's "Capriccio italien" followed by a stage prologue to *The Blue Light* (a solo dance by Igor Schwezoff choreographed by Percy Athos with original music by Becce) before the actual feature. The 1952 German reprise, in comparison, was preceded by the twenty-one-minute short, *Wunder der Bienenwelt* (*Wonders of the Bee World*), a *Kulturfilm* that promised "unforgettable insights into the deeper meaning of miraculous creation." The publicity brochure lists the length of *The Blue Light* as 2,000 meters (73 minutes). The information file on *The Blue Light* in the Stiftung Deutsche Kinemathek also contains the program for the 1938 release and the National-Verleih press booklet for the 1952 version.
32. Riefenstahl, *A Memoir*, 384.
33. In 2006, Pathfinder Home Entertainment issued a subtitled version of the original release as a part of its Leni Riefenstahl Archival Collection. The disc also includes a significantly shorter silent version, a curiosity that circulated during the 1930s in the United States and, even as late as the early 1980s, was still to be found on videocassette. The opening titles credit "Bella Belaze" as having written the story and list "Mathias Waimann" in the role of Vigo. The tacked-on musical accompaniment provides a bizarre pastiche of high and low; the film begins, for instance, with tracks from Fredrick Loewe's score for Vincente Minnelli's *Gigi*.
34. Postwar apologias of Riefenstahl echo a previous century's romantic celebrations of the artist-genius. Take, for instance, Rühle von Lilienstern's special plea for Caspar David Friedrich: "All genius is of an infinite nature, and is, to itself and for all others, the measure and plumbline and substitute for all finite experience. It is safest to let flourish freely, where and when it is encompassed within the process of creation. . . . It behoves genius to break new ground everywhere, and to ripen according to its own

experience, just as it allows no rules from without to intrude upon it, preferring rather to err in the heights and depths than to remain content in the false ground of impoverished certainty. 'Can genius really err?' *Genius*, never!—insofar as it is understood as the divine, creative principle" (quoted in Joseph Leo Koerner, *Caspar David Friedrich and the Subject of Landscape* (London: Reaktion, 1990), 61.

35. Berg-Pan, *Leni Riefenstahl*, 82.
36. National Film press booklet for the 1952 German release (available in the Stiftung Deutsche Kinemathek, Berlin).
37. See Zsuffa, *The Man and the Artist*, 454: "Arnold Fanck was familiar with Renker's novels; in fact, he used the title, with a slight change, of one of Renker's novels, *Heilige Bergen* [sic] (Holy Mountains), for the first film in which Riefenstahl acted, *Der heilige Berg* (the Holy Mountain). Thus, it is most likely that Riefenstahl became acquainted with Renker's works at the very beginning of her film career." Fanck has confirmed this claim.
38. Quoted in Peggy Wallace, "Riefenstahl from 1923 to 1933," 285. Compare the director's similar allegation regarding *Triumph of the Will* in a letter to the editor of *Film Library Quarterly* 5.3 (summer 1972): "Since, right down to the premiere of the film no one from the party, neither Hitler nor Goebbels nor others, got to see as much as one meter of the film, nothing can be said, consequently, of the intention or interference of the political leaders. Just as the film is still to be seen today, it came into being from out of my imagination alone" (5).
39. Gustav Renker, *Bergkristall*, 4th ed. (Gütersloh: Bertelsmann, 1943), 45.
40. Riefenstahl spoke of her work in evocative terms reminiscent of Friedrich's notion that art is "the language of our feeling, or disposition, indeed, even our devotion and our prayers" (quoted in William Vaughan, *German Romantic Painting* [New Haven: Yale University Press, 1980], 74).
41. Likewise, the iconography of the final sequence brings to mind Friedrich's "Morning" and "Morning Mist in the Mountains" as well as "Two Men Contemplating the Moon" and "Rocky Gorge in Elbesandsteingebirge."
42. As in Friedrich, we partake of figures that stand with their backs to the viewer and stare into the distance, small dots against vast expanses, characters who embody yearning, persons wishing to merge with the grandeur before them.
43. Alice A. Kuzniar, "The Temporality of Landscape: Romantic Allegory and C. D. Friedrich," *Studies in Romanticism* 28, no. 1 (spring 1989): 74. Compare Philippe Lacoue-Labarthe and Jean-Luc Nancy, *The Literary Absolute: The Theory of Literature in German Romanticism*, trans. Philip Barnard and Cheryl Lester (Albany: State University of New York Press, 1988), 4: A landscape before which one feels the "sentiment of nature" is romantic. "But romantic, as well, is the sensibility capable of responding to the spectacle, and of imagining, or better, recreating—*phantasieren*—what it evokes."
44. Vigo was played by Mathias Wieman, a strident Nazi activist, one of the first to receive Hitler's commendation as a State Actor ("Staatsschauspieler") in 1937.
45. The couple's entry to the village parallels that of another traveler from the outside world in the embedded story, namely Vigo's.
46. Compare Immanuel Kant, *Observations on the Feeling of the Beautiful and Sublime*, trans. John T. Goldthwait (Berkeley/Los Angeles: University of California Press, 1965), 48.

47. See Martin Swales, *The German Novelle* (Princeton, NJ: Princeton University Press, 1977), 28: "I would argue that the mainspring of much novelle writing is the contact between an ordered and reliably interpreted human universe on the one hand and an experience or set of experiences that would appear to conflict utterly with any notion of order or manageable interpretation on the other. Hence, the novelle derives its peculiar and insistent energy from what one can best describe as a hermeneutic gamble, as a shock confrontation with marginal events. Implicitly, the attempt to make an ordered statement of that which by definition resists the ordering intention is one of the central undertakings within the narrative universe of the novelle."
48. Representative examples include *Das Cabinet des Dr. Caligari* (*The Cabinet of Dr. Caligari*, 1920), *Zur Chronik von Grieshuus* (*Chronicle of the Grey House*, 1925), and *Geheimnisse der Orients* (*Secrets of the Orient*, 1928).
49. See Leni Riefenstahl, *Kampf im Schnee und Eis* (Leipzig: Hesse & Becker, 1933), for her earliest recollections of *The Holy Mountain*, *The Great Leap* (*Der große Sprung*, 1927), *The White Hell of Pitz Palü* (*Die weiße Hölle vom Piz Palü*, 1929), and *Avalanche* (*Stürme über dem Montblanc*, 1930), *The White Frenzy* (*Der weisse Rausch*, 1931), *The Blue Light*, and *S.O.S. Eisberg* (1933). For useful perspectives on the mountain film, see *Fanck—Trenker—Riefenstahl: Der deutsche Bergfilm und seine Folgen*, ed. Klaus Kreimeier (Berlin: Stiftung Deutsche Kinemathek, 1972) and the special issue of *Film und Kritik* 1 (June 1992) entitled "Revisited Der Fall Dr. Fanck: Die Entdeckung der Natur im deutschen Bergfilm" as well as Christian Rapp, *Höhenrausch. Der deutsche Bergfilm* (Vienna: Sonderzahl, 1997) and *Berge, Licht und Traum. Dr. Arnold Fanck und der deutsche Bergfilm*, ed. Jan-Christopher Horak and Gisela Pichler (Munich: Bruckmann, 1997). See also my essay, "Mountains and Modernity: Relocating the *Bergfilm*," *New German Critique* 51 (Fall 1990): 137–161.
50. *From Caligari to Hitler*, 111. Throughout his entire exegesis, Kracauer has little to say about sexual difference. In talking about mountain films, he reduces women to secondary factors in his terse and frequently ironic plot descriptions, desisting from any sustained comment about their constant and conspicuous appearance. He overlooks Junta's erotic attraction and the sexual frenzy she catalyzes in the community's young males. Instead, Kracauer explains the villagers' active hostility toward her as a result of superstition alone: Because the strange woman enjoys sole access to the blue light, residents of Santa Maria consider her a witch (258).
51. Herman Weigel, "Interview mit Leni Riefenstahl," *Filmkritik* 16, no.8 (August 1972): 396.
52. Kracauer described the genre's intended audience harshly in his notice, "*Der Heilige Berg,*" *Frankfurter Zeitung*, March 4, 1927, reprinted in *Von Caligari zu Hitler*, ed. Karsten Witte (Frankfurt am Main: Suhrkamp, 1979), 400: "There may be here and there in Germany small youth groups which attempt to counter everything that they call mechanization, by means of an overrun nature worship, i.e. by means of a panic-striken flight into the foggy brew of vague sentimentality. As an expression of their particular manner of not existing, the film is a masterpiece" (trans. by Thomas Y. Levin).
53. William Vaughan, *German Romantic Painting*, 66.
54. See Hans Feld, "Der Fanck-Film der Aafa," *Film-Kurier*, February 3, 1931. See also the cinematographer Sepp Allgeier's account, *Die Jagd nach dem Bild*, 2nd rev. ed. (Stuttgart: Engelhorns, 1931), especially his description of location shooting on *The Holy Mountain*: "Sometimes we had to lend a bit of a helping hand when nature did

not provide us with camera-ready footage" (p. 62). Compare Joachim Kroll, "Die filmische Landschaft," *Der Deutsche Film* 3, no. 6 (December 1938): Landscapes, according to the author, maintain a photographic interest only to the degree in which they reflect human presence (148).

55. Riefenstahl, *A Memoir*, 89. Riefenstahl also describes Fanck's editing room as a "magic workshop."
56. For a detailed account of the film's production background (whose privileged source of information is Riefenstahl), see Peggy A. Wallace, "'The Most Important Factor Was the Spirit': Leni Riefenstahl During the Filming of *The Blue Light*," *Image* 17, no. 1 (March 1974): 17–29.
57. F. W. Murnau, "Films of the Future," *McCall's Magazine* (September 1928); quoted as reprinted in *Hollywood Directors 1914–1940*, ed. Richard Koszarski (London/Oxford/New York: Oxford University Press, 1976), 217.
58. The phrase comes from Balázs's review of *Nosferatu*, which appeared in *Der Tag* on March 9, 1923, and was included in his collection of notices and essays, *Der sichtbare Mensch*; reprinted in *Schriften zum Film*, ed. Helmut H. Diederichs et al., vol. 1 (Munich: Hanser, 1982), 175–176.
59. "Leni Riefenstahl: Falsche Bauern, falsche Soldaten und was für ein Volk," *Süddeutsche Zeitung*, September 13–14, 1975.
60. See Robin Wood's exemplary reading of *Nosferatu*, "F. W. Murnau," *Film Comment* 12, no. 3 (May–June 1976): 7–8.
61. See Wood, "F. W. Murnau," 8: "One is tempted toward a straight psychoanalytical interpretation: Nosferatu is the symbol of neurosis resulting from the repressed sexuality (repressed *nature*); when the neurosis is revealed to the light of day it is exorcised, but the process of its emergence and recognition has been so terrible that positive life (Nina) is destroyed with it."
62. Earlier Vigo contemplates the sleeping Junta as if he were Count Orlok, leering at her exposed bosom and hovering over her body.
63. Vincent Canby, "Leni Riefenstahl in a Long Close-up," *New York Times*, October 14, 1993.
64. Kracauer, *From Caligari to Hitler*, 259.
65. Sontag, "Fascinating Fascism," 77. Sontag's essay occasioned spirited debate in West Germany when it appeared in the *Die Zeit* on March 2 and March 9, 1975. See Hans Egon Holthusen, "Leni Riefenstahl in Amerika. Zum Problem einer 'faschistischen Ästhetik,'" *Merkur* 29, no. 7 (July 1975): 569–578; see also the special issue of *Frauen und Film* devoted to the "Riefenstahl Renaissance," December 14, 1977.
66. Andrew Sarris, "Notes on the Fascination of Fascism," *Village Voice*, January 30, 1978, 33. Riefenstahl also is struck by Sontag's reliance on *From Caligari to Hitler*, but she chides the American critic above all for branding "thousands of mountains climbers as Nazis or Fascists" (Riefenstahl, *A Memoir*, 622).
67. Sontag, "Fascinating Fascism," 77.
68. Ibid., 93.
69. Junta's metamorphosis mirrors quite poignantly the blend of kitsch and death that Saul Friedländer considers central to the frisson of Nazi aesthetics. See *Reflections of Nazism: An Essay on Kitsch and Death*, trans. Thomas Weyr (New York: Harper & Row, 1984), 29: "The juxtaposition of these two contradictory elements represents the foundation of a certain religious aesthetic, and, in my opinion, the bedrock of Nazi aesthetics as well as the new evocation of Nazism."

70. Junta's face will become an image sold as a souvenir to tourists. See Ludwig Giesz's more general comments about kitsch art and tourism, "Der 'Kitsch-Mensch' als Tourist," in *Der Kitsch*, ed. Gillo Dorfies, trans. Birgid Mayr (Tübingen: Wasmuth, 1969), 170.
71. The 1952 release version begins with Vigo's voiceover, which was recorded after the war by Mathias Wieman: "Locked in the pathless valleys of Santa Maria, the legend of Junta lives on. On quiet evenings, the taciturn peasant tells the wanderer the story of the 'Blue Light.' It is long since existinguished, but on silvery moonlit nights, the secret of beautiful Junta entices the lonely mountaineer to Monte Cristallo's rocky walls."
72. Oskar Kalbus, *Vom Werden deutscher Filmkunst. 2 Teil: Der Tonfilm* (Altona-Bahrenfeld: Cigaretten Bilderdienst, 1935), 66. The high regard for the power of human physiognomy is, of course, a central concern in Balázs's theory of film. Compare the manner in which the villagers in *Lowlands*, played by concentration camp inmates, generally appear in group configurations rather than in sympathetic close-ups.
73. Arnold Berson, "The Truth About Leni: Nazi Collaborator—or Independent Artist," *Films and Filming* 11 (April 1965): 16.
74. Kracauer, *From Caligari to Hitler*, 259.
75. Ernst Bloch, "Nonsynchronism and the Obligation to Its Dialectics," trans. Mark Ritter, *New German Critique* 11 (spring 1977): 27, 30.
76. See Jeffrey Herf, *Reactionary Modernism: Technology, Culture, and Politics in the Third Reich* (Cambridge et al.: Cambridge University Press, 1984).
77. Compare Klaus Theweleit, *Male Fantasies. Vol. 1: Women Floods Bodies History*, trans. Stephen Conway et al. (Minneapolis: University of Minnesota Press, 1987), 215, where he discusses the fascist "language of occupation" and how "it acts imperialistically against any form of independently moving life." One might also compare this scene to the transformation of the real Maria into the vamp robot Maria in Fritz Lang's *Metropolis*.
78. Upon the second release, Riefenstahl would still speak of the film as a collective effort, but her account (as well as the film's credit sequence and advertisements) leaves out the names of significant collaborators like Balázs, Sokal, and Mayer ("Gespräch mit Leni Riefenstahl: 'So entstand *Das blaue Licht*,'" *Film-Kurier*, September 24, 1938. The postwar German version reinstates Balázs as a collaborator, although Riefenstahl continues to claim primary credit for the screenplay—as well as for the direction and cinematography ("Buch, Regie, Bildgestaltung").
79. *Triumph of the Will*, likewise, would change its shape in the course of time. Its release version of March 1935 was 3,109 meters; on January 2, 1939, the film was cut back to 3,030 meters, and on January 28, 1942 to 2,358 meters. In early September 1935, a 16 mm version of 1,237 meters was also released (Klaus Kanzog, *"Staatspolitisch besonders wertvoll": Ein Handbuch zu 30 deutschen Spielfilmen der Jahre 1934 bis 1945* [Munich: Schaubig & Ledig, 1994], 24).
80. Hermann Sinsheimer, "Zwei Legenden: *Das blaue Licht* im Ufapalast am Zoo," *Film-Kurier*, March 26, 1932. The Vienna correspondent for the film journal *Close Up* was equally underwhelmed: "Certainly there are mountains, and water-falls, and moonlight, and clouds and very characteristic old peasants (I have never seen so many wrinkled faces in my life), but it is all so disconnected, and you cannot help thinking that someone feels obliged to show you everything which in his opinion belongs to

a perfect legendary mountain film" (Trude Weiss, "*The Blue Light*," *Close Up* 9, no. 2 [June 1932]: 121). "Magnus," the *Variety* reviewer in Berlin, also expressed mixed feelings in his notice of April 19, 1932: "The picture could have been a worldwide hit but story appeal was ignored. The story does not grip and it is the photography, beautiful in the extreme, and fine production that carry the subject." Riefenstahl, both as director and actress, is unimpressive. "In directing she is lost in repetitions." For a more upbeat assessment of *The Blue Light*'s resonance in the United States, see "Bahnbrechender Erfolg in den Vereinigten Staaten: Amerikanische Pressestimmen über *Das blaue Licht*," *Film-Kurier*, November 6, 1934.

81. Co-producer Harry Sokal has maintained that Riefenstahl threw a temper tantrum, chiding Jewish critics as aliens who lack all understanding of German mentality and spirit. "Thank God," she exclaimed in 1932, "this won't last much longer!" (as cited in Harry R. Sokal, "Über Nacht Antisemitin geworden?" *Der Spiegel*, November 8, 1976, 14). See also Goebbels's diary entry of February 5, 1939: "In the evening, Leni Riefenstahl reports to me on her trip to America. She gives me an exhaustive description, and one that is far from encouraging. We shall get nowhere there. The Jews rule by terror and bribery" (*The Goebbels Diaries: 1939–1941*, trans. and ed. Fred Taylor [Harmondsworth/ New York: Penguin, 1984], 9).
82. "Gespräch mit Leni Riefenstahl: 'So entstand *Das blaue Licht*,'" *Film-Kurier* (September 24, 1938). Also see Günther Schwark's review, "*Das blaue Licht*/Kurbel," *Film-Kurier*, September 28, 1938: "The film, whose artistic merit will remain unforgettable, had a very strong resonance." The January 1939 issue of *Der Deutsche Film* ran an editorial about a German national cinematography, "Gibt es einen deutschen Kamerastil?" 176–177. *The Blue Light* is singled out as an exemplar of a distinctly German camera style.
83. "Riefenstahl File," Berlin Document Center. The "Kaiserhof" hotel was a favorite gathering place for Nazi luminaries.
84. Riefenstahl, *A Memoir*, 135.
85. Zsuffa, *The Man and the Artist*, 230.
86. The original negative of *The Blue Light* had either been lost or, depending on the account, confiscated by the French or stolen by producer Harry Sokal. In any event, the original running time of eight-six minutes was cut back to seventy-three minutes.
87. Riefenstahl, *A Memoir*, 100.
88. Negotiations regarding the ballet version ended in a contract signed on October 27, 1938, in which Riefenstahl granted rights for a dance adaptation that would premiere in Paris and tour Europe. For reasons unknown to Riefenstahl, the undertaking fell through. The film remake was to have been produced in England and directed by Riefenstahl. According to Wallace's dissertation, public controversy in England, including unfavorable articles in *The Daily Express* and other newspapers, led to the cancellation of the project (401–403).
89. Dietrich Kuhlbrodt, "Leni Riefenstahl wieder offiziell," *Die Zeit*, 24 July 1964.
90. See, among other essays and articles, the special issue of *Film Comment* 3, no. 1 (winter 1965), "1965—Comeback for Leni Riefenstahl." The lead piece by Gordon Hitchens, "Interview with a Legend," unabashedly declares the writer's admiration: "One doesn't *interview* Riefenstahl. One listens. And watches. No question—she's a remarkable woman" (6). The number gave rise to lively responses, mainly pro-Riefenstahl, in a subsequent issue of *Film Comment* 3, no. 3 (summer 1965): 82–87. Kevin Brownlow also published a passionate defense of the director, "Leni Reifenstahl

[sic]," *Film* (London) 47 (winter 1966–1967): 14–19. See also Jeffrey Richards, "Leni Riefenstahl: Style and Structure," *The Silent Picture* 8 (autumn 1970): 17–19. Gordon Hitchens played a key role in another American homage to Riefenstahl, a special issue devoted to the director, *Film Culture* 56–57 (spring 1973). Almost two decades later he provided the "American Intelligence Report on Leni Riefenstahl—May 30th, 1945" for *Film Culture* 77 (fall 1992): 34–38. WCBS "Camera Three" in New York aired a two-part program on Riefenstahl in mid-1973. See Amos Vogel's critical commentary, "Can We Now Forget the Evil That She Did?" *New York Times*, May 13, 1973: "The program was created with the active participation of Miss Riefenstahl, whose charisma has already previously inspired other impressionable men to smooth her attempt to transform herself into an innocent, apolitical artist." The international wave of enthusiasm also gave rise to a celebratory special issue on the director in West Germany, the August 1972 issue of *Filmkritik*, replete with a sympathetic interview, notes from the filmmaker's Penthesilea-project, an admiring portrait of Riefenstahl, and a comprehensive filmography. The issue prompted much critical discussion. See, for instance, Rudolph Ganz, "Leni Riefenstahls fragwürdige Renaissance," *Frankfurter Rundschau*, August 25, 1972; Klaus Kreimeier, "Zum Riefenstahl-Heft der '*Filmkritik*,'" *epd Kirche und Film* 25, no. 9 (September 1972); and Gerd Albrecht, "Nochmals: Der Fall Riefenstahl. Gedanken über die Propaganda und ihre Bewunderer," *epd Kirche und Film* 25, no. 11 (November 1972): 18–19.

91. Richard Corliss, "Riefenstahl's Last Triumph," *Time*, October 18, 1993, 91–92. Compare J. Hoberman, "Triumph of the Swill," *Premiere* 7, no. 4 (December 1993): He wryly terms the homage "something like the *Sunset Boulevard* of the Third Reich" (56). For a discussion of the film see Wulf Kansteiner's essay in this volume.
92. Delahay, *Interviews with Film Directors*, 456.
93. Riefenstahl, *A Memoir*, 89.
94. Helma Sanders-Brahms, "*Tiefland*: Tyrannenmord," in *Das Jahr 1945*, ed. Hans Helmut Prinzler (Berlin: Stiftung Deutsche Kinemathek, 1990), 176.
95. J. Hoberman, "Far from Lincoln Center," *Village Voice*, October 7, 1981, 44. The critic provides a striking characterization of Riefenstahl's "narcissistic performance" in *Lowlands*: "Clumsily sexy, she's less Marlene Dietrich in *The Devil Is a Woman* than Maria Montez in *Gypsy Wildcat*."
96. Riefenstahl's memoirs at times read like "The Perils of Leni." There are repeated scenes in which she, an unwary soul, confronts male aggression and unwanted sexual advances. The Minister of Propaganda harasses her in hot-and-heavy tableaux straight out of Harlequin Romances: "He grabbed my breast and tried to force himself on me. I had to wrestle my way out of his arms and dashed to the door, with Goebbels pursuing me. Besides himself with rage, he held me against the wall and tried to kiss me. His eyes were wide open and his face completely distorted" (*A Memoir*, 142). Later, she claims, Hitler makes a pass at her and French journalists tear off her clothes.
97. See Riefenstahl's account of her "fateful meeting" with Hitler in Riefenstahl, *A Memoir*, 106.
98. Gisela von Wysocki, "Die Berge und die Patriarchen: Leni Riefenstahl," in *Die Fröste der Freiheit: Aufbruchsphantasien* (Frankfurt/M: Syndikat, 1980), 75.
99. The filmmaker, to be sure, was the object of much envy and idle gossip as well as abusive humor. Contemporaries called her a "*Bergziege*" (mountain goat-bitch)—or even worse, the "*Reichsgletscherspalte*" (the Reich's glacial crack) (see, for instance,

"Lachen," *Film-Kurier*, March 31, 1934; and Brigitte Jeremias, "Das Jahr 1945," *epd Film* 7, no. 4 [April 1990]: 26).

100. *Triumph of the Will*, she tells Michel Delahaye, was "only a documentary. I showed what everyone was witness to or had heard about" (*Interviews with Film Directors*, 458). Later she insists that she made the film as a documentary and it was only after the film left her hands that it became propaganda. "But what I make with *Triumph of the Will* is normally like newsreels, but I make it in my artistic way" ("Leni Riefenstahl Interviewed by Gordon Hitchens, October 11th, 1971, Munich," *Film Culture* 56–57 [spring 1973]: 102).
101. Quoted by Gunston, "Leni Riefenstahl," 13. See Claudia Koonz, *Mothers in the Fatherland: Women, the Family, and Nazi Politics* (New York: St. Martin's Press, 1987), 6: "The separation between masculine and feminine spheres, which followed logically and psychological from Nazi leaders' misogyny, relegated women to their space—both beneath and beyond the dominant world of men."
102. See Wysocki, 80. Riefenstahl represents, in the words of B. Ruby Rich, "a sort of Amazon among the Nazis, the token exceptional woman who was granted 'permission' by the patriarchy to be privileged in its power in exchange for adopting its values" ("Leni Riefenstahl: The Deceptive Myth," in *Sexual Stratagems: The World of Women in Myth*, ed. Patricia Erens [New York: Horizon, 1979], 208). Rich also argues against critics who would look to Riefenstahl as a feminist role model.
103. Margarete Mitscherlich, "Triumph der Verdrängung," *Stern*, October 8, 1987, 82.
104. Béla Balázs, *Theory of the Film*, trans. Edith Bone (New York: Dover, 1970), 33.
105. Compare Klaus Wolbert, *Die Nackten und die Toten des "Dritten Reiches"* (Giessen: Anabas, 1982), 234: "The beauty of the nude figure in National Socialist sculpture contained . . . a mandate of death. Its excessiveness condemned anyone whose aesthetic claims could not suffice. . . . The fascists murdered programmatically in the name of beauty!"
106. Compare Maholia Dargis, "Queen of Denial: The Life and Lies of Leni Riefenstahl," *Voice Literary Supplement* 123 (March 1994): "Riefenstahl and her defenders would rescue the director and her films from the very history and aesthetics of hate she helped create" (10).
107. "Rede bei der ersten Jahrestagung der Reichsfilmkammer am 5.3.1937 in der Krolloper, Berlin," reprinted in Gerd Albrecht, *Nationalsozialistische Filmpolitik* (Stuttgart: Enke, 1969), 449.
108. See Simon Hofmann, "Das Comeback der Leni Riefenstahl," *Risse: Analyse und Subversion* 5 (summer 2003): "At a time when people seem more concerned with their status as victims than about their own guilt, Leni Riefenstahl's stock could not be higher. The former 'key figure of the Old Right' has become a star of the new German society."

Chapter 8

To Be or Not to Be Wagnerian: Music in Riefenstahl's Nazi-era Films

Celia Applegate

I.

Musically speaking, there is no talking people out of their belief that Richard Wagner composed the score for the Third Reich. We can find plenty of reasons for the persistence of this belief, not least in the unacknowledged influence of the anonymous sound editors who have chosen to score nearly every modern documentary on the Second World War with excerpts from Wagner preludes. The frequent use of the adjective "Wagnerian" or the phrase "Wagnerian *Gesamtkunstwerk*" to characterize the aspirations of those who choreographed public life in the Third Reich also owes something to Walter Benjamin's suggestion that the "logical result of Fascism is the introduction of aesthetics into political life."[1] Thus, for instance, one finds a recent textbook on the Holocaust referring to Hitler's development of his "own vision of politics and power" while inspired by Wagner's "huge casts, imposing music, exaggerated passions, and powerful depictions of Germanic myth."[2] Never mind that Wagner's only opera with a "huge cast" (*Rienzi*) was not based on Germanic myth, or that the Ring cycle, with its remarkably small casts, was not either, depending on what one includes under the adjective "Germanic." And whether one regards the passions expressed in his dramas as exaggerated does depend on one's experience of life. But nowhere does the myth of the Third Reich as Wagnerian prove more influential than when it shapes impressions and interpretations of Leni Riefenstahl's Nazi-era films. *Triumph of the Will* and *Olympia* are routinely identified as Wagnerian *Gesamtkunstwerk* or assumed to use Wagner's music as their scores.[3] As Ray Müller put it to Riefenstahl in his documentary *The Wonderful, Horrible Life of Leni Riefenstahl*, were not the scenes of massed people in *Triumph of the Will*, "teilweise wie eine Wagner Oper?"—at least in part not like a Wagnerian opera? His question was clearly designed to elicit the answer yes, which Riefenstahl declined to provide. Although it takes no effort to discover that Herbert Windt, not Wagner, wrote the score, the suitability of the term *Wagnerian* to describe the music used in these films is rarely examined.[4] Yet examine it we must if we are to understand the character of these musical scores, their place in both German musical tradition and contemporary film music, and their contribution to the films' overall aesthetic and moral-political appeal.

The study of fascist, and specifically Nazi, aesthetics has come a long way since Benjamin's brief, suggestive remarks from the 1930s. We now have a detailed portrait of cultural activities in the Third Reich, and scholars of film, music, art, and dance have made considerable efforts to link the picture that has emerged to the findings of historians on matters of everyday life, coercion, and conformity in the racial state. For Linda Schulte-Sasse writing in 1996, providing a more detailed portrait required an "epistemological reversal" that rejected the view that Nazi films were "of interest only as propaganda" and instead pointed out their ambivalent, contradictory character. Nazi-era films were not simply the conveyor belts of political ideology, but multivalent art forms that could "harbor, transform, exceed, and undermine political ideology."[5] A few years later, in 1999, Lutz Koepnick argued for the interdependence of politics and consumption in the cultural works of Nazism. He suggested that "the charismatic power of public mass events and the lures of privatized consumption" worked together in Nazi-era films, art, and musical productions, both to mobilize the population behind the regime and to isolate individuals in the dreamworlds of leisure culture.[6] Both Schulte-Sasse and Koepnick regarded the work of the Nazi aesthetic as one that worked to create illusory states "of reconciliation, coherence, wholeness" (Schulte-Sasse) or "a utopian unification of modern culture" (Koepnick). And just as historians have urged us to turn away from the obvious (Gestapo headquarters) and toward the everyday (neighborhoods, local networks of acquaintance, business, the family) in order to understand the workings of conformity in the Third Reich, so too have scholars of film and media urged us to turn our gaze away from the oh-so-obvious works of Leni Riefenstahl and her fellow propagandists if we are to make sense both of the regime's astonishing popularity and, connected to that, its lack of aesthetic homogeneity.

Productive though these interpretive moves have proven to be, they have not necessarily led to a better understanding of Riefenstahl's work. Koepnick, for instance, still relies on the trope of Riefenstahl as Wagnerian: He uses phrases like *Gesamtkunstwerk*, a "carefully choreographed spectacle of ethereal bodies and geometrical shapes," theatricality, "glorified gestures of surrender and idealized figurations of death," all Wagnerian in their ultimate point of reference. He sets these images against a more realistic picture of "the stuff dreams were made of," i.e., "racing cars, radios, Coca-Cola, swing, and Hollywood-style comedies."[7] Riefenstahl's work itself remains in Koepnick's revisiting of fascist aesthetics where it was before his return trip took place; he simply suggests that we now see it as only part of a more complex whole, not the whole's quintessence. Its enactment of "homogenizing ritual" made it the foil to the strategies of banal entertainment and consumerist isolationism that the regime pursued simultaneously—strategies that broke "the bonds of old solidarities" and hence prepared the now "atomized individual for the auratic shapes of mass politics."[8] But what if the films themselves contained all these elements, the banal as well as the auratic, the deliberately ordinary as well as the hypertrophied ritualistic? What if, taking a cue from a not uncommon undergraduate response to *Triumph of the Will*, Riefenstahl's work is boring and repetitive—or in the word of Brian Winston, reviewing the 2001 DVD release of the film, "turgid"?[9] This essay will consider Riefenstahl's own (limited) interest in music as well as the work of her chief musical collaborator, Herbert Windt, in order to recover something of the appropriation and the appeal of the everyday that was present even in these products of a person with a highly dramatic, indeed self-dramatizing, aesthetic sensibility.

II.

Although Riefenstahl herself neither composed nor selected the music for her films, her own relationship to music is relevent both for her choice of composer for the film scores and for her substantial involvement in coordinating sound and image in the final product. In both these matters, implicit assumptions about the cultural significance of music reveal themselves and help us to analyze the overall effect of the films. Nothing in the interviews Riefenstahl gave or in her memoirs suggests that she ever regarded music as anything but instrumental. Punning aside, her evident indifference to a long German tradition of taking music seriously on its own terms reminds us that an individual's attitudes cannot be reliably deduced from their social class or milieu. Riefenstahl's supposed membership in the German educated middle class and a youth graced with the obligatory run of piano lessons did not instill in her any strong tendency to regard music as especially profound, especially expressive, or especially German. In her banal telling, she and her brother both had "a love of art and of all things beautiful," but "with the piano as with painting, I had some talent but not enough," and further, "I lacked the passion that I felt so deeply for the art of dance."[10]

Dance is, indeed, the key to Riefenstahl's relationship to music, in her life as in her films. Her exposure to classical music came almost entirely through her involvement with dance, and her responses to music can only be described as kinesthetic. Music was of value to her insofar as it inspired or enabled her to move. The only contemporary composer she discusses in her memoirs is Ferruccio Busoni, the Italian virtuoso pianist, composer, and champion of musical modernism, who worked in Berlin in the decades before the outbreak of war in 1914 and returned to Berlin after the war to teach composition. Riefenstahl encountered him in the 1920s, at a musical salon in Berlin, and wrote about how she spontaneously danced to his piano playing. This allegedly enchanted him to such an extent that he composed a short piano piece to accompany her dancing, sending a handwritten score to her personally with the inscription, *For the dancer Leni Riefenstahl, Busoni*. This Valse Caprice "eventually became one of my greatest successes," wrote Riefenstahl.[11] Likewise, her early training in dance, at the Grimm-Reiter School in Berlin and later at Mary Wigman's celebrated school for modern dance in Dresden, involved her in constant interaction with music, though strictly as accompaniment to dance exercises and performances.[12] During the period of her transition to filmmaking, she insisted, diva-like, on having a piano and pianist (one Herr Klamt) available to her while on location in various mountain lodges, so she could keep up her dance training, and she likewise graciously accepted a gift of a grand piano from the lovesick Arnold Fanck, in order to have a fully equipped dance studio back home in Berlin.[13] In all these quasi-musical anecdotes, the piano (and pianist) is literally and figuratively the instrument of her ambitions as a dancer and dancer-actress.

The music Riefenstahl heard and used in the course of her early training and career also reflected practical considerations. Her own choices of musical accompaniment during her brief career as a solo dancer and choreographer reveal what one comes to expect of Riefenstahl even in her later, more celebrated career as filmmaker—elements of genuine innovation and moments of brilliant inventiveness, combined with aesthetic conventionality, even predictability, and an ambivalent relationship to the modern. An exponent of "the modern dance in Germany," as critic André Levinson described the scene in 1928, she reflected both the synchronist views of the relationship between music and dance and the ambivalent attitude toward modern music.[14] Even in quintessentially modern studios like Mary Wigman's, in which Riefenstahl briefly studied, the use of modernist music was exceptional. Modern music's growing rhythmic complexity and irregularity was part of the problem. The exponents of modern dance in Weimar Germany were all, directly or indirectly, disciples of Émile Jaques-Dalcroze, whose "eurhythmics" posited a natural connection between music and the movements of the human body through the medium of pulse or rhythm. The desirable, "natural" relation between music and dance was thus one in which the musical pulses controlled the bodily movements, with a perfect synchronization as the ideal to which dance aspired. Yet, as Dalcroze himself discovered, the body could not "naturally" accommodate the irregular, rapidly shifting rhythmic texture of much modern music.

Harmony, or rather the move away from western tonality into atonal or twelve-tone music, posed a further aesthetic problem for dancers. Many of the exponents of modern dance in Germany had their roots in the antimaterialist, "life-reform," sun-worshipping milieu of *Körperkultur* and believed that through dance, indeed through physicality itself, modern men and women could recover a harmonic relation to the world, even the world of industry and the machine. Although the more adventurous exponents of this ideal found precisely in atonality the promise of a new harmonization of the world, most dancers, by no means indifferent to the preferences of the paying public, remained wedded to the more familiar expressiveness of nineteenth-century romantic music. Nor were musicians so cheap to hire, or instrumental ensembles so simple to assemble, or the music of living composers so easy to obtain that dancers, even famous ones like Wigman, could afford music accompaniment beyond what a single pianist could produce. Surveying more than 200 concert dance programs from across Europe in the first decades of the twentieth century, Karl Toepfer found a "strong preference" for a list mainly consisting of nineteenth-century romantic composers, including Grieg, Schumann, Chopin, Tchaikovsky, Brahms, Schubert, Mozart, and Dvořák.[15]

Notably absent from the list is Richard Wagner. "Scarcely any dancer," writes Toepfer, "showed the boldness" of Janine Solane, who in 1932 debuted as a solo performer with a lengthy dance set "entirely to the music of Wagner."[16] The problem here was probably musical rather than ideological, for many a dancer, with Rudolf Laban leading the way, had felt powerful affinities with Wagner the dramatist, Wagner the theorist, Wagner the anti-semite and cultural nationalist, and Wagner the vegetarian life-reformer.[17] But the music itself, whether because piano reductions of it were unsatisfactory or because it was simply too modern in harmonic, melodic, and rhythmic terms, did not settle easily into the dancers' repertoire. As for Riefenstahl, she proved to be entirely mainstream in her musical choices, choreographing her solo dances to the music of, among others, Schubert, Chopin, Tchaikovsky, Grieg, and Mikhail Ippolitov-Ivanov.[18]

Chopin, for instance, provided music for a languid piece, all drifting veils and imploring, come-hither arm gestures, which she called "Traumblüte" and modeled on Anna Pavlova's famous "Dying Swan." Along with her "Dance to the Sea," set improbably and with considerable originality to Beethoven's Fifth Symphony, "Traumblüte" proved to be the vehicle by which Riefenstahl first reached the broader filmgoing public.[19] Both dances were featured in Arnold Fanck's 1926 film, *The Holy Mountain*, in which Riefenstahl appears in her first credited role as the dancer Diotima. The trope of "Beethoven Hero," so powerfully represented by the Fifth Symphony in particular, may account for why Fanck, and presumably Riefenstahl, thought this strangely disjointed introductory sequence—in which shots of Riefenstahl perching on rocks and undulating madly on the beach are intercut with shots of crashing waves—formed a suitable introduction to a movie about mountains. Riefenstahl herself, never loath to draw attention to the heroic physical demands required of those who would make movies, later recalled how a lone violinist was "lowered down the cliff by a rope" in order to provide what could only have been the merest snippets from the Fifth, so that she, engaged in "horribly difficult dancing on the slippery rocks in that wild surf," might somehow synchronize movement, music, and waves.[20]

Leni Riefenstahl's early musical experiences reveal, then, a person whose musical choices seemed to have been dictated mainly by a feel for what was the norm in the circles in which she worked and, perhaps, by a preference for music that somehow enabled what she called her "own urge" to "surrender completely to the rhythms of the music."[21] Just as her musical choices traversed a comfortable terrain of classical music already well integrated into the European soundscape and dance world, just as her dancing occupied an aesthetic middle ground within the modernism of expressionist dance, so too did her understanding of how one could integrate sound into the visual world of the film develop neither behind nor ahead of the rapidly emergent conventions of film music. Fortunately for her, she found in Herbert Windt someone with the musical imagination that she seems to have lacked.

III.

In 1929, Riefenstahl acted in her first sound film, Arnold Fanck and G. W. Pabst's *The White Hell of Piz Palü*, and in 1931–1932, she worked on *The Blue Light*, the first film she directed and also, of course, a sound film, scored by the veteran composer of the silent era, Giuseppe Becce (who was already something of a specialist in Alpine films, including *Piz Palü*). In 1932, following the successful debut in Berlin of his opera *Andromache*, Herbert Windt received from Ufa his first commission to compose music for film, the much ballyhooed *Morgenrot* (*At Dawn*, directed by Vernon Sewell and Gustav Ucicky), a "magnificent epic from the annals of German history," according to the prepublicity, and a "film for the German people."[22] This was followed by a number of other film commissions, which established Windt's reputation as one of the few serious composers in Germany able to make the transition to film music. In 1933 he and Riefenstahl were brought together, exactly how is unknown, so that Windt could assemble the film score first for *Victory of Faith (Sieg des Glaubens)* and then, in short order, using much of the same material, *Triumph of the Will*. Riefenstahl turned to Windt in 1936 to score *Olympia* and again in the 1950s to adapt d'Alembert's operatic score, as well as to compose a substantial amount of new music for her *Lowlands* (*Tiefland*) project. Such was the collaboration between the two. Riefenstahl later offered a few words of praise for her collaborator, and Windt for his part made some equally diplomatic and brief expressions of admiration for "Leni Riefenstahl, who has a 'sixth sense' about what is right in musical matters."[23]

What strikes one first about their collaboration is its timing. It came right at the beginning of the sound era, when filmmakers and musicians alike had to rethink the relationship of sound to image in technical but also in aesthetic and theoretical terms.[24] By the time the first sound film was made in the United States in the mid 1920s, filmmakers had already begun to commission original film scores in order to improve the fit between film and sound. Although an improvement on earlier methods of providing music for film, which had relied on compendia of musical snippets organized according to recurrent themes (life, death, love, terror, and so on), the new film scores tended still to consist of a string of musical fragments.[25] The Italo-German film composer Giuseppe Becce, perhaps the prime examplar of this phenomenon, learned early on how to imitate the music of Richard Wagner in film scores, initially because permission to use Wagner's actual music proved too expensive. Becce, whose one and only role in front of the camera was as Wagner himself (in a 1913 bio pic of the composer), also became his musical stunt double, composing hundreds of film scores *à la mode wagnerienne*.[26] He, and many others like him, created the illusion that musical fragmentation could contribute to continuity—or, in knockoff Wagnerian terms, endless melody and, above all, a *Gesamtkunstwerk*.

The principle by which musicians composed their original score was overwhelmingly that of parallelism or manufactured synaesthesia. In its simplest (or most idiotic) form, this was called Mickey Mousing—a descending glissando accompanying an actress down a staircase, for instance.[27] Parallelism could also take more sophisticated forms, but in all cases, wrote Kurt Eisler, there had to "be some meaningful relation between the picture and the music," and the "actual inventive task of the composer is to compose music that 'fits' precisely into the given picture."[28] In any case, most composers never got past conceiving of music's relation to image as some more or less subtle version of the silent film accompanist's rendition of Grieg's "Hall of the Mountain King" while the villain appeared on the screen.[29]

At the same time, the presence of recognizably "classical" music in film scores, even if in bowdlerized versions, gave rise to what Pierre Bourdieu has called "classification struggles," in this case in the form of confusion and consternation over whether the music in films was indeed serious music or, more likely, just entertainment.[30] Writers in scholarly musical periodicals, for instance, lamented the degeneracy, declining standards, and the generally degraded position that music held in the world of film. Such discussions provide further demonstration, as if it were needed, of the pervasiveness of an increasingly widespread nationalist paranoia in the interwar period. Discussions of film and its music, like every other cultural discourse in the years after 1918, easily took on nationalist, even *völkisch* nationalist tones, with denunciations of Americanization, of Jewish influences, of racial mixing, and of any number of other manifestations of degeneration and decline increasingly attached to the particular issues of how one set music to images on the silver screen.

Placing Leni Riefenstahl and Herbert Windt in the midst of these rapid, even dizzying, transformations in social relations, cultural meanings, and political power structures would seem, nevertheless, to be a straightforward task. As we have seen, Riefenstahl herself brought a more or less uninflected version of the synaesthetic, or synchronic, ideal to her film work from her experiences as a dancer. In the ongoing debates about how representational music should be, Riefenstahl would seem an unlikely candidate to find anything amiss in the musical codes of the silent film era. All her biographers, interpreters, accusers, and defenders agree that her overriding concern was with the composition of the visual, not the aural world; she was, in that sense, more than comfortable with an early film culture characterized by what Kathryn Kalinak has identified as "the transcendent power of the image and the dependence of the soundtrack."[31]

But then one must reckon with Herbert Windt, the man in the shadows. Before turning to the relationship of music and image in the films that were, at least in that aspect, their joint creation, we need to take some measure of the talents and musical values he brought to this work. As indicated earlier, Windt represented a different kind of musical figure than Giuseppe Becce.[32] Before the war, Windt had come to Berlin to study piano at the Stern'schen Conservatory, one of the oldest and most important music schools in Germany. He had been there only a few months before he had his fill of formal studies and sought instead a position as assistant musical director (*Hilfskapellmeister*) at Max Reinhardt's Deutsches Theater. With similar restlessness, he volunteered when the war broke out in 1914 and was assigned to a Hussar regiment. He was horribly wounded at Verdun in August 1917, his face partially blown off and an arm permanently damaged. By the time he emerged from multiple efforts at reconstructive surgery, he resembled one of the veterans in a George Grosz painting; he had minimal use of his arm and was thus forced to abandon all hopes of a career as a pianist or conductor. He decided instead to become a composer.

Back in Berlin, Windt's compositional efforts in the 1920s were neither so successful as to allow him to give up working as a theory teacher and journeyman orchestrator, nor so unsuccessful as to make him turn to another profession altogether. A number of his compositions were performed publicly and received respectful notices. One, his "Andante Religioso," even won him a place at the Hochschule für Musik in the composition class of Franz Schreker, whose operas were breaking new ground in their explorations of polytonality and timbre. Through Schreker, Windt fell in with the "Berlin Group," mostly young composers, self-conscious modernists, and active publicists for the "new music."[33] Never entirely comfortable in this particular vanguard, he nevertheless continued to work in what was a recognizably modernist aesthetic, identifying more with Richard Strauss, "the true father of the modern," than with Arnold Schoenberg.[34] In 1928, around the time Riefenstahl was performing her heroic best in her first major hit (*The White Hell of Piz Palü*, 1929), Windt embarked on what he hoped would be his own defining opus, *Andromache*, based on an original adaptation of Racine's play. At this point in their lives, the aesthetic distance between Leni Riefenstahl, glamorous star of melodrama on the silver screen, and Herbert Windt, mutilated minor composer of excruciatingly earnest music, could hardly have been greater. Yet they were drawing closer.

The decision to attempt an artistic breakthrough as a composer of operas, in the tradition of Strauss, Schreker, and—yes, inevitably—Wagner, was a bold one on Windt's part. It required a statement of artistic intent. He published it in 1932, at the time of the opera's premiere under the great Heinz Tietjen and

Erich Kleiber at the Deutsche Staatsoper in Berlin, arguably the most prestigious site in all of Germany. "I will never belong to those self-consciously 'new' composers, who want at any cost to be 'modern,'" he wrote in the *Blätter der Staatsoper* (*Notes from the Berlin State Opera*, a journal for serious opera lovers); "on the other hand, I am not such a reactionary that I would ever undervalue the expanding musical language created by modernism, or ever neglect to make use of those elements of modernist musical language where I think they are appropriate and justified."[35] Despite receiving a gratifying amount of attention and some respectful reviews, *Andromache* did not turn into a major breakthrough for Windt. But the opera—or perhaps his decision at this time to join the Nazi Party?—did bring him to the attention of those conservative nationalists through whom he received his first major film commission to score the overtly nationalist film *Morgenrot*. Almost overnight, he became a composer of film music, most but not all in the heroic mode. *Morgenrot* led to a commission to compose large choral set pieces for Richard Euringer's *Deutsche Passion 1933*, one of the first of the *Thing* plays, those ultimately unsuccessful efforts to create an authentic German theater embodying the *Volksgemeinschaft*.[36] This in turn led to Windt's involvement in the party films with Riefenstahl and many more commissions to score propaganda, documentary, and feature films in the Third Reich (despite what he later called "artistic differences" with Goebbels). He received no honors from a state notoriously fond of bestowing them, and was turned down for things like membership in the Kultursenat, circumstances that weighed in his favor during postwar denazification proceedings.[37]

If the rise of Nazism and the sound film coincided in felicitous ways for Herbert Windt, making him (in those days at least) a rich man, his writings on the subject of film music conveyed a clear refusal to regard his work as in any sense mere entertainment. On the question of the musical score's illustrative function, Windt stood, ironically but not surprisingly, much closer to a left-wing modernist like Kurt Eisler than to Guiseppe Becce or the dozens of other workmanlike compilers of film scores. Deriding the notion that music should either obey the visual action, like a well-trained dog, or fill in visual lulls or transitions with compensatory sound, Windt described his work as one of creating a "dramatic counterpoint" to the visual image, which would widen and deepen the import of what was happening on the screen. Likewise on the question of the use of serious or classical music in films, Windt expressed his opposition. The film score should be an original work of creation, composed by a single artist and complete in itself, not a strung-together series of excerpts from the grab bag of the musical past. As the debate about the status of film music unfolded in the Third Reich, mostly ignored by the serious music community, Windt and a few others like him articulated an ambitious agenda for film music, one that staked a claim to a status equal to that of operatic music.[38] This, then, was not a man who either wanted to compose, or had the reputation of composing, music that would be mistaken for anyone's but his own.

IV.

The score for *Triumph of the Will*, which contains about twelve minutes of Windt's own music in a little over two hours of film, does not overwhelm the ear as fully as the visual images overwhelm the eye. It is, of course, the nature of film, even the sound film, to make a primarily visual impression, and people have observed and analyzed this effect since its earliest days.[39] Nor can one experience the film anymore without being conscious of the hand of Riefenstahl, the "wonderful, horrible" Leni Riefenstahl, in its making. She, after all, gets prominent billing in the film credits and Windt none at all. To be sure, some have found something musical in the rhythmic movement of images, a metaphorical kind of music, to which Riefenstahl herself often laid claim. Martin Loiperdinger, in a similar spirit, calls it a purely musical film ("ein reiner Musikfilm").[40] Still, what the music contributed to the overall effect of the film seems to most observers a relatively minor question, and the bulk of a very bulky scholarly literature on it concerns its visual composition. Riefenstahl herself once articulated what we might call the hundred percent rule. "I always take every precaution," she said in a 1966 interview with Michel Delahaye, "so that the sound and the image never total more than a hundred percent." If the image is "strong," then the "sound must stay in the background." And the converse was also true, although as she herself implied in the interview, the visual usually took precedence.[41] Besides expressing her disdain for the Mickey Mousing phenomenon, this statement also points to the clearest yet most overlooked aspect of the difference between her total works of art (if that is what they were) and Wagner's. For Wagner, despite his attention to costume, theater design, set design, and movement, the music always came first—and remained when all else was gone.

Those who have written about the score have tended to regard its contribution to the film as essential. After all, the case for the potency of the whole Wagner-Hitler nexus in shaping the nature and destiny of the Third Reich depends on the music: no music, no *Gesamtkunstwerk*. In short, the analysis of the music has been driven by the point people have wanted to make about the film overall. People have expected to hear Wagner in the score, and mirabile dictu, so they have.[42] The recent work of Reimar Volker on Windt's propaganda films, in which analysis of the music of *Victory of Faith* and *Triumph of the Will* forms the opening piece of a larger argument about Windt's contribution to the aesthetic footprint of Nazism, is an exception. Concerning Windt's twelve minutes, expanded, and repositioned from the eleven minutes of music he composed for *Victory of Faith*, Volker makes a two-part case for its crucial role in the film as a whole, one comparative (mainly to *Victory of Faith*) and the other cultural-political.

First, compared to the earlier film, which was cobbled together in a more slapdash manner under greater time pressure (and which Riefenstahl essentially disowned), the musical score of *Triumph of the Will* showed growing skill on the part of Windt in deploying music to heighten the intensity of Riefenstahl's visual drama and to add additional layers of cultural resonance. Riefenstahl's decision, for instance, to begin *Triumph* with the famous airplane-over-Nuremberg sequence received in Windt's score a calm, expansive, quietly magisterial accompaniment, in which the string, woodwind, and brass parts work together to create the smooth and unified texture of the music. As the spires of the city and the marching columns of the faithful gradually appear below, the music moves without overt drama into Windt's instrumental version of the party's "*Horst-Wessel-Lied*" (or "*Fahne hoch*"). It does not take up a marching rhythm, and thus sounds unlike the song as routinely sung by SA or Hitler Youth units, the male voices thumping along with the boot-stomping movement of the singers; it does not, in other words, trivialize the troops below. But Windt does begin subtly to raise the level of tension in the music by orchestrating the familiar melody in contrapuntal style, a subdued but distinct brass section taking the lead role with the strings echoing and very slightly elaborating their notes. All of this, as Volker argues, emphasizes the "mythological-sacral" position of the plane and its passengers vis-à-vis the people and city below and, with the introduction of the "*Horst-Wessel-Lied*," identifies the airplane's passenger (if anyone was wondering) as the leader of this movement.[43] It contributes, then, to the transformation that takes place between *Victory* and *Triumph*, from stodgy documentary to skillfully crafted drama—in Volker's terms, from "*Dokument*" to "*Erlebnis*" (experience). "Identical music used in conjunction with identical filmic content," he explains, served in *Victory of Faith* "simply to differentiate one scene from another" but in *Triumph of the Will* "through a more adroit placement of the music viz. the images, it takes on a dramaturgical function: individual moments of a very rapid sequence of images are prepared and accented through the music and iconographic elements of National Socialism are branded."[44]

The same deft placement characterizes the music Windt composed for the scenes of Nuremberg in the early morning, streets empty, sun rising. This scene and its music opened *Victory of Faith*, but in *Triumph of the Will* comes after the arrival, after the procession through the streets of Nuremberg, and after the night rally in front of Hitler's hotel. The music reworks the "Wach auf" chorus from the third act of Wagner's *Meistersinger von Nürnberg*. But Windt's use of Wagner, even as it highlights a difference between the two films (one that was really Riefenstahl's doing, not Windt's), is more essential to the music's resonance in the context of 1934. Placed as it is in *Triumph of the Will*, the music introduces the rally day itself, and the cultural-political import of the choice of Wagnerian quotation—the single authentic Wagner quotation in the whole film—would seem too obvious to require explanation. In 1933, on the occasion of the first production of *Meistersinger* in Bayreuth after the Nazi seizure of power, Goebbels had claimed it for Nazism, as the work "in the entire music literature of the German people" that stood in closest relationship to "the spiritual and intellectual [*seelischen und geistigen*] forces of our times."[45] The quotation of the "*Wach auf*" chorus signaled both a claim to cultural continuity, not only with Wagner's nineteenth century but with the whole panorama of the German past evoked in his drama, and a call to new awakening.

But the quotation is not literal. Windt's orchestration of the theme stays close to Wagner's, but it is not a copy. The entire quotation radically reduces the volume of the Wagner original, including the bold two-note opening of the "*Wach auf*" chorus. In the opera, these notes reverberate as a veritable shout from the assembled people of Nuremberg in the form of a perfect fourth in the key of G major. In Windt's version, these notes barely register, emerging gradually out of near silence as the quietest of a two-note phrase from the horns. In it, and in the brief passage that follows, Windt also slows down the tempo to match the movement of the camera over waking Nuremberg, evoking the equally tranquil image of Wagner's lyrics about the sound of a nightingale calling out of the deep forest and echoing over mountain and valley as the night ends. But as Volker further argues, the cultural resonances of the "*Wach auf*" quotation are not confined to Wagner. By association with the two words themselves—*Wach auf*—the canny listener could be reminded of a sixteenth-century hymn, present in most Protestant hymnals of the modern period and particularly beloved of National Socialists, who often sang it at Nazi festive occasions. This was Johann Walter's "*Wach auf, wach auf, du deutsches Land, du hast genug geschlafen*" ("Awaken, awaken, oh German land, you have slept long enough"), a hymn that probably has its origins in the period of the Peasants' War. The opening two notes of the hymn are, like Wagner's "Wach auf," a rising fourth. A rising fourth also characterizes what Volker identifies as the "Signal Motif," the horn fanfare that appears at many points in twelve minutes of Windt's own composition. It, along with the "*Horst-Wessel-Lied*," the aural counterpart to the swastika, are the two most persistent elements of his score. The means by which Windt weaves these and less prominent motifs in and out of the music, cutting back and forth, sometimes in counterpoint, sometimes in congruence with the rapidly shifting camera angles, all attest to the skill of his scoring of Riefenstahl's visual creation.[46]

Finally, Volker makes clear the distinction between Windt's motific work and Wagner's. Far from replicating Wagner's own texture of overlapping and intersecting signifiers, which comment on, deepen, and sometimes foretell the action on the stage, Windt's motifs are simple phrases that at their most dramatic merely highlight an image on the screen. There is no Hitler motif, nor a Goebbels or a Goering or even an SA or a German people motif, nor do any such signifiers interweave and comment upon one another as they do in Wagner's orchestral writing. Windt, as Volker explains, was not so much a Wagnerian, with that term's suggestion of a monomaniacal discipleship, as he was someone whose techniques of phrase development and patterning signal the combined influence of Bruckner, Wagner, and Strauss. In other words, he was more influenced by the avatars of a loosely similar, late Romantic maximalist style in which he had been trained since his earliest compositional classes. To those who would hear in Windt's various fanfares and other brassy passage work the echoes of Siegfried traveling down the Rhine or Hagen summoning the Gibichung (not a good precedent, in any case) or even the people of Nuremberg gathering on the festival field, Volker points instead to Windt's recent work on the Euringer *Thingspiel*, which in its "mythologizing of National Socialist iconography" represented a more closely fitted and more immediate precedent to the National Socialist festival of the party rally.[47]

Volker's careful musical analysis provides a more nuanced and accurate account of how Windt's music worked and what politico-cultural meanings it actually evoked in *Triumph of the Will*. But two additional perspectives are needed if one is to make any judgment, speculative or otherwise, about the overall effect of the film score. The first concerns the limitations of musical analysis. Even while pointing to some of the more idiotic things recent scholars have said about the "Wagnerian" music of *Triumph of the Will*, Volker rightly acknowledges the significance of such misconceptions for the reception history of the film, an insight that informs Scott Paulin's similar discussion of the seductive appeal of the *Gesamtkunstwerk* idea to film theorists.[48] And as is now well known, the Third Reich had its own Wagner problem, which we could characterize crudely as the large gap between Hitler's love of the music dramas and the public's indifference to them. The literature on Bayreuth is filled with quasi-comic anecdotes about Nazi officials practically ordering soldiers on leave to fill the uncomfortable wooden seats of the Festspielhaus for five-hour performances. In light of such stories, the government's subsidizing of tickets to Bayreuth looks less like official approval than an act of desperation.[49]

Given all this, it would seem that musical analysis, crucial though it is in illuminating one kind of truth about the score, has limited explanatory power in the context of what the untrained ear might have heard. Yet we may have some access to that notoriously unanswerable question. As I have tried to indicate earlier in this essay, there *was* a way in which the general public experienced a quasi-Wagner through the crossover media of film and radio. Versions of Siegfried's horn call, for instance, abounded on the radio and in both the silent and sound film scores that were assembled by the Giuseppe Becces of the music world. Even those who explicitly wanted *not* to invoke the spirit of Wagner did so. In 1924, for instance, Fritz Lang released two silent films, *Siegfried* and *Kriemhild's Revenge*, the screenplays for which had been written by Thea von Harbou and were based not on Wagner's *Ring der Nibelung* but solely on the Nibelungenlied of c. 1200. Seeking to avoid the unavoidable, he asked his friend Gottfried Huppertz (who subsequently wrote the score for *Metropolis*) to undertake the task of writing a musical score. But the point is that the effort to disengage from Wagner proved ultimately futile. Not only did the use of brass instruments in Huppertz's score summon up Siegfried's Rhine Journey from *Götterdämmerung*, but when the films were released in France, Italy, and in the United States, local organizers simply used their own musical scores to accompany the films, all of which were overtly Wagnerian, characterized by the same kinds of creative imitations of Wagner of which Becce had been the pioneer.

So, his own intentions aside, Windt's fanfare music evoked these film music conventions just as powerfully, perhaps more powerfully, than the serious music learned in composition classes or the would-be serious music of the *Thingspiele*. As I have argued elsewhere, place makes a difference in how we recover the cultural meaning of music.[50] From that perspective, the sounding of the Windt fanfare in a movie theater rather than in a concert hall or outdoor *Thing* amphitheater aligned it with different musical associations than those perhaps intended by its composer. And in that perspective also, one cannot help but think that Windt was a man who somehow managed to have his cake and eat it, too. On the one hand, for trained and serious music listeners, in his time and ours, the deftness of his quotations of and references to Wagner and the skill of his blending together of musical themes that were evocative but original to him, forced the knowledgeable to acknowledge his stature as a serious composer. This was clearly important to Windt, who had limited respect for most movie music and particularly detested the vulgarity of dropping pieces of classical music into musical scores.[51] On the other hand, for the general public familiar with the sound of movies, his score *sounded* more than a little bit like other movie scores, and one can imagine people enjoying the pleasure that the middlebrow cultural consumer would feel in making a simple chain of associations: Nuremberg, Wagner, Meistersingers; horn call, Siegfried, Wagner; and so on.

But associations made in this way, by reference to popular media and easily digestible snippets of high culture, do not, returning to Koepnick's analysis, necessarily work to break "the bonds of old solidarities," or prepare the "atomized individual for the auratic shapes of mass politics."[52] They instead constituted gestures of familiarity, which made the new and still unfamiliar rituals of the Nazi regime seem to emerge seamlessly out of the past. Doris Bergen has written that "on the one hand, Hitler revolutionized Germany, but on the other hand, the ways in which he did so seemed undramatic to many participants and observers at the time."[53] This observation applies to the music of *Triumph of the Will* as well, and especially to the seventy-odd minutes of music in the film that Windt himself did not compose. In the technical language of film, much of this music was diegetic; that is, one hears it as part of the narrative, as the sound of bands, occasionally glimpsed, accompanying marching, rallying, waving, speech making, and the like. For most German listeners, who probably understood the oscillations in film scores between diegetic and nondiegetic music only intuitively, the great preponderance of diegetic over nondiegetic music in *Triumph of the Will* only increased the familiarity of this new world. Diegetic music as such is generally considered to heighten the illusion on the part of the spectator of being actually inside the world of the film, but when the diegetic music is as well known as most of this was, it also works in the opposite direction, locating the action of the film in the everyday, experienced, real world. Or, to put this yet another way, music that unmistakably comes into the world of the film from the surrounding culture brings with it what Roger Hillmann has called the "cultural memory of other contexts."[54] In the case of the diegetic music of *Triumph of the Will*, these were powerful memories indeed.

The film's diegetic music falls roughly into three categories: folk songs, German military band marches, and National Socialist *Kampflieder* or fight/official songs. But even these distinctions are at best permeable boundaries, easily crossed. While the Hitler Youth song, "*Vorwärts, Vorwärts*" ("Onward, Onward") was the joint creation of the organization's leader, Baldur von Schirach (lyrics), and Hans Otto Borgmann (tune), its simple, hobbyhorse-like melody had the nagging familiarity of a half-remembered nursery song or a children's camp song.[55] Likewise, the "*Horst-Wessel-Lied*" or "*Fahne Hoch,*" which in Nazi lore was the sole creation of Horst Wessel himself, represented one of the countless reattachments of familiar melodies to new words, in this case a marine reservists' song, "*Vorbei, vorbei, sind all' die schönen Stunden*" ("Gone, gone are all the wonderful times") about the battleship *Königsberg.*[56] In the case of the military marches themselves, from the "*Badenweilermarsch*" to the "*Yorckschen Korps Marsch*" to the "*Husarenmarsch*" (connected to Windt's own wartime regiment), they consisted of something like a review of old favorites, comparable to American listeners hearing the "Stars and Stripes Forever" or "The Battle Hymn of the Republic" or "Dixie" or even "Yankee Doodle Dandy."[57]

The importance of military band music in everyday German life cannot be measured and it is easily exaggerated. In the Kaiserreich, Sunday band concerts constituted a well-loved fixture of leisure practices of many classes, and before the war the military musical ensembles of Germany had an international reputation. German military music was a source of both pleasure and pride for ordinary Germans. The reduction under the Weimar Republic of the number of bands from 560 to a mere 160 was thus extremely unpopular, in ways that have barely been researched.[58] After 1933, the gradual return of prosperity, and of course the commitment of the new regime to German remilitarization, benefited the military bands directly and dramatically.[59] *Triumph of the Will* captures this resurgence and through the musical score tells a story of continuities and new beginnings.

Two especially beloved and culturally resonant pieces of music had prominent places in the score. The first, the "*Grosse Zapfenstreich*" ("Grand Tattoo" or "Grand Taps"), is seen and heard played by the Musikkorps of the Leibstandarte Adolf Hitler, the largest of the military ensembles of the Third Reich, arrayed under Hitler's hotel window during the night rally. In *Triumph of the Will* this rendition represents a modified version of a Prussian ceremonial dating back to the sixteenth century. An ordinary "tattoo" or taps signified the end of the day (the striking of the taps, or the shutting down of the liquor supply), but the elevated, nineteenth-century form of the "*Grosse Zapfenstreich*," performed only in the presence of the monarch himself, represented a military version of evening prayers, or calling down God's blessing on the work of the army.[60] Its function in this context as a serenade to Hitler at once transgressed and appropriated the traditional use of it, thereby carrying a meaning that would have been obvious to the German public: Hitler was head of state and, more important in light of the internal tensions that led shortly before the 1934 party rally to the murder of SA leader Ernst Röhm, the Führer was also supreme commander of the army and heir to a Prussian military tradition in which he himself had, of course, played no part. The music is thus the aural equivalent to a poster from the period (see figure 1) showing the overlapping heads of Frederick the Great, Bismarck, Hindenburg, and Hitler, with the caption, "*Was der König eroberte, der Fürst formte, der Feldmarschall verteidigte, rettete und einigte der Soldat*" ("What the King conquered, the Prince shaped, and the Field Marshal defended, the Soldier has rescued and unified").

Figure 1

The music that accompanied Hitler's review of the Reichswehr conveyed the same message, by which class, regional, and indeed chronological boundaries all dissolved into the present of the Volksgemeinschaft and Führerstaat. At that point in the film, we hear a quiet march version of what is perhaps the best known of German soldier songs, "*Ich hatt' einen Kamaraden*" ("I had a comrade"), the melody and lyrics (by Ludwig Uhland) of which dated back to the Napoleonic Wars and which had taken on nearly unbearable resonance in the slaughter of the First World War. Hitler, reviewing the regular army soldiers to this most familiar of music and most evocative of lyrics, embodies the German people's ability to mourn their losses in the war and, in a filmic moment that demonstrates as clearly as any the ability of the Nazi movement to appropriate the past as well as the future, to gain strength from them. Here, then, more powerfully than could be achieved by loose adaptations of Wagnerian themes, one finds music working, in Windt's formulation, to heighten the sounds of the everyday.[61]

V.

Compared to the dominance of the vernacular and the diegetic in the music of *Triumph of the Will*, Windt's music for *Olympia* sounded more modern, more up-to-date, a dash of tonally ambiguous modernism here, a sparkle of Hollywood glamor there. Windt received more acclaim for his work on this film than on anything else he did, and the same could be said of Riefenstahl. At the same time, their collaboration in the making of the final product of the film was more substantial, a circumstance acknowledged in the opening credits themselves. And yet like *Triumph of the Will*, *Olympia* labors under misapprehensions about its alleged propulsion "by the Wagnerian score of Herbert Windt," variously described as "heroic-lyric" or marked by "false grandeur."[62] Accusations like this go at least as far back as the 1958 hearings of the Filmbewertungsstelle (loosely, the Board of Film Classification, a review board established in 1951 allegedly to determine what films should receive state subsidies) on whether to refuse certification for release in the Federal Republic of Germany of the two-part film. Complaining that the music was "laid on too thick," the review board wrote critically about the suspiciously "stimulating effect" of the film, "ultimately achieved through an intrusive and purposive symphonic score which blares into the ears of the spectator almost unceasingly."[63]

One hardly recognizes the score or the sound track in such a description, yet just like the phantom hearings of Siegfried's Rhine Journey in *Triumph of the Will*, the impressions tell us something important not just about spectators' expectations but about cultural contexts that shape our hearing. Riefenstahl herself argued with vigor and partial accuracy against the accusation of musical intrusiveness. Rightly pointing out that much of the sound track was filled with such diegetic sounds as Richard Strauss's Olympic hymn, Werner Egk's special Olympic fanfares, sports commentary, crowd shouting, and various national hymns at the awards ceremonies, she described Windt's score itself as "purely background music."[64] Of course it was more than that, or rather more effective than that, as Riefenstahl herself acknowledged in less politically fraught circumstances. What Riefenstahl and Windt achieved together in the coordination of music and image in *Olympia* was both the solution of specific practical problems and the heightening of experience that Windt identified around the time of the film's release as his main aesthetic goal. Both these elements of the film's scoring come through in the still impressive coordination of music to image in the marathon sequence. As is well known, Windt had originally written this music in 1936 to accompany the German radio broadcast of the marathon, to fill the gaps in the necessarily discontinuous and uneven coverage of the long race itself. Characteristic of his ambitions for film music, he had come up with a high-cultural solution to this problem that was essentially one of keeping people interested (i.e., entertained) while not very much happened. He composed a three-movement orchestral suite, with a short, quick first movement (in other words a scherzo), a long, extended middle movement, and a last triumphalist finale. In the film, the coordinated and the contrapuntal possibilities of such a three-movement design came into their own. At the outset, Windt's music seems literally to be pacing the runners, driving them on, a characteristic that has led some commentators into the interpretive dead end of dubbing it fascist in the bossiness and regularity of its rhythmic patterns. But in the most effective parts of the whole marathon sequence, the runners' legs seem to move slower and slower (in the famous basket shots, from the heads of the runners), and yet the music rushes on faster and faster, not with bombast or blaring trumpets but with all the more effectively relentless, increasingly frantic strings, joined finally by brass and wind instruments, until the whole sound resolves itself into silence, and then a diegetic trumpet fanfare as the lead runner (from Japan) enters the stadium for the final lap. Windt described this visually contrapuntal music at the time as the runner's "mood, his flight of ideas, his spirit, his will, his driving idea," elevating itself "over the body which begins to tire," the music "flying before him and pulling the body further on."[65] If there is indeed something National Socialist about the movie and its music, then it lies not just in modernist archaisms, gleaming bodies, and feats of strength—traits that, as many post-Sontag commentators have pointed out, can be found in sporting culture the world over, then and now—but in the musical drama of this triumph of the will.

To come back to where this article began, then, the generations of spectators and critics who have heard in the music of Riefenstahl's films something profoundly attuned to the regime from whence it emitted have not been wrong. Yet to limit our understanding of this fit between art and society to various elaborations on Wagnerian themes is to draw the wrong conclusions about the effect and the appeal of this music. Both Windt and Riefenstahl brought to their collaboration musical experiences that encompassed a much broader range of musical life than the term *Wagnerian* could possibly encompass.

NOTES

1. It is probably worth noting that Benjamin himself was not thinking about Wagner or *Gesamtkunstwerk* when he wrote this. Walter Benjamin, "The Work of Art in the Age of Mechanical Reproduction," *Illuminations: Essays and Reflections*, trans. Harry Zohn (New York: Schocken, 1969), 241.
2. Doris Bergen, *War and Genocide: A Concise History of the Holocaust* (New York: Rowman and Littlefield, 2003), 33.
3. Jonathan Petropoulos, for example, an otherwise astute analyst of Nazi aesthetics, misleadingly identifies the music of *Triumph of the Will* as that of Wagner's

Meistersinger von Nürnberg, in his "Leni Riefenstahl, Coy Propagandist of the Nazi Era," *Wall Street Journal*, September 11, 2003.

4. Scott D. Paulin explores the broader "metatheoretical" question of why Wagner's name is "inescapable" within "discourses on film and its music" in "Richard Wagner and the Fantasy of Cinematic Unity: the Idea of *Gesamtkunstwerk* in the History and Theory of Film Music," *Music and Cinema*, ed. James Buhler, Caryl Flinn, and David Neumeyer (Hanover, NH: University Press of New England, 2000), 58–84.
5. Linda Schulte-Sasse, *Entertaining the Third Reich: Illusions of Wholeness in Nazi Cinema* (Durham, NC: Duke University Press, 1996), xviii.
6. Lutz Koepnick, "Fascist Aesthetics Revisited," *Modernism/Modernity* 6, no. 1 (1999): 54. He fully develops and substantiates these arguments in *The Dark Mirror: German Cinema between Hitler and Hollywood* (Berkeley: University of California Press, 2002).
7. Koepnick, "Fascist Aesthetics," 52.
8. Ibid., 54.
9. Brian Winston, "Triumph of the Dull," *Sight and Sound* 11 (2001): 60.
10. Leni Riefenstahl, *A Memoir* (New York: St. Martin's Press, 1992), 11.
11. There is no evidence that Busoni ever published this work she attributed to him under that title, and thus one can only take Riefenstahl's word for it that she was dancing to an original, uncatalogued Busoni work and not the more widely known works titled "Valse Caprice," by Franz Liszt or Cecile Chaminade or Gabriel Fauré, all available in published sheet music in the 1920s. That Busoni wrote such a work for her is not impossible; he did compose a number of short dance pieces, for orchestra and for two- or four-handed piano performance.
12. See Mary Rhiel's essay in this volume.
13. Riefenstahl, *Memoirs*, 46, 57, 61.
14. André Levinson, "The Modern Dance in Germany," *Theatre Arts Monthly* XIII (February 1929): 143–153. The rapidly changing shape of the musical repertoire for early-twentieth-century dance has not been exhaustively studied. The best discussion of music and dance in the early twentieth century is that of Karl Toepfer, *Empire of Ecstasy: Nudity and Movement in German Body Culture, 1910–1935* (Berkeley: University of California Press, 1997), 321–33.
15. Toepfer, *Empire of Ecstasy*, 321.
16. Ibid., 322.
17. That said, Laban's Wagnerian moments seem confined to two points in his life. The first Wagnerian moment came during the First World War, which Laban experienced from the bohemian idyll of Monte Verite in Switzerland, where Parsifal's natural innocence and Tannhäuser's sandals seemed especially attractive to people searching for a new style of life. The second Wagnerian moment came, unsurprisingly, during the first years of the Third Reich, when he wrote, sincerely or opportunistically or both, about the supreme importance of Wagner as a dramatist—"I always say that the greatest German dramatist showed us dancers what to do." See Martin Green, *Mountain of Truth: the Counterculture Begins; Ascona, 1900-1920* (Hanover, NH: University Press of New England, 1986), 110, 123, 244–45; and Lillian Karina and Marion Kant, *Hitler's Dancers: German Modern Dance and the Third Reich*, trans. Jonathan Steinberg (New York: Berghahn Books, 2003), 11–21, 303–338.
18. The latter was not as uncommon a choice as it might seem. Ippolitov-Ivanov was well known at the beginning of the twentieth century as a kind of lesser Rimsky-Korsakov (his teacher). In the national-romantic-exoticist mode, he had immersed himself in

the culture of the non-Russian peoples of Georgia and composed in 1894 a group of instrumental works called *Caucasian Sketches*. Riefenstahl choreographed a dance to the last and most popular of these, the "Procession of the Sardar," a work that, not unlike Ravel's now infamous *Bolero,* combined a moody yet forceful melody in an exoticized minor mode with steadily intensifying rhythmic and dynamic elements. The whole package, with Riefenstahl presumably hurling herself about the stage with ever faster, more frantic movements, earned her, so she reported, tumultuous applause and calls for encores. She called her Ippolitov-Ivanov dance "Caucasian March." See Riefenstahl, *Memoirs*, 37.

19. She had appeared, to be sure, in a previous film, *Paths to Strength and Beauty* (1925), but anonymously, one dancer among many in one of Mary Wigman's ensemble dances, "Der Wanderung."
20. Riefenstahl, *Memoirs*, 56.
21. Ibid., 34.
22. Klaus Kreimeier, *The Ufa-Story: A History of Germany's Greatest Film Company, 1918–1945*, trans. Robert and Rita Kimber (New York: Hill & Wang, 1996), 122 ff.
23. Herbert Windt, "*Tiefland*: the Opera and the Film," unpublished essay dated December 17, 1953, and reprinted as an appendix to David B. Hinton, *The Films of Leni Riefenstahl,* 3rd edition (Lanham, MD: Scarecrow Press, 2000), 124.
24. The scholarly literature on film music is substantial and growing fast. Among the most significant are Claudia Gorbmann, *Unheard Melodies: Narrative Film Music* (Bloomington, IN: University of Indiana Press, 1987); Nicholas Cook, *Analysing Musical Multimedia* (Oxford: Clarendon Press, 1998); James Buhler, Caryl Flinn, and David Neumeyer, eds., *Music and Cinema* (Hanover, NH: Wesleyan University Press, 2000); Caryl Flinn, *The New German Cinema: Music, History, and the Matter of Style* (Berkeley: University of California Press, 2004); Nora Alter and Lutz Koepnick, *Sound Matters: Essays on the Acoustics of Modern German Culture* (New York: Berghahn Books, 2004); Miguel Mera and David Burnand, eds., *European Film Music* (Aldershot/Hampshire: Ashgate Publishing Limited, 2006); Konrad Vogelsang, *Filmmusik im Dritten Reich: die Dokumentation* (Hamburg: Facta, 1990); Ute Rügner, *Filmmusik in Deutschland zwischen 1924 und 1934* (Hildesheim: Georg Olms Verlag, 1988).
25. See, for instance, Giuseppe Becce and Hans Erdmann, *Allgemeines Handbuch der Film-Musik,* 2 vols. (Berlin: Schlesinger, 1927).
26. Interestingly, Paulin's otherwise illuminating article on the Wagner *Gesamtkunstwerk* myth does not mention Becce. See footnote 4 above.
27. Max Steiner, the Viennese-born émigré film composer, took parallelism to comic extremes, as when the clubfooted Leslie Howard, in the 1935 film of Maugham's *Of Human Bondage*, limped around to the accompaniment of a Steiner-eloquent musical motif, not unlike that of Wagner's Mime. See, among the more amusing accounts of the phenomenon, Joseph Lanza, *Easy Listening: A Surreal History of Musak, Easy Listening, and other Mood Music*, revised and expanded edition (Ann Arbor: University of Michigan Press, 2004), 59–60.
28. Kurt Eisler, *Composing for the Films* (London: Continuum, 2007), 69–70.
29. Cook, *Analysing Musical Multimedia*, 65.
30. Pierre Bourdieu, *Distinction: A Social Critique of the Judgment of Taste,* trans. R. Nice (Cambridge: Harvard University Press, 1984); Brian Currid, *A National Acoustics: Music and Mass Publicity in Weimar and Nazi Germany* (Minneapolis, MN: University of Minnesota Press, 2006), 120–123.

31. Kathryn Kalinak, *Settling the Score: Music and the Classical Hollywood Film* (Madison, WI: University of Wisconsin Press, 1993), 7.
32. The best account of Windt's life and work is that of Reimar Volker, *"Von oben sehr erwünscht": Die Filmmusik Herbert Windts in NS-Propagandafilm* (Trier: Wissenschaftlicher Verlag, 2003).
33. Martin Thrun, *Neue Musik im deutschen Musikleben bis 1933*, 2 vols. (Bonn: Orpheus Verlag, 1995), II: 498.
34. He did credit Schoenberg with opening up new compositional paths for him—see Volker, *Sehr erwünscht*, 5–7.
35. "Ich werde nie zu den Neuerern gehören, die um jeden Preis 'modern' sein wollen; anderseits bin ich nicht Reaktionär genug, die Erweiterungen durch die Moderne zu unterschätzen und mich ihrer nicht da zu bedienen, wo ich sie für angebracht und berechtigt halte": Herbert Windt, "Warum Andromache?," *Blätter der Staatsoper* XII, no. 8 (March 1932): 5–6; cited in full in Volker, *Sehr erwünscht*, 7.
36. Henning Eichberg et al., *Massenspiele. NS-Thingspiel, Arbeiterweihespiel und olympisches Zeremoniell* (Stuttgart, 1977); Manfred Frank, "Vom 'Bühnenweihespiel' zum 'Thingspiel.' Zur Wirkungsgeschichte der 'Neuen Mythologie' bei Nietzsche, Wagner und Johst," *Poetik und Hermeneutik* XIV (1989): 610–638; William Niven, "The Birth of Nazi Drama? Thing Plays," *Theatre under the Nazis*, ed. John London (Manchester: Manchester University Press, 2000), 54–95; Johannes M. Reichl, *Das Thingspiel. Über den Versuch eines nationalsozialistischen Lehrstück-Theaters* (Frankfurt/M: Misslbeck, 1988). Rainer Stommer, "'Da oben versinkt einem der Alltag . . .' Thingstätten im Dritten Reich als Demonstration der Volksgemeinschaftsideologie," in *Die Reihen fest geschlossen. Beiträge zur Geschichte des Alltags unterm Nationalsozialismus*, ed. Detlev Peukert, et al. (Wuppertal: Hammer, 1981), 149–173; Rainer Stommer, *Die inszenierte Volksgemeinschaft: Die "Thing-Bewegung" im Dritten Reich* (Marburg: Jonas, 1985).
37. Volker, *Sehr erwünscht*, 7–8.
38. "Sieben Fragen an zwölf Komponisten," *Film-Kurier*, December 31, 1938; and "Musikalische Pionierleistung im Olympia-Film: Herbert Windt: Das Wort 'untermalen' müβte verboten werden," *Film-Kurier*, April 11, 1938. See also "Warum Musik im Film?" *Jahrbuch der Deutschen Musik 1943* (Berlin: Reichsministerium für Volksaufklärung und Propaganda, 1943): 182–85. For a fuller discussion of Windt and the debates about the status of film music in the Third Reich, see Volker, *Sehr erwünscht*, 12–22.
39. To place this tyranny of the visual, or ocularcentrism, in a long historical perspective, see Martin Jay, *Downcast Eyes: the Denigration of Vision in Twentieth-Century French Thought* (Berkeley: University of California Press, 1994); and David Levin, *Modernity and the Hegemony of Vision* (Berkeley: University of California Press, 1993). On the dominance of ocularcentrism over sound in particular, see Alter and Koepnick, eds., *Sound Matters*.
40. Martin Loiperdinger, *Rituale der Mobilmachung: Der Parteitagsfilm* Triumph des Willens *von Leni Riefenstahl* (Opladen: Verlag Leske und Budrich, 1987).
41. Michel Delahaye, "Leni and the Wolf, Interview with Leni Riefenstahl," *Cahiers du Cinema in English* 5 (1966): 49–55.
42. For a rich array of scholars who have fallen into the Wagner trap, see Volker, *Sehr erwünscht*, 75–77.
43. Volker, *Sehr erwünscht*, 58–59, 66–67.

44. Ibid., 68.
45. This radio address of Goebbels is quoted in virtually every text, German and English, on music in the Third Reich. For a particularly strong treatment of the issue, see Reinhold Brinkmann, "Wagners Aktualität für den Nationalsozialismus: Fragmente einer Bestandaufnahme," in *Richard Wagner im Dritten Reich,* ed. Saul Friedländer and Jörn Rüsen (Munich: C. H. Beck, 2000), 106–141 (Goebbels quotation on p. 126).
46. At the same time, Volker's careful analysis of Windt's compositional procedures, in particular his motific work, casts considerable doubt on Riefenstahl's own account of how, frustrated by Windt's seeming inability to conduct his eighty-man orchestra in synchronization with the images, she seized the baton and did the conducting herself (Riefenstahl, *Memoirs,* 165). In order to match particular motif with particular image, as the score succeeds in doing, Windt had to master very precise timing in the compositional process itself, not simply in the performance. Riefenstahl's self-dramatizing account seems built on the assumption that music is music, one just plays it at different tempi—an assumption consistent with her simplistic approach to musical expression altogether.
47. Volker, *Sehr erwünscht,* 79.
48. Paulin, "Richard Wagner and the Ideal of Cinematic Unity."
49. See, for instance, Frederic Spotts, *Bayreuth: A History* (New Haven: Yale University Press, 1996), 195.
50. Celia Applegate, "Music in Place: Perspectives on Art Culture in Nineteenth-Century Germany," in *Localism, Landscape, and the Ambiguities of Place: German-Speaking Central Europe, 1870–1930,* eds. David Blackbourn and James Retallack (Toronto: University of Toronto Press, 2007), 33–54.
51. Volker, *Sehr erwünscht,* 15, 20.
52. Koepnick, "Fascist Aesthetics," 54.
53. Bergen, *War and Genocide: A Concise History of the Holocaust* (New York: Rowman and Littlefield, 2003), 23.
54. Roger Hillman, *Unsettling Scores: German Film, Music, and Ideology* (Bloomington: Indiana University Press, 2005), 27.
55. Borgmann was an accomplished film music composer, whose most famous (notorious) product was the score for the 1933 film *Hitlerjugend Quex.*
56. For a complete account of the melody, lyrics, and anything else one might need to know about the *"Horst-Wessel-Lied,"* see George Broderick, "Das Horst-Wessel-Lied: A Reappraisal," *International Folklore Review* X (1995): 100–127; also available online, http://www.george-broderick.de/ns_docs/ns-horst_wessel_lied.doc (accessed February 28, 2007).
57. See Georg Kandler, *Deutsche Armeemärsche; ein Beitrag zur Geschichte des Instrumentariums, des Repertoires, der Funktion, des Personals und des Widerhalls der deutschen Militärmusik* (Bad Godesberg: Hohwacht Verlag, 1962); and Joachim Toeche-Mittler, *Armeemärsche* (Neckargemünd: Vowinkel, 1971).
58. An important starting point is a short pamphlet by Georg Kandler (1902–1973), which he first wrote as a memorandum to the war ministry, called *Die kulturelle Bedeutung der deutschen Militärmusik* (Berlin: Kandler, 1932).
59. Beyond expanding the musical forces in existing bands and reestablishing ones that had been allowed to dissolve, the new regime also created a number of new musical corps for new military units, including the Luftwaffe, the SS, and the Leibstandarte Adolf Hitler.

60. Bernhard Höfele, *Die Deutsche Militärmusik: Ein Beitrag zu ihrer Geschichte* (Cologne: Luthe, 1999), 137–168.
61. As Windt put it, "und zwar nach innen, nicht nach aussen," or, expansively translated, "and indeed not superficially but in the inner apprehension [of the viewer/listener]." Herbert Windt, "Warum Musik im Film?" 182. The lyrics to "Ich hatt' einen Kameraden" would have come easily to the mind of any German hearing the tune. They are "Ich hatt' einen Kameraden, / Einen bessern findst du nit. / Die Trommel schlug zum Streite, / Er ging an meiner Seite |: Im gleichen Schritt und Tritt. :| // Eine Kugel kam geflogen: / Gilt's mir oder gilt es dir? / Ihn hat es weggerissen, / Er liegt mir vor den Füßen |: Als wär's ein Stück von mir :|, and so on. The German communists and antifascists of the Thälmann Brigade in Spain adopted this tune also, writing new words but in a similar spirit of simple soldierly comradeship and sacrifice.
62. Michael Mackenzie, "From Athens to Berlin: The 1936 Olympics and Leni Riefenstahl's *Olympia*," *Critical Inquiry* 29 (winter 2003): 304–305; Konrad Vogelsang, *Filmmusik im Dritten Reich* (Hamburg: Facta Oblita Verlag, 1990), 12.
63. Transcript of Riefenstahl's appeal to the Filmbewertungsstelle included as Appendix D of Cooper C. Graham, *Leni Riefenstahl and Olympia* (Metuchen, NJ: Scarecrow Press, 1986), 288.
64. Transcript in Cooper, *Riefenstahl*, 288.
65. Windt, in 1938 pressbook, quoted in Cooper, 177.

Chapter 9

The Ups and Downs of Leni Riefenstahl: Rereading the Rhythms of the Memoirs

Mary Rhiel

Diotima's Dance at the Sea from *Der heilige Berg* (*The Holy Mountain*, 1926)

I.

It took Leni Riefenstahl over nine hundred pages to narrate her life story. Adamant about the truthfulness of the past, she cleverly reassures the reader that life is bigger than art. In keeping with her claims that her Nazi-era films were documentaries, she used the "film-as-reality" assertion to convince the reader of the reliability of her life story. In the epilogue to her memoirs she writes: "The events of those years run before my eyes like a film, over and over again, and I am repeatedly confronted with the past, even today."[1] Riefenstahl's investment in convincing her audience that she is telling the truth responds to the one question she has posed over and over again to the public: What crime have I committed?[2] She prepared for the public a voluminous biographical account, published in 1987, that pleads her innocence. So many words, so many pages, however, do not allay our qualms about her; this whirlwind of obsessive verbiage says very little. Indeed, there is general agreement that Riefenstahl has demonstrated that she is either incapable of, or unwilling to, reflect on her involvement with the Nazi regime.

Reading page after page of Riefenstahl's self-serving account of her life might bring one, for a brief moment, to conclude that Paul de Man took the more tolerable path, namely silence. Upon closer examination, however, it becomes clear that his silence has an affinity to these memoirs; despite the rhetoric produced by Riefenstahl, she, too, has said nothing. There are, of course, important differences between these two figures.[3] The strategies of each of them can be read as differing means of coming to terms with anxiety. De Man fetishized absence and its resulting anxiety as a prelude to artistic creation. Riefenstahl, as filmmaker and as memoirist, dances over, around, and through the void as if it did not exist. Thus, the famous photograph of Riefenstahl walking on a ladder over a gaping glacial chasm can stand as an emblem for the production of her persona and art. Nervously, she constantly crosses the abyss, but never acknowledges its existence and power. Words and images flow as a means of containing anxiety. In the argument that follows, I intend to link the flow of her words in her memoirs, as well as the rhythmic editing of her films, to her foundational training in modern dance in the interwar period.

Riefenstahl's memoir is a narrative of defense and counteraccusation. Without hesitation she usurps the position of the counterstory narrator, i.e., the victim, in order to destroy all other versions of her life that construct her guilt as a perpetrator of Nazi ideology. She presents herself as a woman of high integrity, who has suffered terribly at the hands of men and history. She explained her attraction to Hitler as a product of a personal (not political) relationship with a man of extreme charisma, who renders all who enter his aura helpless. So, although her formal trial as Nazi war criminal took place over forty years before the appearance of her memoirs, she calls up a variety of discourses and narrative strategies in the closing argument for her defense.

The timing of the publication of her life story is telling. Her memoirs appeared at a poignant historical moment in the postwar West: The last living survivors and witnesses of the Holocaust and World War II were passing away, Germany's relationship to the present and past was changing as it unified within a transforming Europe, and modernist political institutions and practices had been undeniably surpassed by global, multinational formations.

Perched on the cusp of this transitional epoch, Riefenstahl's retrospective account of her life assumed a conservative and nostalgic place in the pantheon of memory work that flourished in the twilight of the millennium. Her memoirs anticipated the confluence of what more recent scholarship has called the "globalization of memory and the rediscovery of German suffering."[4]

In view of Riefenstahl's self-justification, de Man's disdain for autobiographical confessional writing may seem an appropriate response to Riefenstahl's memoirs. Peter Brooks views confessions as invitations to the listener/reader to join in a confessional game. Brooks worries about a dynamic in which the autobiographical disclosure of one's foibles in life involves the reader in a dialogic process, in which guilt is spread to the reader by virtue of identification with the autobiographical subject. If the writer of the memoir operated and operates as a subject who accommodated easily to the dominant social, institutional, and discursive orders of his or her time and culture, then the autobiographical act can presuppose a strong sense of fraternity with the reader. Such a memoir operates under the sign of sympathy and understanding, under the belief in humanistic acts of identification and empathy, which in effect obliterates differences.[5] Violence as a referential act or as a historical event loses significance when posed against the desire for the secure identity positions, promised through such an act of self-revelation, in which one would express remorse and ask for forgiveness.

Not that Riefenstahl expressed or even feigned remorse. Indeed, there is little in her memoirs that admits to ethical or moral error, beyond, that is, her admission that she found Hitler charismatic and was successfully hoodwinked into believing in him. Yet the confessional impulse propels the narrative, if not in content, then as a speech act. Riefenstahl's voluminous account of her life is heavy on the side of excuse making. Her text, by exposing her private thoughts and intentions, functions as an excuse for making Hitler's most powerful propaganda films, and legitimates her question: What crime have I committed? Thus her memoirs have in common with confessional discourse an underlying desire for absolution, an emotion that, according to Brooks, implicates the reader in a cycle of guilt production that becomes meaningless with respect to historical events, because what is at stake is not referentiality,[6] but the desire of the text to give the reader digestible psychological "explanations."

We may thus concede that confessions may be suspect if they unselfconsciously use the language of self-naming as a means toward final exoneration. However, "confessions" need not operate under the sign of the modern, i.e., they need not aim to achieve final absolution. "Confessions" can represent interventions into dominant discursive orders whose reliance on the reign of "truth" demands conformity, at the very least, and enacts extreme violence at the limit. As complex as is its relation to the context into which it asserts itself, a "confession" can acknowledge one's participation in violent systems/acts while conceding simultaneously to the inevitability of one's blindness. Such "confessions" accept the inadequacy of language to represent totalities, of the self or of historical events. They can assume a position in relation to the crime, a position that is historically and institutionally contingent; that operates as an intervention into the creation of collective, cultural identities; that is not afraid of affect, but that does not rely upon final absolution.

II.

Given the self-exonerating project of the Riefenstahl narrative, one might ask: Why read it and/or write about it? With respect to the reception of Riefenstahl's memoirs, there has been, as one might expect, a range of responses. The overall reaction falls into a postwar pattern that Eric Rentschler has called an "impasse between moral castigation and aesthetic vindication."[7] But in this volume, we have acknowledged the need to move away from our postwar fixation on Riefenstahl as either a persecuted film genius or an evil Nazi pinup girl.

In answer to the above question, such a move demands that we re-evaluate some of the terms of our critique of "Riefenstahl" and her films. Their aesthetic—the use of rhythmic camera movements and editing, the photographic shots of faces and bodies against the open sky, the framing of the mass ornament—calls for investigation as part of the cultural discourses of the Weimar era, particularly as these concern her early training in dance. Rather than reading her memoirs as an expression of either the creative artist or as the etchings of a guilt-ridden fascist subject par excellence, her memoirs are interesting because they, in fact, duplicate the dominant narrative pattern of her Nazi-era films. Riefenstahl's Nazi-era films have been called innovative for the creation of drama in the repetition of alternating rhythms that she establishes through editing. Indeed, her memoirs show us that she has not lost the knack for creating theatrics through movement. Her text takes the reader to alternating highs and lows of love and rejection, comfort and fear, mania and depression, illness and vitality. Her admirers are engaged by the excitement of the ride: John Simon's review in the *New York Times Book Review* goes so far as to claim that the memoir "does not contain a single un-spellbinding page."[8] Others found it painfully boring and ideologically reprehensible. Whether one experiences the "read" as a thrill or a bore, we need to trace the genealogy of this particular narrative rhythm, and finally to ask what it has to do with Nazi visual culture.

My initial attempt to understand the back and forth between extreme emotional states was focused, typically enough, on Riefenstahl as an individual in need of psychological analysis.[9] After all, it is a commonplace in trauma studies to attribute oscillations between emotional states to trauma. That was what I thought described the Riefenstahl narrative perfectly. The narrative builds in intense emotion as she evokes Goebbels's sexual attack on her in the forest at the edge of Berlin, yet when her father dies, she mentions it more or less in passing. We ride pages of absolute manic activity as Riefenstahl plans and films *Triumph of the Will* or *Olympia*, only to fall into valleys of immobility caused by illness or depression. Occasionally, at the emotional peak of some experience, like the opening night of *Triumph of the Will*, Riefenstahl actually claims to have fainted.

The problem with such an analysis is that it posits "Riefenstahl" as the victim stuck in a vicious pattern of posttraumatic stress disorder. However, upon recognizing that her Nazi-era films were edited according to the same aesthetic principle of the repetition of hills and valleys, it becomes clear that the narrative pattern of the memoirs was not that of an individual trauma victim, but rather followed an aesthetic principle that Riefenstahl described as the melody of her shots: "There are valleys, there are peaks. Some things have to be sunk down, some have to soar."[10] This fluctuating pattern of the memoirs, moreover, is characterized not by difference or oscillation, but by a repetition of those oscillations that cover the entire nine hundred pages. This movement creates a compulsive, rhythmic sameness. This, too, resembles in an important way the aesthetic of her propaganda documentaries, films in which there is movement without change, i.e., narrative progression.[11] Difference without change, oscillating patterns of movement: In order to better understand this organizing aesthetic principle, it is necessary to look at the social and aesthetic qualities of modern dance culture in the interwar years and their influence on Riefenstahl.

III.

Bringing dance and Riefenstahl's aesthetic into an intertextual relation is not completely arbitrary. Riefenstahl began her career as a passionate and moderately successful solo modern dancer. She studied with Weimar Germany's most famous dancer/choreographer, Mary Wigman. Riefenstahl's time with Wigman was, however, short-lived because she found Wigman's choreography too abstract and was unwilling to relinquish her position as a soloist in order to participate in the school's group choreographies. As a result, she returned to her favorite teacher of *Ausdruckstanz*, dancer/choreographer Jutta Klamt in Berlin. Here I will offer a short discussion of the dominant discourses of rhythm in general, as well as in the development of expressive dance specifically, in the interwar period in order to explore the roots of her aesthetic.

Before World War I, body movement pedagogy consisted primarily of rationally applied sets of rhythms and repetitions for various parts of the body. These were developed largely by the dance and movement pedagogue Emile Jaques-Dalcroze at Hellerau. In the interwar years, Rudolph Laban's theory, based on rhythmic oppositions, grounded much of the movement work that was used in the vast majority of modern dance schools.[12] However, as Carl Toepfer points out, there was a transition in the role that rhythm played in dance culture after the Great War: "By the end of World War I, Dalcroze's definition of rhythm appeared too narrow and mathematical to satisfy the German appetite for a more radical, ecstatic, and transformative definition of rhythm that yielded a distinctly 'German' expression of modernity."[13] This postwar transition to a vocabulary that was less mechanistic and rationalized is indicative of the general postwar trend to make sense of modern life, particularly given the recent phenomenon of mass technological warfare. Dance and the body movement culture were arenas in which the recuperative language of wholeness dominated. This fact is all the more important given how popular these movements were, especially among young women.

Rhythm as a mode of self-understanding links modern dance to other intellectual and cultural trends of the interwar period. Michael Golston asserts that "rhythm was ready by 1913 to become deployed in generative theoretical relationships with/in a significant array of social, political, and scientific discourses."[14] Let us take Ludwig Klages, an important philosopher and popularizer of *Lebensphilosophie*, as an example. His influential book on rhythm, *Vom Wesen des Rhythmus (On the Essence of Rhythm)* was published in 1923. Michael Mackenzie's essay on Riefenstahl's *Olympia* shows clearly the relationship between Klages and the role of rhythm in Weimar and Nazi culture, a pivotal discourse in which he locates Riefenstahl's film aesthetic. In the rhythms of nature, Klages finds a preservation of the life force, which so many intellectuals found was endangered by modern industrial life. He posits rhythm as the realm in which vitalistic forces protect the modern subject from the deadening, mechanistic time of the industrial age. He distinguishes between *Takt* and *Rhythmus. Takt* is repetitive movement. It is the product of human intellectual activities, as exemplified in the movement of machines. According to Klages, it is soulless and destroys rhythm.[15] *Rhythmus,* in contrast, flows; it contains the attributes of waves of water and as such is universal. The function of rhythm, according to Klages, is to rejuvenate the life force threatened by modernity's machine time. As Mackenzie has shown, there are direct links between Klages, dance, and later Nazi ideology, although, according to him, Riefenstahl does not participate in the latter's racialization of rhythm. He sees *Olympia*, especially in its glorification of Jesse Owens, as constructed in a discourse of rhythm that is particular to Weimar's culturally conservative discourse of the body à la Klages. He asserts further that Riefenstahl did not take the leap to Nazism's inability to "tolerate the image of its nonwhite other."[16]

MacKenzie's argument is perceptive as it relates to the sameness of Riefenstahl's aesthetic, which is rooted in the cultural conservatism of Weimar discourses of the body. However, I will show here that Riefenstahl's aesthetic prepares the ground for gendered positionalities in which passivity is masked as activity. Such a position was fundamental to Nazism's cultural appeal. That is not to say, however, that there is an inherent "fascist aesthetic" of which Riefenstahl's films are a paradigmatic example. Rather, in dance discourse we find a profound moment of historical continuity and adaptability from the Weimar era into the early Nazi years. Prior to that period, in the years between 1923 and 1924, Riefenstahl gave at least seventy solo dance performances. Most reviews show that she was received as an up-and-coming star in the world of modern dance in Germany. We find the only visual record of her dancing in her first appearance as an actress in Arnold Fanck's Alpine film, *The Holy*

Mountain (1926). Here she dances in the prologue, which is set on rocky cliffs overlooking the sea. Her character, Diotima, dances in pairs of movements that mirror each other: First she swings to the left, then right, then she moves across the frame in one direction, only to reverse herself and cross the frame again in the other direction. The dance itself is crosscut to the ocean's waves that swell and crash on the rocks. One source states that two principles guided the cutting of the sequence—"the visual matching of the shape of the dance with the curve of the surf and, more importantly, the kinesthetic pulse of a dance movement with the rhythmic crash or caress of the waves upon the shore."[17] The critical literature sees the crosscutting in the prologue as constructing a typically neoromantic, antirationalist relationship to nature, a precursor to *Blut und Boden* ideology. I would argue, however, that the neglected aspect of this sequence, namely the to-and-fro motion, needs analytical attention. In the repetitive rhythms of the sequence is the locus of an important continuity between aspects of Weimar dance culture and Nazi aesthetics.[18]

Indeed, the back-and-forth movement of Riefenstahl's seaside dance acquires a more complex meaning when compared to another interwar text, a text in which the alternations of here and there, of back and forth, are set in the historical context of war trauma. This text is part two of Sigmund Freud's *Beyond the Pleasure Principle*, in which Freud discusses the child's *fort/da* game. Putting this psychoanalytic narrative into a larger cultural context is the stepping-stone for understanding the relationship between the rhythms of Riefenstahl's aesthetic signature, modern dance, and Nazi-era culture. Freud wrote *Beyond the Pleasure Principle* during a period in which the popularity of modern dance culture exploded in Germany, right after World War I. The essay opens with a timely discussion of traumatic neurosis, "related," says Freud, "to the terrible war that gave rise to a great number of illnesses."[19] He continues with a short discussion of the traumatic circumstance and its effect on the victim and then moves on to a discussion of the childhood game. We know, of course, that the rhythmic alternation of throwing and finding the toy, a staging of disappearance and return, was, Freud posited, the means by which the child not only masters the mother's absence, but also, due to the repetition of the activity, finds pleasure in it. Freud notes that at the outset the child is in a passive situation and thus overwhelmed by the experience. But by repeating it, he takes an active role. When the boy's father leaves for the front, the boy has now a strategy for dealing with his absence. Freud ends the second part of *Beyond the Pleasure Principle* with a move from child's play to artistic play, which, in the case of tragedy, for example, "does not spare the spectators the most painful experience and yet can be felt by them as highly enjoyable."[20]

The narrative progression of this subsection of Freud's seminal text has larger cultural and multidimensional relevance. Its significance, of course, depends upon the context through which it is read. For the purposes of this essay, it is the Great War and its aftermath that comprise the frame for interpreting the significance of the child's activities. We often learn of *fort/da* in isolation from the war trauma that frames the discussion of the child's game, yet the mark of war that begins and ends this section is far from incidental. Freud began the *fort/da* narrative with the actual victim of trauma, i.e., with the subject who is active in the traumatic situation, namely the soldier. But if we take Freud's narrative progression, which leapt from talking about soldiers' post-traumatic stress to a child's game, then we move from the subject actively experiencing the traumatic situation, to the problems faced by those who have an indirect, that is passive, position in relation to the trauma.

Freud tells us that the good child, the passive one, is the child who does not raise a fuss over the mother's absence. His repetitions are productive because they lead toward acceptance of the loss. Arguing by analogy to the war setting, the good citizen is culturally defined as the adaptable "woman," who would learn to manage the horror over the losses of the battlefield. The means for the transformation of loss into pleasure is to be found in aesthetic activity. In this historical instance, we are led to modern dance. Moving Freud's theory of repetitive movement as a gendered theory into its strategic relation to war trauma is illuminating for the rest of this discussion, because the essay describes strategies that were at work in constructing particular subject positions. These were ideologically inscribed as passive in relation to the active traumatic situation. The repetition compulsion of the little boy, who goes through the rhythms of throwing and recovering the lost object, illuminates the crucial role that rhythm plays within predominantly female dance culture.

Indeed, Riefenstahl's dance performances in *The Holy Mountain* work rhythmically and narratively in a way that is similar to the way the *fort/da* movement is embedded in Freud's essay.[21] Eric Rentschler's important essay, "Mountains and Modernity," offers insight into the centrality of gender analysis for understanding Alpine films (*Bergfilme*) by pointing out that female figures are central to the narrative economy of the genre.[22] In that context, Diotima's dance "catalyzes the film's story, a story revolving around the energies her image and presence arouse in two men."[23] The film's story shows two men in love with Diotima, and as a result of one man's traumatizing discovery of her affection for the other, a murder/suicide takes place in the rugged mountain landscape. While climbing together, the jealous lover pushes his friend over the cliff, but in a moment of remorse, he refuses to let go of the rope that would let the other man fall to a sure death. Joined by the climbing rope, the two men die in the freezing temperatures that accompany that stormy mountain night. The jealous mate is thus transformed into the ultimate male buddy in a sequence in which male bonding triumphs over Diotima's lure. The frozen bodies, reminiscent of the armored bodies of which Hal Foster and Andreas Huyssen write,[24] have a double purpose: They give a dramatic ending to a story that, in Rentschler's words, "confronts the fearful dynamics that ensue when men dream too ardently about a woman."[25] The two climbers simultaneously create an image of impenetrability, a final defense against the lure of "woman," which, as Klaus Theweleit showed in *Male Fantasies*, was central to the fascist-modernist fantasy. In the following, I would like to re-frame the reading of the film's story by linking Diotima's dance in the prologue to the child's *fort/da* rhythms.

Such a re-framing has the effect of inscribing a "feminine" subject position as not just the victim of a paranoid masculine modern subject. In fact, the "feminine" rhythms can be seen as preparing the ground for the fantasmatic support of men and women assuming discursive positions supportive of the Nazi regime. As Rentschler notes, the credits of the film contain Fanck's dedication to "my friend who was killed in the war, the mountain climber, Dr. Hans Rohde."[26] Indeed, just as Freud's essay begins with trauma related to war loss, so the film begins with a soldier/friend's death in the war. Diotima's dance follows the narrative trajectory of Freud's narrative in which a subject who is passive in the traumatic situation engages in a repetitive, rhythmic activity, an activity that is related by virtue of its narrative proximity to war trauma. In both cases, the to-and-fro motion is productive in that it prepares the subject for further loss: in Freud's piece, the boy manages the disappearance of the father to the war front; in the film narrative, Diotima loses both men to the mountains.

The rhythmic repetition that comprises the dance, then, can be said to work in a way that suggests not a strengthening of individuation through activity, but rather an activity that unproductively re-stages the loss, and in doing so, constructs a subject who is tied to loss in a fundamental way. Evoking Slavoj Žižek's essay on Richard Wagner's uniting of music and drama, we can see that bringing the rhythms of dance into a narrative relationship with the drama of *The Holy Mountain* is a crucial moment in the film's conferring of death with its mythical dimensions.[27] In fact, the film ends with a close-up of Diotima's face, a face emptied of expression, caught in the numbed state of memory of her two admirers.[28] Thus, the prologue has a double function: It responds to the literal naming of death in the dedication, and it constructs a subject who can transform factual death through stylization into myth. After all, the death of the two friends is only meaningfully heroic if there is a subject who can give them life after death. The function of the dance is thus to tie the feminine position into an activity that naturalizes the losses she endures and that elevates her suffering by linking it to the redemption of the masculine.

The historical appeal of repetitive rhythms had among its many contradictory effects the transformation of shattered prewar dreams, dreams that associated war with a catastrophic destruction that was supposed to generate new utopias, into another myth of coherent and masterful male subjects. This aesthetic activity prepares for the central role that the mythification of death will play in Nazi culture as well.[29] This discussion, however, should not be understood as a wholesale condemnation of *Ausdruckstanz*, nor as a suggestion that all rhythm is politically suspect. These are historical issues.[30] In the Weimar era, especially early on, modern dance was not a completely homogeneous movement. There were numerous schools and choreographers who had much in common, but who also approached dance in a variety of ways. However, if we stress the links between second-generation modern dance and its particular historical circumstances, then *Ausdruckstanz* must be seen as productive of contradictory effects, one of which associates modern dance as a popular movement to the war that came both before and after it. Susan Manning, in her book on Mary Wigman, is sensitive to these multiple effects of *Ausdruckstanz*. She posits that perhaps one reason for the traditional exclusion of modern dance from the many histories of Weimar culture is that it "counters the master-narrative of a sharp break between Weimar and Nazi culture."[31] Manning observes that "in contrast to the other arts, where the majority of leading artists before 1933 either emigrated or withdrew into 'inner emigration,' only a minority of the leading choreographers before 1933 emigrated."[32] In other words, dance did not save practitioners from participation in Nazi culture. In fact, it served to connect them to it.[33]

The most powerful evidence that rhythmic movement constituted a major interface between Weimar dance and Nazi choreography is found in the writings of Nazi dance ideologues themselves, most of whom were major figures in the world of *Ausdruckstanz* in the 1920s. Not surprisingly, Nazi constructions of rhythm and its role in national life are achieved through its racialization. Rhythm is no longer an aesthetic quality, but an expression of a racial category. It dominated Nazi prescriptions for dance and performance, thereby eliminating the variety of styles and varying degrees of abstraction that were typical of German Ausdruckstanz at the time.

The rhythm guru of the Weimar period, Rudolph Bode, understood rhythm to be the fundamental unit of life. Bode's concept of bodily rhythms, which served ideologically to protect against an excessive rationality that was associated with technological and social developments, was united with a distinctly "German" notion of rhythm and bodily movement.[34] Bode has become the poster boy of the elision of rhythm and German identity, a link that attracted him to Nazism already in the nineteen twenties. In 1933, he was named "the director of the "Körperbildung und Tanz Division of the Kampfbund für deutsche Kultur and director of the gymnastics and dance section of the Reichsverband Deutscher Turn-, Sport- und Gymnastiklehrer im NS-Lehrerbund."[35] The link between rhythm and Nazism is not about rhythm as such, but rather emerged from the content that rhythm carried in the dance discourse of this time. For Bode, rhythm that dwells in the blood demonstrates the essence of Germanness. Another important Weimar dance critic, Fritz Böhme, slid into the Nazi dance world through the merging of rhythm and race ideology. He wrote in 1936:"We are a self-contained people, and only if we feel the urgency of our unity will it emerge in our gestures and in our rhythmic expressive movements."[36]

Major figures in the world of Nazi dance culture were the husband-and-wife team Jutta Klamt and G. Jo Fischer-Klamt, she as choreographer/teacher, he as ideologue. As mentioned above, Jutta Klamt was Riefenstahl's primary teacher of modern dance. Her husband, Fischer-Klamt, once a student of Laban, was a climber in the highly politicized world of Nazi dance. By 1937, he came into favor as Laban was being pushed out of his leading position in the Nazi dance bureaucracy. In the 1930s he taught Rassenkunde (race science).[37] Lilian Karina, in her book *Tanz unterm Hakenkreuz*, uses the Klamts as an example to typify the ease with which modern dance practitioners and theoreticians slid into the Nazi regime as active participants.[38]

Prior to the Nazi takeover, Fischer-Klamt, in an essay published in 1929 in the newsletter of the Jutta Klamt Society, *Koerperrhythmus und TANZ* (*Body Rhythm and Dance*), wrote about the vehicle that linked the bodily movements of the dancer to the larger social order, theorizing as such the emerging importance of kinesthetic identification. He said that the work of famous dancers has thrust itself "tief in das Wesen des Menschen," (deep into the essence of man), which outlives the moment of the experience: "Connections resound between the body and the powers that the body mobilizes; between the dancer's body and the audience's body, the totality of which is brought into motion through the experience."[39] Rhythm, in other words, connects the individual to the collective. The link to Nazi-era discourse emerges in the notion of a collective *Schwingen* that is created by the linking of the dancer to the racial community through an experience of rhythmic movement. The audience, in turn, is linked to the experience via a kinesthetic identification with the dancer(s). This generates the notion of a spectatorial position that is at one with the movement (aesthetic and political).

These community formative aspects of rhythm are central for an understanding of Riefenstahl's Nazi-era films, particularly *Triumph of the Will*. We have no record of her own writing that linked rhythm and race, but her films are part of the dominant cultural vocabulary in which that connection was taken for granted. The language of rhythm is one that permeated Riefenstahl's own cultural world. Though Riefenstahl was adamant about making beautiful, and not political, films, her own description of her Nazi-era filmmaking has political/historical resonance: ". . . the feeling for dance is very similar to the feeling for cutting, especially in a documentary. For me, the documentary is like a dance. They are both rhythm."[40] And even if we assume that Riefenstahl remained blind to the political content ascribed to rhythm, highly unlikely though that is, Nazi-era film "critics" were not, to which a 1936 assessment of her work attests: "The director had 'communicated the political experience in the form of an artistic experience by transforming the rhythm of the real event into a cinematic rhythm.'"[41]

In summary, Riefenstahl's dance in *The Holy Mountain* is representative of the repetitive nature typical of the popular body movement culture. Modern dance and exercise cultures were immensely popular, not only in the cities but also in the provinces.[42] Indeed, I posit that the interwar obsession with modern dance and exercise culture—by virtue of its kinesthetic identification and rhythmic repetitions—wanted to have a lulling effect; it represents a subject position in opposition, for example, to Walter Benjamin's anxiety preparedness, which acts as a defense against fascism. Riefenstahl's artistic foundations are in dance. The kinesthetic identification that underpins the effectiveness of modern dance is transformed by her into film through camera movement and editing.

I hope that it is clear by now that this essay does not aim to explain "Riefenstahl" in a totalistic way. The judgment that she was highly ambitious and opportunistic still stands, but the reliance on psychological traits as historical explanation does not allow us to learn from the extreme violence the Nazis perpetrated. Instead, I look to understand complicity as a culturally constructed choice, which asks us to include ourselves and our present in the search for cultural practices that help us naturalize death, violence, and loss endemic to our own time. Specifically, the Nazi past teaches us to question whose death we legitimize or make heroic, and how, and at whose expense.

As I have suggested in this study, aspects of dance and body practice facilitated the acceptance of a culture that permitted violence against Jews, homosexuals, political resisters, and others while it glorified the death of "Aryans." Certain kinds of rhythmic, repetitive movement organized subject positions that relied on the ability to accept, master, and find pleasure in a life of loss and risk. Such subjects feel helplessness with poignancy, mastery with victimization. These are the same rhythms that punctuate the unfolding of Riefenstahl's own life story.

NOTES

I would like to thank Neil Christian Pages and Ingeborg Majer-O'Sickey for their careful readings of drafts of this essay.

1. "Wie ein Film sind die Erlebnisse jener Jahre unzählige Male vor meinem Augen abgelaufen-und bis auf den heutigen Tag werde ich mit der Vergangenheit konfrontiert" Leni Riefenstahl, *Memoiren* (München und Hamburg: Albrecht Knaus Verlag, 1987), 913. Published first in English as *The Sieve of Time* (London: Quartet Books Limited, 1992). Quoted in the U.S. publication as *Leni Riefenstahl: A Memoir* (New York: Picador USA, 1995), 655.
2. Ray Müller's film, *The Wonderful, Horrible Life of Leni Riefenstahl*, ends with Riefenstahl posing the familiar question: "What am I guilty of?"
3. I do not seek to conflate these two figures, rather I find thinking them together oddly productive. Of course, de Man was dead upon the discovery of his wartime journalism. Still, Shoshana Felman's essay justifies de Man's silence from within his intellectual tradition. See: Shoshana Felman, "After the Apocalypse: Paul de Man and the Fall to Silence," in *Testimony: Crises of Witnessing in Literature, Psychoanalysis, and History*, ed. Shoshana Felman and Dori Laub (New York: Routledge, 1992), 120–164.
4. Bill Niven, "The Globalization of Memory and the Rediscovery of German Suffering," in *German Literature in the Age of Globalization*, ed. Stuart Taberner (Birmingham: University of Birmingham Press, 2004), 220–246. Niven, however, would not consider Riefenstahl's memoir as a part of the blurring between "victim memory and perpetrator memory" in the transnational setting. In his view, the emergence of

self-empathy around German suffering is best achieved when there is a parallel focus on German crime, a quality that does not typify the memory work under discussion here.

5. See Doris Sommer on the issue of sympathy and identification between reader and writer. "Taking a Life: Hot Pursuit and Cold Rewards in a Mexican Testimonial Novel," in *The Seductions of Biography,* ed. Mary Rhiel and David Suchoff (New York and London: Routledge, 1996), 147–172.
6. Peter Brooks, "Storytelling Without Fear: Confessions in Law and Literature," *Law's Stories: Narrative and Rhetoric in the Law*, ed. Peter Brooks and Paul Gewirtz (New Haven and London: Yale University Press, 1996), 122.
7. Eric Rentschler, *The Ministry of Illusion: Nazi Cinema and Its Afterlife* (Cambridge, MA, and London: Harvard University Press, 1996), 30.
8. John Simon, "The Führer's Movie Maker," *New York Times Book Review,* September 26, 1993, 1.
9. In an effort to break from the postwar focus on Riefenstahl as artistic genius versus evil Nazi, Catherine Soussloff reads the oscillations of Riefenstahl's memoirs as a symptom of additive patterns, in which success and failure must repeat endlessly. Using Gregory Bateson, Soussloff's analysis of Riefenstahl's memoirs relate it to a "flawed epistemology that reifies an indomitable self that seeks impossible forms of control, forgetting what it cannot control to fate." See Catherine Soussloff, "Leni Riefenstahl: The Power of the Image," *Discourse* 18, no. 3 (Spring 1996): 20–44 (36).
10. David Hinton, *The Films of Leni Riefenstahl* (Metuchen, NJ: Scarecrow Press, 1991), 14. Quoted in Alan Marcus, "Reappraising Riefenstahl's *Triumph of the Will* 4 (2004): 75–86 (81).
11. Many scholars have commented on this stylistic feature. Brian Winston, for example, finds *Triumph of the Will* aesthetically uninteresting due to its repetitive sameness. See Brian Winston, "*Triumph of the Will,*" *History Today* 47, no. 1 (1997): 24–28. Roy Schwartzmann points out in his essay that the viewer becomes a direct participant in the events of the rally because of the absence of narrative intermediaries and narrative progression, a move that he maintains reduces critical distance (139). See Roy Schwartzmann, "Racial Theory and Propaganda in *Triumph of the Will,*" in *Authority and Transgression in Literature and Film*, ed. Bonnie Braendlin and Hans Braendlin (Gainesville, FL: University Press of Florida, 1996): 136–153. Terri Gordon writes also of movement outside of narrative development as key to the film's identificatory power that she calls a "kinetic force . . . that seeks to draw the spectator in." (185). See Terri J. Gordon, "Fascism and the Female Form: Performance Art in the Third Reich," *Journal of the History of Sexuality* 11, no. 1–2 (2002): 164–200.
12. See Karl Toepfer, *Empire of Ecstasy: Nudity and Movement in German Body Culture 1920–1935* (Berkeley, Los Angeles, London: University of California Press, 1997). He writes about Laban: "Every movement entailed a countermovement; thus, breathing was the complement of the pause, symmetry the complement of asymmetry. Bending unfolded against arching, the swing against the turn, the flight against the fall, the spiral against the lateral profile, stamping against tip-toeing, stretching against coiling, advancing against retreating, the ring against the line, the left hand against the right, the head against the torso." 103.
13. Ibid., 125.
14. For a larger discussion of the role of rhythm in the development of modern cultural and political practices, see Michael Golston, "'im anfang war der rhythmus': rhythmic

incubations in discourses of the mind, body, and races from 1850–1944." *SEHR* 5, Supplement: Cultural and Technologies of Fascism (December 1996): 1.

15. Ludwig Klages, *Vom Wesen des Rhythmus* (Kampfen auf Sylt: Niels Kampmann Verlag, 1934), 15.
16. Michael MacKenzie, "From Athens to Berlin: The 1936 Olympics and Leni Riefenstahl's *Olympia*," *Critical Inquiry* 29 (2003): 335.
17. Peggy Ann Wallace, "An Historical Study of the Career of Leni Riefenstahl from 1923 to 1933." Diss. University of Southern California, 1975, 127–128.
18. Jürgen Trimborn wrote that it was this sequence in particular that first drew Hitler's attention to Riefenstahl. Jürgen Trimborn, "Der Tanz an das Meer: Ein Porträt der Tänzerin Leni Riefenstahl," *Tanzdrama Magazin* 48 (1999): 20–23.
19. Sigmund Freud, *Beyond the Pleasure Principle*, trans. and ed. James Strachey (New York and London: W. W. Norton, 1961), 6.
20. Ibid., 11.
21. There is, however, no foundational relationship between Freud's text and Riefenstahl's version of modern dance. In fact, the political trajectory of the *fort/da* narrative is versatile and could be offered as a treatment against a fascist paradigm.
22. Eric Rentschler, "Mountains and Modernity: Relocating the Bergfilm" *New German Critique* 51 (fall 1990): 137–161 (153).
23. Ibid., 154.
24. Andreas Huyssen, "Fortifying the Heart-Totally: Ernst Jünger's Armored Texts" *New German Critique* 59 (spring/summer 1993): 3–23. Also, Hal Foster, "Armor Fou," *October* 56 (spring 1991): 64–97.
25. Rentschler, "Mountains and Modernity,"155.
26. Ibid., 154.
27. Slavoj Žižek, "'There Is No Sexual Relationship': Wagner as Lacanian," *New German Critique* 69 (fall 1996) 7–35. Žižek, too, sees rhythm as occupying an important place in the cultural life of the twenties and early thirties. Speech, however, resists "inclusion into this 'symphony of life'" (19). As a result, when speech as "natural" conversation enters film, the musical score "serves as the means of its (the action on the screen) stylization, confers on it its mythical dimension" (19).
28. The blank face was a feature of modern dance that was admired by many literary modernists, among them Yeats and T. S. Eliot, according to Terri A. Mester, author of *Movement and Modernism: Yeats, Eliot, Lawrence, Williams, and Early 20th Century Dance* (Fayetteville: University of Arkansas Press, 1997). The blank gaze of the dancer, according to Yeats, allowed for the creation of the impersonal and the formal (Mester, 33). T. S. Eliot also "extolled the virtues of impersonality in the dancers"(Mester, 74). The impersonal face of the dancer, then, is a vehicle of artistic abstraction, which links the individual to the universal. In Nazism, the face provides the link between the individual and the racialized national community, as exemplified by the low-angled close-ups of blankly gazing faces that pepper Riefenstahl's film *Triumph of the Will*.
29. An illustration of the framing of interwar feminine subject positions in relation to the war is contained in the script from a Lothar Schreyer dance choreography. Lothar's "Kreuzigung" dance (1920) was choreographed to this poem: "Mother: / in light / my son / is silent / (noise tones) / Mistress: Men scream / Men go into / battle / I dance / I." Quoted from Karl Toepfer, *Empire of Ecstacy: Nudity and Movement in German*

Body Culture (Berkeley, Los Angeles, London: University of California Press, 1997), 137.

30. There has been much attention paid to dance history and theory. Sally Banes wrote the following in *Writing Dance in the Age of Postmodernism* (Hanover and London: University Press of New England, 1994), 50: "For dance history to take its place on the stage as a branch of cultural history, dance historians need to show that dancing bodies have not simply created divertissements. Perhaps then cultural historians will be convinced to take seriously the centrality of dance in our culture."
31. Susan Manning, *Ecstasy and the Demon: Feminism and Nationalism in the Dances of Mary Wigman* (Berkeley, Los Angeles, London: University of California Press: 1993), 5.
32. Ibid., 6.
33. Lilian Karina's book, *Tanz unterm Hakenkreuz*, gives a vivid account of the politics of modern dance in the Nazi era. She shows how modern dance, unlike Expressionist painting or literature, was defended by choreographers and ideologues of the Nazi period as not a decadent art form but rather as expressive of a deeply German quality. There seemed to have been consensus among choreographers, dancers, and theoreticians alike that *Ausdruckstanz* was and is German in origin and character, as opposed to ballet, for example, which was the product of foreign influence. "Ballett sei geistlos und zeigte stilisierte Figuren, Ballettschulen würden ausserdem ausländisch geleitet. Der Ausdruckstanz sei hingegen im Sinne Nietzsches die Kunst des bewegten und tänzerischen deutschen Menschen, Medium eines zum Instrument erzogenen Körpers aus der tiefe des deutschen Gemüts and des deutschen Gefühlslebens." Lilian Karina/Marion Kant *Tanz unterm Hakenkreuz: Eine Dokumentation* (Berlin: Henschel Verlag, 1996), 136–137.
34. Toepfer, *Empire of Ecstacy*, 128.
35. Ibid.
36. Fritz Boehme, "Die Aufgabe des Tänzers der Gegenwart," In . . . *jeder Mensch ist ein Tänzer: Ausdruckstanz in Deutschland zwischen 1900 und 1945*, ed. Hedwig Mueller and Patricia Stoeckemann (Giessen: Anabas-Verlag Guenter Kaempf, 1993), 124. In German it reads: "Wir sind ein geschlossenes Volk und auch in der Gebärde und im rhytmischen Bewegungsausdruck wird diese Einheit, wenn sie nur als Notwendigkeit gefühlt wird, emporwachsen."
37. Karina, *Tanz unterm Hakenkreuz*, 130.
38. Ibid., 46.
39. G. Jo Fischer, *Koerperrhythmus und TANZ: Mitteilungsblatt der Jutta Klamt-Gemeinschaft* III/IV (1929): 1. "Zusammenhänge klingen auf zwischen dem Instrument Körper und den Kräften, die sich dieses Instrumentes bedienen, zwischen dem Instrument des Tänzers und dem Instrument des Zuschauers, dessen Totalität durch das Erlebte zum Schwingen gebracht wird."
40. Wallace, *An Historical Study of the Career of Leni Riefenstahl from 1923 to 1933*, 83.
41. "Gibt es einen deutschen Kamerastil?" *Der deutsche Film* 3, no. 7 (1939): 176–177. Quoted in Rainer Rother, *Leni Riefenstahl: The Seduction of Genius*, trans. Martin H. Bott (London and New York: Continuum, 2002), 96.
42. See for example, Karl Toepfer's work. He says there that the demand for "bodily expressivity was very strong during the Weimar era, and even quite provincial cities could boast not one but two or three schools for gymnastic/dance instruction." Toepfer, *Ecstacy and the Demon*, 135.

Part Four

"Riefen-Star"

Chapter 10

Control and Consumption: The Photographs of Leni Riefenstahl

Guinevere Narraway

In a 1997 interview with the German newsmagazine *Der Spiegel*, Leni Riefenstahl asserted that she wanted to make "the beautiful" visible to people and to thereby rescue it.[1] The "beautiful" in question here were the Sudanese Nuba, who became Riefenstahl's photographic subjects in the early 1960s, and the coral reef ecologies of a number of the world's seas and oceans, which Riefenstahl had been photographing since the mid-1970s. While she continued to deny that there was political intent driving the phenomenal potency of images and their juxtaposition in the Nazi-era films *Olympia* and *Triumph of the Will*, Riefenstahl here in the *Spiegel* interview uncharacteristically claimed a political motivation for her photographic work. Riefenstahl's prioritization of aesthetics in these photographs, however, confounded her averred liberal humanist aims as much as it had aided her effective representation of National Socialist ideological principles in the films she made during the Third Reich. Prioritizing form over content, Riefenstahl constructed the Nuba as a "primitive" people of untouched beauty. Indeed, at precisely the time when the discipline of anthropology was entering a crisis instigated by a poststructuralist critique of its own assumptions, Riefenstahl firmly placed herself, through quasi-ethnographic texts and photographs, as a monological authority who would speak on behalf of a purportedly "dying" culture.[2]

Ultimately, however, Riefenstahl's attempts to deny the embeddedness of the Nuba in "civilization" became untenable, and thus after a decade or so of gazing upon them, she turned her colonizing eye to the more obliging sphere of the nonhuman that she found in the world of the coral reefs. In her underwater photographs, too, there is as little evidence as in those of the Nuba of an attempt to "save" something. Refusing to locate her subjects in context—a move that would have potentially enabled them to escape her mastery—and depending on the perpetuation of certain discourses of Otherness, Riefenstahl succeeded in her photographs of both the Nuba and the coral reefs in producing the human and the nonhuman as commodities. Riefenstahl claimed that her initial desire to visit Africa was stimulated by Hemingway's evocation of the continent in his 1935 *Green Hills of Africa*, but that she found her inspiration for a film project in a newspaper article about the contemporary slave trade. What was to be a documentary on the subject, she claimed, developed later into the idea for a feature film called *Black Cargo*. Riefenstahl began work on the project in the mid-1950s, but filming soon ground to a halt when she failed to secure sufficient financial backing.

In 1962, Riefenstahl returned to Africa, specifically to Sudan, in search of the Nuba. Her inspiration this time came from a photograph of two Nuba wrestlers taken in 1949 by the British photojournalist George Rodger.[3] The description of her journey to "discover" "her" Nuba is vintage Riefenstahl.[4] In her memoirs and in the photographic volume *The Last of the Nuba*, she emphasizes and enumerates the adversities that she overcame in achieving her goal: the near impossibility of the journey itself, the lack of comforts and amenities, the seeming hopelessness of the search for what was probably a long-vanished culture. When she and her party, an anthropological team from Tübingen, finally enter the Nuba Mountains, Riefenstahl evokes the landscape as virtually primordial—"[b]locks of stone and age-old trees gave the landscape an almost mythical character"—and as very nearly defying their modern transport.[5] Her first vision of the Nuba themselves is rapturous: Painted and ornamented, these dancing figures are fantastical "beings from another planet."[6] All of a sudden, she recounts in *The Last of the Nuba*, "[h]ands reached out towards me, faces laughed at me and I immediately sensed that I was among good people."[7] In this moment, Riefenstahl claims to lose all sense of time. This withdrawal into a world without time and context becomes characteristic of her experience with the Nuba where events are frequently "unreal," "fantastic," dreamlike, or, in one particular case, "like a mystical vision from an ancient myth."[8] In thus escaping the temporal through an obsolete evocation of the "primitive" as undynamic and without history—in opposition to the Western, the "civilized" as of history—Riefenstahl escapes her own past and finds what, according to Claudia Lenssen, she had sought in Africa: "an originary experience (*Ursprungserlebnis*) as a rebirth of her self."[9] Riefenstahl corroborates this assessment, recalling in her memoirs that at the end of her first visit to Africa, she had forgotten "the harsh years; I felt reborn."[10]

Over the next thirteen years, Riefenstahl made seven trips to Sudan in order to capture the Nuba on film. The best-known products of these expeditions are the two coffee-table books, *The Last of the Nuba* and *People of Kau*.[11] The former volume is the result of a decade spent on and off with the Mesakin Nuba, whom Riefenstahl had encountered on her initial visit. The book, self-consciously constructed as an ethnographic "study," is divided into five chapters, each dealing with what is notionally one of the chief aspects of Mesakin Nuba culture. After the publication of this volume, Riefenstahl returned in the early 1970s to the village where she had taken most of her original photographs.

Much to her dismay, she found that the village bore markers of modernity that she could no longer overlook and featured signs of poverty that she could no longer construct as "natural" (and therefore unassailable). To Riefenstahl, the Mesakin Nuba had crossed over from the state of nature to the realm of culture and had thus fallen from grace. No longer "beautiful," these, Riefenstahl's first subjects, were abandoned. In their place, she sought out the Southeast Nuba who, at least superficially, remained in the ur-state that she sought. While it took Riefenstahl almost ten years to amass the photographs that appeared in *The Last of the Nuba*, *People of Kau* is the result of just two brief visits—one of which lasted only a matter of days. *People of Kau* contains less text than *The Last of the Nuba* and Riefenstahl makes less effort to give it the appearance of supposed "objective knowledge." This is a far more explicitly personal text. Moreover, if the images in the earlier book evoke their subjects as archetypes rather than as individuals, this statement is even more apropos of the photographs in the later book. At times, the *People of Kau* gives the reader/viewer the sense of looking through a catalogue rather than at a volume of documentary photography. This is particularly so in the section entitled "The Art of Masking," which predominantly features headshots of young men displaying facial art.[12]

As with *The Last of the Nuba*, in *People of Kau* Riefenstahl once again attempts to create a sense of the fantastic and timeless about her subjects. Even her inspiration to search for the Southeast Nuba is, Riefenstahl professes, the result of a kind of epiphanic dream in which two Southeast Nuba fighters appear to her.[13] Yet while *The Last of the Nuba* devotes at least some attention to the everyday life of the Mesakin Nuba—for example their agrarianism—this second volume focuses on what Riefenstahl invokes as the aesthetic and ritualistic aspects of Southeast Nuba culture.[14] The Nuba photographs were a huge commercial success. They stimulated fresh interest in Riefenstahl and marked the beginning of her new career as photographer. Since the war, she had largely been persona non grata—particularly in Germany. However, as a consequence of the success of the two volumes of photographs, she was welcomed back into the public sphere, albeit not without controversy.[15] Perhaps one of the most important outcomes of the ensuing "reassessment" of Riefenstahl was a renewed critical analysis of her films: where once they had been predominantly understood as propaganda, their aesthetic value was now acknowledged.[16] But this revision of the reception and understanding of Riefenstahl's films did not simply lead to an unproblematic celebration of the formal qualities of her work—although this was the case in some quarters—it also raised questions concerning the relationship between art and politics.[17] Riefenstahl herself was fundamentally uninterested in addressing such questions. In regard to the films she made during the Nazi period, she doggedly maintained that her perspective was one of documentary objectivity. Nonetheless, the issue of the interrelationship of aesthetics and politics continued to inform discussions of her work, including the volumes on the Nuba, and here her position was more complex, including claims to scientific objectivity, artistic sensibility, and political motivation.

In heading off possible criticisms of her Nuba photographs, Riefenstahl to some degree stuck to her tried-and-true claim to impartiality. In response, for example, to Schreiber and Weingarten's suggestion in the *Spiegel* interview that she stages her subjects, she alleges that the Nuba "just look like that."[18] This claim, of course, denies Riefenstahl's own authorial voice as well as the conventions to which her photographs subscribe. First, Riefenstahl's approach to her subjects collapses them together with the material form of the image in that the aesthetically pleasing—young, muscular, slender, able-bodied—Nuba become subsumed by Riefenstahl's general pictorial goals. That is, Riefenstahl is as interested in color and composition, for instance, as she is in representing the Nuba "as they are." Indeed, those Nuba who cannot conform to her aesthetic demands, who cannot contribute to making a materially "beautiful" photograph—the sick, the old, the disabled—barely feature, if at all.[19] Second, Riefenstahl's refusal to acknowledge her role in meaning making in the Nuba photographs is integrally bound up with her realist approach and the assumptions of representational transparency and certainty that go with it.

Psychological and photographic theory in the late 1960s and early 1970s questioned exactly this "objectivist view of the photograph as a simple record."[20] However, the Western assumptions about visual perception that these theories threw into doubt—if not rejected—frequently continue to inform even anthropology's images of the Other.[21] Elizabeth Edwards highlights the dangers of this realist tradition in ethnographic photography by elaborating on how it informs representations of traditional cultures in the postcard.[22] Such an approach reverberates with the commercial aspects of Riefenstahl's Nuba projects. Ludewig argues that Riefenstahl's approach to the Nuba should be seen within the tradition of the nineteenth and early twentieth century European artist who "pursued, in ... encounters with the 'other', a sense of wholeness that had been lost in the fragmentation, inequality and the propensity for alienation of their home societies."[23] Yet the commercial quality of Riefenstahl's photographs and her need to justify her work through the scientific discourse of anthropology perhaps more strongly situate Riefenstahl's work on the Nuba at the intersection of the ethnographic and the touristic outlined by Edwards. Here the authorial voice is elided. The difference between "the connotating expression and the thing itself" is obscured by an assumed verisimilitude.[24] As Edwards argues, ethnographic-style postcards "draw the legitimating structure of their images from precisely the realist, positivist assumptions of a knowable and recordable world which have informed the conventional use of the camera within anthropology."[25] This positivist discourse, which informs both Riefenstahl's representation of the Nuba and our reception of her images, is further supported, as with the postcard featuring a traditional culture, by the "ethnographic" text that accompanies and provides a notional caption for the photographs. Furthermore, visual and written texts together convey an idea of completeness, as if they capture the whole of Nuba culture, suggesting closure rather than an openness that forces the viewer to actively reflect on what they are seeing.[26]

The viewer's active engagement is also suppressed in Riefenstahl's images by the evocation of traditional culture as immutable. Again, consonant with the discourse of tourism, the "real" or "authentic" is understood as timeless and undynamic.[27] Indeed, Riefenstahl's form of "salvage ethnography" depended on the Nuba remaining forever untouched yet on the verge of vanishing. Having already constructed the narrative of their disappearance prior to her arrival—the drama of Riefenstahl's initial search for the Nuba hinges on the fact that they probably no longer "exist" and that she is already "too late"[28]—Riefenstahl's images of the Nuba were always a re-creation of their "authenticity." Her approach was, in Fatimah Tobing Rony's terms, "taxidermic": "[P]osited as already dead, long since passed by in the steeplechase of history, the 'vanishing' Native is 'redeemed' through taxidermic reconstruction."[29] Thus as with the touristic photograph/postcard, Riefenstahl's photographs demand no more of the viewer than that they gaze at what seemingly was and is and ever shall be.[30] Edwards points out how perfectly the photograph operates within this discourse for "still photographs stand diametrically opposed to the flow of life," a contention of both Roland Barthes and Christian Metz.[31] Photography traps and preserves the person photographed, who, due to the passage of time, has inevitably irrevocably changed. Inherently, Metz notes, photography "suppresses from its own appearance the primary marks of 'livingness,' and nevertheless conserves the convincing print of the object: a past presence."[32]

Here we can start to see the correlation, noted by Christopher Pinney, between photography and the "ethnographic present" (the use of the present tense in ethnographic accounts).[33] While photography effects the temporal distantiation of its object through its production of "an immediate memento mori" in the moment of exposure,[34] the ethnographic present denies "coevalness" by placing the Other outside the "dialogic situation."[35] Photography is thus the perfect tool for Riefenstahl's narration of "the last of the Nuba." It facilitates her speaking *of* the Nuba, not *to* them, and enables a mystification of their existence as an eternal recurrence that lies in a locked past. However, the power relations at work in Riefenstahl's photographs are not solely to be found in the discourses in which they trade, but also in their literal production. In her memoirs, Riefenstahl blithely describes Africa as "the dark, mysterious and still barely explored continent."[36]

It is perhaps therefore unsurprising when James Faris argues that Riefenstahl's subject matter and the "intellectual notions" behind her photographs are essentially unchanged from colonial images of the Nuba from the 1920s.[37] The fundamental difference, Faris contends, between early photographs and the work of later photographers such as Riefenstahl is the disavowal of the photographic apparatus. Comparing amateur photographs of

Nuba wrestling from 1929 with later representations of the Nuba (and targeting Riefenstahl's work in particular), he notes the gradual obfuscation of power hierarchies through photographic technique. Discussing the images from 1929, he observes, for example, that we are conscious of peering with the photographer over other people's shoulders for a view of the wrestlers, or that the photographic subjects themselves address the photographic apparatus in a way that, in turn, draws the viewer's attention to it.[38] In contrast, the advanced technology of contemporary photography, such as long-focus lenses and high-speed film, enables the viewer to feel unobtrusively present.[39] Indeed, without her high-tech "arsenal," Riefenstahl, as she herself points out, would have had far less success capturing the Southeast Nuba on film: "Although I had no difficulty in photographing the natives on my earlier expeditions and was thus able to manage with focal lengths of 21 to 135 mm., the timidity and hostility of the Kau Nuba compelled me to do most of my work on this occasion with very powerful telescopic lenses."[40] Photographic technology thus enabled both Riefenstahl's intrusion on the life of the Southeast Nuba and the concealment of this intrusion.

Through his comparative analysis, Faris demonstrates how colonial photographs of the Nuba illuminate the power relationship between the Western "master" and the performing non-Western Other that is obscured in the work of later photographers like Riefenstahl. Additionally, he exposes how the analogous power relationships inherent in photographic practice are revealed in the colonial images while they remain hidden in later photography: As technique has become more sophisticated and technology more advanced, the photographer has increasingly been able to assert dictatorial power over her/his subject, covertly controlling all that appears within the frame (and all that does not) and thus determining what counts as knowledge.[41]

This is manifestly the case in Riefenstahl's work. While she herself observes the embeddedness of the Nuba in the modern world, she endeavors to obscure it.[42] She notes, for example, in her description of her first encounter with the Mesakin Nuba that there was an official school within a few miles of the Nuba village and that "a good number of Nuba were already wearing clothes."[43] Nonetheless, in her photographs she still represents the Nuba as a people "from another planet." And again in *People of Kau* while Riefenstahl notes, for instance, the presence of Nuba in Arab dress at the fights she photographs, they are absent from the images—these show only that "primitive beauty"[44] of the "uncivilized" Nuba. Yet despite the reliance of Riefenstahl's photographic work—and her defense of this work—on the realist tradition, Riefenstahl herself openly confesses to staging many of her photographs. She recalls, for example, that she bribed a reluctant Nuba woman to model for her[45] and that she and Horst Kettner, Riefenstahl's partner and assistant, tried to convince clothed Nuba men to pose naked for the camera on their 1968/69 expedition.[46] The confusion of staging and documentary in Riefenstahl's work is highlighted by the layout of *Mein Afrika*.[47] Here Riefenstahl includes two stills from the uncompleted film project *Black Cargo*. The captions for the photographs are at the back of the book and would possibly be overlooked and remain unread, leaving the reader/viewer with the impression that these fiction stills are "authentic" images of traditional life.

Yet even Riefenstahl could not fully control her subjects. Frequently, "civilization" penetrates her photographs, one supposes despite her wishes. Looking more closely at many of the images, artifacts of modernity—a T-shirt on a funeral mourner for example, or a pair of old sneakers on a naked female tattoo artist—can be found. One particular photograph offers what is arguably the most striking combination of the "exotic" and the quotidian, of Riefenstahl's version of the "beautiful" and its opposite: the vision of an otherwise naked man wearing a pair of brown business shoes as he helps to carry a dead leopard through a village. Although Riefenstahl claims that the Islamic authorities were determined to clothe the Nuba, and while she notes that the Nuba did business with passing traders, her photographs would, at first glance, seem to belie that the government has had any impact on traditional life or that the Nuba possess any manufactured goods.[48] One has to look carefully to spot what Riefenstahl's technique clearly works hard to conceal.

Through the omissions in the photographs, Riefenstahl attempts to "produce" an untouched people. More than that, in both her written and her visual texts she constructs the Nuba as a terra incognita, an undiscovered "nature." Not only, as Ludewig observes, does Riefenstahl draw analogies in her writing between the Southeast Nuba and native fauna, but she characterizes both the Mesakin and the Southeast Nuba in terms used to define nature.[49] In her celebration of their art, for example, Riefenstahl describes a culture that is paradoxically precultural in its "authenticity":

> The South-East Nuba have an exceptional gift of imagination and feeling for graphic design. Even modern artists are inspired with awe and admiration by the way in which they attune one colour with another and combine ornaments, lines and stylized figures into a harmonious unity. Their mode of facial and physical decoration, which contains elements of both classical and modern painting, springs from the very fount of true art. Nobody knows where they acquired this incredible talent. It has ecaped investigation until now and will always remain a mystery.[50]

Although Riefenstahl conceives of Nuba culture in Eurocentric terms here, she evokes it as "natural" and without history. As "nature" or "of nature" the Nuba are, according to the dominant (Western) narrative within which Riefenstahl operates, without agency and available for appropriation.[51] Indeed, appropriation or a kind of colonization of the Nuba was exactly Riefenstahl's project as she approached them armed to the teeth with photographic technology. However, much to her frustration, she gradually found herself unable to exert sufficient control over her subjects who were clearly not isolated in time and space—as her own photographs paradoxically revealed. Thus, her reflections on the Mesakin Nuba appear in her memoirs as a trajectory of disappointment from "paradise" to "paradise altered" to, finally, "paradise destroyed."[52] Riefenstahl's first response to the undeniable "coevalness" of the Mesakin Nuba is to turn to the pathetic fallacy as she finds their allegedly negative transformation in the late 1960s reflected in purported changes in the natural environment: The sky is no longer always blue, but rather is now nonspecifically "different"; the temperature mysteriously vacillates between being unbearably hot and uncomfortably cold; the air is hazy, denying Riefenstahl the beautiful sunsets of her earlier visits.[53]

Riefenstahl's temporary solution to this crisis was, as I noted earlier, to replace the Mesakin Nuba with the Southeast Nuba. Ultimately though, Riefenstahl took a far more emphatic and secure step away from conceptions of culture and civilization. In the late 1960s, as she perceived—or, more accurately, constructed—the negative change in the Mesakin Nuba brought about by their increasing contact with modernity, Riefenstahl "discovered" a new world, the coral reefs of the Indian Ocean, and in the course of the 1970s the reef life of the Indian Ocean, the Red Sea, and the Caribbean became her new photographic subjects. In marine ecologies, Riefenstahl once again found that "nature" that the Nuba no longer represented, and in snorkeling and diving she recaptured what she had lost in Africa. As she notes in the introduction to the photographic volume *Coral Gardens*, "I could not believe that an hour had gone by already. I had lost all sense of time."[54] Once more, Riefenstahl instrumentalized the same conception of nature as ahistorical that she had deployed with regard to the Nuba in order to evade temporality and its consequences. Now "the boundless silence" of the underwater world sheltered her "from the outside world, removing all problems and worries."[55]

Concomitantly, this newly found beautiful, allegedly pure, and fragile nature furnished her with fresh opportunities for mastery. In the coral reefs, she could again incorporate the Other into her self—presuming to know and understand it—and expand her self into the Other—presuming that her interests coincided with its interests.[56] Now she could truly avoid seeing anything that did not "fit within the composition of the image itself," producing, as Georg Seesslen argues, "nature" that imitated her "art."[57]

In Riefenstahl's hands, photography is an instrumental and objectifying mode of knowledge and control, but in order to further examine her work it is useful to consider that the photograph can open up new ways of seeing. This opinion finds one of its earliest expressions in Benjamin's idea of the "optical unconscious"—the ability of photographic technique to reveal realities invisible to the naked eye.[58] Among Benjamin's examples is the revelation of architectural and artistic forms in Karl Blossfeldt's magnifications of plants in his 1931 volume of botanic photography *Urformen der Kunst (Art Forms in Nature)*. In relation to Blossfeldt's work, Benjamin argues that rather than dominating nature, photography can "take off the 'veil' that our 'laziness' has thrown over the old nature."[59] Blossfeldt's magnifications change our perspective on the plants by disclosing "an unsuspected wealth of forms and analogies which we never imagined existed in the plant world."[60] However, such cultural production that provokes, rather than foreclosing, thought is only possible, Benjamin argues elsewhere, when the means of production is not appropriated by capitalism and the state.[61] Under these conditions, photography would only produce "reified dream images" of the democratic promise held by technology.[62]

Riefenstahl had already produced highly effective "dream images" for the state in her Nazi-era films. In contrast, her work on the Nuba, and later on the coral reefs, fulfilled what Benjamin calls the "economic function of photography," which is "to supply the masses, by modish processing, with matter which previously eluded mass consumption."[63] Ines Walk believes that this "free enterprise side" of Riefenstahl's Nuba photographs has been "greatly underrated" and that Riefenstahl's consumerist intentions, particularly with regard to producing *People of Kau*, are clear in the large amount of equipment (about 1.5 tons of it) and telephoto lenses that Riefenstahl required to shoot the material for the second book.[64] Yet Riefenstahl attempted to attach a liberal political goal to her photographic work. This contrasted with her retrospective explanation of her work under National Socialism, which she largely maintained had no political motivation. At the end of the brief written sections of both *Coral Gardens* and *Wonders under Water*, her volumes of photographs of coral reefs and sea life, Riefenstahl makes an environmentalist plea, writing in the latter, for example, "I would also like to think that my pictures might help a little to protect this wonderful underwater world from the increasing destruction which our civilization causes. I therefore urge all those who are concerned about Nature to play a part in saving these last remaining corners of paradise."[65] In the case of the Nuba, Riefenstahl's aim is to create a "permanent record ... in the annals of the once Dark Continent," securing their memory in perpetuity.[66] This latter salvage operation is even less ambitious than her attested desire to contribute "a little" to saving the reefs. Conveniently, neither aim conflicts with the fact that her work posits and demands an imagined ideal nature that is completely independent of—or hyperseparated from—culture.[67] Having constructed the Nuba, for example, as timeless and nature-bound (*naturverbunden*), Riefenstahl does not need to engage with them as the poor of the developing world. Consequently, she bemoans the founding of schools for the Mesakin Nuba and finds the appearance of the Southeast Nuba "ridiculously distorted" when they start wearing glasses.[68] When the Southeast Nuba flock to her and Kettner for medical attention, Riefenstahl vacillates between viewing their need as genuine and dismissing their request for drugs as a result of their "primitive" superstition that the medication has "supernatural powers."[69]

Ultimately however, Riefenstahl sees helping the Southeast Nuba as either a hindrance to her work or as a way of gaining her subjects' trust. Her prioritization of aesthetics, of getting a beautiful shot, over a politics of social justice is perhaps most evident in her response to changes in Nuba culture. Filming the Nuba dressed in ragged clothing and adorned with plastic bottles and empty tin cans "would have been a waste of celluloid."[70] Once paradise has been despoiled, once the appearance of the Nuba recalls that of beggars in European slums, her "one desire" becomes "to get away as soon as possible." [71] Thus, while Riefenstahl asserts that she wants to save "the beautiful," that which endangers it is only ever superficially enunciated in her work. As I have observed above, she routinely elides the sociopolitical networks in which her subjects are inevitably embedded: She shows effectively little interest in the changing politics and ongoing conflicts in Sudan that impact on the way of life and survival of the Nuba; she removes from view the causes of environmental destruction that threaten coral reefs around the world. Riefenstahl's one-sided, consumerist images of the "beautiful" do not provoke the viewer to thought—and thereby to the political action required to "save" anything. We can level the same criticism at her work that Benjamin leveled at Albert Renger-Patzsch's photographs in *Die Welt ist schön (The World Is Beautiful)* when he aligned them with the images of advertising in their valorization of surface aesthetics at the expense of context.[72]

When Schreiber and Weingarten ask her in the *Spiegel* interview, "If you photograph a Greek temple and a rubbish heap is next to it, you would leave out the rubbish?" Riefenstahl famously replies, "Absolutely. Reality does not interest me."[73] Riefenstahl makes this assertion, probably one of her most honest, just moments after her claim that the Nuba photographs are purely observational. The commercial success of the Nuba volumes is founded on just this lack of interest in reality on Riefenstahl's part and on her simultaneous ability to deploy the discourses of verisimilitude to maintain the fantasy that the Nuba remain outside "civilization." The consumption of the photographs is premised on Riefenstahl's claim that the Mesakin Nuba have "still kept their primeval innocence,"[74] that the Southeast Nuba "led a traditional tribal existence and were [...] entirely shielded from the outside world and untroubled by the influences of modern civilization,"[75] and by Riefenstahl's ability to create images that convincingly convey these fictions. Fulfilling her own and the consumer's need for a mythical people, Riefenstahl's subjects become increasingly decontextualized.[76] This finds its formal expression in *People of Kau* in shots of individuals where the background is deliberately blurred.[77] In representing the Nuba "as if they were not involved in the present world systems,"[78] Riefenstahl circumnavigates the political and environmental problems of the region that had been building for decades.[79]

In fact, rather than saving "the beautiful," Riefenstahl encourages and engenders its consumption. In the case of the coral reefs, she literally appeals to us as consumers in her denunciation of environmental degradation: "For who wants to dive on an already denuded reef?"[80]; "Only very rigorous action can save the diver's paradise at this late date."[81] The nature of Riefenstahl's implied call to environmental activism here ironically highlights her work as an example of what Heidegger conceives of as modern technology's "challenging" (*Herausfordern*) of nature, whereby nature becomes "standing-reserve," raw material available at all times for exploitation and consumption.[82] But it is not only the nonhuman that can become standing-reserve. In fact, this was precisely the impact of Riefenstahl's photographs on the Nuba: The success of her books led to an influx of tourists to the area who paid young men to decorate themselves. According to Frances Harding, the tourists' conduct transformed the social practice of the Nuba into a form of entertainment.[83] The Nuba became standing-reserve for the tourist industry. They became, in the words of Faris, "a zoo."[84] Those "aged, or clothed, or producing, or in school ... [were] driven away to cater to the nude, scarred, bleeding, decorated, dancing."[85]

In "Fascinating Fascism," Susan Sontag reads Riefenstahl's images of the Nuba as a continuation of her work during the Nazi period. For Sontag, the Nuba photographs reflect an aesthetic of purification that also characterizes her Nazi-era films. We find this aesthetic articulated in a 1972 review of *Olympia* in the *Süddeutsche Zeitung*: "Euthanasia become film. Everything ordinary, everything relative filtered away, cut out. An idealizing projection of that which was being prepared.... A symphony of horror."[86] I have argued here for an interpretation of Riefenstahl's work on the Nuba that would serve as an alternative to that of Sontag. Riefenstahl herself inadvertently supports this reading. Revealing her inability to reflect on her own work, she includes an image of herself in *People of Kau* that lays bare the meaning and consequences of her images. Here, with a camera slung around her neck, she leads by the hand a towering naked Nuba man who carries her photographic equipment. The technologized white woman clearly dominates the physically powerful nonwhite male. But more than this, as she leads him through the rocky wilderness into his technologized future, she makes him complicit in his own consumption and exploitation. Recollecting the end of her final journey to collect material for *People of Kau*, Riefenstahl writes that "[t]he question of whether our film would contain any of the strange and vanishing fascination of this unusual tribe nagged at me during our long trip home."[87] Here we find familiar tropes concerning Otherness in which the quotidian of home is contrasted with the exotic "primitive" from another (soon to be past) time. Judging from the sales of *People of Kau*, Riefenstahl's colonizing discourse was eminently marketable. Indeed, rather than "fascinating fascism" I would argue that Riefenstahl's work on the Nuba comes closer to Rony's "fascinating cannibalism" wherein it is the consumer who, like Riefenstahl, is the "savage" who devours the body of the Other.[88]

NOTES

I would like to thank the editors for their support and advice during the writing of this chapter.

1. Mathias Schreiber and Susanne Weingarten, "Realität interessiert mich nicht," *Der Spiegel* interview with Leni Riefenstahl, *Der Spiegel* 34 (1997): 205. All translations are my own unless otherwise indicated.
2. Regarding anthropology's self-reflexive move, see James Clifford, introduction to *Writing Culture: The Poetics and Politics of Ethnography*, ed. James Clifford and George E. Marcus (Berkeley: University of California Press, 1986), 8–9. See also Clifford's discussion and critique of ethnographic method and writing in "On Ethnographic Authority," *Representations* 2 (spring 1983): 118–146.
3. Riefenstahl tellingly omits the fact that Rodger is noted as the first photographer to capture the horror of Bergen-Belsen in the immediate aftermath of World War II.
4. Riefenstahl's use of the possessive here, although deeply problematic, is not exceptional. As Clifford writes in 1983: "The possessive form, 'my people,' has until recently been familiarly used in anthropological circles; but the phrase in effect signifies 'my experience.'" Clifford, "On Ethnographic Authority," 130. Although Riefenstahl's use of "'my' Nuba" is self-conscious, her repeated use of the phrase throughout her work appears to be born out of a desire to assert the legitimacy of her knowledge of the Mesakin Nuba. The phrase therefore functions not only in terms of asserting the dominance of the Western "knower" over the "native," but is also deployed by Riefenstahl to delegitimize those who might criticize her work.
5. *Leni Riefenstahl: A Memoir* (New York: Picador, 1995), 468. The "ancient trees" motif returns in 1973, when Riefenstahl searches for the Southeast Nuba. See ibid., 590.
6. *The Last of the Nuba* (London: Collins, 1976), 11.
7. *Leni Riefenstahl: A Memoir*, 468.
8. Ibid., 614. Other "Others" are also evoked as timeless in Riefenstahl's work. See for example her description of her encounter with a Bedouin boy in ibid., 419.
9. "Leben und Werk," *Leni Riefenstahl*, ed. Filmmuseum Potsdam (Berlin: Henschel, 1999), 94. See also Alexandra Ludewig, "Leni Riefenstahl's Encounter with the Nuba: In Search of the Sublime," *interventions* 8, no. 1 (2006): 83–101. Riefenstahl's search for solace—and selfhood—in Africa is central to Ludewig's argument here.
10. *Leni Riefenstahl: A Memoir*, 498. It seems ironic that George Rodger's "escape" to Africa was initiated by the trauma of his experience as a war correspondent—in particular the horror of seeing the concentration camp Bergen-Belsen—while Riefenstahl, who was inspired by Rodger's work, arguably went to Africa to flee the consequences of her own complicity with the Nazis. With regard to George Rodger's motives for traveling to Africa see Bruce Bernard's introduction to *George Rodger: The African Photographs* (British Council: London, 1997), 7.
11. *The Last of the Nuba* appeared in Germany in 1973 under the title *Die Nuba: Menschen wie von einem anderen Stern* (literally *The Nuba: People as if from another planet*). *People of Kau* (*Die Nuba von Kau*) appeared in Germany in 1976. Riefenstahl also published a book of photographs called *Mein Afrika* (literally *My Africa*) in 1982, whose problematic title was transposed accurately into the English as *Leni Riefenstahl's Africa* in the United Kingdom and as *Vanishing Africa* in the United States. The volume is a cross section of Riefenstahl's work in Africa. It contains photographs of many traditional cultures including that of the Nuba.
12. Regarding the obviation of individuality in *People of Kau* see also Ines Walk, "Bildproduktion und Weltmodell," in *Leni Riefenstahl*, 164.
13. See *People of Kau*, trans. J. Maxwell Brownjohn (London: Collins, 1976), 8; *Leni Riefenstahl: A Memoir*, 588–589. James Faris argues that Riefenstahl had in fact come

across the Southeast Nuba in his book *Nuba Personal Art,* which was published in 1972. James C. Faris, "Leni Riefenstahl and the Nuba Peoples of Kordofan Province, Sudan," *Historical Journal of Film, Radio and Television* 13, no. 1 (1993): 96. It is, of course, equally possible that Riefenstahl may have become aware of the existence and culture of the Southeast Nuba through George Rodger's photographs of them from the 1940s.

14. Susan Sontag overlooks Riefenstahl's discussion of Nuba farming practices in the *Last of the Nuba* in order to make the volume's contents conform to her paradigm of "fascist aesthetics." See Sontag, "Fascinating Fascism," *Under the Sign of Saturn* (New York: Doubleday, 1991), 73–105. This scathing critique of Riefenstahl's Nuba photographs originally appeared in the *New York Review of Books* in 1975.
15. See Rainer Rother, *Leni Riefenstahl: Die Verführung des Talents* (Berlin: Henschel, 2000), 173–189.
16. Ibid., 175.
17. Ibid.
18. "Realität interessiert mich nicht," 205.
19. The sick and the old make a brief appearance in *The Last of the Nuba* but are absent from *People of Kau.*
20. Terence Wright, "Photography: Theories of Realism and Convention," *Anthropology and Photography 1860–1920,* ed. Elizabeth Edwards (New Haven: Yale University Press, 1992), 29–31.
21. See Elizabeth Edwards, "Beyond the Boundary: a consideration of the expressive in photography and anthropology," *Rethinking Visual Anthropology,* ed. Marcus Banks and Howard Morphy (New Haven: Yale University Press, 1997), 53–80.
22. Ibid.
23. "Leni Riefenstahl's Encounter with the Nuba," 85.
24. Edwards, "Beyond the Boundary," 60. Regarding the dominance of the referent in photography see Christian Metz, "Photography and the Fetish," *October* 34 (autumn 1985): 82.
25. "Beyond the Boundary," 60.
26. For counterexamples of the "coherence" of the touristic image see ibid., 64–67.
27. Ibid., 62.
28. Riefenstahl, *Leni Riefenstahl: A Memoir,* 462, 467.
29. *The Third Eye: Race, Cinema, and Ethnographic Spectacle* (Durham, NC: Duke University Press, 1996), 195–196.
30. See Edwards, "Beyond the Boundary," 62.
31. Ibid., 62; Roland Barthes, *Camera Lucida: Reflections on Photography,* trans. Richard Howard (London: Vintage, 2000); Metz, "Photography and the Fetish," 83–85.
32. "Photography and the Fetish," 85.
33. Christopher Pinney, "The Parallel Histories of Anthropology and Photography," *Anthropology and Photography 1860–1920,* 80.
34. Pinney, "The Parallel Histories of Anthropology and Photography," 80.
35. See Johannes Fabian, *Time and the Other: How Anthropology Makes Its Object* (New York: Columbia University Press, 1983), 80–87. Put rather schematically, in this work Fabian critiques anthropology's denial of what he calls the "coevalness" of cultures.
36. *Leni Riefenstahl: A Memoir,* 462.
37. James Faris, "Photography, Power and the Southern Nuba," *Anthropology and Photography 1860–1920,* 214.

38. Ibid., 214, 215. Interestingly, even when Riefenstahl's subjects do look directly into the camera, our attention is not drawn to the photographic apparatus. For example, in the "Art of Masking" section of *People of Kau*, the consumer quality of the shots merely has the effect of, in Benjamin's terms, eliminating aura. See Walter Benjamin, "The Work of Art in the Age of Mechanical Reproduction," *Illuminations*, ed. Hannah Arendt, trans. Harry Zorn (London: Pimlico, 1999), 216–217.
39. Faris, "Photography, Power and the Southern Nuba," 214–215.
40. *People of Kau*, 224.
41. See Elizabeth Edwards, introduction to *Anthropology and Photography 1860–1920*, 7
42. See Lenssen, "Leben und Werk," 95.
43. *Leni Riefenstahl: A Memoir*, 470, 471.
44. Riefenstahl, *The Last of the Nuba*, 10.
45. *People of Kau*, 210–211.
46. *Leni Riefenstahl: A Memoir*, 558–559. The Nuba too have claimed that Riefenstahl staged a number of her photographs. See Faris, "Leni Riefenstahl and the Nuba Peoples of Kordofan Province," 96. Riefenstahl herself writes that "[w]ith money, you get only posed shots; and once the natives start posing, a real photographer is doomed." Riefenstahl, *Leni Riefenstahl: A Memoir*, 607. Implicitly, Riefenstahl did not see herself as bribing her subjects because she gave them beads and mirrors rather than money.
47. See note 12.
48. Faris refutes Riefenstahl's claim that the Sudanese government imposed Islam on the Nuba population. Faris, "Leni Riefenstahl and the Nuba Peoples of Kordofan Province," 96.
49. Ludewig, "Leni Riefenstahl's Encounter with the Nuba," 93.
50. *People of Kau*, 220.
51. See Val Plumwood, "Nature as Agency and the Prospects for a Progressive Naturalism," *Capitalism Nature Socialism* 12, no. 4 (December 2001): 3–32.
52. *Leni Riefenstahl: A Memoir*, 554, 588.
53. Ibid., 559. This use of the pathetic fallacy could be seen as a habit instilled in Riefenstahl by her work on the *Bergfilm* where the imbuing of mountains and weather with emotions is prevalent.
54. *Coral Gardens*, trans. Elizabeth Walter (London: Collins, 1978), 8.
55. Riefenstahl, *Wonders under Water* (London: Quartet Books, 1991), 7.
56. In an interview with Alice Schwarzer, Riefenstahl describes her love of nature in terms of unity: "I myself feel like a bee or a fish." "Leni Riefenstahl. Propagandistin oder Künstlerin?" *Emma*, no. 1 (January/February 1999): 47.
57. "Blut und Glamour," in *Leni Riefenstahl*, 210. See the English traslation in this volume.
58. Walter Benjamin, "A Small History of Photography," *One-Way Street and Other Writings*, trans. Edmund Jephcott and Kingsley Shorter (London: Verso, 1985), 243.
59. Susan Buck-Morss, *The Dialectics of Seeing: Walter Benjamin and the Arcades Project* (Cambridge, Massachusetts: MIT Press, 1991), 158.
60. Walter Benjamin, "New things about plants," *Germany—The New Photography 1927-33*, ed. David Mellor (London: Arts Council of Great Britain, 1978), 20.
61. See "The Author as Producer," *Understanding Brecht*, trans. Anna Bostock (London: NLB, 1977), 85–103; "A Small History of Photography," 240–257.
62. Buck-Morss, *The Dialectics of Seeing*, 143.
63. "The Author as Producer," 95.
64. Walk, "Bildproduktion und Weltmodell," 163–164.

65. *Wonders under Water*, 7.
66. *The Last of the Nuba*, 11.
67. For more on the function of hyperseparation in the culture/nature dualism, see Val Plumwood, *Feminism and the Mastery of Nature* (London: Routledge, 1993), 49–52.
68. *Leni Riefenstahl: A Memoir*, 558, 636.
69. *People of Kau*, 212.
70. Riefenstahl, *Leni Riefenstahl: A Memoir*, 557.
71. Ibid., 588.
72. Benjamin, "A Small History of Photography," 254–255; Brian Stokoe, "Renger-Patzsch: New Realist Photographer," *Germany—The New Photography 1927–33*, 98.
73. "Realität interessiert mich nicht," 205.
74. *The Last of the Nuba*, 11.
75. *People of Kau*, 6.
76. Walk rightly contends that the consumer is complicit in the exploitation of the Nuba. Walk, "Bildproduktion und Weltmodell," 168.
77. Ibid., 163. See also Riefenstahl's discussion of this technique in *People of Kau*, 224.
78. Clifford, introduction to *Writing Culture*, 10.
79. See Leif O. Manger, "Traders, farmers and pastoralists: economic adaptations and environmental problems in the southern Nuba Mountains of the Sudan," *The Ecology of Survival: Case Studies from Northeast African History*, ed. Douglas H. Johnson and David M. Anderson (London: Lester Crook, 1988), 155–172.
80. *Coral Gardens*, 19.
81. Ibid.
82. Martin Heidegger, "The Question Concerning Technology," *The Question Concerning Technology and Other Essays*, trans. William Lovitt (New York: Harper & Row, 1977), 3–35.
83. "Presenting and Re-Presenting the Self: From Not-Acting to Acting in African Performance," *TDR* 43, no. 2 (summer 1999): 132.
84. "Leni Riefenstahl and the Nuba Peoples of Kordofan Province," 96.
85. Faris, "Photography, Power and the Southern Nuba," 216.
86. Quoted in Rother, *Leni Riefenstahl: Die Verführung des Talents*, 249.
87. *Leni Riefenstahl: A Memoir*, 619.
88. Rony, *The Third Eye*, 10.

Chapter 11

Representing the Body in Cyberspace: Riefenstahl's Self-staging (Notes on Leni Riefenstahl's Web Page)

Martina Thiele
Translated by Ingeborg Majer-O'Sickey and Neil Christian Pages

I.

From the depth of the sea a body glides upward into brilliant blue light: This is Leni Riefenstahl. The scene is from her last film, *Impressions under Water*, broadcast by the Arte television channel in 2002 in honor of her one hundredth birthday. Leni Riefenstahl is one of the most controversial artists of the twentieth century. Her involvement with the National Socialists and the effects of her work are the topic of countless publications. What has received less attention, however, is the extent to which Riefenstahl herself contributed to the design of her public persona. Inasmuch as she was a star-maker (Hitler, key Nazi hangers-on, top athletes, the Nuba), she also created her own stardom. In order to fill the gap in scholarship around Riefenstahl's construction of her public persona, my study intends to analyze one of the latest incarnations of Riefenstahl, namely her Web site (http://www.leni-riefenstahl.de).[1]

Riefenstahl's public statements were always attempts at self-justification. The question arises, however, as to whether her images are always consonant with her self-justifications. At first glance, Riefenstahl's oeuvre seems diverse. Consider her appearances as a dancer and as an actress in the Alpine films (*Bergfilme*) in the guise of an extreme sportswoman. Consider the films under her own direction: *The Blue Light*, *Lowlands*, *Impressions under Water*, and of course, her "documentary" work from the Nazi period, *Triumph of the Will* and the *Olympia* films. Consider, finally, her photography. The similarities between the photographic images and the films may lie in her technical and narrative strategies and in the way she stages the body.

As is well known, Riefenstahl's works resonated widely, and we are witnessing now both a Riefenstahl renaissance and a rehabilitation of sorts. Filmmakers cite her, gaining inspiration from her mise-èn-scene and montage. Volker Schlöndorff praises the so-called Riefenstahl cut; and George Lucas's *Star Wars* trilogy and Paul Verhoeven's *Starship Troopers* shamelessly cite scenes of the masses in *Triumph of the Will*. In addition, Roxy Music put Riefenstahl's images on the cover of *Flesh + Blood*, and Rammstein inserts her images into their music videos. Advertisers, too, brand their products with Riefenstahl's images (Fachinger Champagne, Davidoff Cool Water, Volkswagen). Evidently, Riefenstahl's creations, and especially her self-creations, invite a fascination that is timeless. Riefenstahl the person appeared to defy time as well. Claudia Lenssen wrote of Riefenstahl's "five lives" as synonymous with her five careers (dancer, actor, director, photographer, and deep-sea diver), but Riefenstahl was never simply one or the other. Clearly, she was much more: model, extreme athlete, boss/supervisor, defendant, ethnologist, and above all, maker of images and public relations manager of her persona.[2]

II.

Before addressing the issue of Riefenstahl as a transmitter of "fascistic" ideas of the human body, I would like to chart a historical mapping of the use of metaphors of the body more generally. Their use is not a modern occurrence of the twentieth century. As early as antiquity, for example, in a speech by Menenius Agrippa provided by Livius, we find notions of people as an organism in which each member and organ would fulfill its function. Similar corporeal metaphors appear in texts about the French Revolution. As the natural sciences gained strength in the nineteenth century, metaphors of the body were marked by biologist-social-Darwinist elements on a continuum toward racism.[3] The National Socialists instrumentalized these images in order to transmit the message that individuals and their bodies were significant only in their function as a part of the whole national community (*Volksgemeinschaft*). The health of the nation was said to be endangered by a virus manifest in the foreign, urban, industrial, bureaucratic, and intellectual. The "Jewish" and all non-"Aryan," they claimed, embodied these in turn. The Nazis were convinced that a healing of the national body (*Volkskörper*) could be achieved only through radical measures. Notably, the word-concept *Volkskörper* even appears in the index to Hitler's *Mein Kampf*, in which Hitler writes of a "progressive pacifist-Marxist paralysis of our *Volkskörper*," in other words, its "racial contamination."[4]

Goebbels's speeches used the body metaphor, too, but it was not restricted to descriptions of the Jews. In his speech after the assassination plot against Hitler on July 20, 1944, the Propaganda Minister avoided speaking directly about the assassins. Instead, he invoked an image of a national body in danger of being infected by disease. "I am personally convinced," Goebbels said to his party comrades, "that the excising of this putrid pustule from the German *Volkskörper* could have brought on a temporary weakness, but it will eventually lead to enormous strengthening of that body. This is exactly like the human organism: whenever such a boil makes life difficult or even impossible for a human being, it must be cut open."[5] The Nazi concept of the body included stature, size, strength, invincibility, functionality, and structural harmony. If these traits were not natural, then one could attain them through sports, training, and reproductive controls. In contrast to this concept were old age, sickness, handicap, asymmetry, and diversity. The ideal body concept was interpreted as "Aryan"; its opposite was non-"Aryan" and connected to the Jews. Ultimately, these propagandistic images served as a justification for war and mass murder.

In the following I call images "fascistic" when they depict a confrontation between two body concepts or when they emphasize exclusively elements such as size, stature, posture, uniformity, and functionality. In these images, the Other (ugly, abnormal, etc.) is defamed, omitted, or erased. The question is to what extent these constructions, with their labels "beautiful" or "ugly," determine Riefenstahl's work. For example, to what extent are Riefenstahl's choices in the *Olympia* films determined by notions of athletic competition or attributable to the Nazi *Zeitgeist*? It is possible that fascist, in particular Nazi, aesthetics and Riefenstahl's gaze complemented each other, but it is not possible to ascertain who or what influenced whom. In order to substantiate the charge of a "fascist" aesthetic in Riefenstahl's work, one must take into account her work on the Web.

III.

My analysis of Riefenstahl's home page is subtended by two premises: first, that she not only staged others' bodies but also her own, offering it as a model for emulation; and second, that her photography and films share, in addition to narrative and technical strategies, physical (body) stagings. To support these two premises, I analyze—in addition to auto/biographical discourse—the way in which she stages others (important Nazi figures, the *Volk*, athletes, the Nuba) and herself. This analysis will interrogate claims of continuities in her work, especially as it relates to her different self-stagings. On Leni Riefenstahl's home page, image building of others and of herself converge. Even in later years she was never intimidated by technical innovation. Recognizing the possibilities of the new medium of the Internet, Riefenstahl hired the Berlin firm "maldonado" to set up her own Web page (http://www.leni-riefenstahl.de). The page is done in black, red, and white and is well organized both in terms of design and information. Images and text are balanced, and the page is user-friendly. Users can decide whether they wish to continue in English or German.

Following the introductory page, we meet Riefenstahl in six black-and-white photographs, three at the top and three at the bottom of the page. They show

Riefenstahl as a dancer and as an actress in the Alpine films and in the film *Lowlands*. There is also a so-called working shot of her that was taken during the shooting of the *Olympia* films. In the middle of this grouping, the name LENI appears in white capital letters, and beneath it, RIEFENSTAHL, in red. To the left of the name is a list of categories: BIOGRAPHY, FILMOGRAPHY, PHOTOGRAPHY, THE NUBA, BOOKS, NEWS, SHOP. Clicking on BIOGRAPHY, users discover how Riefenstahl sees herself and how she wishes to be seen. Twenty-six photographs accompany short texts that tell her life story. Both the visual and written texts omit any negative information. Of particular interest is the way Riefenstahl designs the physical body. As we analyze Riefenstahl's imaging of her life and work, we are bound to ask which information and images were chosen and which ones were left out, whether consciously or subconsciously.

The text of the biography page and the titles that accompany the photographs are printed in cursive. The text comments on and evaluates the images. The order is chronological: 1. Baby Leni, 2. Leni's parents, 3. Leni (ten years old) with her brother (seven years old), and 4. Leni as a teenager (sixteen years old). The caption reads "Leni Riefenstahl was born in Berlin in 1902. She studied painting and started her artistic career as a dancer. She became already so famous after her first dance hat [sic] Max Reinhardt engaged her for the *'Deutsches Theater.'*" Contrary to the blurb on her Web site, though, the reviews of Riefenstahl's dancing from the period were not all praise. Dance critic Fred Hildebrandt wrote in the *Berliner Tageblatt* in 1923:

> When we see this perfectly shaped, tall creature stand in the music, we have a promise, an inkling that there are joys to be had in dance . . . ; of an incarnation of powerful grace, of an exemplary beauty, of the likeness of God. But then this girl begins to unfold her body and the promise disappears, the brilliance fades, the sound rusts. What does move is a miraculous mannequin, surely animated by a desire for space, by a thirst for rhythm, by a longing for music. However, from this desire the space does not come alive. In this thirst rhythm dries up. . . . This is the desire, the thirst and the longing of a silly and uninspired virgin.[6]

Eighty years later, film critic Andreas Kilb agreed with Hildebrandt's assessment. In a retrospective teleology, Kilb sees the critique as an apt description of the content of Riefenstahl's later work:

> What we have here is the gesture of a beauty that is created through power, a mechanical, lifeless intensity. . . . Through muscle contractions Riefenstahl wanted to conjure by force a grace she did not possess, just like in her so-called documentary films, which are not documentaries. In a similar way, the event [that she films] is contracted into a series of images that are always the same: the cuts and counter cuts in perpetual back-and-forth: the athlete and the masses, the *Führer* and the *Volk*.[7]

Riefenstahl the artist enjoyed looking back at her dancing career. Even though it was not easy for the girl from the bourgeois home to become a dancer, she was able to get her way. Against her father's will, she became a student of Mary Wigman's dance school; she practiced tirelessly, and created her own choreographies. In an interview with Alice Schwarzer, Riefenstahl said that dancing "was the most enjoyable for me because I could do all of that with my body by myself."[8] Her dance career ended when she injured her knee. She then went on to become an actress whose roles in a number of films—*The Holy Mountain* (1926), *Giant Leap* (1927), *The White Hell of Piz Palü* (1929), *Storm over Mont Blanc* (1930), *The White Dream* (1931), *The Blue Light* (1932), and *SOS Iceberg* (1933)—brought her world renown. Riefenstahl's move into an acting career was thus not voluntary. Impressed by Arnold Fanck's Alpine films, she approached him for a starring role in his next production. Because Fanck's films strove for maximum authenticity in dangerous ascents and descents, she learned mountain climbing and skiing. Riefenstahl's first starring role was in *The Holy Mountain*, where she played the dancer Diotima, an outsider between two men (played by Luis Trenker and Ernst Petersen). Although the shoots were exhausting and Riefenstahl, frequently in life-threatening situations, sustained injuries, she did not give up, earning the respect of her colleagues. But she was not satisfied and felt typecast as an athletic heroine. Indeed, the protagonist of Fanck's films was always nature, the mountains, avalanches, and bad weather, followed by men as the second important element. They tamed nature—and it was only then that a heroine was needed.

Riefenstahl recalls in her memoirs that she used the early 1930s to learn filmmaking and to plan her own project, the film *The Blue Light*.[9] Even though the film crew from Fanck's productions collaborated closely with Riefenstahl on the film, she has taken exclusive credit for it. Notable is the fact that the Hungarian filmmaker and critic Béla Balázs received only minor mention as having collaborated on the screenplay; her former partner Hans Schneeberger is listed only under "Photography." In *The Blue Light*, Riefenstahl takes on the double role of director and protagonist. She thus has final say behind and in front of the camera. The film can, apart from its stylistic qualities, be seen as a breakthrough. As Claudia Lenssen writes, Riefenstahl embodied "the paradigm shift from the classical, female object of spectacle for the voyeuristic gaze" to the position of a "technically well-versed camerawoman," in that she "united in her persona both the schizophrenic double role of the model before the camera and that of the controlling art director behind it."[10] In *The Blue Light*, shot in a fairy-tale-like, surreal style, Riefenstahl portrays the outsider Junta, who lives by herself in the mountains. She alone knows the path to the precious crystals. In the village below she is decried as a witch. The painter Vigo finds her, but he cannot prevent the villagers from persecuting Junta and from robbing her of the crystals.

The film is replete with sexual connotations. Junta is seen as a threat to the reigning sexual order. The character is styled into a proud, wild creature, and her demise is predestined. Riefenstahl excels in the role of Junta. Without doubt, there are similarities between Riefenstahl the director and Junta the independent character. Both are determined to decide their own fate; Junta her living space and Riefenstahl her working space. Once again, critics discover tendencies in *The Blue Light* that they see manifest in the films she would make during the Third Reich. As journalist Peter W. Jansen noted in an obituary for Riefenstahl:

> This film, seemingly so distant from political fascism, already contains the entire cult iconography, the emphatic gestures toward the light as well as toward bodies, the rhetorical figure of the arabesque, the arrangement of a fragmented world to a harmonized-holy image of the world, the move from terrible isolation and loneliness to a community around the warm campfire.[11]

Film enthusiasts Hitler and Goebbels were spellbound by *The Blue Light* and especially by its female protagonist, Leni Riefenstahl. She in turn was spellbound by Hitler's political speeches. After a campaign speech in Berlin in the spring of 1932, she wrote him and asked for a meeting. On that occasion Hitler later made her an offer: "Once we are in power you will make my films."[12] Riefenstahl's home page does not mention this meeting, nor are there any photographs of her with Hitler and other prominent Nazis. Following her baby and childhood photos are images entitled "5. Leni as a dance student," "6. Leni as a dancer," "7. Leni in boarding school," "8. Leni as a young lady," "9. Leni in Africa (1963)," and "10. Leni scouting for locations in Kenya." Between images eight and nine, forty years are missing. After "Leni as a young lady," we see her for the first time in color as an elderly woman of sixty-one. Even so, she appears much younger. Now a blonde, she smiles directly into the camera. She holds a camera in one hand, and with the other she touches her hair. The strap of her colorful summer dress has slipped off, displaying her bare shoulder. The text that accompanies these images offers us the following information, paraphrased here: Her greatest success was the "documentary" film *Triumph of the Will*, named after the Nazi Party Congress of 1934 in Nuremberg; the film received the gold medal at the Venice Film Festival and the gold medal at the Paris World Fair. The caption also informs us that this film destroyed her career because it was no longer recognized as a work of art after World War II, but rather was judged to be a propaganda film. We further learn that Riefenstahl's two-part *Olympia* film (*Festival of Nations* and *Festival of Beauty*) had a similar fate. It also won the highest honors, the gold medal (for the director's cut of the film) in Paris (1937) and the first prize as the world's best film in Venice (1938) as well as the Olympic Diploma of the International Olympic Commitee; it was named as one of the world's ten best films in the United States in 1956. Three photographs from the 1930s and 1940s document perhaps the most important period in Riefenstahl's life. Two are studies of her at work and one is a very personal photo of Riefenstahl with her husband, Major Peter Jacob, on their wedding day in 1944. The working photos reveal Riefenstahl as the decisive artist behind the *Olympia* films. Her eye serves as the camera's eye in the shot of her cameraman Walter Frentz, who sits on the camera cart next to her while she looks through the lens. The image of Riefenstahl at the cutting table is revealing as well. Dressed in a white lab coat, she resembles a medical doctor who looks through a microscope. Here, too, Riefenstahl does not look directly at the camera, but rather at the negatives before her. Instead of a stethoscope, strands of film are hanging from her neck. In contrast to these images of an emancipated woman, the photograph with her husband communicates a different message. She leans against her husband's shoulder and looks down instead of into the camera. Next to her husband, who is dressed in his uniform, Riefenstahl appears delicate in a simple white dress (note that she is not wearing a wedding dress). Her hair is longer and curlier than in other photos. Her smile is sad, as if she were thinking about her husband's impending departure. The image is not exactly uplifting or optimistic. The page continues with Riefenstahl's career after the 1960s and her work as a photographer. The gap is remarkable. We can find only a few of the images that she produced between 1933 and 1945 (from the *Olympia* films) on her home page, but none from *Victory of Faith*, *Triumph of the Will*, or *Day of Freedom*. Erased also is the immediate period after World War II and the 1950s. In the following, I wish to turn to those images that are omitted from the home page.

IV.

Even though under the protection of Hitler and Goebbels, Riefenstahl met with resistance from the Nazi Party's film bureau during the shoot for the first of the three party rally films. The film bureau claimed exclusive rights to all the films that were made about the party congresses. As is well known, Riefenstahl was not satisfied with *Victory of Faith*. Apart from the fact that she could not control the shooting, Riefenstahl cited enormous time pressure that resulted in a lack of composition and in technical errors. Today, some of the shots of Hitler strike us as unwittingly comical. In *Victory*, Hitler is not yet the messianic figure that Riefenstahl will construct of him one year later, in 1934 in *Triumph of the Will*. Neither *Victory of Faith* nor *Day of Freedom* provided suitable vehicles for glorifying Hitler—that vehicle would be *Triumph of the Will*, which the Nazi film press called a "symphony," a "monumental painting," and a "sacred christening." It is also the basis upon which Riefenstahl's reputation as a filmmaker for the Nazis rests. After the murder of the SA chief Ernst Röhm and the death of Field Marshall Hindenburg, the film recognized Hitler as Germany's supreme ruler.

The film's main theme is the relationship of the German *Volk* to Hitler. It depicts the people awaiting Hitler as a messiah, and the orchestration of the rally recalls a religious ceremony. In the opening sequences, the film orchestrates Hitler's arrival as the people's love story, replete with rituals of subjugation.[13] The subjugated masses are female. Later, the *Volk* becomes masculinized, dressed in uniforms and orderly, thus mirroring the politics of the ideal fascist body. All that is formless or "badly formed," all that is individual, pliant, and supple stands in opposition to the "fascist" aesthetic of the body. Siegfried Kaltenecker explains the forced disappearance of all non-"Aryan," nonmasculine, nonheterosexual self-portraits by linking this move to the Nazis' desire to counter the increasing presence of images of independent women and homosexuals during the 1920s; thus, they constantly worked to demonstrate a heterosexual "masculinity" and toughness.[14] The military parades and party congresses were designed to demonstrate the discipline of the NSDAP (Nazi Party). Boys and men doing morning calisthenics or washing themselves are transformed into uniformed figures standing at attention with stony faces and erect bodies. It is always clear that the individual is part of the larger movement. The theme here is to show what they have in common, the unity of the *Volk*, or as Kracauer put it, the "mass ornament." Instead of individuals, the film produces a rectangular tapestry of human beings who bow before Hitler. The camera looks down upon these masses, while the masses look up to Hitler. The latter is the dominant perspective of Hitler. This is only one of many cinematic techniques in Riefenstahl's arsenal that include use of light and shadow and montage. As Elke Schmitter notes, "Riefenstahl showed us how to make a monument from a body, how to make a character actor from an unremarkable face, and how to make a charismatic hero from a madman with a mustache."[15]

Riefenstahl proudly referred to the technical perfection of the film, and pointed to innovations such as the camera elevators at the flagpoles, which allowed new ways of seeing, and the light domes and innovative camera perspectives. Even though certain scenes were produced and others added in postproduction, Riefenstahl always insisted that the film should be understood as a document of what took place. Her primary argument is that it is indeed a documentary because of the absence of voice-over commentary. She also argued that there were no anti-semitic references in the film.[16] However, Riefenstahl's work report (*Behind the Scenes of the Party Congress Film*) from 1935 testifies to the fact that *Triumph of the Will* was a meticulously staged film.

The quality of and sensational shots in the *Olympia* films (*Festival of the People* and *Festival of Beauty*) are also marked by technical innovation. The cameras offer unusual perspectives and become mobile, at times accompanying the runners in the famous marathon sequence in accelerated motion, at other times in slow motion. Or again, the cameras are positioned during the broad jump in a way that even the spraying sand can be captured. Riefenstahl includes the spectators as well. Tracking shots frequently show the jubilant spectators in the stadium. Hitler—himself no athlete—watches excitedly, even jumping up with encouraging shouts, clearly pleased at the German athletes' achievements. The *Olympia* films are seen as a milestone in the history of sports films as well as a prototype for the fascist cult of the body. They represent the competitive athletic body as part of a larger, more important movement than the Olympics, namely the National Socialist movement. The prologue constructs a line of succession from Greek antiquity to German National Socialism in order to show the regime as the epitome of civilization. The predominant film strategy that Riefenstahl uses to create this impression is the dissolve (antique statues morph into moving, competing athletes, and so on).

After the prologue, the film then presents both female and male athletes of various nations. Male athletes predominate. Historian Daniel Wildmann, whose study focuses on the manner of representation of bodies in the *Olympia* films, sees the opposition of "Aryan"/non-"Aryan" as more important than the male/female one: "The male body is not determined by its relationship to the female body. Rather, it is shown as a positive [determinate], i.e. as an 'Aryan' body as opposed to a non-'Aryan' one."[17] Similarly, Wildmann does not focus on the black/white opposition and on attempts to use the sequences with black athletes to show that Riefenstahl's film was not racist. What interests Wildmann is the erasure of the Jewish body in the *Olympia* films, in which that body is not visible but is nonetheless "present" as an absent body that is the "negative opposition" to the "Aryan" body."[18] Wildmann thus argues that the *Olympia* films predict the destruction of the Jewish body: "Riefenstahl simultaneously hides the operation of exclusion while showing only its result, namely the completed project." In this way, he concludes, Riefenstahl was even more radical than the anti-Semitic images of Jews featured in Julius Streicher's *Der Stürmer*.[19]

Such an argument is troublesome in at least two of its aspects: first, because it is based on the Nazi opposition of "Aryan"/Jewish bodies: and second because Wildmann accuses Riefenstahl of having omitted something that was nevertheless introduced as an imaginary presence. One would first have to ascertain what the film includes and what it excludes. This entails that one accept that no work of art, no human expression, can make the claim for totality.[20] In interviews, Riefenstahl was often asked to explain what she did not show. In response she maintained that she strove to omit that which is unsightly, and it was precisely because the world contained so much that was unsightly that she wanted to keep it out of sight. She was not interested in "objective" reality.[21] Crucial to Wildmann's argumentation is the issue of mimetic desire: Desire here is not an anthropological fact but rather a historically contingent and changeable construct. As he argues, the other body is presented as exemplary and desirable with the goal that viewers also form their bodies in ways that are desirable for others. Similarly, Riefenstahl said of the *Olympia* films that they should "become a motivation and symbol for youth so that they would become even more beautiful and faultless."[22] In other words, her film would awaken a mimetic desire through which viewers would emulate their idols. The constant representation of perfect bodies in these films appears to have been successful in their historical context. Hilmar Hoffmann recalls the films: "The magic of the flags, the flair for hyperbolized sacredness, the songs that simulated a community deeply impressed us boys back then. We wanted to be like the blond drummerboy on the screen and we wanted to go through fire for the Führer."[23]

After the party congress and the *Olympia* films, Riefenstahl became the star director of the Nazis. She reveled in her fame and dreamed of a new project, the filming of Heinrich von Kleist's *Penthesilea*, which was thwarted by the outbreak of World War II. While filming on the front, she witnessed the massacre of Polish civilians. According to her own story, she was shocked, and thus returned to Berlin and to an earlier film project that had been shelved, *Lowlands*. In *Lowlands*, a story in the tradition of her directorial debut (*The Blue Light*), Riefenstahl again plays dual roles, director and protagonist, and once again, the protagonist (Martha) is an outcast who is caught between two men. Set in Spain, the film needed the appropriate atmosphere and extras. Riefenstahl, who plays a "gypsy," took her extras from the Maxglan camp near Salzburg, where Sinti and Roma inmates were held. After the film shoot, they were deported to concentration camps. After 1945, Riefenstahl claimed not to have known about the deportation: "The Gypsies, adults and children alike, were our favorites. We have seen most of them after the war again."[24] *Lowlands* did not premiere until 1954 and is therefore considered a so-called transitional film (*Überläuferfilm*). It was not as successful as Riefenstahl's previous works.[25]

When and if ever Riefenstahl distanced herself from the Nazis is a matter of dispute. One side of the debate focuses on Riefenstahl's escapism and distance from reality during the war and asserts that her obsession with unrealizable film projects is evidence of that distancing process. The other side argues that she neither admitted nor took co-responsibility for the terror of the regime. The pertinent question would be when Riefenstahl herself felt discomfort. She contended that for her it was 1939, the year the war began, and not 1945, the year it ended, that she experienced a caesura.[26] This is a strange utterance since, after all, Riefenstahl's life changed dramatically after Germany's capitulation. She lost her privileges, was incarcerated, interrogated, "denazified," and classified as a "fellow traveler" (*Mitläuferin*). She fought to restore her reputation and refused to accept that she was seen not as an ambitious artist but rather as the privileged filmmaker and propagandist for the Nazi regime. She, however, saw herself as an artist who was unfairly persecuted and blacklisted, particularly since other filmmakers from the period, Wolfgang Liebeneiner or Veit Harlan for example, were already working again. Others in the film industry judged her as difficult, her projects too expensive and convoluted, and she received no offers. But Riefenstahl would not have been Riefenstahl had she given in to these difficulties. Instead, she reinvented herself.

V.

Riefenstahl's interest in Africa was born after she read Ernest Hemingway's *Green Hills of Africa* and saw a photograph of Nuba wrestlers by George Rodger. In 1956, she traveled to Kenya for the first time. In the early 1960s, she journeyed to Sudan where she photographed the Nuba. Even though her film project on modern slavery, titled *Black Cargo* (*Die schwarze Fracht*), failed, she was able to sell the stills from the expedition to international magazines. Later Riefenstahl produced coffee-table books of her Nuba photographs. On her home page the transition from filmmaker to photographer is explained in the following, here taken verbatim from the English-language pages of the Web site:

> As a photographer too, she soon gained the world's elite after the war. Photo reportages about her stay with the Nuba were published in the magazines *Stern, The Sunday Times Magazine, Paris Match, L'Europeo, Newsweek* and *The Sun*. Mainly her illustrated books *The Nuba* and *The Nuba of Kau* earned her further honours and awards.

Added to this text are images of Riefenstahl as she hugs a black child and lets a baggage carrier work for her. The titles accompanying the photos are quite revealing: "14. Leni Buna Nuba—Leni loves the Nuba; 15. A Nuba is carrying Leni's camera bag at 45 degrees above zero in the Sudan." For Riefenstahl, the Nuba are the manifestation of the Other, the distant, and the natural. She observes them in their daily lives, during competitive games, and festivities. Her appellation "my Nuba" seems proprietary. While the first photographs in *The Nuba* are marked by a sense of wonderment and curiosity, the next collection, *People of Kau*, reveals more distance and aesthetic calculation. In her later journeys to the Sudan, Riefenstahl is equipped with highly sophisticated technology, looking like a veritable image hunter. While she did not eschew paying the Nuba, she complained that they changed each time she visited, both in their outward appearance and in their increasingly demanding behavior toward her. In the Nuba photographs, nudity functions as a sign of naturalness and flawlessness. Unlike in the *Olympia* films, here the genitalia are not covered. According to Riefenstahl, "the Nuba are only naked as long as they are young and beautiful. The girls until they become pregnant and the men until they abandon their knife fights, which are the highest point of their physical development." Here, Riefenstahl's remarks are based on the ethnologist Fabris, who writes, "The Nuba say that when the body is no longer beautiful, strong and healthy it is useless to adorn it. If they do so, they will be laughed at. Their ideal is the healthy and beautiful body."[27] For Riefenstahl, clothing is a sign of the harmful influence of civilization.

Riefenstahl was not only drawn to Africa or to the highest peaks, as in the earlier Alpine films, but also to the deepest oceans. Inspired by Jacques

Cousteau, she learned scuba diving, was certified at the age of seventy-one, and became an underwater photographer. Her underwater photographs energized discussions of the continuities in her work.[28] On her home page, Riefenstahl's deep-sea photography is an occasion to present further artistic achievements and awards. The color photographs there show her sitting on the side of a boat, clad in a diving suit, her blond hair in disarray. Riefenstahl soon became a master of the craft, and her two collections *Coral Gardens* (*Korallengärten*) and *Wonders under Water* (*Wunder unter Wasser*) were international sensations. She was also at work on writing her life story, published in 1987. Riefenstahl's memoirs have appeared in thirteen countries. In 1993, Ray Müller's *The Wonderful, Horrible Life of Leni Riefenstahl (Die Macht der Bilder)* gave her an opportunity to explain her life and artistic work. The film was an international success and received an Emmy award in the U.S. and the Special Prize of the Film Critics Association in Japan.

Many more or less famous people wanted to be photographed by or with Riefenstahl. Each image of her with a celebrity assisted in her rehabilitation. While we do not see her with Hitler and Goebbels on her Web page, she is shown with Mick and Bianca Jagger, Juan Antonio Samaranch, the Müller-Wohlfahrt family, and with Siegfried and Roy on her 101st birthday. Other photographs show a heavily damaged helicopter and Riefenstahl lying down, her face encrusted with blood. The text claims that she had traveled to the war-ravaged Sudan to look for her old acquaintances. The remarkable decision to travel to this war-torn region was taken after twenty-three years of silence from her Nuba friends; Riefenstahl claimed the long delay in her return was because she was denied a visa. Only after a long wait and difficult negotiations was it possible for the team to travel (accompanied by military protection) to the Nuba mountains. Thousands of Nuba welcomed Leni Riefenstahl. Upon her arrival she learned that her best friends had fallen victim to the civil war. She was deeply moved. During her search for surviving friends, new outbreaks of hostilities forced the team to flee by helicopter, which then crashed after a pit stop in El Obeid.

That Riefenstahl published photographs of herself as a victim of the crash does not contradict her previous stagings as an invincible fighter. Indeed, one can read these images as signs of her indestructibility, followed as they are by photographs of her at her 98th and 101st birthday celebrations. She smiles—almost childlike—into the camera, surrounded by flowers, balloons, stuffed animals, and champagne. The contrast between illness and convalescence, old age and youth, that is constructed in this montage is also present in interviews from the period. Shortly before her 100th birthday she noted:

> I often feel like a wreck. My emotions, thoughts, and my work are affected. I am very tired. . . . It is terrible to lose control over one's body. It is so awful that I often ask myself whether I still want to live. I have always loved movement. . . . Every morning I overcome my inertia and tell myself: I must do

> it. And so it works. . . . I am not giving up. That's something I was born with.[29]

This is Leni Riefenstahl's very personal "Triumph of the Will." The older she became, the more she tried to offer her body and lifestyle as a model, engendering a kind of "mimetic desire." Even the last image on her home page, of Riefenstahl in the Maldives in 2003, counters the message offered by the text, namely the announcement of her death: After a long, hardworking, and successful life, Leni Riefenstahl died shortly after her 101st birthday. She passed away at 10:50 p.m. on September 8, 2003, in her house in Pöking at the Starnberger See. She was buried on Friday, September 12, in the Ostfriedhof in Munich.[30] The final photograph on Riefenstahl's home page shows her in a full portrait with a shadow. She seems to move toward the viewer, walking on a white sandy beach against a background of an azure-blue sea and sky. The impression is that she walks out of the sea toward the viewer. Her hair is blond and windblown and she smiles, animated and energetic, so that it is hard to believe that she was a century old when the photograph was shot.

VI.

That fact that Riefenstahl was considered a beautiful woman both helped and hurt her. Bianca Jagger called her "one of the great beauties of her time," and added that "she has had to fight against many prejudices, namely the one that a beautiful woman is not necessarily dumb and spoiled, but that a beautiful woman can be intelligent and original." Jagger showed empathy toward Riefenstahl, noting that "the sad thing about a woman with such creative powers is that she was thwarted by politics."[31] Is this assessment correct? I think not. Politics did not stop Riefenstahl, at least not after 1945. And before 1945, political forces fostered her talent and used it for their purposes. Both parties profited. Riefenstahl was able to work fairly independently and her projects were always funded.

The privileges she enjoyed during the Nazi period were also a function of the fact that she was a woman, although she never had to bend to the dictates of the Nazi image of women. Until 1933, she was an ambitious actress who never shied away from extreme physical performances. Thereafter she was celebrated as a genius. A genius need not conform. During her entire life, Riefenstahl staged herself as a workaholic. She spoke of the nights she spent at the editing table, the high expectations, and the deadline pressures. Her personal life had always been subordinated to her professional life; her films were her children. Hitler shared this view of her. We know little of her relationships with men, however. But in her own version of the story, Hitler was not her "type," and she made an enemy of Goebbels after she rebuffed him. We also know that she married Peter Jacob in 1944 and divorced him three years later. She called Horst Kettner, forty years her junior, her life partner.

Riefenstahl exhibited traditionally "masculine" characteristics—determination, persistence, courage, and ambition—and in so doing conformed to patriarchal norms. Whenever she could not prevail with iron will, Riefenstahl used "feminine wiles." She instrumentalized her appearance in similar ways; here, too, she combined so-called masculine and feminine features. Her body, while prototypically female, was not soft and round, but well trained, muscular, and slender. Her attire was at times very feminine (we see her in evening dresses or brightly colored summer skirts) and at other times simply functional. As she stated in 1999 in an interview with Alice Schwarzer, editor of the feminist magazine *Emma*, she was "100% man and 100% woman."[32] Riefenstahl's vaulting over these gender restrictions opened additional spaces for her. Other hurdles, too, seemed easy for her to manage—dichotomies like nature/culture and body/spirit, for example. As a young woman, Riefenstahl represented herself as natural and athletic, posing as a tomboy in ski pants or a pilot's jacket. As she aged, she appeared more feminine, with makeup, dyed blond hair, brightly colored clothing, and high heels. Undoubtedly, her success lies in the ambivalence of her physical staging, in her Amazon-like demeanor and fluid gender roles. Pop stars like Madonna, David Bowie, and Mick Jagger have taken a page from her; indeed, the latter two have never denied their admiration for Leni Riefenstahl.

VII.

The question of continuities in Riefenstahl's work has been a recurring topic. In the German newsmagazine *Der Spiegel*, Matthias Schreiber and Susanne Weingarten asked Riefenstahl if there was not some connection between the Nazi idolization of the superior, strong race as seen in the male bodies of *Olympia* and the later images Riefenstahl made of the Sudanese Nuba. Riefenstahl responded: "I couldn't use an ugly man, could I? And as for the Nuba, that's what they look like. I didn't know that before my trip to Africa. Of course, one could photograph the Nuba in a way that would not show their beauty. But I wouldn't be able to do that."[33] As Susan Sontag suggested, Riefenstahl is not racist in questions of beauty.[34] Her images of others, however, do often depict power relations, in which the "below" and "above" as well as the "who-against-whom" are clearly marked. Human beings are shown in a struggle against one another or against natural forces, depicted in athletic competition, as superior or subordinate to one another.

Siegfried Kracauer, Susan Sontag, Wilhelm Bittorf, and Georg Seesslen have been central figures in the debate about the continuities in Riefenstahl's work, arguing that the Alpine films, the Nazi-era films, and the postwar photographs exhibit continuities in their "fascist" perspective. Others, like Elke Schmitter, have argued that Riefenstahl's work is marked rather by an "artistic conglomeration of futurism, a cold gaze, a false naturalness, a love for the monumental, and a neo-classical cult of beauty."[35] These elements can be found in other artists' work as well. Whether genuinely fascist or simply grandiose kitsch, the question remains as to whether the images that show Riefenstahl are aesthetically similar to those that she produced. Her Web page offers unequivocal answers. Here, as in her other work, nothing is left to chance. The selection of photographs and texts follow the same structural principle. The unpleasant is omitted. Every image appears composed; all elements—from the composition of the photographs and the perspective to the use of light and shadow—are strategically chosen. There are no "snapshots." Riefenstahl has seen to it that everything is properly set up and that she appears in the best light.

Judged in this context, Riefenstahl remained true to herself. Her gaze upon others did not change. As she described it in a 1965 interview, she was always in search of the "beautiful, harmonious, forthright, [and] strong."[36] This evidently explains the popular appeal of her images. After all, even though beauty may be a social and cultural construct, this does not change its power as image. As Sontag put it, "Although the Nuba are black, not Aryan, Riefenstahl's portrait of them evokes some of the larger themes of Nazi ideology: the contrast between the clean and the impure, the incorruptible and the defiled, the physical and the mental, the joyful and the critical."[37] According to this precept, Riefenstahl provides what most people want. What remains is the legitimate allegation that the monumental weight of her images contributed by way of her conscious erasure of the Other to its disappearance—and that this work has sharpened the discrepancy between the represented and real bodies. The debate on aesthetics becomes, as does everything about Riefenstahl, political.

NOTES

1. This translation is an abridged and adapted version of Martina Thiele's "Körper ins rechte Bild gerückt. Selbstinszenierungen der Leni Riefenstahl am Beispiel ihrer Homepage," *Identitätsräume. Nation, Körper und Geschlecht in den Medien. Eine Topographie,* ed. Brigtte Hipfl, Elisabeth Klaus, and Uta Scheer (Bielefeld: transcript, 2004), 172–200. The translator has not translated the passages from the German Web site, but instead refers to the English-language pages there: http://www.leni-riefenstahl.de/eng/bio.html. German citations, unless otherwise noted, have been translated by the translator, with the German sources listed in the endnotes.
2. See Claudia Lenssen, "Die fünf Karrieren der Leni Riefenstahl," *edp-Film* I: 27–31.
3. See Claudia Schmitz-Berning, *Vokabular des Nationalsozialismus* (Berlin and New York: Walter de Gruyter, 2000), 667.
4. Adolf Hitler, *Mein Kampf* (Munich: Zentralverlag der NSdAP, 1941), 361.
5. Helmut Heiber, *Goebbels Reden,* vol. II (Düsseldorf: Droste, 1972), 371.
6. Andreas Kilb, "Die Sehnsucht der Jungfrau. Leni Riefenstahls Kinematographische Sendung," *Frankfurter Allgemeine Zeitung* (August 22, 2002): 38.
7. Ibid., 38.
8. Alice Schwarzer, "Propagandistin oder Künstlerin?" *Emma* 1 (1999): 39.
9. Leni Riefenstahl, *Memoiren* (Cologne: Taschen, 2000), 137.

10. Claudia Lenssen, "Sie hält sich warm an ihrem Exhibitionismus," *taz*, August 8, 2002, http://www.taz.de/index.php?id=archivseite&dig=2002/08/22/a0163 (accessed October 24, 2007).
11. Peter W. Jansen, "Die Sprache der Körper. Mit Ornamenten und Arabesken: Die Filmregisseurin und Fotografin Leni Riefenstahl ist im Alter von 101 Jahren gestorben," *Frankfurter Rundschau* (September 10, 2003): 11.
12. Riefenstahl, *Memoiren*, 158.
13. Rainer Rother, *Leni Riefenstahl. Die Verführung des Talents* (Berlin: Henschel, 2000), i.
14. See Siegfried Kaltenecker, "Weil aber die vergessenste Fremde unser Körper ist. Über Männer-Körper-Repräsentationen und Faschismus," in *The Body of Gender: Körper/Geschlechter/Identitäten*, ed. Marie Luise Angerer (Vienna: Passagen, 1995), 97.
15. Elke Schmitter, "Triumph des Widerwillens. Leni Riefenstahl, die in dieser Woche hundert Jahre alt wird, ist weltberühmt—und findet doch in der Bundesrepublik bis heute kaum Anerkennung. Was eigentlich können die Deutschen ihr nicht verzeihen?" *Der Spiegel* 34 (2002): 158.
16. AP-Report, "Leni Riefenstahl nennt frühere Filme 'stubenrein,'" in *Frankfurter Rundschau* (August 12, 2002): 11.
17. Daniel Wildmann, *Begehrte Körper Konstruktion und Inszenierung des "arischen" Männerkörpers im "Dritten Reich"* (Würzburg: Königshausen & Neumann, 1998), 12.
18. Daniel Wildmann, "Kein Arier ohne Jude". Zur Konstruktion begehrter Männerkörper im "Dritten Reich," *Körper-Konzepte*, ed. Julika Funk and Cornelia Brück (Tübingen: Narr, 1999), 81.
19. Wildmann (1998), 139, 134.
20. Wildmann's notion of the ex-negativo plays a central role in debates about cinematic representations of the Holocaust. For example, in the context of Steven Spielberg's *Schindler's List* the controversy was whether the director showed the rescue of a few hundred Jews as a reference to the murder of millions. See also Martina Thiele, *Publizistische Kontroversen über den Holocaust im Film*, 467.
21. See Jörn Rohwer, "Wie viele Leben haben Sie gelebt, Frau Riefenstahl?" *Zeit-Magazin* (August 19, 1997): 9–13. The interviewer asked Riefenstahl: "If you photographed a Greek temple and there was a pile of garbage next to it, would you leave out the garbage?" Riefenstahl answered "Of course. I'm not interested in reality. I also don't show the destruction of nature by industry. Rather, I show the wonders of nature —among other reasons because one can see what one loses if it is destroyed.... I do want to make the beautiful visible and save it. I have a well developed social conscience."
22. Leni Riefenstahl, "Schönheit und Kampf in herrlicher Harmonie. Geleitwort zum Olympia-Film," in *Licht Bild Bühne* 31 (1938): 1.
23. Hilmar Hoffmann, "Zum 100. Mein neuer Film"—Ihr Werk, ihr Verhältnis zu Hitler, ihr Tauchprojekt: Leni Riefenstahl spricht mit Hilmar Hoffmann," *Die Welt* (January 7, 2002): 28.
24. Riefenstahl, *Memoiren*: 361ff. Legal disputes about the use of extras from the concentration camp at Maxglan were ongoing until 2002, when Riefenstahl was instructed by the court to cease claiming that she has seen all extras from the camp again and that none were harmed. See N. N. "Wissen oder Nichtwissen," *Süddeutsche Zeitung* (August 23, 2002): 11.

25. The troublesome and contentious context of the production of this film is absent from Riefenstahl's Web site, as is the photograph of her in Poland during the massacres of civilians.
26. Leni Riefenstahl, "'Ich bereue doch.' Leni Riefenstahl über ihren 100. Geburtstag, ein Leben im Schatten Hitlers and die Sehnsucht nach dem Tod." Interview with Mareen Linnartz and Herbert Fritz. *Frankfurter Rundschau Magazin* 127 (April 27, 2002): 4–5.
27. Leni Riefenstahl, *Die Nuba von Kau* (Munich: dtv, 1982), 48.
28. The film critic and director of the Munich film museum, Enno Patalas, reports that Riefenstahl had asked him why Sontag has come to the conclusion that the fish were photographed like SA men: "Susan Sontag was not amused when I told her this." See Patalas, "Die schönste Festrrede von allen. Hart wie Riefenstahl: Erinnerungen eines Betroffenen an die Regisseurin von *Triumph des Willens," Frankfurter Allgemeine Zeitung* (February 19, 2004): 35.
29. See Lenssen (2002).
30. On the English language site, the reader only receives this terse notice: "Leni Riefenstahl died on Monday September 8, 2003, in Poecking, Germany. She died only a few weeks after her 101st birthday."
31. Bianca Jagger, "Leni's back and Bianca's got her," *Interview* 5, no. 1 (1975): 35.
32. Alice Schwarzer, "Propagandistin oder Künstlerin?" *Emma* 1 (1999): 32–47.
33. Riefenstahl, *Memoiren,* 205.
34. Susan Sontag, "Verzückt von den Primitiven II. Die Ekstase der Gemeinschaft. Leni Riefenstahl oder die anhaltende Faszination faschistischer Kunst," *Die Zeit* 175: 22.
35. Schmitter, 156ff.
36. Michel Delahaye, "Leni and the Wolf, Interview with Leni Riefenstahl," *Cahiers du Cinema in English* 5 (1966): 49–55: 55.
37. Susan Sontag, "Fascinating Fascism," *Under the Sign of Saturn* (New York: Farrar Straus Giroux, 1975).

Chapter 12

In the Rearview Mirror: Curating Riefenstahl, Filmmuseum Potsdam, 1999

Ingeborg Majer-O'Sickey

I. Berlin U2

For a brief period in late 1998, Berlin subway riders learned to ignore a graffiti shocker at Bahnhof Zoo. Someone had written across the underground wall, "THERE'S NO BUSINESS LIKE SHOAH-BUSINESS." The slogan had been washed off by February 1999 when I rode the U2 from Nollendorfplatz to Bahnhof Zoo to catch the train to Potsdam. I was on my way to interview Dr. Bärbel Dalichow, the director of the Potsdam Filmmuseum and the curator of the first comprehensive retrospective of Riefenstahl's life and work in Germany (on view from December 1998 to March 1999).[1]

The stark truth of the message about the commodification of the genocide of millions of European Jews will always be there as a palimpsest. One might therefore begin by reading the scrawled message in sociological terms by way of Siegfried Kracauer's "surface phenomena" as he explained in *The Mass Ornament*:

> Every typical space is brought about by typical societal relations that express themselves in it without the distracting intervention of consciousness. All that is denied by consciousness, all that which is otherwise deliberately overlooked, takes part in its construction. The spatial images are the dreams of society. There, where the hieroglyphics of some spatial image or other have now been decoded, the ground of social reality presents itself.[2]

I read "THERE'S NO BUSINESS LIKE SHOAH-BUSINESS" as one of these "surface phenomena" in the sense that a metonym (business) replaces the Shoah by way of marking it a commodity. In our context "all that is denied by consciousness, all that which is deliberately overlooked" may refer to memory—historical, urban memory to be precise. In other words, this unsettling phrase foregrounds the "social reality" of fifty-four years of commodification of the Shoah. What has been "deliberately overlooked" and "takes part in the construction of consciousness" lurks underneath; it resides in the cultural memory of genocide. In this sense, I see the connection between Kracauer's "surface phenomena" and the graffiti on the underground wall as a palimpsest that shares points of contact that relate to the way capitalism (constitutive of the modern city space) participates in the burying of historical trauma.

It seems reasonable to speculate that the anonymous graffiti artist confronted the subway riders with a "memorialization fatigue" that many shared. In Berlin especially, the commemoration and memorialization debate was experiencing an all-time high in 1998/1999.[3] It may have been a cipher for the fear of failing the test of *Vergangenheitsbewältigung* at the latest fin-de-siècle. On the level of public discourse surrounding the "German Question," the angst that the twentieth-century would end without having finally dealt with the Shoah is one aspect of this problem.[4] For months, heated debates took place in the Bundestag about what would be a fitting memorial to the Jewish victims of the Nazis. The public airwaves and newspaper pages were full of analyses of Martin Walser's Peace Prize Address (*Friedenspreisrede*) in the Paulskirche in Frankfurt, where his own "guilt fatigue," as some pundits would have it, was actually not the major point of the speech. Rather, Walser complained about what he saw as the media's misuse of the Holocaust, or, as he put it, their use of the Holocaust as a "moral club."[5] The ensuing war of words gave Walser's unfortunate rhetorical phrase (*moralische Keule*) the status of a deadly virus whose symptoms, rather than its underlying cause, became the topic of public discourse that involved all who read newspapers or watched the news and talk shows in Germany. The Ignatz Bubis–Martin Walser dispute that followed would take another couple of years to settle down. Mixed in with this intense debate about coming to terms with the past was the controversy about architect Daniel Libeskind's stark design for the Jewish Museum in Berlin, which swirled around the—at that time—empty, three-storied, 9,500-square-meter museum. And finally, the international competition for the design of a Holocaust memorial in Berlin was also a hotly debated topic in the public forum.[6]

I would like to take the reading of "THERE'S NO BUSINESS LIKE SHOAH-BUSINESS" in another direction—into the realm of visual culture as it relates to the fascination with fascism.[7] As we shall see in a moment, the intersecting note between the subway artist and Leni Riefenstahl is the use of the wall in a Berlin underground station as a screen that is akin to a cinematic screen. Both projected (albeit more than four decades apart and for entirely different reasons) a dream—or nightmare for that matter—onto the screen of the underground space and made it into a "visually distinct ornament." This ornament is "oriented not toward the mental field but toward the sphere of social consciousness."[8] In order to connect the contemporary slogan scrawled at Bahnhof Zoo and Riefenstahl's memory of a life-changing moment in 1923, I will quote at length from a crucial passage in Riefenstahl's memoirs. Here she frames her transition from dancer to actress with a dream narrative that places her in the reality screen of the subway station at Nollendorfplatz in Berlin:

> Exhausted, I stood waiting on the platform, gritting my teeth as my knee began to throb again. My eyes wandered over the colors of the posters on the opposite wall until abruptly they focused on something: a male figure clambering over a towering mountain chimney. Underneath, the poster said "*Mountain of Destiny (Berg des Schicksals)*—a Film about the Dolomites by Dr. Arnold Fanck." Still tormented by thoughts about my future, I stared hypnotized at the poster, at those steep walls of rock, at the man swinging from one wall to the next.
>
> The train arrived at last and came to a halt between the poster and me. It was the train that I had been waiting for so impatiently, but I let it steam off again, to unblock my view of the poster. As if awakening from a trance, I saw the train vanish into the tunnel of Kleistrasse [sic]. *Mountain of Destiny* was running at the Mozart Hall, on the other side of the square, so I forgot about going to the doctor and instead went out into the street. Several minutes later I was sitting in the cinema. . . . The very first images of mountains, clouds, alpine slopes and towering rock fascinated me. I was experiencing a world that I did not know, for I had never seen such mountains. I knew them only from postcards, on which they looked rigid and lifeless. But here, on the screen, they were alive, mysterious, and more entrancingly beautiful that I had ever dreamed mountains could be. As the film went on I became more and more spellbound. I was so excited that even before it ended I had made up my mind to get to know those mountains. Filled with a new yearning, I left the theatre. That night it took me a long time to fall asleep as I debated with myself through the wakeful hours whether I was really enthralled by nature or by the artistry of the film. I dreamed of wild mountain crags, I saw myself running across talus slopes, and always, the leading performer in the film, the symbol of all the feelings aroused in me, seemed to be the steep tower of rock: the Guglia.[9]

Both the subway graffiti and Riefenstahl's text create the subway space as a place of otherworldliness that has to do with traumatic memory. Ironically, both texts result in a memorialization of sorts. They also share an excess of affect. While the subway writer states a truth as shock, Riefenstahl's narrative is neither verifiable nor falsifiable. As is always the case with autobiographical accounts, they are only real as representation. What is verifiable is that her story claimed to represent a dramatic shift from her ontological status in the urban uncanny to the alpine sublime. The narrative also represents, I would argue, a shift from Riefenstahl's practice of a thoroughly modernist sensibility (in her *Ausdruckstanz*) to an acting practice that was steeped in neoromantic sensibility.

It is important to also keep in mind that the scenario Riefenstahl created is evocative of the Berlin subways of the Weimar period. Her alienation from the metropolis is the unstated premise in her neoromantic thinking; it is overshadowed by her flight into a white utopia. Indeed, the train—as a cipher for the modern metropolis—only obscures her utopian vision for a moment. Riefenstahl's mythologizing invites a comparison to Siegfried Kracauer's rich passages about the tunnel under the tracks at Charlottenburg Station, which he describes as a "clattering hellish passage, a sinister cohesion of bricks, iron, and concrete, joined together for eternity."[10] As Henrick Reeh points out, "The tunnel space does not produce in Kracauer a feeling that he is viewing a more or less beautiful piece of architecture; rather—on the borderline between aesthetics and ethics—it provokes a Grauen—a feeling of horror and loathing..." in short, the "Urban Uncanny."[11] Quite characteristically, Riefenstahl uses purple prose (in her memoir) and the "silvery gaze"[12] (in Müller's film) to transcend the "Urban Uncanny." In the urban uncanny, the space of the subway is itself a complex text.[13] It is from this site that Riefenstahl escaped to the cinema. Imagined as palimpsest, Riefenstahl's "original" text inspires the creation of yet another visual text, best rendered in a screenplay with Brechtian *Verfremdungseffekte* (distanciation effect) to highlight the constructedness of her (historical) narrative that would look something like this:

> Cut one: A placard with THERE'S NO BUSINESS LIKE SHOAH-BUSINESS. Blank screen.
> Cut two: Riefenstahl waits on the platform for the train at the Nollendorfplatz subway station. (She is, as she tells it in her memoirs, in her early twenties.)
> Cut three: Blank screen with an intertitle that tells us that Riefenstahl's fictional self looks at the memory of a poster that was affixed to the wall across the tracks.
> Cut four: Full shot of the poster of Arnold Fanck's 1923 *Mountain of Destiny*.
> Cut five: Medium long shot of Riefenstahl in her early nineties, reinventing the "original" scene (1923/1987) for a sequence in Ray Müller's 1993 biopic, *The Wonderful, Horrible Life of Leni Riefenstahl (Die Macht der Bilder)*, on the platform at Nollendorfplatz.[14]
> Cut six: A placard with the date 1998 moves aside the image of Riefenstahl—with the (still) silvery gaze she had in Müller's sequence—to make room for our graffiti artist, who overwrites the earlier pronouncement with "THERE'S NO BUSINESS LIKE RIEFENSTAHL-BUSINESS."

The reader will ask herself with some justification what such a scenario achieves—other than demonstrating a metonymic connection between two events that have to do with the culture industry generally and the commodity fetishism inherent in memorialization in particular. Since the goal of my essay is to set the stage for the first exhibit of Leni Riefenstahl's life and work within a "society of the spectacle," it seems appropriate to set in motion thoughts about her self-presentation.[15] Riefenstahl's self-staging—indeed, her self-articulation—is recorded in hundreds of images (photographic as well as cinematic and as blatant advertisements on her Web site) with the overwhelming iconographic goal of personifying indestructibility, agelessness, harmony, and beauty.[16] Indeed, for this reason, one can say that her self-construction over some seven decades provides a classic case in point for the feminist theoretical insight that women see themselves as image, seen by others. Mary Ann Doane's apt description of the ontology of female spectatorship shows that, "for the female spectator there is a certain overpresence of the image—she is the image."[17] A scene such as the one I created above distances the image (Riefenstahl as surface) from its content (Riefenstahl as subject/object) so that the placards brought onto the walls of the subway disrupt a seamless identification with Riefenstahl's romantic narration of a life-altering event.

The passage I cited earlier from Riefenstahl's memoirs reveals her bipolar relationship to the *Zeitgeist* with remarkable clarity and shows ways that she triangulated visuality, subjectivity, and sexual desire by way of an image (in her dream).[18] Her triangulation is a result of her "recall" of a moment of deep caesura in her life. For consideration of this aspect, Kracauer's sociological perspective needs to be supplemented by way of Freud's notion of "deferred action" (*Nachträglichkeit*). As Laplanche explains this concept, "the recall of the first scene . . . sets up the upsurge of sexual excitation, catching the ego in reverse, and leaving it disarmed. . . ."[19] Indeed, one might go so far as to say that Riefenstahl gives the poster episode and her cinematic experience of the Guglia the status of an over-determined dream.[20]

Riefenstahl staged the event of her conversion from dancer to actress in her memoirs and restaged it in Müller's film by framing her "destiny" at a distance. Both stagings of her memory testify to what is well known about her, namely that she avoided at all cost a reflective process in remembering. The denial is made visible, it seems to me, in her radical emptying out of all people around her in the subway event, in both her memoir and in its reenactment in Müller's film. While it is remarkable that we meet no one but Riefenstahl on the platform of the subway station, and while it may betoken Riefenstahl's well-known self-centeredness, it is also true that the city space lends itself, as Georg Simmel has shown, to being subjectivized. As contemporary commentators on the metropolis—from Benjamin to Kracauer and Simmel—have noted, it is difficult to create "the analogy between an individual and an urban-collective subjectivity."[21] As David Clarke emphasizes, "The modern city was . . . the world as experienced by the stranger, and the experience of a world populated by strangers—a world in which a universal strangehood was coming to predominate."[22] In other words, "emptiness" may indeed have been the best solution for staging Riefenstahl's subjective experience of the urban uncanny.

The vehicle for Riefenstahl's escape is the dream factory cinema. Her flight to the cinema was not an uncommon reaction on the part of alienated city dwellers in Weimar Berlin. As Miriam Hansen observes, in Weimar Berlin: "It was both part and prominent symptom of the crisis as which modernity was perceived, and at the same time it evolved into a social discourse in which a wide variety of groups sought to come to terms with the traumatic impact of modernisation."[23] In both her memoir and her performance in Müller's film, Riefenstahl claims that she went to see *Mountain of Destiny* "every evening for a week, I couldn't stand Berlin anymore."[24] Is it any wonder, then, that she shrinks the period from her activity as dancer to viewer (of the poster and the film) to actor (in the *Bergfilme*, the Alpine films) to director of feature and "documentary" films in as dizzying a speed as her editing cuts appear in *Triumph of the Will*? The mass unemployment in Germany, the violent clashes in the streets, the hunger and misery in Berlin get one paragraph in her re-membering of the past. The astonishing creative drive (in theater, film, literature, cabaret, and so on) in Berlin during the 1920s gets very little play in her memoirs, and then only if she can stage herself as its protagonist. After she joined the *Bergfilm* director Arnold Fanck and his group, and certainly by the time she directed and starred in *Das blaue Licht* (*The Blue Light*, 1932), she had turned her back to the metropolis Berlin, and become a *Bergfilm/Heimatfilm*-maker of sorts.

Not surprisingly, Riefenstahl's work in Fanck's Alpine films (*Bergfilme*) is generally discussed in terms of its antimodernism. In fact, the roots of these films lie in late nineteenth- and early twentieth-century neoromantic "back to nature" movements like the *Lebensreformbewegungen*. The latter attempted to achieve a bodily harmony or a consonance between the rhythm of the body and the rhythms of nature. A filmic example is the prologue to Fanck's 1925/1926 *The Holy Mountain (Der heilige Berg)*, in which the character Diotima (played by Riefenstahl) dances in rhythmic movements to the waves of the sea.[25] (As some commentators have justly pointed out, the Fanck group's antimodernist stance is somewhat disingenuous. Without modern technology, their neoromantic attitudes would not find cinematic articulation.) It is important to recall that Riefenstahl's neoromantic attitude toward modernity paid off well in the capitalist systems in which she worked. It got her Hitler's commission for *Triumph of the Will* (*Triumph des Willens*, 1934). It also resulted in the commission (she claims by the Olympic Committee) to film the 1936 Olympics in two blockbuster films, *Festival of Nations* and *Festival of Beauty* (*Fest der Völker* and *Fest der Schönheit*). It also paid off after a short period of treading water right after World War II. By the 1960s, she had switched to taking photographs of the Nuba and in the 1970s, she went underwater to photograph and film life in the ocean. Benedikt-Taschen celebrated Leni Riefenstahl with "opulent photo books."[26] In time for her one hundredth birthday on August 22, 2002, Taschen also brought out a coffee-table book that reportedly went for 1,250 Euros a copy.[27] The Filmmuseum Potsdam, too, profited from the public's fascination with fascism. Although certainly not a moneymaking venture during its three-month run, the exhibit of Riefenstahl's life and work in the Filmmuseum Potsdam was exceedingly rewarding as an investment.[28] The indestructible Riefenstahl had made a financial rebound. There is no business like Riefenstahl-business.

II. The Visit to Potsdam

"Writing about Leni Riefenstahl invites trouble" ("*Wer sich Ärger einhandeln möchte, sollte über Leni Riefenstahl schreiben*").[29] This statement opens Bärbel Dalichow and Claudia Lenssen's article "Focus Riefenstahl" in the catalogue that accompanied the retrospective of her work at the Filmmuseum Potsdam. In print, the statement sounds rather innocuous. Paper, it is said, is patient. In person, Bärbel Dalichow, curator and director of the museum, offered a rather more bristly version. "Riefenstahl is a difficult person," she said with exasperation, "so, if you want trouble, work on Leni Riefenstahl."[30] Evidently, three months into the organization and planning for the Riefenstahl exhibit, Dalichow and her staff's nerves had been stretched to a breaking point. Nevertheless, it seems that Dalichow is used to difficult projects. She has become known as a mover and shaker in the cultural life of her native Potsdam. Having joined the Filmmuseum Potsdam as its director in 1981, Dalichow has curated, among numerous other shows there, the popular permanent exhibit, "Berlin-Hollywood," and is a prolific writer on cinema.[31]

The following day, February 7, the museum expected Leni Riefenstahl's visit, "Der Besuch der alten Dame" as one reporter quipped, citing the title of Friedrich Dürrenmatt's play "The Visit," whose original German title means literally, "the visit of the old lady."[32] For months, German newspapers headlined now-you'll-see-her-now-you-won't articles. Riefenstahl had been slated to come to the opening on December 4, 1998. She sent her regrets the day before, citing her recovery from pneumonia. The previous evening, German TV viewers could see the ninety-six-year-old filmmaker as she was interviewed, apparently in good health. Recalling the reasons for Riefenstahl's no-show, Dalichow cited "a mixture of illness and unease" that had kept the filmmaker from the opening. Riefenstahl had wanted to meddle—*wollte sich einmischen*—in some of the decisions the show's coordinators had made. For this reason, tensions arose and the Dalichow-Riefenstahl interview could not be published. In addition, explained Dalichow, Riefenstahl was not pleased with the earlier title for the exhibit "Schönheit und Schuld" ("Beauty and Guilt"), and eventually the offending title was changed to simply: "Leni Riefenstahl." Ines Walk, one of the show's coordinators and a contributor to the comprehensive catalogue, speculated that Riefenstahl's no-show also had to do with her wanting to "make sure the show was well-received by the public before coming to Potsdam."[33]

Nervous anticipation of Riefenstahl's visit contributed to a tense atmosphere when I arrived at the museum on February 6, 1999, for my interview with Dalichow. What kind of trouble, other than Riefenstahl's meddling, might Dalichow have referred to? When I posed this question, Dalichow vacillated between candor and discretion. Indeed, I need not have asked it. Even those who know no more about Riefenstahl's persona than information gleaned from Ray Müller's 1993 biopic can see that it would be difficult to curate an exhibit whose subject was the living Riefenstahl and to whom the curator was beholden for materials from that subject's own personal archive. If nothing else, the viewer will remember Riefenstahl's intensity, her passion, and the stubborn way she clung to her opinions. Müller framed Riefenstahl's desire for control throughout the film. In life as well, her desire for control in relation to her work is evident. Approaching her one hundredth birthday, Riefenstahl planned to establish her own museum in her adopted town of Pöcking on Lake Starnberg in Bavaria.[34] Other potential troubles could be found in the filmmaker's penchant for lawsuits (she won fifty of fifty lawsuits involving her person). And finally, Dalichow feared that trouble might come from voices in the press, from pesky left-wing intellectuals, print journalists, and even from the radical right.[35]

Riefenstahl's involvement in the show clearly complicated Dalichow and her team's intent—to "demystify without remystifying."[36] Indeed, from my conversation with Dalichow, it became apparent that she saw as her most difficult task the danger of creating the appearance of having staged an homage, as has been the case with Eiko Ishioka's 1980 Riefenstahl show at the Tokyo Sheibu-Museum with its banner "Pure Schönheit" (Pure Beauty).[37] Time and again, Dalichow stressed that she and her team strove to inspire critical thinking in the show's visitors. Providing a balance would, she hoped, keep both the political left and right at bay.

To live up to her own idea of courage was evidently important for Dalichow personally; as for me—I admired her chutzpah.[38] In November 1998, about a month before the opening of the exhibit and more than three years into the project, she emphasized that it took courage to stage a Riefenstahl exhibit at this particular historical moment. In an interview with the *Berliner Morgenpost* that advertised the exhibit, Dalichow said,

> Evidently, up until now, no one has felt like becoming a target for insinuations and accusations. What is lacking is a certain distance to the most painful issues in our history. This is evident in some of the hysterical reactions to the *Wehrmachtsausstellung* [the traveling exhibit on the human rights abuses and crimes against humanity committed by the Wehrmacht during World War II] and to Walser's speech. These reactions show that public discourse about the Nazi period is still only possible on well-trodden paths.[39]

If the museum's staff was nervous about Riefenstahl's visit the next day, I was glad to be out of the miserable February weather. During my walk from the train station to the Filmmuseum Potsdam it began to sleet. The museum building and its charming downstairs café were well worth the trek through the freezing rain. Formerly the royal stables of Prussian kings, the baroque Marstall that houses the café and the museum was built in 1685 as an Orangerie by architect Johann Arnold Nering. From 1714, the building served as the stables for the royals living in the *Stadtschloss* (City Palace). Three decades later, Frederick II of Prussia commissioned his architect Georg Wenzelaus von Knobelsdorff (of Sansscouci fame) to change the Marstall's appearance to its current baroque style.[40] Established in 1981, the film museum was called "Filmmuseum der DDR" ("Film Museum of the GDR") until 1989, when the State of Brandenburg took over its administration and rechristened it Filmmuseum Potsdam.[41]

Just up the road from Potsdam are the famed film studio grounds of Babelsberg and the Babelsberg Movie Park. The ghosts of history reside here, too: Former home to Bioscop (ten years), UFA (twenty-three years), and DEFA (forty-six years), today this is the home of a state-of-the-art facility for all sorts of international film and television productions.[42] One should always approach the Filmmuseum Potsdam from the west, so as to get into the proper film-historical frame: Here, German cinema greats worked under five different political regimes. Silent stars rolled their eyes for the likes of Lang, Murnau, and Wiene; Sternberg learned how to create Dietrich's cheekbones; Detlef Sierck discovered Zarah Leander's erotic screen presence and helped German film fans get over the loss to Hollywood of Garbo, Dietrich, and Bergman. Veit Harlan staged his wife, Kristina Söderbaum, here, and DEFA made (among many other unforgettable films) *Paul und Paula.*[43] Viewers of Müller's 1993 *The Wonderful, Horrible Life of Leni Riefenstahl* will recall the comical sequence in which Riefenstahl walks on the cobblestones toward the studios on the Babelsberg grounds. At first, Riefenstahl argues energetically that she cannot walk and talk at the same time. Then, overtaken by her desire to recall the good old days at the Babelsberg studios, she proves that she can do two things at the same time after all.

The Potsdam retrospective was so successful that it was extended from February 28, 1998, to March 14, 1999.[44] In addition to the displays about her work and life, the museum had arranged film screenings and panel discussions in the museum's cinema.[45] For me the panel discussion "Pop Will Eat Itself," with Kai-Uwe Kohlschmidt as moderator, was perhaps the most memorable of the events that accompanied the show. The audience was asked to contemplate fascinating fascism in current pop culture, including a screening of the heavy metal group Rammstein's music video "Stripped." Kohlschmidt, in his day-job as singer in the group Sandow, came across as a self-proclaimed *enfant terrible*, regaling the audience with statements about how pop culture couldn't care less about politics. It seemed (that night at least) that dismissing Riefenstahl, Rammstein, and other fascistic-aesthetic wannabes was the only way to be cool. Here is a sample from Kohlschmidt: "She [Leni Riefenstahl] was once important because she was taboo. But it's been broken." And: "It [the retrospective of Leni Riefenstahl's work] wasn't worth it. . . . Everything has been normalized, made into mediocrity (*Mittelmaß*), like commercials for detergent."[46] Regrettably, Kohlschmidt remained stuck in the middle of the road himself. His nomination of Riefenstahl as a "has-been" ignored—among other realities—the fact that the exhibit managed to put the Filmmuseum Potsdam on the map internationally.[47]

Before meeting with Dalichow in her upscale post-IKEA office above the museum's exhibition space, I had another look at the exhibit. As the exhibition plan showed, one of the main challenges of the curators was the relatively small space they had available to display an immense amount of filmic, photographic, and textual material from the life and career of the by now ninety-six-year-old Riefenstahl. The arrangement seemed sensible to me on my first visit. The diagram of the exhibit included labels of the arrangement according to periods in her life. What struck me in this second visit, however, was the aesthetic consonance between Riefenstahl's postwar self-staging (especially in her memoirs and on her Web site) and the curators' display. Indeed, since the exhibit was not only on Riefenstahl's work but also about her life, it is not particularly surprising that Riefenstahl's artistic and physical longevity marked the show. Evidently, Dalichow and Lenssen admired Riefenstahl's "strength of character, her ability to succeed and her obsessive working habits": These character traits are, as these two curators emphasize in the introduction to the catalogue, "part of the American dream that is dreamed all over the world. Riefenstahl could be the originator of the adage, 'You can make it if you really want to.'"[48]

One could not help but be struck by the curators' re-petitioning of Riefenstahl's self-promotion of herself as sole creator of her own cult of beauty and of a toughness in both body and character.[49] Impressions of an ageless and indestructible artist were reproduced throughout with photographs and texts. These include images of her barefooted climb up an impossibly steep cliff in Fanck's film and of her broken body on a stretcher after her helicopter crashed in Africa. Combined with an artificial agelessness (images of the seventy-year-old in her incarnation as a photographer of the Nuba, dancing), the exhibited material re-staged (perhaps inadvertently) Riefenstahl's self-promotions over the past thirty years.[50] The question is how could the exhibitors have deconstructed the Riefenstahl myth, given that they needed her collaboration in opening her personal archives to them? It seems that the desire to please the living icon was insurmountable. What resulted, then, was a multiple reproduction: Riefenstahl's own lifelong cult of strength and beauty reproduced, logically enough, one of the most important National Socialist tenets, that of "Strength and Beauty." The Filmmuseum Potsdam, in turn, reproduced the aesthetic of the Nazi period and Riefenstahl's staging of it.

III. The Interview and Beyond

The following is an abridged version of my interview with Dalichow.[51]

Ingeborg Majer-O'Sickey: Frau Dalichow, how did you come to the idea of undertaking the exhibit of Riefenstahl's work and life?

Bärbel Dalichow: Well, I should mention that in our programming meetings, we had been talking about an exhibit about film production during the

Third Reich for some time. The way I came up with the idea of doing a retrospective show of Riefenstahl was actually quite strange. When I was in the U.S. in the summer of 1995 I saw Ray Müller's *Die Macht der Bilder* [*The Wonderful, Horrible Life of Leni Riefenstahl*] on TV. By coincidence, right at this time we were screening this film together with the Olympia films in the cinema of our museum. So, after I got back, I did some research about what had been done with her work to date, and since there hadn't been any exhibits that treated both her life and work, I wrote a letter to Müller and then to Riefenstahl. About a year later, she sent me a postcard from Indonesia in which she agreed to the exhibit. So, that's how it all started.

IMOS: What was most important to you about how the exhibit would show Riefenstahl's work and life?

BD: I wanted the least bias possible. We planned the exhibit in a space and arranged it in ways that help viewers get beyond preconceived notions about Riefenstahl's work and persona. I think that the fact that we come from the former GDR is important here. We knew nothing about her, and we didn't have these institutionalized ideas about her. For that reason I believe that we came to the task with a less encumbered point of view. In the West, her very name stands for all sorts of positions vis-à-vis German *Vergangenheitsbewältigung* [coming-to-terms-with-the-past]. There, she has two functions: On the one hand, she's a stand-in for identification, and on the other for dis-identification. We never had this problem in East Germany. She was an unknown.

IMOS: Would you elaborate on this last point a bit?

BD: First of all, Riefenstahl was nothing in the GDR, so she could not serve as an alibi for anyone. And second, there are folks—especially West German, left-oriented intellectuals—who are constantly talking about the dangers of Riefenstahl's work today. I don't buy into this. And, by the way, I disagree that there should be a ban on showing her films in the open market.[52] I think that you have to have the right conditions politically for her—or other artists'—work to be dangerous. We don't have such conditions here at this time. What is important is that these films can be seen and that the power relations of those days can be seen as their context. That's where the reading room that's part of the exhibit can be useful to those visitors who actually want to learn about her work and life.

IMOS: You and Claudia Lenssen started your introduction to the catalogue with the words: "*Wer sich Ärger einhandeln möchte, sollte über Leni Riefenstahl schreiben*" ["Whoever wants to make trouble for themselves should write something about Leni Riefenstahl."] Would you elaborate on this?

BD: Well, there are basically two things. One, working with a living artist is always fraught with difficulties. And, of course, Riefenstahl had to be involved quite a bit. After all, we wanted the material that she has in her private archives. So, we were sort of at her mercy. Not a comfortable position to be in, to be sure. And as we had to do all of the research through catalogues upon catalogues on her turf, in her house, you can imagine that there was some tension. We sometimes felt like we were sitting under the sword of Damocles. Second, Riefenstahl is at a point in her life where she expects some consideration, some recognition of her life's work. At the end of the day, of course, we don't have control over how the exhibit is going to be received. In relation to this question, it's interesting that film people—and some of them profess to admire her work—declined to come to the opening of the show.[53]

IMOS: In a few weeks it will be over. So far, the show has been received well by the press, and the number of visitors is still impressive. There were no demonstrations, neither from the left nor from the right. There is one more hurdle, obviously. Riefenstahl's visit tomorrow. What are you afraid of most?

BD: That she'll like it. If she says that she likes it, all the talking heads will dismiss our work and call it an homage. That would be devastating. The political left, too, will brand it as an homage. And the political right will praise us. Either way, it would be a nightmare.

The next day, Leni Riefenstahl arrived in the museum to take a tour of the presentation of her work. After the tour, Dalichow had arranged a press conference in the museum's cinema. Reporters from all the major German media (mostly print) were assembled. One of the first questions was, of course, "How did you like it?" Riefenstahl: "The exhibit is beautiful and very correct" ("*Die Ausstellung ist wunderschön und sehr korrekt*"). An "objective homage"? It seemed to me that Dalichow, who was sitting next to Riefenstahl on the dias, had a resigned look on her face.

Leni Riefenstahl and Bärbel Dalichow view the exhibit. Photograph courtesy of the Filmmuseum Potsdam.

Riefenstahl and Dalichow at the press conference. Photograph courtesy of the Filmmuseum Potsdam.

Riefenstahl's lifelong cult of training her body, which she practiced in her dance training, skiing, mountain climbing, and deep-sea diving, still registered in her graceful movements as she walked through the exhibit. Remarkably, Riefenstahl's flawless performance during her stroll through the show and on the stage in the museum's conference room belied her recent bout with pneumonia. While watching the ping-pong ball game of innocuous questions and predictable answers during the press conference, one could hardly dodge the question of the connection between her physical performance of various forms of social and symbolic control and Riefenstahl's own body as site for racialist history (*Geschichte* and *Geschichten*). The title of Susanne Conze's 1999 study, *Körper macht Geschichte—Geschichte macht Körper (Bodies Fashion History—History Fashions Bodies)*, reminds us that an interrogation of either field cannot exclude one or the other.[54] This issue was not raised, of course. Riefenstahl has never been mistaken for an intellectual. Watching Riefenstahl's self-staging at the museum in February 1999 in the context of its staging of her life and career evokes issues that have to do with the "woman's body," long a site for the interrogation of social and psychical phenomena. Scholarship about the gendered body covers the range of disciplinary fields in ways that have legitimated the combining of seemingly disparate fields. For all that, the appearance of a particular woman is rarely the topic of inquiry in feminist scholarship.[55]

Leni Riefenstahl presented a specific challenge in this context, since she maintained her hyperbolic self-staging until her death, four years later. Doane's observation cited above bears repeating: ". . . for the female spectator there is a certain overpresence of the image—she is the image."[56] Seeing Riefenstahl articulate herself that afternoon, one noticed in her body language patriarchal regulatory practices that pertained to women of Riefenstahl's generation and class (leaning forward in an accommodating manner and flirtatiously smiling). In fact, watching Riefenstahl's performance recalled Joan Rivière's findings about successful women performing their gender (in her 1929 essay "Womanliness as Masquerade"), where she presents her experiences with successful career women in her practice as a psychoanalyst. Rivière observed that successful women who consulted her in her practice sought approval from men (a.k.a. father figures) through hyperfeminine mannerisms.[57] Slender and well toned, Riefenstahl moved ramrod straight through the exhibit and climbed the steps onto the podium, not pleased that Dalichow made efforts to assist her. She told the photographers: Five minutes for photos, no more. She asked them to use softening filters, and posed this way and that.[58] Apparently, the right side of her face was her preferred side.

Riefenstahl's appearance calls to mind a costly walking and talking *Gesamtkunstwerk*—her blond curls perfectly coiffed, unruffled by the sharp February winds. Her pricey, cuddly mohair sweater with appliqués and the silk scarf worked in harmony with her cream-colored stretch pants that reached into white, fur-lined ankle boots—the costume fit Riefenstahl's answers (well rehearsed, perfectly coordinated, smooth). Indeed, when I saw Riefenstahl on the dais, I was reminded of the women in my mother's circle of friends. Born in the early 1920s, they grew up in a similar cultural atmosphere in which reigned a cult of physical beauty (promulgated by the *Lebensreform* movement) and neoromantic ideas in fine art were highly valued. It is Riefenstahl's penchant for constructing beauty and harmony that many German women of a certain age admire most. Yet many women in that generation are unwilling to concede that what they praised in Riefenstahl aligns them with the National Socialists' rejection of "degenerate art." These women also refuse to refract their admiration of Riefenstahl's toughness, longevity, and her alacrity of a person twenty years their senior through the National Socialists' injunctions that the individual's body is a property of the state and is for this reason required to remain "healthy and strong" (*leistungsfähig*).[59] *Zeitzeugen* (witnesses of the period) I have spoken to always bookended their discussions of her work during the Third Reich (during which they were teenagers) with hyperbolical observations: Riefenstahl was the first, most ambitious, most talented, and most importantly, the toughest ("*eine gute Preussin*") female filmmaker of her generation. These judgments eclipsed any critical content of our discussions. The press and critics continue to echo this judgment nearly one and all.[60]

The organizers of the Leni Riefenstahl exhibit are professionally trained to think about and to exhibit the past in a critical manner. The question arises then: What should the Filmmuseum's exhibit have done in order to demythologize Leni Riefenstahl? My sense is that it should have questioned Riefenstahl's own myth that she was the first, most ambitious, or most talented German female filmmaker of her generation. Evidence shows that she was not. There is, for example, Hanna Henning (1884–1925), the most prolific female film director, screenwriter, and producer in German silent cinema. During her brief eight years as a film industry worker, she directed forty-two films, having written the screenplay for fifteen and having been the producer for five of these films. Although many of her films received critical praise, her production company went bankrupt in 1925 and that same year Henning died of pneumonia at the early of age forty-nine. Henning's versatility in the film industry is remarkable not only because of her ability to write, direct, and produce, but also due to the varieties of genre she worked in: from light-hearted comedies and children's films (the so-called "*Bubi-Filme*") to heavy melodramas, most notably the 1919 *Die Siebzehnjährigen (The Seventeen-Year-Olds)*. At the same time as she directed the 1921 films *Die Furcht vor dem Weibe (Fear of Women)* and *Am roten Kliff (On the Red Cliff)*, Henning made a foray into documentary filmmaking.[61]

Another example is Lotte Reiniger (1899–1981). She was a trailblazer with her animated films—called *Sillouettenfilme*—predating even Walt Disney. In 1919, Reiniger animated wooden rats for Paul Wegener's film *Der Rattenfänger von Hameln (The Pied Piper of Hamelin)*. That same year she directed *Ornament des verliebten Herzens (Ornament of a Heart in Love)*, in 1923 *Die Abenteuer des Prinzen Achmed (The Adventures of Prince Achmed)*, and in 1928 *Doctor Dolittle und seine Tiere (Doctor Dolittle and His Animals)*.[62] And Leontine Sagan (1989–1974) comes to mind. Her 1929 film *Mädchen in Uniform (Girls in Uniform)* predated Riefenstahl's directorial debut by three years. Both Sagan and Reiniger had to leave Germany when the Nazis came to power.

Of the film industry workers who stayed, Thea von Harbou (1888–1956) was more productive than Riefenstahl by far. Although Harbou loathed self-promotion, she was quite ambitious, becoming the second highest paid screenwriter during the Nazi period.[63] She directed two films, *Elisabeth und ihr Narr* (1933; *Elizabeth and the Fool*) and *Hanneles Himmelfahrt* (1934; *Hannele's Trip to Heaven*). Furthermore, Harbou wrote over fifty screenplays, about half during the Weimar Republic (she worked with Fritz Lang, her husband for a time), and the other half during the Nazi era. Olga Tschechowa (1897–1980), dubbed the "Grande Dame of German Film" (Hans J. Wollstein) was—without the kind of financial support that Riefenstahl enjoyed—also a productive and creative film actress, director, and, after World War II, entrepreneur. Born in Alexksandropol (then in Tsarist Russia), Tschechowa was discovered by F. W. Murnau. Murnau gave her the leading role in *Schloss Vogelöd* (1921; *Haunted Castle*). This silent film catapulted her to fame. She starred in over forty silent films during the early 1920s. In 1929, she directed *Der Narr Seine Liebe (The Fool of Love)*. Shortly after World War II, Tschechowa founded her own film production company (Venus-Film Olga Tschechowa) and starred in a number of films. By 1950, she had launched an immensely successful cosmetics line (Olga Tschechowa Kosmetik Gesellschaft).

The list could go on: I have only chosen a few of the interesting film industry workers as examples. Thus, the simplest way that Dalichow & Co.'s exhibit might have avoided a reproduction of Riefenstahl's self-promotion as an icon of the original, the first and only female genius in the German film industry, would have been to situate her work in the context of the film industry workers I mention above. This could have been achieved by screening films made by Riefenstahl's female colleagues, and by offering a panel discussion that would have expanded the visitor's frame of reference. Such events would have gone a long way toward demystification.

During our warm-up to the interview, Dalichow made the point that the exhibit in Potsdam wanted to get out of well-trodden paths and affect a shift in paradigm as to how to present Riefenstahl. Perhaps the will required for a paradigm shift was lacking. A more generous interpretation would be that it was not possible because Riefenstahl was too energetically involved in the exhibit. If so, then the statement Dalichow and Lenssen made at the outset of their introduction to the catalogue might better have read: "Writing about and staging a show about a living artist invites trouble." But this conclusion misses the point. Riefenstahl had fashioned herself as a lone female genius of the German film industry. For all the protests and laments against labeling her a Nazi, it is indeed the major reason for her fame. At the danger of overstating it, Riefenstahl herself kept alive the fascinating aspect of the scent of fascism that (still) adheres to her persona. It was, then, the task of the Filmmuseum Potsdam to remove the one marketing aspect that drew so many visitors to the show, that of fascinating fascism. The irony is, of course, that such a decommodification would have exacted its price. To return to the truism I cited at the beginning in amendment: "There is no business like the same old Riefenstahl-business."

NOTES

For their unflagging support of my work on women in National Socialism, I am profoundly grateful to my mother, Gudrun Majer (1924–2006) and my brother, Helge Majer (1942–2006). I also appreciate Bärbel Dalichow's generosity and frankness during our interview, and am indebted to Barbara Mennel and Mary Webster for thoughtful critiques of earlier versions of this essay. I thank the editors for their careful readings and suggestions. All translations are my own unless otherwise noted.

1. Earlier exhibits include a film-only retrospective at the Venice Biennale (1959); the "Leni Riefenstahl-life" at the Bank Mura Complex in Japan (1991); Ray Müller's *The Wonderful, Horrible Life of Leni Riefenstahl* was presented in New York City's Museum of Modern Art (1993); film retrospectives were held in Leipzig, Kuopio (Finland),

Milan (1995), and in Rome (1997). A commercial exhibit of Riefenstahl's photographs at the Schlüter Gallery, Hamburg, was unabashedly designed to sell photographs, especially Riefenstahl's Nuba photographs.

2. Siegfried Kracauer, *Das Ornament der Masse* (Frankfurt/M: Suhrkamp, 1963), 69–70.
3. A headline in the December 16, 1998, *Berliner Zeitung* cited the administrator of the *Gedenkstätte Deutscher Widerstand* in Berlin as saying that there are enough Holocaust exhibits (*Es gibt genug Holocaust-Ausstellungen*).
4. I suggest at least three aspects to what I call "memorialization fatigue": an anxiety of not living up to the task; an ennui toward an intensifying and ubiquitous public discourse about atonement through creating memorials; and lingering anti-semitic sentiment.
5. I find Christian Semler's critique in his article "In Walsers Gewissensgärtchen," *taz*, December 17, 1998, one of the most sensible among the dozens of responses by bona fide commentators of Walser's speech. He answered Walser's complaint that the media attempts to prescribe how his conscience should react to the Holocaust by noting that "Walser's evocation of 'conscience' is already chemically cleansed from conflict situations" in which moral decisions have to be made. Semler also criticizes Walser's move of privatizing public concerns: "He transforms public matters into a private desire to come to terms with the [Nazi] past in his own way. . . . All the while Walser sees himself surrounded by moralists who wield the 'moral club' he mimics the old drama from the hero, who follows his own moral drum, who has to resist publicly directed conformist edicts."
6. Ulrich Clewing, a reporter for the *taz*, observed in his article "Linien der Zerstörung," *taz*, February 1, 1999: "The symbolic connotations that Libeskind has given the Jewish Museum are so strong that some visitors comment that it is no longer necessary to build a Holocaust Memorial. This building is a Holocaust Memorial tout court." As Clewing also reports, "over 8,000 visitors will have worked their way through the building in the six hours of the so-called 'long night of museums' . . . they take possession of the world famous building." The judges of the competition settled on Peter Eisenman's steles.
7. I am alluding, of course, to the title of Susan Sontag's seminal essay, "Fascinating Fascism" from 1975. A recent example of the fact that fascism fascinates were the high viewer numbers garnered by the *ZDF*/History Channel series *Hitler's Women* (*Hitlers Frauen*). The series included segments on Zara Leander, Winifred Wagner, and Magda Goebbels, among others. A segment on Leni Riefenstahl was aired in fall 2002.
8. See Henrik Reeh, *Ornaments of the Metropolis. Siegfried Kracauer and Modern Urban Culture* (Cambridge, MA: MIT Press, 2004), 162, 205, for example. While there exists no definitive conceptual explanation of the "ornament" in Kracauer's work, Henrik Reeh distinguishes between two meanings of the term. Reeh identifies a "double concept of the ornament": "It is at one and the same time surface and an abstraction that conveys meaning. . . . The formally abstract is thereby enriched by a semantic dimension. The two-dimensional abstraction becomes linked to a third, interpretive dimension. This constellation means that the concrete and the abstract, form and meaning meet. It is only this new—admittedly frail—unity that confirms the ornament's special *raison d'être* and cognitive value."
9. Leni Riefenstahl, *A Memoir* (New York: St. Martin's Press, 1992), 41–42.

10. Siegfried Kracauer, *Straßen in Berlin und anderswo* (Frankfurt/M: Suhrkamp Verlag, 1964), 62.
11. Reeh, *Ornaments of the Metropolis*, 145.
12. The term "silvery gaze" (*Silberblick*) in relation to Riefenstahl comes from Claudia Lenssen, "Leben und Werk," *Leni Riefenstahl*, ed. Filmmuseum Potsdam (Berlin: Henschel Verlag, 1999), 35. She suggests that Riefenstahl "seems to be looking at the spectator at the same time as she appears to be looking through him. . . . She thus appears both present and absent at once, ungraspable, as if an apparition." I would suggest that this "silvery" look appears, in fact, as a self-directed gaze. It presents itself to the camera as an empty eye, emptied of everything but the narcissistic self.
13. It is a space that fosters extreme anonymity at once as it creates an inescapable physical intimacy. It is also the site of the transitory, of arrival and departure. Its potential as a space that engenders violence is brilliantly thematized in the film *Kontroll* (Nimrod Antal, 2003).
14. Riefenstahl seems to equivocate in her memoirs when she says, "I stood alone on the elevated subway platform at Nollendorfplatz" (41). In Müller's film the sequence is shot underground.
15. See Guy Debord, *The Society of the Spectacle*, trans. Fredy Perlman et al. (Detroit: Black and Red, 1977).
16. See Martina Thiele's essay, "Representing the Body in Cyberspace: Riefenstahl's Self-staging" in this volume.
17. Mary Ann Doane, "Film and the Masquerade: Theorizing the Female Spectator," in *The Sexual Subject: A Screen Reader in Sexuality*, ed. John Caughie and Annette Kuhn (London and New York: Routledge, 1992), 231. Riefenstahl's self-staging indicates that she dramatized her own specuralization to the point of hysteria, which renders Doane's description even more powerful.
18. I refer here to Riefenstahl's enactment of the "New Woman" in Weimar on the one hand (independent, adventurous, enterprising), and on the other, her internalization of and collaboration with male power. In addition, Riefenstahl's bipolar response to the urban modern can be seen in her very activity of looking, investigating, and consuming of the poster and the film (in short, of the dream)—a thoroughly modern urban activity.
19. Jean Laplanche and J. B. Pontalis, "Fantasy and the Origins of Sexuality," *International Journal of Psycho-Analysis* 49 (1968): 4.
20. See J. Laplanche and J. B. Pontalis, *The Language of Psycho-Analysis*, trans. Donald Nicholson-Smith (New York, London: W. W. Norton & Company, 1973), 292. I mean "over-determined dream" in the sense that Laplanche and Pontalis explain this Freudian term in entry (b): "The fact that formation of the unconscious (symptoms, dreams, etc.) can be attributed to a plurality of determining factors. This can be understood in two different ways. The formation is related to a multiplicity of unconscious elements which may be organized in different meaningful sequences, each having its own specific coherence at a particular level of interpretation."
21. Reeh, *Ornaments of the Metropolis*, 118–122
22. David B. Clarke, "Introduction: Previewing the Cinematic City," *The Cinematic City* (London and New York: Routledge, 1997), 4.
23. Miriam Hansen, "America, Paris, the Alps: Kracauer (and Benjamin) on Cinema and Modernity," *Cinema and the Invention of Modern Life*, ed. Leo Charney and Vanessa Schwartz (Berkeley: University of California Press, 1995), 365–366.

24. Riefenstahl, *A Memoir*, 42.
25. For a detailed discussion of this film, see Mary Rhiel in this volume.
26. *Süddeutsche Zeitung*, August 16, 2002, Kultur.
27. *Die Welt*, August 16, 2002, Kultur.
28. An average of 500 people visited the exhibit each day, and there were usually long lines for tickets. How quickly the volatile Riefenstahl could stop the flow of ticket sales became evident when, in 2003, Riefenstahl (at this point one hundred years old) blocked her loan of the artifacts to other exhibitors because of protests engendered by an exhibit of about 300 Riefenstahl artifacts in the *Haus der Geschichte* in Bonn. See "Riefenstahl-Rezeption nach 1945. Ausstellungen." http://.ruhr-uni-bochum.de/riefenstahl/ (accessed July 7, 2007).
29. See Annie Thompson, Associated Press, "Rare Look at Nazi-era Filmmaker: Retrospective Examines Leni Riefenstahl's Cinematic Propaganda, Other Works." See http://welcometosilentmovies.com/news/newsarchive/leni.html (accessed June 2, 2007).
30. Dalichow and Lenssen, "Focus Riefenstahl," *Leni Riefenstahl*, ed. Filmmuseum Potsdam (Berlin: Henschel Verlag, 1999), 7.
31. Interview, February 7, 1999. Filmmuseum Potsdam.
32. Dalichow is also author of a number of books on cinema and representation, including *Zur Ästhetik von Debütfilmen der DEFA in den 80-er Jahren, Hans Albers: Ein Leben in Bildern,* and *Sandmann Auf Reisen: Eine Ausstellung.*
33. Brigitte Werneburg, "Der Besuch der alten Dame," *taz*, February 8, 1999. The quip was repeated by Christine Dankbar, in her article in the *Berliner Zeitung*, May 6, 2000, where she commented on the commercial exhibit of photos from Riefenstahl's childhood in Berlin. See also, "Riefenstahl-Rezeption nach 1945, Ausstellungen." See http://.ruhr-uni-bochum.de/riefenstahl/ (accessed July 7, 2007).
34. See note 29.
35. See note 29.
36. Dalichow feared that the radical right wing would be very enthusiastic about the show and that its radical constituents would celebrate the exhibition as a kind of Riefenstahl revival. She reasoned that a stamp of approval from right-wing extremist groups would invalidate the museum's project and judge it as uncritical, thus allowing left-oriented intellectuals and the media to dismiss the exhibit. None of these fears were warranted. The exhibit received a positive response in most of the press reports. The authors of the report by the University of Bochum push the point that perhaps Dalichow was disappointed that there was relatively little protest in the press. See http://ruhr-uni-bochum.de/riefenstahl/n (accessed July 7, 2007).
37. See Brigitte Werneburg, "Kraft durch Pose. Die erste deutsche monographische Werkschau zu Leni Riefenstahl in Potsdam," *taz*, December 4, 1998.
38. Eiko Ishioka is quoted as having said that the exhibit "was not to inform or to illustrate or to criticize, but to celebrate." See http://.ruhr-uni-bochum.de/riefenstahl/n (accessed June 7, 2007).
39. Uwe Schmitt, in his article "Dienst an den höheren Beweggründen" satirized Dalichow's chutzpah in the *Frankfurter Allgemeine Zeitung*, December 5, 1998. "Mut zu leben bescheinigt sich die Direktorin Bärbel Dalichow, die Polizeischutz angefordert hatte gegen die erwartete Randale und von drohenden Anrufern und immer wieder umgeschriebenen Katalogtexten berichtet wie von einem Fronterlebnis."

40. Cited in "Riefenstahl-Rezeption nach 1945." See http://.ruhr-uni-bochum.de/riefenstahl/n (accessed July 7, 2007).
41. For a history of the Marstall building see http://www.filmmuseum-potsdam.de/en/352-0.htm (accessed October 26, 2007).
42. The museum's budget, including twenty-nine full- and part-time employees, was funded by the state of Brandenburg Ministry of Culture. Although the museum recorded high visitor numbers (110,000), Brandenburg's state administrators have cut budgets and thus impacted the museum. See "Läuft fürs Filmmuseum schon der Abspann?" http://www.welt.de/print-welt/article561630/ (accessed July 7, 2007).
43. Of note is the museum's permanent exhibit on the nearly one-hundred-year (1912–2000) history of Babelsberg. The collection comprises over 3,000 pieces—from early film cameras to developing and editing equipment.
44. In fact, on February, 6–7, 1999, DEFA would celebrate its forty-fifth anniversary. Among the commemorators were DEFA veteran filmmakers Frank Beyer and the GDR's Chief Indian Gojko Mitic. Concomitant to this event, the founding of the DEFA Foundation—nine years in the planning—was announced in Berlin. The foundation will concern itself with the restoration, preservation, and archiving of DEFA's films. See Ralf Schenk, "45 Jahre Filmgeschichte in einer Hand," *Berliner Zeitung* 31 (February 6–7, 1999).
45. Putting the Riefenstahl exhibit into a contemporary context of Berlin cultural life in February 1999, it is important to remember the yearly International Film Festival (the Berlinale) in Berlin. Julian Stringer's observation about similar events that foreground visual culture—from theater to beauty contests—is well taken: Noting the "touristic and commodified aesthetic" in the city space of Berlin, he cites the opening remarks of the Berlinale by Berlin's mayor. These remarks put into stark relief the interdependency of venues within the culture industry: "Along with the great variety of films presented during the festival, the lineup of international film stars adds yet another highlight to the already rich cultural agenda of the Berlin winter season. . . . While you are enjoying encounters with exciting new worlds of cinema from all the five continents, don't forget the real world outside, off the silver screen, and take a little time to discover the streets and squares of Berlin: there is much to be seen in the city's many museums, theaters, and exhibitions." Julian Stringer, "Global Cities and the International Film Festival Economy," in *Cinema and the City: Film and Urban Societies in a Global Context*, ed. Mark Shiel and Tony Fitzmaurice (Oxford: Blackwell, 2001), 134–144: 140. The original text appeared in "Welcome: Governing Mayor of Berlin," *Moving Picture Berlinale Extra* (February 11–12, 1998): 3.
46. All of Riefenstahl's films, except *Sieg des Glaubens (Victory of Faith)*, were shown as an accompaniment to the exhibit. In addition, film specialists Ines Walk, Guido Altendorf, and Matthias Struch gave introductory information about the nightly screened features.
47. Quoted in Volker Oelschläger, *Süddeutsche Zeitung*, February 2, 1999. One wonders, of course, how he would explain the 900,000 visitors to the 2002 Riefenstahl exhibit at the *Haus der Geschichte* in Bonn. http://www.welt.de/print/article120926 (accessed July 7, 2007).
48. What made the panel discussion especially controversial was Ulf Poschardt's (he is managing editor of the *Zeitmagazin* of the *Süddeutsche Zeitung*) tiff with Kohlschmidt on the question of whether the plan to make a documentary film on the Paralympics

in Sydney was a counterpoint to Riefenstahl's idealization of beauty and an inopportune "idealization of cripples," ibid., n.p.

49. See Dalichow and Lenssen, "Focus Riefenstahl," in *Leni Riefenstahl*, ed. Filmmuseum Potsdam (Berlin: Henschel, 1999), 9.
50. A monitor at the entrance to the exhibit showed visitors a spectacular image of Riefenstahl under water in a diving suit. Riefenstahl was not certified as a diver until in her seventh decade, and her young face is shocking in this context.
51. Furthermore, the exhibit reproduced the myth that Riefenstahl was the lone creator of her two most successful films, *Triumph of the Will* and the *Olympia* films. In fact, few scholars note that the idea of Riefenstahl as the lone genius flies in the face of logic. A notable exception is Hamilton Burden, who makes the point that her cameramen (among them Hans Ertl, Guzzi Lantschner, and Willy Zielke) were their own directors during the filming. Indeed, it is only logical that Riefenstahl could not give direction to the more than forty cameramen and over thirty assistants who filmed *Triumph of the Will*. Riefenstahl always mentioned her cameramen with admiration and affection, but these film industry workers never had the ability (or desire?) to occupy center stage themselves.
52. The meeting lasted about an hour, the interview approximately twenty minutes. I have removed only redundant material.
53. To date, certain Nazi propaganda films (like Riefenstahl's *Triumph of the Will* and Harlan's *Jud Süss*) can only be screened in educational settings.
54. Uwe Schmitt, "Dienst an den höheren Beweggründen," *Frankfurter Allgemeine Zeitung*, December 5, 1998. Schmitt claims that the cultural minister Michael Naumann, along with Wim Wenders, Klaus Brandauer, and some film stars, had been asked to give the opening speech, but declined. Mick Jagger, Hans Magnus Enzensberger, and Quentin Tarantino declined to give "Grußadressen" for the catalogue. Schmitt noted that "this is how cowardly the art world is."
55. See Bielefelder Graduiertenkolleg Sozialgeschichte, ed., *Körper Macht Geschichte—Geschichte macht Körper: Körpergeschichte als Sozialgeschichte* (Bielefeld: Verlag für Regionalgeschichte, 1999).
56. A notable exception is Gerd Gemünden and Mary R. Desjardins, eds., *Dietrich Icon* (Durham, NC, and London: Duke University Press, 2007). Many of the essays in the volume brilliantly problematize issues such as aging and femininity, stardom as masquerade, the representation of ambiguous sexuality and the status of her legendary legs and voice in cultural iconography.
57. Mary Ann Doane, *Femmes Fatales: Feminism, Film Theory, Psychoanalysis* (London: Routledge, 1991), 20.
58. Joan Rivière, "Womanliness as a Masquerade," *International Journal of Psychoanalysis* X, 1929. Reprinted in Hendrik M. Ruitenbeek, ed., *Psychoanalysis and Female Sexuality* (New Haven: College and University Press, 1966). Rivière presents three case studies whose common thread is that "women who wish for masculinity may put on a mask of womanliness to avert anxiety and the retribution feared from men" (210). In her study of female spectatorship, Doane points to three central problems with Rivière's interpretation. One is that Rivière's essay (as well as its reception) privileges the field of sexuality "born as it is of power and its effects," ignoring "another field of power relations—that of race." *Femme Fatales* (38). Second, Rivière's case study "makes femininity dependent upon masculinity for its very definition," and the third,

Rivière sees masquerade as "socially inappropriate," rather than viewing it as an expression of playfulness. Ibid., 37.

59. Riefenstahl gave Ray Müller similar instructions: "I need soft light, don't you understand?" *Die Macht der Bilder* (1993).
60. Stefanie Grote, "Object Mensch. Körper als Ikon und Ideologem in den cineastischen Werken Leni Riefenstahls. Ästhetisierter Despotismus oder die Rezipprozität von Auftragskuns und Politik im Dritten Reich." Diss., Europa-Universität Viadrina, 2004, 27.
61. A notable exception is Lars Quadfasel's highly critical and acerbic description of Alice Schwarzer's interview with Riefenstahl (*Emma* 1, 1999), which celebrates Riefenstahl as a feminist. Quadfasel rejects Schwarzer's "Riefenstahl-Portrait Vergangenheitsbewältigung als Kaffeeklatsch" and rightly dismisses her claim that Riefenstahl should be seen as a feminist icon. See Lars Quadfasel, "Leni bei den Emmas," *Jungle World,* February 13, 1999, n.p.
62. See http://www.film-zeit.de/home (accessed September 15, 2007).
63. Grote, 253.
64. See Reinhold Keiner. *Thea von Harbou und der deutsche Film bis 1933* (Hildesheim: Olms, 1991) and Karin Bruns, *Kinomythen 1920–1945: Die Filmentwürfe der Thea von Harbou* (Stuttgart: J. B. Metzler, 1995).

INDEX